New Frontiers in Economics

This book brings together essays from leading economists analyzing the new
directions that subdisciplines of economics have taken in the face of modern
economic challenges. The essays represent invention and discovery in the
areas of information, macroeconomics and public policies, international trade
and development, finance, business, contracts, law, gaming, and government,
as these areas of study evolve through the different phases of the scientific
process. It offers not only a wealth of factual information on the current
state of the economy, but also theoretical and empirical innovations that
conceptualize reality and values in different ways from their predecessors.
The new concepts presented here can guide practitioners in their search for
ways to resolve problems in the various areas. Together, the essays offer the
reader a balanced look at the various fields, approaches, and dimensions that
comprise future directions in economic theory, research, and practice. The
extensive introduction by the editors not only summarizes and reviews the
implications of the contributions presented in the volume, but also examines
how scientific progress takes place, with special reference to economics and
finance.

Michael Szenberg is Distinguished Professor of Economics at the Lubin
School of Business, Pace University. He is the author or editor of many books,
including *Economics of the Israeli Diamond Industry* (1973) with an Introduction by Milton Friedman, which won the Irving Fisher Monograph Award,
and *Eminent Economists, Their Life Philosophies* (1992). Professor Szenberg
has received the Kenan Award for excellence in teaching. He serves as the
editor-in-chief of *The American Economist* and as a consultant to private and
government agencies.

Lall Ramrattan holds a Ph.D. from the New School University. He is an
instructor at the University of California, Berkeley. He has published articles
in several major journals and serves as an associate editor of *The American
Economist*.

NEW FRONTIERS IN ECONOMICS

Edited by

MICHAEL SZENBERG

Pace University

LALL RAMRATTAN

University of California, Berkeley

Foreword by

PAUL A. SAMUELSON

CAMBRIDGE
UNIVERSITY PRESS

PUBLISHED BY THE PRESS SYNDICATE OF THE UNIVERSITY OF CAMBRIDGE
The Pitt Building, Trumpington Street, Cambridge, United Kingdom

CAMBRIDGE UNIVERSITY PRESS
The Edinburgh Building, Cambridge CB2 2RU, UK
40 West 20th Street, New York, NY 10011-4211, USA
477 Williamstown Road, Port Melbourne, VIC 3207, Australia
Ruiz de Alarcón 13, 28014 Madrid, Spain
Dock House, The Waterfront, Cape Town 8001, South Africa

http://www.cambridge.org

First published 2004

Printed in the United States of America

Typeface Times Ten 10/13 pt.   *System* LaTeX 2_ε [TB]

A catalog record for this book is available from the British Library.

Library of Congress Cataloging in Publication Data
New frontiers in economics / edited by Michael Szenberg, Lall Ramrattan.
p.   cm.
Includes bibliographical references and index.
ISBN 0-521-83686-7 – ISBN 0-521-54536-6 (pbk.)
1. Economics – History – 20th century.   2. Economic policy – History – 20th century.
I. Szenberg, Michael.   II. Ramrattan, Lall, 1951–
HB87.N487   2004
330′.09′04 – dc22   2003065442

ISBN 0 521 83686 7 hardback
ISBN 0 521 54536 6 paperback

B'H

To my Mother, Sara, my Father, Henoch, and my Sister,
Esther, in Memoriam

who exemplified the Proverbs' words:

Happy are those who find wisdom
She is more precious than jewels
And nothing you desire can compare with her . . .
Her ways are ways of pleasantness and all her paths are peace

To Naomi – the oldest of my children
and to Jacob – the youngest of my grandchildren

To my wife, Noreena Ramrattan,
To my children – Devi and her husband Arjun, Shanti, Hari, and
Rani and to my grandchildren – Soham and Lakshmi.

It is not what we think, rather, it is what we have not thought of.

Jerome Wiesner

Contents

Contributors

Kyle Bagwell
Professor of Economics, Columbia University

Peter Bossaerts
William D. Hacker Professor of Economics and Management, California Institute of Technology

John Y. Campbell
Otto Eckstein Professor of Applied Economics, Harvard University

Michelle R. Garfinkel
Professor of Economics, University of California, Irvine

Perry Mehrling
Professor of Economics, Barnard College and Columbia University

James Poterba
Mitsui Professor, Public Finance and Corporate Finance, Massachusetts Institute of Technology

Mathew Rabin
Edward G. and Nancy S. Jordan Professor of Economics, University of California, Berkeley

Debraj Ray
Julius Silver Professor of Economics, New York University

Stergios Skaperdas
Associate Professor of Economics, University of California, Irvine

Robert W. Staiger
Professor of Economics, University of Wisconsin

Joseph Stiglitz
2001 Nobel Laureate and Professor of Economics and Finance, Columbia University

Alan O. Sykes
Frank and Bernice Greenberg Professor of Law and Faculty Director for Curriculum, University of Chicago Law School

Foreword: Eavesdropping on the Future?

Paul A. Samuelson

An evolving discipline – whether it be history or economics or astrophysics or immunology – is ever dynamically changing. Two steps forward and X steps back, so to speak. Periodically, the scholarly group registers more or less self-confidence, self-esteem, and complacency. We careerists are happiest when recent past achievements have seemed to be successful, but when still there are completable tasks dimly visible ahead.

Human nature is much the same in every generation. We each want to leave our distinctive initials on the subject – fulfill our fond teachers' hopes for us but (if possible) do it by bettering their obsolescent achievements. Paradoxically then, it can be just when a science is at a high point in its Kondratieff wave that discontent begins to ferment. It has been said, "Newton did everything, and that set back English mathematics for almost a century while the action moved toward continental writers such as Euler, the Bernoullis, Lagrange, and Laplace." The bright shine of Keynes in the first half of the last century subsequently shadowed economics at Oxbridge. And because Nature abhors a vacuum, that gave my generation of American economists – American-cum-Hitlerian refugees – the opportunity to peddle at the vanguard of the bicycle race. Today's textbooks at every stage – beginning, intermediate, and advanced – are notably similar. Once upon a time, you could have learned a different economics at Madison and Austin and Berkeley than at Cambridge or Chicago. Now there is no hole to hide in.

Such conditions generate discontented minorities who seek to bypass peer-reviewed journals and huddle together in volumes of proposed alternative economics. The basement of Harvard's Widener Library is a cemetery for past similar efforts. Thus during the 1920s Rexford Tugwell edited such a collection that tempted some of that era's brightest and best. When I am gone, maybe nobody will be left to remember that particular effort.

Here is my advice. When in doubt, give my new efforts a hearing. Many feel a calling to break new ground; in the end, few will end up finding their efforts chosen. But the yea-sayer does do less harm than the naysayer, in that the Darwinian process of adverse testing will in time (most likely?) separate the useful from the useless, the trivial from the profound.

I have reported more than once what the late New School scholar Hans Neisser told me toward the end of his life. In paraphrase he said, "My friend, fellow immigrant Jacob Marschak, was right and I was wrong. When each new innovation came along – game theory, Keynes' notions of effective demand, econometric identifications – he embraced them all with enthusiasm, even overenthusiasm. I held back, worrying about the holes in those doughnuts. In the end things did more or less get sorted out. Those open-minded individuals experienced more fun and maybe did accelerate that sorting out process."

Perhaps I should warn against a common trap. Often you may hear yourself saying, "But this is not new, and neither is that." Alfred North Whitehead once opined, "Nothing new was ever said for the first time by the person who was saying it." Each generation has a need to put into its own goatskins the wine it drinks. Few of my MIT students will call themselves "Keynesians" as Solow, Modigliani, and I might. They are "neo-Keynesians," "neo-neo-Keynesians," and even "anti-Keynes Keynesians." But make no mistake about it. Their writings and views are light-years away from the macro I learned at the University of Chicago. And the common core of their beliefs is scarcely country miles away from the vulgar IS-LM diagrammatics that Harrod, Hicks, and Hansen distilled out of Maynard's intuitive explorations.

I echo what my mother would have said: to potential readers of this book: "Try the new stuff. It might even turn out to be good for you."

Preface

The underlying notion in this volume is the importance of the new directions that subdisciplines of economics have taken. The contents of this volume – ten essays – give us a broad perspective on the changes that the economics discipline is undergoing. Clearly, there are omissions, and our selection will not satisfy every reader. Putting on our entrepreneurial robe, we canvassed the younger leading scholars and asked them to contribute essays about the direction in which they perceive their area to be moving. The contributors were free to determine their own approach, although we did ask them to minimize the mathematical content to a descriptive level, certainly avoiding proofs in order to make the target audience as broad as possible. We did not find it necessary to use length as an essential criterion for reaching a balanced presentation of the subject areas.

Acknowledgments

The subject of this volume – seeing beyond what is apparent and thinking otherwise – is the brainchild of Scott Parris, the senior economics editor of Cambridge University Press. During a conversation over a cup of coffee at the ASSA meetings, I responded to the idea, and on a napkin we immediately jotted down the names of possible candidates. The authors extend special thanks to Scott Parris for shepherding this book through the four referees and two editorial boards, one in the United States and the other in the UK. No author could wish for a more supportive editor or for a better publisher with which to work. Cambridge University Press is known for the quality and the care it takes with every book it produces. It has taken several years for this volume to be completed. I asked my collaborator, Lall Ramrattan, to join me as the coeditor of this work. Many papers in this volume initially appeared in the *American Economist*, of which I am the editor; they are reprinted here with changes.

In bringing this volume to fruition, we have benefited greatly from the support and assistance of many individuals. The most important debt goes to Paul A. Samuelson – who continues to extend to me many kindnesses, and unhesitatingly agreed to pen the foreword to this volume – and to the contributors to this collection. Their cooperation made the editing a pleasant task. We thank them for their congenial partnership.

I wish to thank as well the four anonymous referees and the members of the two editorial boards for their enthusiastic support of this work and their thoughtful comments. Progress from draft manuscript to final version was aided by Abraham Goldstein, Diana Ward, and Gary Yohe. They are all hereby thanked.

Along the way, I have benefited at Lubin from the collegiality and deep friendship of the members of the Finance and Economics Department: Lew Altfest; William C. Freund; Surendra Kaushik; Matt Morey; Jouahn Nam; Joseph Salerno; P. V. Viswanath; Berry Wilson, the Director of the Center for Global Finance; Jorge Pinto; and the two academic Associate Deans, Peter Hoefer and James Russell. I would like to single out Aron Gottesman for special thanks. His many insightful comments and editorial emendations immeasurably improved the final product. My deep gratitude is extended to Lynette Wailoo, Associate Dean of Lubin School of Business, for her warmth and intellectual support.

I value the camaraderie that has prevailed at the Center for Applied Research at Lubin which was helpful to our research efforts over the last four years. I also owe much gratitude to Iulie Ismailescu, my dedicated and talented past assistant and now adjunct assistant professor at Pace University who is studying for her Ph.D. in Finance at the University of Massachusetts. My graduate assistants over the years – Ester Budek, Priya Hariani, Scott Hinman, Richard Nilsen, and Justyna Tuniewicz – have contributed to the fraternal atmosphere that pervades the Center and have assisted me enthusiastically with this project as well as with numerous other projects. My gratitude for their generosity is extended to all these individuals.

In addition, no list of debts would be complete without acknowledging the trust, generosity of spirit, and assistance of Carmen Urma, the Coordinator of the Finance Department; Nicola Simpson, the Secretary of the Center for Applied Research; and Andrea Pascarelli, the Center's Editorial Assistant.

Special appreciation and thanks are owed to the members of the Executive Board of the Honor Society in Economics for being a source of support: Professors Mary Ellen Benedict, James Bradley, Jr., Stanley L. Brue, Kristine L. Chase, Robert R. Ebert, William D. Gunther, Shirley Johnson-Lans, Charles F. Phillips, Jr., and Robert S. Rycroft.

Putting a book together is a stressful endeavor. My coeditor, Lall Ramrattan, shared the work with me while I was assuming the new and challenging responsibilities of Chair of the Finance and Economics Department at Lubin, which necessitated transforming the department. To do so successfully for an academic department of close to fifty faculty members, many of whom hold tenure positions, is as challenging as restructuring an organization employing thousands of individuals. It was quite an experience! Lall was really terrific, and I want him to know how much his support meant to me.

Most of all, I renew my indebtedness to Arthur L. Centonze, Dean of the Lubin School of Business, Pace University, for his wise counsel, unfailing support, and encouragement in ways too numerous to list. My heart warms with gratitude to all of those mentioned.

While the book was being compiled, my mother, Sara Szenberg of blessed memory, passed away. She possessed great wisdom and personified the marriage of steadfastness and flexibility, of steel and velvet. She knew not only what to say, but also how to say it. She exhorted us that a smart person knows what to say, but a wise person knows whether to say it. I very often think of her.

It is to my children, Naomi and Avi, their spouses Marc and Tova, and to my grandchildren, Elki, Batya, Chanoch, Devora, Ephraim, Ayala, and Jacob, that I affectionately dedicate this book. They provide emotional sustenance and are a joyous gift and blessing to my wife and me.

The eighteenth-century printer cried out, "Thank God I am done with Johnson!" after completing the laborious task of preparing for publication the dictionary by Samuel Johnson, the dominant figure of eighteenth-century literary London. I would hope that those mentioned in this section have not had the same urge with this volume.

M. S.

My family has been very patient with me, and without such cooperation my participation in this project would not have been possible. I sincerely appreciate the patience they showed for the time I spent away from the family for this endeavor.

I am indebted to the person who really made economics attractive to me, even when I was in elementary school – my untimely deceased brother, Suruj Rattan. His death has robbed us of a person who would have made meaningful contributions to economics. My participation in this volume as an economist can certainly be traced to the influence he had on me. With the same breath, I also thank my Mother, in memoriam, for her encouragement, both spiritually and academically. She taught me my first lesson in economics: "Poverty is a crime." My three other brothers and my three sisters receive special thanks for seeing me through school.

I feel very privileged to collaborate with Mike on this book. Mike's heart is as big as his brains, his generosity knows no bounds, and he has sheltered me like an elder brother from the conflicts and confrontations of the review process. I hope he will understand when I say that this book is really dedicated to him.

L. R.

Introduction

A story is told of the poet William Blake's friend, who overheard someone remark that Blake was cracked. The friend's memorable response was, "Yes, but it is the sort of crack that lets in the light!" In this volume, we look at how the younger leading practitioners of the various branches of economics are examining the new directions of the economics discipline in the face of modern economic challenges. This collection of articles represents invention and discovery in the areas of information, trade, development, finance, business, law, gaming, and government as these areas of study evolve through the different phases of the scientific process. Because the authors are presenting new theories that conceptualize reality and values in different ways from their predecessors,[1] some essential background material on methodology will be discussed first.

Thomas Kuhn's description of the scientific process – as modified by Latsis (1976), Lakatos (1977), Laudan (1977), and others – seems to capture the dynamics of change in knowledge represented in this volume. Whereas Kuhn used the term "paradigm shift" to characterize change in the practice of "normal science," Lakatos used the term "problem shift." These two classifications also are empirically based in that they ask substantive questions about objects in the domains of their disciplines

---

[1] The authors exhibit here their natural ability to be original. Moving a discipline into new directions is equivalent to breaking the rules, which requires the innate ability to transform the subject matter. An anecdote from the world of music illuminates the point. Anton Halm, a minor composer, asked Beethoven for his opinion of the piece Halm had composed. Beethoven responded that the piece contained "errors." Halm then protested that Beethoven, too, disregarded rules. Beethoven's classic retort to Halm was: "I may do it, but not you." Beethoven's new paradigm resulted in the Ninth Choral Symphony.

1

(Laudan 1977, 15, 77), the concern being fitting theory to facts (Bechtel 1988, 53; De Marchi and Blaug 1991, 2). Another concern of both classifications is how practitioners solve problems. Kuhn's notion of a "puzzle-solving" solution is stated unambiguously, whereas Lakatos's desire for "proof" in problem-solving led him to a conversion experience (De Marchi and Blaug 1991, 11). Both views are somewhat alike in their treatment of anomalies. For Kuhn, normal science deals with questions as they come up. Particular articulations of a paradigm or a new direction "may well be criticized, falsified and abandoned; but the paradigm itself is unchanged. It remains so until enough 'anomalies' accumulate" (Laudan 1977, 73). For Lakatos, creative research can defend a paradigm from anomalies (Mayo 1996, 275); therefore, anomalies should not be a distractor (De Marchi and Blaug 1991, 5). However, Kuhn and Lakatos part company, particularly in their treatment of rationality. Although Kuhn relies mostly on "taste or persuasion" as the criteria for evaluating acceptance of new directions (Bechtel 1988, 57),[2] Lakatos sees changes through Popper's rational spectacle (Mayo 1996, 274).

According to Quine, "The falsity of the observation categorical does not conclusively refute the hypothesis. What it refutes is the conjunction of sentences that was needed to imply the observations. In order to retract that conjunction we do not have to retract the hypothesis in question; we could retract some other sentence of the conjunction instead" (Quine 1990, 13–14). This method is now called the Duhem-Quine's (DQ) "holistic" hypothesis. It imparts the lesson that one cannot appraise a single hypothesis, but only a joint distribution of hypotheses. For the economist, such a bundle of hypotheses contains familiar terms, such as core elements, auxiliary theories, *ceteris paribus* and other assumptions, definitions, statistical specifications, measurements, lag structures, identifications, error terms, and boundary conditions. This bundling of

---

[2] The same phenomenon can be observed in the literature. Morris Dickstein demonstrates how in the post–World War II period, once marginalized writers – writers who were Jewish, black, Southern, or homosexual (e.g., Norman Mailer, Philip Roth, Saul Bellow, Joseph Heller, Bernard Malamud, J. D. Salinger, Ralph Ellison, James Baldwin, Jack Kerouac, Truman Capote, and John Barth) – would gradually "be integrated" into the once-decorated rites of American literature and ultimately "would become American literature and viewed as literary icons." See his *Leopards in the Temple: The Transformation of American Fiction: 1945–1970* (Cambridge, MA: Harvard University Press, 2002). The title of the book is taken from the once outsider-author Franz Kafka's parable: "Leopards break into the temple and drink to the dregs what is in the sacrificial pitchers; this is repeated over and over again. Finally, it can be calculated in advance and it becomes part of the ceremony."

hypotheses makes it difficult to reject a movement toward new directions. For example, it is easy to change one of the "umpteen" assumptions and save the bundle from being rejected. This way any statement can remain true by making sufficient accommodation in the bundle of hypotheses. Kuhn and Quine, therefore, stand on the same ground in rejecting the analytic–synthetic concepts that is the justification of *a priori* concepts through empirical observations as a guide to new changes. For Kuhn, there is no neutral language to compare old and new directions (Bechtel 1988, 56), and therefore he relied on the art of persuasion to win people over in accepting a particular new direction.

Kuhn (1970) was keen in pointing out similarities between his and Popper's view. Among his comparisons, Kuhn finds that their observations were both theory-laden. But although they are in agreement that scientific knowledge grows through its accumulation, they disagree over the type of revolution that might take place. For Popper, science "grows by a more revolutionary method rather than accumulation – by a method which destroys, changes, and alters the whole thing" (Popper 1962, 129). Popper has taken a rather broad-based approach to scientific revolution that not only involves falsification, but also notions of excess content, verisimilitude, objective knowledge, discovery via evolution, and situational determinism (De Marchi and Blaug 1991, 2). We will revisit situational determinism through the works of Latsis (1972, 1976).

ANALYTIC AND SYNTHETIC ASPECTS OF NEW DIRECTIONS

Broadly speaking, Kuhn describes how traditional theories emerge from a pseudo to a normal scientific state. In the process, problems that have the potential to evolve into crisis points make their appearances. Over time, during crisis points, more and more skillful students who are members of an "invisible college" attempt to solve those problems. The likely scenario is that the practitioners have never met, but they know about each other's problem–solution through common sources such as books and journals in which they publish their findings. As a rule, they agree more than disagree about their commitment to a paradigm, and because a paradigm does put many theoretical problems to rest, it is hard to give it up even at sword's point. But anomalies can be tolerated only for a time, until a normal science prevails again in the form of a new direction or a new paradigm. The resolution may represent a paradigm shift, where an old paradigm may just drop dead, or, as Max Planck put it, "It is not that old theories are disproved, it is just that their supporters die out"

(Mohr 1977, 136). Paul A. Samuelson (1999, XI) rephrased it so vividly: "Science advances funeral by funeral." In this volume, we find examples of budding paradigms that usurped older ones, as well as examples of paradigms that represent only a partial break with their predecessors.

Following Thomas Kuhn, a paradigm represents a universally recognized achievement that would answer questions by way of new models, tools, standards, and methods. One problem with this concept is that it represents more than a particular theory or model, but economists have been accustomed to deal with those ambiguities. Much as the "invisible hand" concept in economics clears the market but cannot be precisely defined, the paradigm concept explains the scientific process but also cannot be precisely defined. Because of a lack of certain specific items in our vocabulary, Kuhn offers twenty-one definitions to characterize the concept (Masterman 1970). Therefore, we would like to focus more on how a paradigm explains new directions in economics.

A new direction in economics may start off with a very basic, fuzzy concept that holds out some potential for solving problems in a discipline. We are reminded of how the portfolio theory started. When Harry Markowitz first presented the theory as his dissertation in economics, Milton Friedman, a member of his defense committee, remarked that there is no room for portfolio theory in economics, whereupon Markowitz asserted that it did not have a role in the past, but is now part of economics (Varian 1993, 162). Similarly, in the hands of Hume, Fisher, Marshall, and Keynes, the quantity theory of money suffered a long gestation period, but it was not until it was revised by Tobin and Baumol and restated by Friedman that it explained facts well and became a universally accepted pillar of the monetarist paradigm.

Economists are interested in new directions in their discipline because there is something for practitioners to learn, even from their rudimentary phase. They are given a set of instructions on how to extend and articulate the concepts that enables their research with the promise that it will potentially solve their problems. For instance, "The study of exemplars enables one to acquire the ability to apply symbolic generalizations to nature" (Suppes 1977, 486). If someone were to look at a group of swans and describe or point ostensibly to a swan, that individual would tend to observe such common features as whiteness and length and curvature of the neck. Exemplars tell us how to apply symbolic generalizations to natural phenomena and single out which law or symbolic generalization is applicable. We not only apply them to nature, but such generalizations, when manipulated, can also lead to newer techniques or new discoveries. Also, we can have opportunities and occasions to use auxiliary generalizations; as Kuhn (1970, 274) observes,

similarity–dissimilarity relationships are ones that we all deploy every day, un-problematically, yet without being able to name the characteristics by which we make the identifications and discriminations. They are prior ... to a list of criteria which, joined in a symbolic generalization, would enable us to define our terms. Rather they are parts of a language-conditioned or language-correlated way of seeing the world. Until we have acquired them, we do not see the world at all.

Kuhn further explains, starting from a law-sketch (Newton's Second Law of Motion: $f = ma$), that we manipulate the model into one form for freely falling bodies, another for the pendulum, and yet another for coupled harmonic oscillators. We learn how to use words, as well as what entities are in the world and how these entities behave. During the learning process, we acquire the ability to reason from words like "duck" to "there is a duck swimming." Only one step remains in the application of law-sketches like Newton's law of nature; namely, to figure out how to pair mass with force and acceleration (Suppes 1977, 503–4).

For Kuhn, we make progress when we can explain observations using a theory. With theory, scientists fit models to nature or explain facts. Quine (1990, 7) maintains that our research is theory-laden; even a simple observation of a sentence with the word "water" has the theory H_2O behind it. In addition to theory, we need to keep one eye on beliefs and the other on rationality. When a problem cannot be solved, a crisis period develops. Scientists use their imagination to come up with new theories, new paradigms to resolve the crisis. Many new competing schools may develop, each trying to make its paradigm dominant. They may do so by converting many practitioners to their paradigm, which gives it social dominance, much like a state developing power through hegemony. This is a new ingredient in the scientific process. The new direction – the process of a paradigm change – does not rely on logic, reason, or axioms, making several things hard to accept. We would like to know whether the theoretical and empirical values of the new path carry any of the "genes," so to speak, of the older path. In spiritual and religious undertakings in which beliefs are central, we are told not to compare things, not to covet. Yet, Kuhn's position is that two paths cannot be compared even if we wish to do so. The paths may be "incommensurable" because no neutral language is available to enable such comparison. The observation may be reported in different ways, or the same word as used in different paths may have different meanings.

The movement toward new directions is central to this volume and therefore deserves to be illustrated. First, Kuhn points to the theory of combustion to illustrate the discontinuity between paths, where, for example, the oxygen paradigm took over the phlogiston theory. In the case of Einstein's theory of relativity, Newton's laws dominated. Although the latter were subsumed within the new view, the lives of scientists who studied classical mechanics became overturned. This is tantamount to a revolution taking place. Oftentimes, in order to converge to a universal agreement regarding a scientific revolution, we may be required to grasp concepts that lie not only beyond our senses, but also beyond reason itself. Kuhn views the scientist's decision to persuade or convert others to follow the scientist's point of view as integral in accepting a new direction (with social and belief baggage). To emphasize the latter, Kuhn offers a new and more encompassing term: namely, "disciplinary matrix" – "disciplinary" because the practitioners share common beliefs in a discipline and "matrix" because it is composed of ordered elements of various sorts, each requiring further specification (Kuhn, in Suppes, 463).

Also, we would like to know whether or not one or several new directions would dominate in a normal scientific environment and when the actual dominant process is affected. Kuhn originally advocated the naive falsification process in which one path is replaced with another just when it is confronted with a wrong prediction. However, his thoughts for the replacement of a path with "disciplinary matrix" changed things quite a bit. In the latter view he redescribed "theoretical change in science as comprising an unending sequence of smaller revolutions or 'micro-revolutions'" (Toulmin 1972, 114).

FROM KUHN TO LAKATOS: "PARADIGM SHIFT" VS. "PROBLEM SHIFT"

Lakatos emphasized that scientists are "thick-skinned" people, in that they do not give up their cherished beliefs in any immediate fashion. Rather, they stay with their degenerating theories in the hope of turning them around from a scientific point of view. Marxism comes to mind as a good example, as does Keynesian economics. For Lakatos, we will be armed not with a single path but with a series of paths. Lakatos preferred to use the term Methodology of Scientific Research Programme (MSRP) to evaluate the state of scientific knowledge. He considers the research states to be either "degenerating" or "progressive." In economics, beta risk coefficients, marginal propensity to consume, and elasticity

coefficients – or what Ward calls the normal scientific activity of re-
fining constants (1972, 10) – are continually being evaluated and ap-
praised, yet no one will question the scientific practice of trying to refine
constants.

While Lakatos's view of a research program has a home in the economic literature, we need to spell out what counts as progress and the
different implications progress has for our volume. If scientists are willing to change ideas only in a "protective belt" without a willingness to
change or replace elements of the cherished or blind beliefs that form the
"hard core" of their research program, then progress can occur only in
the protective belt, where promising new theories and empirical applications are accommodated. The "hard core" remains intact, particularly
when we have a promising new program. Lakatos made it clear that we
cannot test the "hard core." We must invent "auxiliary hypotheses" to
form a "protective belt" around the hard core for the purpose of testing. In the process, we will "call a problem shift progressive if it is both
theoretically and empirically progressive, and degenerating if it is not.
We 'accept' problem shifts as 'scientific' only if they are at least theoretically progressive; if they are not, we 'reject' them as 'pseudoscientific'"
(Lakatos 1970, 118).

Because we may witness swings between progressive and degenerative
states of a research program in the "protective belt," an observed state
of the program cannot be considered final enough to warrant the giving
up of an acceptable path. On the contrary, a "budding" research program
may require protection for a time. This version of sophisticated falsification replaces the naive one originally proposed by Kuhn that supports the
rejection of a theory because it has failed to predict for the first time. For
instance, the Keynesian model was not falsified when it failed to predict
double-digit inflation in the 1970s. Rather, expectation elements in the
protective belt were postulated. Macro textbooks now carry aggregate
demand, which has displaced the IS and LM curves, along with aggregate
supply curves. When IS and LM are now used, they have different meanings. In the introductory book by Taylor (2001), for instance, IS and LM
demonstrate interest rate policies.

Latsis showed how to appraise economic theory through Lakatos's
MSRP, by an appeal to Popper's "situational logic,"[3] meaning, a typical
situation in which a person acts according to the aims and knowledge of

---

[3] "[T]he situational logic plays a very important part in social life as well as in the social
sciences. It is, in fact, the method of economic analysis" (Popper 1945, 47).

the situation. He argued that basically perfect and monopolistic competition share the same "hard-core" elements, but the latter is distinguished by the use of a small modification of the situational assumptions of perfect competition (Latsis 1972, 214). Even with the new amendments to Lakatos, methodologists seem to be split about when a new direction occurs. On the one hand, Cross (1982) thinks it is helpful to explain new directions in macroeconomics. On the other hand, Hausman (1989) thinks it is still unsettled and advances a more eclectic view. We take the position in this volume that the methodology for Duhem-Quine through Popper, Lakatos, and Latsis is still useful to observe and that it explains changes in the modern branches of economics.

IMPLICATIONS OF PARADIGMS

This volume makes general and specific implications of Kuhn's and Lakatos's view of new directions for economics. Some, including Kuhn, consider the social sciences as still in their immature stage. If one were to visit Keynesian economics for the first time, one might not perceive any general agreement or harmony between the hydraulic Keynesians[4] and post-Keynesians. Yet these schools form an "invisible college" in which practitioners all over the globe share their research in a designated journal such as the *Journal of Post Keynesian Economics*. But no universal agreement about the Keynesian revolution has been reached. Therefore, we may only be at the doorstep of the first stage of the new directions of Keynesian economics. From one point of view, economics may very well be at the "data gathering" stage, comparable to the Kepler state of the physical sciences, waiting for its Newtonian characterization. From another point of view, Adam Smith might have achieved such a characterization through his principle of the maximizing individual in society (Gordon 1965).

Kuhn and Lakatos have methodological implications for the use of mathematics in economics, and some of the contributors in this volume have not hesitated in applying math. Kuhn spoke of law-sketches, Lakatos of methodology from the side of mathematics. However, if we are to look for a representative mathematical or research program in economics, all fingers point to Paul A. Samuelson, who is said to be the first to advocate

---

[4] Hydraulic Keynesians is a term that refers to the Keynesian system of the 1940s and 1950s. It assumes stable macroeconomic aggregates – such as expenditures, output, and income – but not prices or quantity per unit of time. The government, under this system, can make deliberate policy choices to steer the economy.

the use of mathematics to explain, predict, and explore economic phenomena (Puttaswamaiah 2002, 10).

In a description of his methodology, Samuelson wrote, "Always when I read new literary and mathematical paradigms, I seek to learn what descriptions they imply for the observable data," emphasizing his preference for inductive over deductive science (Samuelson 1993, 242). We learn early on that his use of words like "literary" could mean the use of a differential equation as well as prose (Samuelson 1966, 1771). The official Palgrave dictionary considers the "descriptive" aspect of Samuelson's methodology, and sets it apart from what Samuelson calls the "F-Twist" theory, Friedman's brand of positivism that emphasizes "instrumentalism." The distinction is that economic theories can describe data, or they can be used as instruments to predict or measure data (Eatwell et al. 1987, 455). Machlup mentions, however, that Samuelson's methodology has undergone dynamic changes over time (Samuelson 1972, 758).

Latsis' work on the microeconomic front (1972, 1976) has extended Karl Popper's view of situations and situational logic, which according to Popper forms "the method of economic analysis" (Popper 1971, v. II, 97). According to Latsis, on the one hand, economic agents act in social situations that constrain their rational choices, minimizing the role of psychological assumptions in explaining their actions. On the other hand, "behaviour is animated by the principle that rational agents act appropriately to the 'logic of the situation'" (Latsis 1972, 208–9). The term "situational determinism" has evolved to represent the neoclassical program. Profit maximization is similar to a person running out of a "single exit" available in a burning cinema. The course of action in such a straitjacket situation allows the agent to reach a unique equilibrium from objective conditions such as cost, demand, and technology (Latsis 1972, 210–11). Latsis' concern with whether to include or exclude psychological assumptions in the theory of a firm splits research into three areas: (1) "Situational Determinism," where psychological assumptions are situational minimal; (2) "Economic Behavioralism," where psychology plays a role; and (3) "Organizational Approach," which sheds light on the firm's internal structure and decision making.

A. Informational Implications

The incorporation of information into economic theories and models has taken new directions. The change has not been quite parallel to the development in the physical sciences, which has moved from a data-gathering stage up to Kepler to a model-incorporating stage with Galileo and Newton. Rather, in economics, we have witnessed price-seeking alongside price-taking markets since the time of Adam Smith. The main paradigm of price-taking is that information is self-centered, promulgating the doctrine that only the market can gather the information efficiently and not a central or social planner. This doctrine reached its climax with the work of Hayek's "The Sensory Order" (1952), where it was postulated that information resides in the brain cells of each individual, and therefore cannot be organized, except via the spontaneous order of the market mechanism.

Today, the tools of the marginal revolution are invoked to depict equilibrium within a search domain; that is, the agent will search until the marginal cost of the search equals the marginal benefit of the search. But we can discern changes in new directions implicit in that process. We list here at least four major strands of changes: (1) Adaptive agents are allowed to adapt information about their past errors into current decisions. (2) Rational agents are assumed to use rational information, conditioning their decision on a full information set. (3) Signaling agents can signal in a game-theoretic environment their expected security level with regards to cooperation or noncooperation with one another. (4) Efficiency agents are efficient decision makers. As such, this can involve paying a wage rate that is greater than the marginal product of labor.

B. Behavioral Implications

When John Watson (1913) introduced the subject, behavioral facts were limited to reflexes and conditioned reflexes obtained mostly from the study of animals, such as rats and dogs. This view of behavioralism did not draw on the fully capable mind of the economic agent in his or her study of market rules or rivals' reactions. Rabin proposes that through modern surveys and experiments, the cognitive, conative, and affective aspects of individual economic agents (consciousness, feelings, and state of mind) can be better understood. Standard neoclassical economics does not incorporate such subtle factors, which may have contributed to its decline.

Behaviorists propose that predictions that consider the conduct of economic agents will outperform those that have only structural premises.[5]

---

[5] Structural premises refer to traditional models such as perfect competition and monopoly. In behavioral models, such as in Cournot, Bertrand, and Nash, behavioral assumptions are assumed to reach a market solution.

Surprisingly, time-honored concepts such as Smith's desire to better one's condition; the propensity to truck, barter, and exchange; and the propensity to procreate; along with Keynes' psychological law of savings, are played down in the behavioral approach. But Latsis (1972, 225) argues that psychological assumptions are minimized, as the major concern of the economic agent is whether to stay in business. Rabin's position on behavioral methodology corresponds with Latsis (1972) in suggesting that behaviorism can be perceived as a rival research program to the impaired neoclassical theory. Such an approach is devoid of self-effort on the part of the economic agent. No individual economic agent has his/her own perceptions of the rival's intention or the rules of the game because behavioralism focuses on "a collection of different goals pursued by a collection of people in executive positions in a business organization" (Machlup 1978, 522). With this focus, individual behavior can only be studied. For instance, we can study price behavior, product strategy, research and development expenditures, advertising expenditures, and legal tactics of the economic agents as they are revealed through a production or utility function.

Behavioralism does not represent revolutionary change, a paradigmatic shift, a complete mutation of the hard core, or heuristics of the neoclassical program. Rather, it seems to be more potent in the area of expanding and articulating such changes. We may have the potential to observe "micro revolution" in the sense of Toulmin (1972). This does not negate entry and exit strategies. The economic agents make choices that are influenced by psychological, physical, and institutional factors. The research program is reduced to choosing whether to maintain the current utility level or an alternative that will yield the highest utility. This is situational determinism analogous to Latsis' decision maker choosing whether to exit or stay in business.

Progress in the behavioral world involves more complex decision making. Perhaps models will be developed "first in their application to a single decision maker and later to a complex decision-making structure" (Latsis 1972, 230). If we use game theory as an approach to the new brand of behavioralism, then Latsis' two-stage approach is no longer necessary. In game theory, it is possible to represent multiple objectives of several players. The emphasis on psychological assumptions can be represented through allowing player-specific perceptions of the rules of the game, as well as other players' intentions. For instance, players may have different perceptions of the number of players in the game. As Latsis (1976, 26) argues, a situation of an n-person game is a possibility. But the value of "n" may differ across players, and each of the n-players may have their own perceptions of the outcome process. This analysis will include Latsis' situational determinism as a special case whenever we can reduce a multi-stage game to a single-stage game. The single exit situation is then the decision-making process of a player making the choice between a resultant payoff vector for a given set of perceptions and bargaining processes, against one for another set of perceptions and bargaining processes.

C. Experimental Implications

Moving from Rabin to Bossaerts and Campbell in Part I, the financial section looks at new directions as we move from the classical to the more enhanced strategic and experimental viewpoints. It has generally been asserted that the social sciences are not as capable of experimentation as are the physical sciences. However, when one considers the abstract character of the physical scientist's laboratory against the universal nature of the social scientist's laboratory, any advantage to the former fades in comparison. As Machlup notes, where precise measurement is possible, such as in the decision to overtake a car on the road, the physical scientist's approach is not followed. Rather, the necessary calculation is done intuitively.

In economics, two forms of experimental directions are popular. Smith (1989, 166) identifies the maximizing principle of the economist's and the psychologist's points of view. The need for these new directions rests on the desire to abandon *a priori* beliefs or auxiliary assumptions of their theory when they fail to serve their interests in reality. This is precisely Lakatos' theoretical contribution. It postulates that in cases where theory lags behind facts, research programs are in a state of deterioration (Worrall and Currie 1978, I, 6). A new direction is delayed through sophisticated falsification in which only elements in the protective belt and not in the hard core are abandoned. For a change to occur, the evidence of falsification must be accepted, which "thick-skinned" scientists ignore until a better theory is found (ibid.). Smith (1989, 163) suggests that this shift from the experimental point of view is facilitated by focusing on filling in the gap of knowledge that lies between decision theory and behavior, between how economic agents think and how they behave in experimental markets.

Bossaerts' analysis strengthens the "auxiliary assumption" of the traditional econometric models in asset pricing through experimentation. From the naive falsification perspective, Kuhn can argue that auxiliary assumptions only prolong the life of a bad model, much like those of epic cycles in Ptolemaic astronomy that set back science by about 2,000 years. However, given a second thought, Kuhn would adopt a more sophisticated position, making room for the addition of auxiliary assumptions. Bossaerts' work examines those assumptions and finds that some of them may be progressive to the extent that they find validation for his first proposition; namely, that expected excess returns are proportional to the market "beta." The approach is, in the first place, a symbolic generalization of the traditional Arrow-Debreu model to allow experimentation.

D. Strategic Implications

Campbell's work is more strategic. Focusing on strategies rather than on behavior lifts progress away from crude behavioral assumptions of the Cournot types (where rivals are held to their previous level of observed behavior) to broader practical situations that have many solutions.

Equilibrium exists for both pure and mixed strategies. John Nash (1951, 286) demonstrates that "a finite noncooperative game always has at least one equilibrium point." Given a closed, bounded, and convex simplex, any function that carries mixed strategy pairs that are close together into other mixed strategy pairs that are also close together will have a fixed-point which will be the equilibrium pair in mixed strategies.

To summarize, Thomas Kuhn describes normal and revolutionary scientific activities that explain well how new directions in a discipline take place. From the normal point of view, the models are "scientific achievements that for a time provide model problems and solutions to a community of practitioners" (Kuhn 1962, VIII). However, as new economic events are confronted over time, anomalies develop to the extent that "not only is there no means of rationally assessing two competing paradigms, there is no way of rationally comparing them at all" (Shapere 1971). In this volume, we identify extreme cases in which a new direction exhausts or usurps an old one. Perhaps it is because laws, customs, and administrative institutions survive during such changes. We find evidence that new and old ways of explaining phenomena coexist and therefore blur the distinction between revolutionary and evolutionary accounts of scientific advances in the domain of economics (Toulmin 1972, 118, 122).

We demonstrated that the developments that pitted structuralism against behavioralism represent normal scientific activity and not revolution. This argument also has some important implications for behaviorism as a budding rival research program, in terms of whether it can accommodate psychological assumptions and how it should be developed.

Presumably, game theory presents itself as a promising tool, if not a rival research program to the neoclassical theory of a firm.

The new direction approach calls for an examination of the shared beliefs of the "scientific community" (Kuhn 1977, 450). However, to get around the purely sociological, psychological, or historical perspectives, we looked at the works of a particular segment of the scientific community; namely, the works of younger outstanding scientists. The participants in this volume represent a substratum of the "invisible college" in the sense that they are from top institutions in the country.

PART I. INFORMATIONAL BEHAVIORAL ECONOMICS AND FINANCE

JOSEPH E. STIGLITZ, *INFORMATION AND THE CHANGE IN THE PARADIGM IN ECONOMICS*

Stiglitz's paper is firmly based on Kuhn's methodology of paradigm shift. The section labeled "From the competitive equilibrium paradigm to the information paradigm" clearly addresses the differences in the two paradigms. Basically, traditional neoclassical economics treats information by explicitly including an information variable "I" in a production function. Such functions are meshed with similar specifications for consumer behavior in a general equilibrium setting. Assuming some stylized facts, a main result of the neoclassical paradigm is that factors are rewarded their marginal product. The new paradigm of efficiency wage theory, for instance, predicts and explains that it can be advantageous for the producer to pay a wage that exceeds the worker's marginal product of labor. This would be true if the employer is experiencing a high rate of turnover of its skilled workforce.

Stiglitz's information paradigm evolved at a time when anomalies in the area of economic development emerged. One such anomaly, which Stiglitz traced to Gary Fields (1972), indicated that private and public returns to education are not the same. Fields' paper indicated that private returns were higher perhaps because people tend to go after the credentials. This was a setback to human capital and productivity theories. Stiglitz's information paradigm explains such anomalies within a full equilibrium framework. Such a framework proceeds from the necessity to condition marginal product on available information. It results in a paradigm that focuses most on incentives and mechanisms to process information between employer and employees.

The new paradigm presents a progressive research program in the Lakatosian sense that pervades modern research in many directions. Information asymmetry was a hard nut to crack. Broader problems include moral hazard and adverse selection problems. These problems give practitioners of the new paradigm an ample supply of problems and puzzles to solve, creating a new normal scientific approach in Kuhn's terminology. The new paradigm also has some novelties in that wages can exceed the marginal product of labor. What is more significant is that it moves the focus from money to credits and it encompasses both fixed and flexible wage theories.

MATTHEW RABIN, *BEHAVIORAL ECONOMICS*

Rabin's paper deals with deep methodological issues in establishing new directions in economics. The classical and neoclassical frameworks provide a "development-by-accumulation" path to knowledge in economics that has lasted for over 200 years. However, the works of several new researchers in the neglected area of behavioralism – such as those by Thomas Schelling, George Akerlof, Daniel Kahneman, Amos Tversky, and Richard Thaler – are not at home in the neoclassical approaches, but have been flowering in top economics departments and journals across the country. Rabin's paper addresses the movement toward the behavioral path that has been occurring for some time. It argues for a progressive shift from hard-core assumptions such as full self-control, pure rationality, all-in-all self-interest, and narrow definitions of agents toward basic but budding research based on empirical knowledge from experiments, surveys, and traditional methods on human preferences, cognition, and behavior.

PETER BOSSAERTS, *EXPERIMENTS WITH FINANCIAL MARKETS:*
IMPLICATIONS FOR ASSET PRICING THEORY

This article introduces experimentation to the mix. It distinguishes the econometric approach to asset pricing that uses experimentation on the grounds that there are too many "auxiliary assumptions." Bossaerts makes these assumptions progressive through the experimenter control. In particular, he finds that "careful control of aggregate risk and information can dramatically enhance the significance of experimental results." Also, he finds validation for equilibrium at the point where expected return is proportional to covariance with aggregate risk, and only mixed results for the role of markets in aggregating information.

While experimentation in this essay is not illustrative of the physical scientist's laboratory, it still includes the element of control. As mentioned above, Bossaerts discusses predictions of models where control is present from the angles that a financial market both "aggregates" and "equilibrates." Such predictions through experimentation are meant to test basic markets such as the NASDAQ and NYSE. This approach represents a new direction because it presents a new way of seeing things. For instance, although it is possible to compute asset prices directly from general equilibrium models, we can compute them only indirectly from a financial market experiment. However, within a framework of asset pricing theory, such calculations are possible because one need not rely on risk aversion and endowments data. Overall, the author presents experimentation within asset pricing theory as only a budding research program that requires further experimentation. It is progressive in the sense that it recovers the rational expectation equilibria.

JOHN Y. CAMPBELL, *TWO PUZZLES OF ASSET PRICING AND
THEIR IMPLICATIONS FOR INVESTORS*

Because finance is an important source of growth in the global economy, our need to understand risk and return in a rational way has been elevated to the forefront of financial analysis. Campbell examines two puzzles of asset pricing, one dealing with equity premium and the other with equity volatility. He explains why models that linked asset prices to aggregate consumption and dividend behavior do not explain crises. He investigates problems from exemplar questions, such as why average stock returns are so high, given their volatility and consumption behavior and where the volatility comes from. Symbolic generalizations from intertemporal marginal rate of substitution of investors, stochastic discount factors (SDFs), consumption models, the Power Utility Function, and lognormal and heteroskadistic distributions are considered.

PART II: MACROECONOMICS AND PUBLIC POLICIES

PERRY MEHRLING, *WHITHER MACRO?*

Sometimes paradigms can be referenced to the authors, their work and policies, and the degree of articulation of the new approach, rather than to distinctions among approaches. Mehrling's essay considers and illustrates those sources for many first directions in macroeconomics prior to Keynes and up through Solow, Lucas, Romer, Mankiw, and other modern contributors.

The essay exemplifies new directions in modern Keynesian macroeconomics. It points to shifts from (1) the Keynesian consensus of the 1960s, (2) the supply to demand-driven usable cores, (3) the monetarist model of the Friedman type, and (4) the new classical and real business cycle types. Mehrling supports a new direction based on the IS-LM diagram, with a possible "demand can create its own supply" twist in the sense of Solow (1997, 232). More specifically, the new path is based on reality, empirical observations, or – more simply – on the practical affairs of government and businesses in the new macroeconomies concerned with high growth and productivity and low inflation and unemployment. But the approach, although shifting, is a stable one. A government may wish to keep inflation and output in a well observable corridor of their target values, through using an interest rate it can control, such as the federal funds and discount rates. Chaotic variations in their values, as notoriously demonstrated during the Great Depression of the 1930s and the frequent inflation episodes of the 1970s, are exceptions to the rule but have perhaps created a larger role for government through accounting for about a quarter of a country's GDP.

Such a usable core of the modern Keynesian system has the novelties of being dynamic where actual values converge to their natural levels, short- and long-term relationships are unified or merged through applying short-term coefficients to the convergence process, and the distinction among regions using the gold or commodity standard is played down. The theory is also easily adapted to the global economy, perhaps taking macroeconomics back to the topical world of banking and finance, the way Keynes and Hawtrey initially viewed macroeconomics.

The new direction provides an ample number of problems to be solved by its practitioners and consequently is quite vibrant. It creates concerns of big government in the wider global market. Problems have grown, as well, in the areas of health care, social security, and education. These problems may potentially force further changes in several areas: integrating money into general equilibrium models; overcoming puzzles, such as those raised by Farmer (1993) as to why the price of money and the money rate of interest are positive; extending the Gurley and Shaw (1960) puzzle of inside and outside money to include currency as a promise to pay; and other puzzles of the hierarchical nature of monetary systems. Macro theories may also shift with the complexity of new equilibrium concepts such as multiple and sunspot equilibria, complex dynamics, heterogeneous agent problems, and Taylor's expansion rule beyond the financial and banking areas.

JAMES M. POTERBA, *RECENT DEVELOPMENTS IN AND FUTURE PROSPECTS FOR PUBLIC ECONOMICS*

Poterba takes on the new directions in public economics during the last three decades. He features the incentive problems from the tax design point of view, a new foundation to understand how taxes and social insurance programs affect economic agents such as households and firms and social support for policy design in the areas of taxing and spending.

This essay demonstrates how new paths in the area of public economics have evolved during the last few decades. It concentrates on empirical advances, where new directions allow both step-by-step as well as rapid advances of knowledge. In regard to the former, we can surmise reconstructed approaches for the future in relation to environmental issues, the economics of aging, privatization, open economies, social programs, taxation, transfer payments, and national security. In regard to the latter, we see increased availability of public use of data sets, rapid advance of econometric methods for the analysis of both cross-sectional and panel data on household behavior, and the presence of several substantial tax reforms during the 1980s and 1990s, such as ERTA 1981 and TRA 1986.

PART III: INTERNATIONAL TRADE AND DEVELOPMENT

KYLE BAGWELL AND ROBERT W. STAIGER, *ECONOMIC THEORY AND THE INTERPRETATION OF GATT/WTO*

Bagwell and Staiger have traced new directions for GATT/WTO during the last fifty years through the political institutions. They identified how the most recent 1994 Uruguay Round of GATT has extended and articulated the institutional approach to new areas.

The novel achievement of GATT is a drastic cut in ad valorem tariffs from 40 percent to 4 percent. The winning over of countries toward the new direction is evidence of this shift. GATT began with twenty-three member nations and now includes more than 140. To provide an economic interpretation for the new path, the authors discuss the political–economic objectives of negotiating governments, traditional terms of trade externalities, and the need for self-policing in trade agreements. In this context, the authors identify two hard-core elements of the new system; namely, reciprocity that invokes the *ceteris paribus* assumption on world price, and enforcement, which is learned through repeated games of cooperation and noncooperation.

DEBRAJ RAY, *WHAT'S NEW IN DEVELOPMENT ECONOMICS?*

Development economics is in a state of flux. The convergence concept in growth and development is hardly a decade old and is already being challenged, at least by the multiple equilibra notion. A desired investment may be denied because a complementary investment did not materialize, and not due to model parameters. In the budding multiple equilibria model, policies shift from "tweaking" parameters, such as savings and fertility rates, toward "pulling" the economy out of an equilibrium. Because the new direction makes equilibrium either good or bad, once the bads are replaced, a policy measure need not be persistent or permanent. The new approach also minimizes differences in population and culture, and has an intertemporally inactive role for government.

To an extent, the author argues that the convergence path represents a degenerating program because its auxiliary assumptions embedded within its *ceteris paribus* clauses are untenable. Other variables such as fertility rates and savings cannot be held equal, and complexities such as differences in culture and government role in development must be dealt with in a new way. The new direction aims at a substantial reduction or elimination of assumptions in favor of a "first principle" or "original cause" model, in which cultural differences and governmental interventions are viewed from a new perspective.

PART IV: CONTRACTS, LAW, AND GAMING

MICHELLE GARFINKEL AND STERGIOS SKAPERDAS, *CONTRACT OR WAR? ON THE CONSEQUENCES OF A BROADER VIEW OF SELF-INTEREST IN ECONOMICS*

This essay examines the rivalry between two models that originated from Edgeworth's work; namely, war and contracts. The authors argue that the models limp along on one leg, that leg being the contract curve. They want to stabilize its gait by bringing on the other leg – a progressive research program since Adam Smith has endowed it with "self-interest." Their essay proceeds to extend and articulate Edgeworth's model by the exemplars of conflict and appropriation.

This new direction requires economists to expand their empire in order to enlist the help of other disciplines. Economists must usurp the model's dark side – which is based on conflict – and manage it properly in order to transcend the tradeoff of production and appropriation. From a model point of view, the absence of property rights would put in place a mechanism of conflict to enable distribution. The new direction manages conflict situations in a way that would avoid the waste of resources such as high security cost that takes away from economic activity. It minimizes competition by groups and individuals for political influence and advantages. The new path can manage conflict situations through third-party interventions, empathy, ethical norms and beliefs, or even religion and law.

ALAN O. SYKES, *NEW DIRECTIONS IN LAW AND ECONOMICS*

This essay demonstrates how practical cases, such as *United States v. Microsoft* and the "patient bill of rights," force practitioners of the legal paths to look for coherent and acceptable theoretical solutions to problems in the field of economic law. It focuses on the practical state of affairs in modern criminal law, international law, and insurance law, in which the legal practitioners have to feel their way through issues that are not yet codified or that lack precedents or guidance from a public policy perspective.

Sykes underscores that the underlying new direction is established on reality or empirical support. The puzzles are articulated from a cost–benefit specification in the form of cost net of transfers; fines versus incarceration; taxes on wealth and human capital; and the role of stigma in deterrence, marginal deterrence, and shaming penalty. The new puzzle confronts such problems as fines not being used as much as expected; some criminals walking away with large sums of verifiable wealth; deterrence in the form of "three-strikes" laws tending to increase the homicide rate; crime rates in cities depending on the percent of female heads of households; and factors such as race and the prevalence of guns influencing the crime rate. Add to this the recent exposure of corporate crimes, and you have a truly challenging puzzle.

Fundamental puzzles in the area of international law abound in the form of enactments, codifications, enforcements, policing of agreements, and human rights agreements. The new direction points to unilateral sanctions that promise "tit for tat" equilibrium solutions, either through self-interest conditions – with their mutual advantage to the players – or the credible threat of sanctions. The new approach is articulated in the concepts of optimal contracting under treaties, terms of trade, protection for organized industries, the free rider problems under the most favored nations practice, and under protectionism through regulation and tariffs. The budding research programs are attracting a significant amount of work in the traditional conflict areas of war, human rights, dumping, the patterns of private rights, and maritime law.

In the area of insurance law, the author underscores how practical occurrences bring up new puzzles ranging narrowly from "per occurrence" claims to broader terrorist and catastrophic events in insurance coverage. The new direction examines problem–solution in the areas of insurance regulation, particularly at the national versus state levels, and the ease of entry and exit in lines of coverage that remain puzzling. More challenging conundrums await in the area of common law decisions in insurance contracts that are complicated with moral hazard problems. A principal–agent problem exists in the area of liability policies, in which the insurer can settle a case against the insured. Solutions are sought in areas that would maintain private and social optimality, as well as in the maintenance of harmony between judgments and the policyholder's ability to pay.

REFERENCES

Bechtel, William. *Philosophy of Science: An Overview for Cognitive Science*. Lawrence Erlbaum Associates, 1988.

Blaug, Mark. *The Methodology of Economics*. New York: Cambridge University Press, 1980.

Cross, Rod. "The Duhem – Quine Thesis, Lakatos and the Appraisal of Theories in Macroeconomics." *The Economic Journal* 92 (June 1982): 320–40.

De Marchi, Neil, and Mark Blaug. *Appraising Economic Theories: Studies in the Methodology of Research Programs*. Northampton, MA: Edward Elgar Publishing Company, 1991.

Eatwell, J., P. Newman, and M. Milgate, eds. *Palgrave: A Dictionary of Economics*. Grove's Dictionary, Inc., 1987.

Farmer, Roger E. A. *The Macroeconomics of Self-Fulfilling Prophecies*. Cambridge, MA: MIT Press, 1993.

Fields, G. "Private and Social Returns to Education to Labor Surplus Economies." *Eastern Africa Economic Review* 4 (June 1972): 41–62.

Gordon, Donald F. "The Contribution of the History of Economic Thought to the Understanding of Economic Theory, Economic History, and the History of Economic Policy." *American Economic Review* 55 (1965): 119–27.

Gurley, J. G., and E. S. Shaw. *Money in a Theory of Finance*. Washington, D.C.: Brookings Institution, 1960.

Hausman, Daniel M. "Economic Methodology in a Nutshell." *The Journal of Economic Perspectives* 3 (Spring 1989): 115–27.

Hayek, Friedrich. *The Sensory Order*. Chicago: University of Chicago Press, 1952.

Heilbroner, Robert. "Economics as a 'Value-Free' Science." *Social Research* 40 (1973): 129–43.

Kuhn, Thomas. *The Structure of Scientific Revolutions*. University of Chicago Press, 1st ed. 1962, 2nd ed. 1970.

Kuhn, Thomas. "Logic of Discovery or Psychology of Research?" and "Reflections on My Critics." In *Criticism and the Growth of Knowledge,* edited by I. Lakatos and A. Mustgrave. Cambridge: Cambridge University Press, 1977: 91–196.

Kuhn, Thomas. "Second Thoughts on Paradigm." In *The Structure of Scientific Theories*, edited by Frederick Suppes. Urbana, IL: University of Illinois Press, 2nd ed. 1977: 459–82.

Lakatos, Imre, and Alan Musgrave, eds. *Criticism and the Growth of Knowledge.* Cambridge: Cambridge University Press, 1977.

Latsis, Spiro. "Situational Determinism in Economics," *The British Journal for the Philosophy of Science* 23 (1972): 207–45.

Latsis, Spiro. *Method and Appraisal in Economics*. New York: Cambridge University Press, 1976.

Laudan, Larry. *Progress and Its Problems: Towards a Theory of Scientific Growth*. Berkeley: University of California Press, 1977.

Loasby, Brian J. "Hypothesis and Paradigm in the Theory of the Firm." *The Economic Journal* 81 (December 1971): 863–85.

Machlup, Fritz. *Methodology of Economics and Other Social Sciences*. New York: Academic Press, 1978: 425–50.

Masterman, Margaret. "The Nature of a Paradigm." In Imre Lakatos and Alan Musgrave, *Criticism and the Growth of Knowledge*. London: Cambridge University Press, 1970: 59–89.

Mayo, Deborah G. "Ducks, Rabbits, and Normal Science: Recasting the Kuhn's Eye View of Popper's Demarcation of Science." *The British Journal for the Philosophy of Science* 47 (1996): 271–90.

Mohr, H. *Lectures on Structure and Significance of Science*. New York: Springer-Verlag, 1977.

Nash, J. "Non-Cooperative Games." *Annals of Mathematics* 54 (1951): 286–95.

Nell, E. J. "Economics: A Revival of Political Economy." In *Ideology in Social Science*, edited by R. Blackburn. London: Fontana, 1972: 76–95.

Popper, K. R. *The Logic of Scientific Discovery*. New York: Basic Books, 1959.

Popper, K. R. *Conjectures and Refutations*. New York: Basic Books, 1962.

Popper, K. R. *The Open Society and Its Enemies*. Princeton University Press, 1971.

Puttaswamaiah, K. ed. *Paul A. Samuelson and the Foundations of Modern Economics*. New Brunswick: Transaction Publishers, 2002.

Quine, W. V. *Pursuit of Truth*. Cambridge, MA: Harvard University Press, 1990.

Samuelson, Paul A. *Collected Scientific Papers of Paul A. Samuelson, Volume II*, edited by Joseph E. Stiglitz. Cambridge, MA: MIT Press, 1966.

Samuelson, Paul A. *Collected Scientific Papers of Paul A. Samuelson, Volume III*, edited by Robert C. Merton. Cambridge, MA: MIT Press, 1972.

Samuelson, Paul A. "My Life Philosophy: Policy Credos and Working Ways." In *Eminent Economists, Their Life Philosophies*, edited by Michael Szenberg. London and New York: Cambridge University Press, 1993.

Samuelson, Paul A. "Foreword." In Michael Szenberg, *Passion and Craft, Economists at Work*. Ann Arbor, MI: University of Michigan Press, 1999.

Shapere, Dudley. "The Paradigm Concept." *Science* 172 (1971): 706–9.

Shapere, Dudley. *Reason and the Search for Knowledge: Investigation in the Philosophy of Science*. Boston: D. Reidel Publishing Company, 1984.

Smith, Vernon. L. "Theory, Experiment and Economics." *The Journal of Economic Perspectives* 3 (Winter 1989): 151–71.

Solow, Robert. "Is There a Core of Usable Macroeconomics We Should All Believe In?" *American Economic Review*, 87 Proceeding (May 1997): 230–2.

Suppes, Frederick, ed. *The Structure of Scientific Theories*. Urbana, IL: University of Illinois Press, 2nd ed. 1977.

Szenberg, Michael. *Eminent Economists, Their Life Philosophies*. London and New York: Cambridge University Press, 1993.

Szenberg, Michael. *Passion and Craft, Economists at Work*, with a Foreword by Paul A. Samuelson. Ann Arbor, MI: University of Michigan Press, 1999.

Taylor, J. B. *Principles of Macroeconomics*. Boston, MA: Houghton Mifflin, 2nd ed. 2001.

Toulmin, Stephen. *Human Understanding*. Princeton University Press, 1972.

Varian, Hal. "A Portfolio of Nobel Laureates: Markowitz, Miller and Sharpe." *The Journal of Economic Perspectives* 7 (Winter, 1993): 159–69.

Ward, Benjamin. *What's Wrong with Economics?* New York: Basic Books, 1972.

Woozley, A. D. *Theory of Knowledge*. London: Hutchinson & Co. 1949, reprinted 1969.

Worrall, John, and Gregory Currie. *The Methodology of Scientific Research Programmes, Vols. I and II*. New York: Cambridge University Press, 1978.

PART I

INFORMATIONAL BEHAVIORAL ECONOMICS AND FINANCE

Information and the Change in the Paradigm in Economics

Joseph E. Stiglitz[1]

INTRODUCTION

Information economics has already had a profound effect on how we think about economic policy, and is likely to have an even greater influence in the future. Many of the major political debates over the past two decades have centered around one key issue: the efficiency of the market economy, and the appropriate relationship between the market and the government. The argument of Adam Smith suggested, at best, a limited role for government. The set of ideas that I will present here undermined Smith's theory and the view of government that rested on it.

I began the study of economics some forty-one years ago. At the time, it seemed to me that if the central theorems that argued that the economy was Pareto efficient – that, in some sense, we were living in the best of all possible worlds – were true, we should be striving to create a different world. As a graduate student, I set out to try to create models with assumptions – and conclusions – closer to those that accorded with the world I saw, with all of its imperfections. My first visits to the developing world in 1967, and a more extensive stay in Kenya in 1969, made an indelible impression on me. Imperfection of information, the absence of markets, and the pervasiveness and persistence of seeming dysfunctional institutions, like sharecropping, attracted my attention. I had not seen before the massive unemployment that characterized African cities, unemployment that could not be explained either by unions or minimum wage laws (which, even when they existed, were regularly circumvented).

---

[1] This is a shortened version of a more elaborate essay. The full version appears in two parts in the Fall 2003 and Spring 2004 issues of *The American Economist*.

There was clearly a massive discrepancy between the models we had been taught and what I saw.

My attention centered around the assumption of perfect information. Previous work in economics had assumed that information was perfect, or even if imperfect, information was *fixed*; individuals beliefs did not change *within the model* as a result of what they saw. No one, of course, believed that this was the case. The hope – and it was no more than a hope – was that a world with perfect information would provide a good description of an economy, so long as information was not too imperfect. Our research showed that our hope was not well grounded; that even a little bit of imperfection in information could have large effects. And, of course, in many circumstances the imperfections of information may be overwhelming.

One of the main developments to follow from the analysis of information imperfections for the functioning of markets is the construction of *macroeconomic* models that help explain why the economy amplifies shocks and makes them persistent, and why there may be, even in competitive equilibrium, unemployment, and credit rationing.

The profound implications for economic policy of the paradigm are illustrated by recent events. Some of the huge mistakes which have been made in policy – in for instance the management of the East Asia crisis or the transition of the former communist countries to the market – might have been avoided if there had been a better understanding of issues, like bankruptcy and corporate governance, to which the new information economics called attention. And the so-called Washington consensus policies, which have predominated in the policy advice of the international financial institutions over the past quarter century, have been based on market fundamentalist policies that ignored the information-theoretic concerns, and this explains at least in part their widespread failures.

Information affects decision making in every context – not just inside firms and households. More recently, I have turned my attention to some aspects of what might be called the *political economy* of information: the role of information in political processes, in collective decision making. For two hundred years, well before the economics of information became a subdiscipline within economics, Sweden had enacted legislation to increase transparency. There are asymmetries of information between those governing and those governed, and just as markets strive to overcome asymmetries of information, we need to look for ways by which the scope for asymmetries of information in political processes can be limited and their consequences mitigated.

THE HISTORICAL SETTING

I do not want to review and describe in detail the models of information asymmetries that have been constructed in the past thirty years. I do want to highlight some of the dramatic impacts that information economics has had on how economics is approached today, how it has provided explanations for phenomena that were previously unexplained, how it has altered our views about how the economy functions, and, perhaps most importantly, how it has led to a rethinking of the appropriate role for government in our society. Much of the work was motivated to see how the standard models could embrace problems of information imperfections. Following Marshall's dictum *"Natura non facit saltum,"* it was hoped that economies in which information was not too imperfect would look very much like economies in which information was perfect. As I noted above, one of the main results of our research was to show that this was not true; that even a small amount of information imperfection could have a large effect on the nature of the equilibrium.

And of course, that was precisely what we wanted. Something was wrong – seriously wrong – with the competitive equilibrium models that represented the prevailing paradigm when we went to graduate school. It seemed to say that unemployment did not exist, that issues of efficiency and equity could be neatly separated, so that economists could neatly set aside problems of inequality and poverty as they went about their business of designing more efficient economic systems.

It is hard to reconcile the competitive equilibrium model with a host of other predictions and empirical puzzles. In microeconomics, there were tax paradoxes (such as why did firms seemingly not take actions which minimized their tax liabilities), security market paradoxes (such as why did asset prices seem to exhibit such high volatility), and behavioral puzzles (such as why did firms respond to risks in ways which were markedly different from that predicted by the theory). In macroeconomics, the cyclical movements of many of the key aggregate variables – such as consumption, inventories, real product wages, real consumption wages, and interest rates – are hard to reconcile with the standard theory; and if the perfect market assumptions were even approximately satisfied, the distress caused by cyclical movements in the economy would be much less than seems to be the case.

The problem that we saw with the models that we were taught was not only that they seemed wrong, but that they also left a host of other problems unexplained. IPOs typically sold at a discount. Equities, which provided far better risk diversification than debt, play such a limited role in financing new investment.

Worse still, some – seeing the obvious contradictions between what they saw and the predictions of the competitive equilibrium model – sought to assign the blame for the failure elsewhere. They saw unemployment as largely reflecting an interference (for example, by government in setting minimum wages or by trade unions in using their monopoly power to set wages too high) with the free workings of the market, with the obvious implication: unemployment would be eliminated if markets were made more *flexible*, that is, unions and government interventions were eliminated.

The economics profession was reluctant to let go of the perfect market model. Some, like G. Stigler, while recognizing the importance of information, argued that once the real costs of information were taken into account, even with imperfect information, the standard results of economics would still hold. Information was just a transactions cost. For the more mathematically inclined, information could be incorporated into production functions of, say, goods by inserting an "I" for the input "information," and "I" itself could be produced by inputs, like labor.

Other economists sought to narrow the scope of the arenas in which the standard competitive arena did not work. P. A. Samuelson could not ignore the bouts of unemployment that had plagued capitalism since its inception; he talked of the neoclassical synthesis, in which once government restored the economy to full employment, the standard theory would once again apply.

Interestingly, these economists ignored the warnings of the nineteenth century and earlier masters on how information concerns might alter the analyses. For instance, Smith, in anticipating later discussions of adverse selection, wrote that as firms raise interest rates, the best borrowers drop out of the market. If lenders know perfectly the risks associated with each borrower, this would matter little; each borrower would be charged an appropriate risk premium. It is because lenders do not know the default probabilities of borrowers perfectly that this process of adverse selection has such important consequences.

Together with a number of co-authors, we began a systematic assault on the competitive equilibrium paradigm, looking at how introducing information imperfections would alter most of the important conclusions. It seemed to me, for instance, massive unemployment was just the tip of the iceberg, of more pervasive market efficiencies that were harder to detect. If markets seemed to function *so* badly some of the time, certainly they must be malperforming in more subtle ways much of the time, and that was what Bruce Greenwald and I were able to show – that whenever information was imperfect (or markets incomplete), the market was essentially never (constrained) Pareto efficient. We showed that Keynes was right, that there could be persistent unemployment, but that the standard Keynesian models – derived from Hicks' IS-LM framework, focusing on wage and price rigidity – provided only a part of the story. Even with wage and price flexibility, there could be serious macroeconomic problems. Given the nature of the debt contracts, falling wages and prices led to bankruptcy and economic disruptions, actually exacerbating the economic downturn. Had there been more wage and price flexibility, matters might have been even worse. Our critique of the rigid wage/price stories went further: Because neither government nor unions imposed the limitations on wage and price dynamics in many sectors of the economy, at the very least, those who argued that the problem was wage and price rigidities had to look for other *market* imperfections, and any policy remedy, including a call for greater flexibility, had to take those factors into account. Our imperfect information models provided an *explanation* of the slow adjustment of wages and prices.

In the next section, I shall explain how it was not just the discrepancies between the standard competitive model and its predictions that led to it being questioned. The model was not robust – even slight departures from the underlying assumption of perfect information had large consequences.

But before turning to those issues, it may be useful to describe some of the concrete issues that underlay the beginnings of my research program in this area. Key to my thinking on these issues was the time between 1969 and 1971 that I spent at the Institute for Development Studies at the University of Nairobi with the support of the Rockefeller Foundation.

Education as a Screening Device

One of the critical policy issues posed was how much should the government invest in education, particularly secondary and tertiary education. As we looked at the Kenyan labor market, it became clear that the standard human capital model provided only a part of the explanation of what was going on. Individuals wanted a higher credential in order to get a job. There was a high level of unemployment, and those with better credentials often seemed to go to the head of the queue.

G. Fields, a young scholar working at the Institute of Development Studies in Kenya, developed in 1972 a simple model suggesting that the private returns to education – the enhanced probability of getting a good job – differed from the social return; and that it was possible that as more people get educated, the private returns got higher (it was even more necessary to get the credential) even though the social return might decline. Fields' work did not provide a full *equilibrium* analysis: wages were fixed, rather than competitively determined. This led me to ask, what would the market equilibrium look like if wages were set equal to mean marginal products *conditional on the information that was available*? And what were the *incentives* and *mechanisms* for employers and employees to acquire or transmit information? Within a group of otherwise similar job applicants (who therefore face the same wage), the employer has an incentive to identify who is the most able, to find some way of *sorting* or *screening* among them, *if it could keep that information private*. But it often cannot, and if others find out about the true ability, the wage will be bid up, and the employer will be unable to *appropriate* the return to the information. At the very beginning of this research program we had thus identified one of the key issues in information economics: the difficulty of *appropriating* the returns.

On the other hand, the employee, *if he or she knew his ability* (that is, if there were *asymmetries of information between the employee and the employer*) and he or she knew that his abilities were above the average of those in the market, had an incentive to convince the employer of his ability. But someone at the bottom of the ability distribution had an incentive not to have the information revealed. Here was a second principle that was to be explored in subsequent years: there are incentives on the part of individuals for information not to be revealed, for secrecy, or, in modern parlance, for a lack of transparency. This raised a question: how did the forces for secrecy and for information disclosure get balanced? What was the equilibrium that emerged? I will postpone until the next section a description of that equilibrium.

Efficiency Wage Theory

A central concern was the high urban unemployment, seemingly caused by migration from the rural sector. M. Todaro and J. Harris had formulated a simple model of labor migration from the rural to the urban sector where high urban wages attracted workers, and they were willing to risk unemployment for the chance of those higher wages. How could you explain the high wages, which were well in excess of the minimum wage? It did not seem as if either government or unions were *forcing* these high wages. Here again one needed an equilibrium theory of wage determination. I recalled, during an earlier stint at Cambridge, discussions with H. Leibenstein in which he had postulated that in very poor countries, higher wages lead to higher productivity. It might not pay firms to cut wages, if productivity was cut more than proportionately, even if there was an excess supply of labor. The key insight was to recognize that there were a variety of other reasons why, when information and contracting were imperfect, productivity might depend on wages. In that case, it might pay firms to pay a higher wage than the minimum necessary to hire labor; such wages I referred to as *efficiency wages*. With efficiency wages, there could exist an equilibrium level of unemployment. I explored four explanations for why productivity might depend on wages (besides through nutrition). The simplest was that lower wages lead to higher turnover, and therefore higher turnover costs that the firm bore. It was not until some years later than we were able to explain more fully – based on limitations of information – why it was that firms had to bear these turnover costs.

Another version of the efficiency wage related to the work I was beginning on asymmetric information. Any manager will tell you that you attract better workers by paying them higher wages, an application of the general notion of adverse selection. If all firms were paying the market-clearing wage, it might pay a firm to offer a higher wage, to attract more able workers. The efficiency wage theory meant that there could exist unemployment *in equilibrium*. It was thus clear that the notion that had underlain much of traditional competitive equilibrium analysis – that markets *had* to clear – was simply not true if information were imperfect.

It was also clear that higher wages provided workers with a greater incentive to work harder. (This was an information problem: if information were perfect, workers would be paid only in proportion to the effort they exerted.) It was not until several years later that Carl Shapiro and I formulated the now-standard general equilibrium version. We recognized that if all workers are identical, and all firms paid workers the same wage, then if it paid one firm to pay a high wage, it would pay all of them. But if a worker was then fired for shirking, and there was full employment, he or she could immediately get another job, at the same wage. The high wage would provide no incentive. But if there was unemployment, then there was a price for shirking. A fired worker would have to remain in the unemployment pool for some time before getting another job. The higher the unemployment rate, the longer he or she would have to wait. We showed that *in equilibrium* there *had* to be unemployment: unemployment was the discipline device that forced workers to work. In practice, of course, workers are not identical, so problems of adverse selection become intertwined with those of incentives; being fired does convey information – there is typically a stigma.

There was a fourth version of the efficiency wage, in which productivity was related to *morale* effects, perceptions about how *fairly* they were being treated. Although I briefly discussed this version in my earlier work – anticipating, in some ways, the development of what has come to be called *behavioral macroeconomics* – it was not until almost twenty years later that the idea was fully developed, in the important work of G. Akerlof and J. L. Yellen.

Sharecropping and the General Theory of Incentives

Incentives are at the core of economics – some economists have even gone so far as to say that incentives is the *main* economic issue. As I suggested earlier, if information were perfect, the incentive problem would not be particularly complicated. Individuals would be paid if and only if they did the contracted-for work, and thus would have the incentive to do what they promised. But any visitor to a developing country cannot but be struck by the fact that one of the prevailing contractual arrangements seems to undermine incentives. Sharecropping is a common form of land tenancy in a developing country, in which the worker surrenders half (sometimes two-thirds) of the produce to the landlord in return for the use of his land. Surely, this must enervate incentives to work hard. If that was the case, why was sharecropping so common? I argued that it represented a compromise, between risk bearing and incentives. The underlying *information* problem was that the input of the worker could not be observed, but only his output, and his output was not perfectly correlated with his input. The sharecropping contract could be thought of as a combination of a rental contract *plus* an insurance contract, in which the landlord "rebates" part of the rent if crops turn out badly. There is not full insurance (which would be equivalent to a wage contract) because such insurance would attenuate all incentives. The adverse effect of insurance on incentives to avoid the insured against contingency is referred to as *moral hazard*. I analyzed the *equilibrium* sharecropping contract, and in doing so effectively analyzed equilibrium in insurance markets in which moral hazard was important. I argued that the incentive problems were isomorphic to those facing modern corporations, for example, in providing incentives to their managers. There followed a large body of literature on optimal and equilibrium incentive schemes, in labor, capital, and insurance markets.

Later work would show the relationship between this information problem and other information problems. Even if farmers were willing to bear the risk, there is a problem with rental contracts: the tenant may not have the money to pay the rent in advance. This problem could be overcome if individuals could borrow money. But capital market imperfections – limitations on the ability to borrow, which themselves arise from information imperfections – explain why this "solution" does not work.

Equilibrium Wage and Price Distributions

The huge disparity between wages in the urban and rural sectors was only one example of similar workers receiving markedly different wages. The same seemed to hold true within the urban sector. One version of the efficiency wage theory described above argued that firms pay high wages to lower turnover costs. Firms with higher training costs might pay higher wages. But the consequence of raising the wages depends, of course, on what other firms pay. The challenge was to formulate an *equilibrium* model, in which there was a wage distribution, which led firms to pay different wages – the distribution of wages that had originally been postulated. The implication was that wage discrepancies might not be explicable solely in terms of differences in abilities.

FROM THE COMPETITIVE EQUILIBRIUM PARADIGM
TO THE INFORMATION PARADIGM

Much of the research in the profession was directed not at reconciling the discrepancy between the predictions of the standard model and reality, but shoring up the intellectual foundations of the existing theories. Much of the attention was directed to the underlying *mathematics*, at, for instance, the assumptions of convexity and continuity. With these assumptions one could prove the *existence* of equilibrium and its (Pareto) efficiency. The question was, could these mathematical assumptions be dropped, and some version of these central theorems still be valid? The standard proofs of the fundamental theorems of economics did not even list in their enumerated assumptions those concerning information: the perfect information assumption was so ingrained it did not have to be explicitly stated. The *economic* assumptions to which the proofs of efficiency called attention concerned the absence of externalities and public goods. The market failures approach to the economics of the public sector discussed alternative approaches by which these market failures could be corrected, but these market failures were highly circumscribed.

The standard paradigm talked about scarcity, but ignored other information problems faced by consumers and firms every day. It ignored, for instance, imperfections of information concerning the prices and qualities of the various objects that are for sale in the market, the quality and efforts of the workers they hire, and the returns of investment projects. There were no shocks, no unanticipated events: at the beginning of time, the full equilibrium was solved, and everything from then on was an unfolding over time of what had been planned in each of the contingencies. It argued that institutions did not matter – markets could see through them, and equilibrium was simply determined by the laws of supply and demand. It said that the distribution of wealth did not matter. And it said that (by and large) history did not matter – knowing preferences, technology, and initial endowments, one could describe the time path of the economy.

Work on the economics of information began by questioning each of the underlying premises, each of the central theorems. The convexity assumptions which corresponded to long-standing principles of diminishing returns were no longer plausible. It was not just that the cost of acquiring information could be viewed as fixed costs. R. Radner and Stiglitz showed that there was a *fundamental nonconcavity in the value of information*, that is, under quite general conditions, it never paid to buy just a little bit of information. R. A. Arnott and Stiglitz showed that such problems were pervasive in even the simplest of moral hazard problems (where individuals had a choice of alternative actions, for example, the amount of risk taking to assume.) Although we had not repealed the law of diminishing returns, we had shown its domain to be more limited than had previously been realized.

M. Rothschild and I showed that under natural formulations of what might be meant by a competitive market with imperfect information, equilibrium often did not exist – even when there was an arbitrarily small amount of information imperfection. While subsequent research has looked for alternative definitions of equilibrium, we remain unconvinced. Most of them violate the natural meaning of competition, that is, where each participant in the market is so small that he or she believes that he or she will have no effect on the behavior of others.

The new information paradigm went further in undermining the foundations of competitive equilibrium analysis, the basic "laws" of economics, which include: the law of demand and supply, the law of the single price, the law of the competitive price, and the efficient markets hypothesis. Each of these cornerstones was rejected, or was shown to hold under much more restrictive conditions than had previously been believed to be the case.

- When prices affect "quality" – either because of incentive or selection effects – equilibrium may be characterized by demand not equaling supply; firms will not pay lower wages to workers, even when they can obtain such workers, because doing so will raise their labor costs; firms will not charge higher interest rates, even when they can do so, because of an excess demand for credit, because doing so will increase the average default rate, and thus lower expected returns.
- The market will be characterized by wage and price distributions, even when there is no exogenous source of "noise" in the economy, even when all firms and workers are (otherwise) identical.
- In equilibrium, firms will charge a price in excess of the marginal costs, or workers are paid a wage in excess of their reservation wage. The "surplus" is required to provide the *incentive* for maintaining a reputation.
- Even in situations where reputation rents were not required, information imperfections gave rise to market power – there is *imperfect competition* – which results in firms charging prices in excess of marginal cost.
- The efficient markets hypothesis held that prices in the stock market fully reflected all information. But if that were the case, then there would be no incentive for anyone to expend money to collect information. Work with S. Grossman showed that the price system both imperfectly aggregated information and that there was an equilibrium amount of "disequilibrium."

The most fundamental reason why markets with imperfect information differ from those in which it is perfect is that actions (including choices) convey information, market participants know this, and this affects their behavior.

Willingness to provide a guarantee conveys information about a firm's confidence in the product. On average, those willing to take an insurance policy with a large deductible are those less likely to have an accident. A firm may, at the same time, not assign an employee to a highly visible job, because it knows that the assignment will be interpreted as an indication that the employee is good, making it more likely that a rival will try to hire the person away.

The problem in constructing an equilibrium model, as we emphasize below, was that participants in the market know that their actions convey information, and this affects their behavior; but those observing their behavior know that their behavior has been altered. There is, as a result, a most complex interdependence, which had to be unraveled. For instance, an individual with a high probability of having an accident might buy, it would seem, a high deductible in order to fool the insurance firm into thinking that he or she was, in fact, one of those individuals with a low accident probability. But the insurance company would know this, and the individual would know that the insurance company would know what he or she was trying to do, it appeared that analyzing the equilibrium was not going to be easy.

There is another fundamental reason that a world with imperfect information differs from that with perfect information. Underlying standard competitive market analysis was the assumption that a complete set of markets existed. But in fact, many important markets (especially for risks) do not exist. The question was why. One of the early insights by Akerlof was that markets in which adverse selection is important may be thin or absent. The absence of particular markets, for example, for risk, has profound implications for how *other* markets function. The fact that workers and firms cannot buy insurance against many of the risks which they face affects labor and capital markets; it leads, for instance, to labor contracts in which the employer provides *some* insurance. But the design of these more complicated – but still imperfect and incomplete – contracts affects the efficiency, and overall performance, of the economy.

In the next section, I want to present a somewhat more systematic account of the *principles* of the economics of information.

Some Problems in Constructing an Alternative Paradigm

But before turning to that issue, I want to discuss briefly some methodological issues. One of the keys to success was formulating simple models in which the set of relevant information could be fully specified – and so the precise ways in which information was imperfect could also be fully specified. Perhaps the hardest problem was modeling equilibrium. It was important to think about both sides of the market – employers and employees, the insurance company and the insured, lender and borrower. Each had to be modeled as "rational," in some sense, making inferences on the basis of available information. Each side's behavior too had to be rational, based on beliefs about the consequences of their actions; and those consequences in turn depended on what inferences others would draw from those actions. Finally, one had to think carefully about what was the feasible set of actions: what might each side do to extract or convey information to others.

As we shall see, the variety of results obtained (and much of the confusion in the early literature) arose partly from a failure to be as clear as one might about the assumptions. For instance, the standard adverse selection model had the quality of the good offered in the market (say of used cars, or riskiness of the insured) depending on price. The car buyer (the seller of insurance) knows the *statistical* relationship between price and quality, and this affects his or her demand. The market equilibrium is the price at which demand equals supply. But that is an equilibrium if and only if there is no way by which the seller of a good car can convey that information to the buyer – so that he or she can earn a quality premium – and if there is no way by which the buyer can sort out good cars from bad cars. Typically, there are such ways, and it is the attempt to elicit that information which has profound effects on how markets function.

In the new theories, long-standing conclusions were thrown aside. Economists had long simply assumed that equilibrium required zero profits or demand equaling supply. The new theories said that these conclusions might not be correct. One had to rethink all the conclusions from first premises. For many economists this was hard, and unsettling.

We made progress in our analyses because we began with highly simplified models of *particular* markets, that allowed us to think through carefully each of the assumptions and conclusions. From the analysis of particular markets (whether the insurance market, the education market, the labor market, or the land tenancy/sharecropping market), we attempted to identify general principles, to explore how these principles operated in each of the other markets. In doing so, we identified particular features, particular *informational assumptions*, which seemed to be more relevant in one market or another. The nature of competition in the labor market is different than that in the insurance market or the capital market, although they have much in common. This interplay, between looking at the ways in which such markets are similar and dissimilar, proved to be a fruitful research strategy.

SOURCES OF ASYMMETRIES OF INFORMATION

Much of the earlier work on imperfect information began with the assumption of information asymmetry – that some individuals know more than others. (Although in this essay I focus on information asymmetries, it is important to recognize that information economics is far broader.) Workers know more about their ability than does the firm; the person buying insurance knows more about his or her health, whether he or she smokes and drinks immoderately, than the insurance firm; the owner of a car knows more about the car than potential buyers; the owner of a firm knows more about the firm than a potential investor; the borrower knows more about his or her risk and risk taking than the lender.

Some of these information asymmetries are inherent: the individual naturally knows more about himself than does anyone else. But many of the information asymmetries are endogenous. Some of the asymmetries arise naturally out of economic processes. The current employer knows more about the employee than other potential employers; a firm may find out a great deal of information in the process of dealing with his or her supplier that others may not know; the owner of a car naturally knows the faults of the car better than others – and in particular, he knows whether or not he has a lemon. While such information asymmetries inevitably arise, the extent to which they do so and their consequences depend on how the market is structured, and the recognition that they will arise affects market behavior.

Creating Asymmetries and Imperfections of Information

But whereas many information asymmetries (and information imperfections more generally) might seem to arise naturally, some are deliberately created. Managers of firms attempt to *entrench* themselves, increasing their bargaining power, for example, vis-à-vis alternative management teams, and one of the ways that they do this is to take actions which *increase* information asymmetries. Similarly, the presence of information imperfections give rise to market power; and firms can exploit this market power through "sales" and other ways of differentiating among individuals who have different search costs. The price dispersions which exist in the market are *created* by the market – they are not just the failure of markets to arbitrage fully price differences *caused* by shocks that affect different markets differently.

OVERCOMING INFORMATION ASYMMETRIES

I now want to discuss briefly the ways by which information asymmetries are dealt with and how they can be (partially) overcome.

Incentives for Gathering and Disclosing Information

There are two key issues: what are the *incentives* for obtaining information, and what are the *mechanisms?* We noted earlier that although some individuals have an incentive to disclose information, those who are less able have an incentive not to have the information disclosed. In the simplest models, I described a process of unraveling: if the most able could establish his or her ability, she would; but then all but the most able would be grouped together, receiving the mean marginal product of that group; and the most able of that group would have an incentive to reveal his or her ability. And so on down the line, until there was full revelation.

The other side of the market has an incentive too to gather information: an employer that can find a worker that is better than is recognized by others will have found a bargain; his or her wage will be determined by what others think of him or her. The problem, as we noted, is that if what the employer knows becomes known to others, the wage will be bid up, and it will be unable to appropriate the returns on its investment in information acquisition. The economy, in effect, has to choose between two different imperfections: imperfections of information or imperfections of competition. Of course, in the end, there will be both forms of imperfection. (If markets were fully informationally efficient – that is, if information disseminated instantaneously and perfectly throughout the economy – then no one would have any incentive to gather information, so long as there was any cost of doing so. That is why markets cannot be fully informationally efficient.)

Mechanisms for Elimination or Reducing Information Asymmetries

In simple models where individuals know their own ability, there might seem an easy way to resolve the problem of information asymmetry: let each person tell his or her true characteristic. The underlying problem arose from the fact that individuals did not necessarily have the incentive to tell the truth. Assume employees knew their abilities. An employer might ask, what is your ability? The more able might answer honestly. As we have seen, the least able would have an incentive to lie, to say that he or she was more able than he was. Talk is cheap. There had to be some other ways by which information could be credibly conveyed.

Screening by Examination

The simplest way by which that could be done was an exam. As I constructed a simple competitive equilibrium model, two further general principles became apparent: *the gains of the more able were largely at the expense of the less able*; by establishing that an individual is of higher ability, thereby leading, in equilibrium, to higher wages, he or she simultaneously establishes that others are of lower ability. The private returns to expenditures on education exceed the social returns. It was clear that there were important *externalities* associated with information, a theme which was to recur in later work.

But a more striking result emerged: there could exist multiple equilibria, one in which information was fully revealed (the market identified the high- and low-ability people) and the other of which it was not (called a pooling equilibrium). The pooling equilibrium Pareto dominated the equilibrium with full revelation.

This work, done some thirty years ago, established two results of important policy consequences, which remarkably have not been fully absorbed into policy discussions even today. First, markets do not provide appropriate incentives for information disclosure. There is, in principle, a role for government. And second, expenditures on information may be too great.

The Simplest Adverse Selection Model

But most information is gleaned not through examination but through observing *behavior* in the marketplace. Within the insurance literature, it had long been recognized that the willingness to purchase insurance at a particular price conveyed information to the insurance company. Akerlof recognized that this phenomenon was far more general: the willingness to sell a used car, for instance, conveyed information about whether the car was or was not a lemon. Greenwald showed how adverse selection applied to labor and capital markets: the willingness of an employer not to match the bid of a competitor conveyed information about the current employer's judgment of that individual's ability; the willingness of insiders in a firm to sell stock at a particular price conveyed information about the insider's view of the price relative to the expected return. Akerlof's insight that the result of these information asymmetries was that markets would be thin or absent helped explain why labor and capital markets often did not function well. It provided part of the explanation for why firms raised so little of their funds through equity. Stigler was wrong: imperfect information was not just like a transaction's costs.

The consequences go well beyond just an absent or missing market. Weak equity markets meant that risks could not be divested, leading firms to act in a risk averse manner, explaining some of what would otherwise seem to be anomalous aspects of firm behavior. These capital market imperfections, in turn, played a central role in the macroeconomic theories to be described below.

The fact that current employers have more information than others means that labor mobility will be limited: a firm attempting to recruit a worker away from his or her existing employer is more likely to succeed if it bids too much, a version of the winners' curse. Because other firms know this, they will be reluctant to hire "used labor": the used labor market is thin, just as the used car market is thin. Firms, knowing this, may attempt to exploit those who come to work for them; and because workers know this, before they go to work for a firm, it affects the terms at which they are willing to work. The labor market is affected both *before* the asymmetry of information is created in the process of hiring and after.

The Simplest Adverse Incentive Model

Individuals differ not only because of inherent characteristics (some are more able than others), but also because of actions, of *choices*. A worker can work harder, a borrower can undertake greater risk, and the insured can undertake greater care. The employer would like to know how hard its worker is working; if it could, the employer would specify that in the contract; the lender would like to know the actions which borrowers will undertake; if it could, the lender would specify that in the contract. These asymmetries of information about *actions* are as important as the earlier-discussed asymmetries about characteristics. Just as in the adverse selection model, the seller of insurance may try to overcome the problems posed by information asymmetries by *examination*, so too in the adverse incentive model, it may try to *monitor* the actions of the insured. But examinations and monitoring are costly and, although they yield some information, typically there remains a high level of residual information imperfection. Just as in the adverse selection model, the seller of insurance recognizes that the average riskiness of the insurance applicants is affected by the terms of the insurance contract, so too the level of risk taking can be affected. And similar results hold in other markets. Borrowers' risk taking is affected by the interest rate charged. It turns out, accordingly, that there are many close parallels between adverse selection models and adverse incentive models.

Efficiency Wage Theory, Credit Rationing

The simplest adverse incentive (and adverse selection) models – while a marked step forward in recognizing that "quality" depends on price – were seriously deficient. There is in fact no law that requires the insurance firm to sell to all who apply at the premium it announces, the lender to lend to all who apply at the interest rate it announces, the employer to employ all those who apply at the wage it announces. In adverse selection and incentive models, what mattered was not only the supply of customers or employees or borrowers, but also their "quality" – the riskiness of the insured or the borrower, the returns on the investment, the productivity of the worker.

Because "quality" may increase with price, it may pay an employer to pay a higher wage than the market clearing wage, or for the lender to lend at an interest rate that exceeds the market clearing interest rate. This is true whether the dependence on quality arises from adverse selection or adverse incentive effects (or, in the labor market, because of morale or nutritional effects). And what matters is that there be imperfect information, not asymmetries of information. The healthy who decide not to buy insurance at a high premium do not need to *know* that they are healthy; they could be as uninformed as the insurance company, but simply – perhaps because of their health – have different preferences, for example, they may prefer to spend more of their money on recreational sports.

The consequence, as we have noted, is that market equilibrium may be characterized by demand not equaling supply: in equilibrium, the interest rate may be lower than that at which the demand for loans equals the supply – there may be credit rationing, as Stiglitz and A.Weiss showed; just as in the labor market the wage rate may be higher than that at which the demand for labor equals the supply – there may be unemployment.

Conveying Information through Actions

These models showed that firms did not passively have to accept the market price. They could pay higher wages or charge lower interest rates than that prevailing in the market. But there were a wider set of actions that firms and individuals could undertake, either to convey information (to signal who they were) or to extract information. An insurance company wants to attract healthy applicants. It might realize that by locating itself on the fifth floor of a walk-up building, only those with a strong heart would apply. The willingness or ability to walk up five floors conveys information. More subtly, it might recognize that how far up it needs to locate itself, if it only wants to get healthy applicants, depends also on the premium charged. Or it may decide to throw in for free a membership in a health club, but charge a higher premium. Those who value a health club – because they will use it – willingly pay the higher premium. But these individuals are likely to be healthier.

There are a host of other actions that convey information. The quality of the guarantee offered by a firm can convey information about the quality of the product; only firms that believe that their product is reliable will be willing to offer a good guarantee. The guarantee is desirable not just because it reduces risk, but because it conveys information. The number of years of schooling may convey information about the ability of an individual. More able individuals may go to school longer, in which case the increase in wages associated with an increase in schooling may not be a consequence of the human capital that has been added, but rather simply be a result of the sorting that occurs, the information that is conveyed. As we have noted, the size of the deductible that an individual chooses in an insurance policy may convey information about his or her view about the likelihood of an accident or the size of the accidents he or she anticipates – *on average*, those who are less likely to have an accident may be more willing to accept high deductibles. The willingness of an entrepreneur to hold large fractions of his wealth in a firm conveys information about his beliefs in the firm's future performance. If a firm promotes an individual to a particular job, it may convey information about the firm's assessment of his or her ability.

Once one recognizes that actions convey information, two results follow. First, in making decisions about what to do, individuals will not only think about what they like (as in traditional economics) but also how it will affect others' beliefs about them. If I choose to go to school longer, it may lead others to believe that I am more able, and I will therefore decide to stay in school longer, not because I value what is being taught, but because I value how it changes others' beliefs concerning my ability. This means, of course, that we have to rethink completely firm and household decision making.

Second, we noted earlier that individuals have an incentive to "lie" – the less able to say that they are more able. Similarly, if it becomes recognized that those who walk up to the fifth floor to apply for insurance are more healthy, then I might be willing to do so even if I am not so healthy, simply to fool the insurance company. If it becomes recognized that those who stay in school longer are more able, then I might be willing to do so, even if I am less able, simply to fool the employers. Recognizing this, one needs to look for ways by which information is conveyed *in equilibrium*. The critical insight in how that could occur was provided in a paper with Rothschild in 1976. If those who were more able, less risk prone, more creditworthy *acted* in some observable way (had different preferences) than those who were less able, less risk prone, less creditworthy, then it might be possible to design a set of *choices*, which would result in those with different characteristics in effect *identifying* themselves through their *self-selection*. One of the reasons that they might behave differently is that they *know* they are more able, less risk prone, more creditworthy – that is, there is asymmetric information. But it is only one of the bases for self-selection.

Monopoly and Self-Selection

The problem of *sorting* occurs, of course, not just in competitive markets. In many ways, analyzing the problem of sorting through self-selection in monopolies is far easier, because the monopolist can frame the entire choice set facing the individual. Under standard theories of monopoly, *with perfect information*, firms would have an incentive to price discriminate perfectly (extracting the full consumer surplus from each). If they did this, then monopoly would in fact be non-distortionary. Yet most models assumed no price discrimination (that is, the monopolist offered the same price to all customers), without explaining why they did not do so, and argued that monopoly was distortionary. Our work showed how, given limited information, firms could price discriminate, but could do so only imperfectly. They would normally charge a different price per unit depending on the quantity purchased: if it was possible for them to charge different prices depending on the quantity purchased, they would do so. Distortions arose from the imperfections of information, from the fact that discrimination was imperfect; there were costs associated with the discrimination mechanisms.

Subsequent work by a variety of authors such as S. Salop in 1977 and J. L. Adams and J. Yellen in 1976 explored a variety of ways by which a monopolist might find out relevant characteristics of its customers. (For an insurance company, the relevant characteristics are not only the likelihood of having an accident, but also the degree of risk aversion, the premium that an individual would be willing to pay to divest him- or herself of risk.)

The economics of information thus provided the first coherent theory of monopoly.

Self-Selection and Competitive Equilibrium

The reason that analyzing monopoly was easy is that the monopolist could structure the entire choice set facing its customers. The hard question is to describe the full competitive equilibrium, that is, a set of insurance contracts such that no one can offer an alternative set which would be profitable. Each firm could control the choices that it offered, but not the choices offered by others; and the decisions made by customers depended on the entire set of choices available. In our 1976 paper, Rothschild and I succeeded in analyzing this case.

Three striking results emerged from this analysis. The first I have already mentioned: under plausible conditions, given the natural definition of equilibrium, equilibrium might not exist. There were two possible forms of equilibria: pooling equilibria – in which the market is not able to distinguish among the types – and separating equilibria, in which it is. The different groups "separate out" by taking different actions. We showed that there never could be a pooling equilibrium – if there were a single contract that everyone bought, there was another contract that another firm could offer which would "break" the pooling equilibrium. On the other hand, there might not exist a separating equilibrium. The cost of separation was too great. Any putative separating equilibrium could be broken by a profitable pooling contract, a contract which would be bought by both low-risk and high-risk types.

Second, even small amounts of imperfections of information can change the standard results concerning the existence and characterization of equilibrium. Equilibrium, for instance, never exists when the two types are very near each other. (As we have seen, the competitive equilibrium model is simply not robust.)

Third, and relatedly, we now can see how the fact that actions convey information affects the *equilibrium*. In particular, our analysis here reinforced the earlier analysis of adverse selection about markets not functioning well. In perfect information models, individuals would fully divest themselves of the risks which they face, and accordingly would act in a risk neutral manner. With imperfect information, they do not fully divest themselves of risk.

Sorting, Screening, and Signaling

In the case where say, the insurance company or employer or employee takes the initiative for sorting out applicants, self-selection is an alternative to examinations as a sorting device. In the case where the insured, or employee, or borrower, takes the initiative for identifying him- or herself as a better risk, a better employee, a borrower more likely to repay, then we say he or she is *signaling*. But of course, in equilibrium both sides are aware of the consequences of alternative actions, and the differences between signaling and self-selection screening models lie in the technicalities of game theory, and in particular whether the informed or uninformed (employee or employer, insured or insurance company) moves first.

Still, some of the seeming differences between signaling and screening models arise because of a failure to specify a *full* equilibrium. There are many educational systems which "separate" – that is, the more able choose to go to school longer, and the wages at each level of education correspond to the productivity of those who go to school for that length of time. But all except one are not *full equilibrium*. Assume, for instance, there were two types of individuals, a low ability and a high ability. Then if the low ability goes to twelve years of schooling, then any education system in which the high ability went *sufficiently* long – say more than fourteen years – might separate. But the low ability would recognize that if it went to school for eleven years, it would still be treated as low ability. Thus the *full* equilibrium is that where the low ability goes to school the efficient amount (based on standard human capital theory), and the high ability goes to school the least amount that it can such as to *separate* itself out from the low ability (assuming that that amount is greater than the efficient amount.) The contention that there is an infinite number of equilibria is wrong, *in a reasonably specified model*.

THEORY OF CONTRACTS AND INCENTIVES

As I noted earlier, the contracts that had characterized economic relations in the standard competitive model were extraordinarily simple: I will pay you a certain amount if you do such-and-such. If you did not perform as promised, the pay was not given. But with perfect information, individuals simply did not sign contracts that they did not intend to fulfill. Insurance contracts were similarly simple: a payment occurred if and only if particular specified events occurred.

The work on sharecropping and on equilibrium with competitive insurance markets showed that with imperfect information, a far richer set of contracts would be employed, and thus began a large literature on the theory of contracting.

In the simple sharecropping contracts of Stiglitz, the contracts involved shares, fixed payments, and plot sizes; more generally, optimal payment structures related payments to *observables*, inputs, processes, outputs. Because what went on in one market affected others, the credit, labor, and land markets were *interlinked*; one could not decentralize in the way hypothesized by the standard perfect information model. The economics of imperfect information thus provided the basis of the *theory of rural organization* in developing countries.

The basic principles were subsequently applied in a variety of other market contexts. The most obvious was the design of labor contracts.

Payments can depend too on *relative* performance; relative performance may convey more relevant information than absolute performance. If a particular company's stock goes up when all other companies' stock goes up, it may say very little about the performance of the manager. B. Nalebuff and I analyzed the design of these relative performance compensation schemes (contests). One of the strong arguments for competitive, decentralized structures is that they provide information on the basis of which one can design better incentive pay structures than those which rely on the performance of a single individual only.

Credit markets too are characterized by complicated contracts. Lenders would specify not only an interest rate, but also impose other conditions (collateral requirements, equity requirements) that would have both incentive and selection effects. Indeed, the simultaneous presence of both selection and incentive effects was important: in the absence of the former, it might be possible to increase the collateral requirement *and* raise interest rates, still ensuring that the borrower undertook the safe project.

Incentives in Market Equilibrium

Incentives are based on rewards and punishments. In modern economies, the most severe punishment that one can impose is to fire an individual. But if the individual could get a job just like his or her current one, then there would be no cost. Good behavior is driven by earning a surplus over what one could get elsewhere. Thus, in labor markets, the wage must be higher than what the worker could get elsewhere (which may be zero, if there is unemployment); hence, equilibrium must be characterized by unemployment, or a wage distribution. In the goods market, firms must feel a loss when they lose a customer because of a shoddy product, so the price must exceed the marginal cost of production. Thus, the long-standing presumption that in competitive equilibrium price equals marginal cost *cannot* be true in markets with imperfect information. Thus, information economics stripped away another of the long-standing presumptions of the standard competitive model.

EQUILIBRIUM WAGE AND PRICE DISTRIBUTIONS

The "law of the single price" is another pillar of standard theory: the same good has to sell, in equilibrium, for the same price everywhere. Economists have long recognized that prices do differ, and since Stigler's classic paper (1961), there has developed a large body of literature exploring one of the consequences: that individuals invest in a search looking for the lowest price. Stigler and most of the search literature took the price or wage distribution as a given, however. They did not ask how it arose, or even, given the search costs, could it be sustained. For instance, if search costs are relatively low, one might have thought (if one bought the older theories) that markets would look very much like they would with zero search costs, in which case there would be no price or wage distribution. It is not surprising that given that information is costly, when there are shocks to the economy – the demand for a good goes up in some locale, so prices there rise – prices are not fully arbitraged instantaneously. But much of the wage and price dispersion cannot be related to such "shocks."

Our analysis of efficiency wage theory provided an alternative explanation. We showed that it paid firms to pay more than they had to, for example, in order to reduce labor turnover costs. But it might pay some firms to pay higher wages than others.

As I began to analyze these models, an important insight occurred: there could be a wage distribution even if all firms were identical, including, having the same costs. It was clear that even small search costs could make a large difference to the behavior of product and labor markets. This was a point that P. Diamond in 1971 had independently made in a highly influential paper, which serves to illustrate powerfully the lack of robustness of the competitive equilibrium theory. He had shown that even with arbitrarily small search costs, the equilibrium price could be the monopoly price. Salop and I showed that in situations where there were even small search costs, markets would be characterized by a price distribution. If everyone were charging the same price, it would pay some firm either to raise its price knowing that high-search cost customers would not lose, or to lower its price to steal customers from its rivals. The standard wisdom that said that not everyone had to be informed to ensure that the market acted perfectly competitive was simply not in general true.

EFFICIENCY OF THE MARKET EQUILIBRIUM AND THE ROLE OF THE STATE

Economists over the preceding three decades had identified important market failures – such as the externalities associated with pollution – that required government intervention. But the scope of market failures was limited, and thus the arenas in which government intervention was required were limited.

Our early work in the economics of information suggested that when information was imperfect, markets might not be efficient. We had shown, for instance, that incentives for the disclosure and acquisition of information were far from perfect; imperfect appropriability meant that there might be insufficient incentives, but the fact that much of the gains were "rents" – gains by some at the expense of others – suggested that there might be excessive expenditures on information. One of the arguments for unfettered capital markets was that there were strong incentives to gather information; if one discovered that some stock was more valuable than others thought, if you bought it before they discovered the information, then you would make a capital gain. This price discovery function of capital markets was often advertised as one of its strengths. But the issue was, although the individual who discovered the information a nanosecond before anyone else might be better off, was society as a whole better off? If having the information a nanosecond earlier did not lead to a change in real decisions (for example, concerning investment), then it was largely redistributive, with the gains of those obtaining the information occurring at the expense of others. Another example illustrates what is at issue: Assume hundred-dollar bills were to fall, one each at the left foot of each student in my class. They could wait to the end of the lecture, then pick up the money; but that is not a Nash equilibrium. If all students were to do that, it would pay anyone to bend down and quickly scoop up what he or she could. Each realizing that immediately picks up the bill at his foot. The equilibrium leaves each no better off than if he or she had waited – and there was a great social cost, the interruption of the lecture.

There are other potential inefficiencies associated with information acquisition. Information can have adverse effects on volatility. And information can lead to the destruction of markets, in ways that adversely affect welfare.

The fact that markets with imperfect information worked differently – and less well – than markets with perfect information was not, by itself, a damning criticism of markets. After all, information is costly, and taking into account the costs of information, markets *might* be fully efficient. Stigler had essentially argued for this perspective, but without proof. Our research showed that this assertion – or hope – was simply not correct. The early work just cited had established that when markets are absent or imperfect, market equilibrium might be *constrained* Pareto inefficient; that is, taking into account the absence of the market, everyone could be made better off. Moreover, because asymmetries of information give rise to market power, and *perfect* competition is required if markets are to be efficient, it is perhaps unsurprising that markets with information asymmetries and other information imperfections are far from efficient.

Although it was not surprising that markets might not provide appropriate incentives for the acquisition and dissemination of information, the market failures associated with imperfect information are far more profound. The intuition can be seen most simply in the case of models with moral hazard. There, the premium charged is associated with the *average* risk, and, therefore, the average care taken by seemingly similar individuals. The moral hazard problem arises because the level of care cannot be observed. Each individual ignores the effect of his or her actions on the premium; but when they all take less care, the premium increases. The lack of care by each exerts a negative externality on others.

The essential insight of my work with Greenwald was to recognize that such externality-like effects are pervasive whenever information is imperfect or markets incomplete – that is always – and as a result, markets are essentially never constrained Pareto efficient. In short, market failures are pervasive.

There were two other implications. The first was the non-decentralizability of efficient market solutions. The notion that one could decentralize decision making to obtain (Pareto) efficient resource allocation is one of the fundamental ideas in economics. Greenwald and I showed that that was not in general possible. Again, a simple example illustrates what is at issue. An insurance company cannot monitor the extent of smoking, which has an adverse effect on health. The government cannot monitor smoking any better than the insurance company, but it can impose taxes, not only on cigarettes, but also on other commodities which are complements to smoking (and subsidies on substitutes that have less adverse effects). Earlier work with A. Braverman had shown the consequences of this non-decentralizability, the interlinkage of land, labor, and credit markets in agrarian markets of developing countries.

Markets are also interlinked over time. *Intertemporal linkages* impair the efficacy of competitive processes, as we have already noted. Standard theory stated that if an employer does not treat an employee well, he or she simply moves to another firm. But informational asymmetries impair labor mobility, partially locking the employee into his or her employer, or the borrower into his or her creditor. Whereas with perfect information and perfect markets, some of the consequences of this reduction in ex post competition could be corrected by the intensity of ex ante competition, there is little reason to believe that is in fact the case with imperfect information.

One of the sources of the market failures is *agency problems*, such as those that arise when the owner of land is different from the person working the land. The extent of agency problems – and therefore of market failures – thus depends on the distribution of wealth. This was most evident in our discussion of sharecropping, in which the separation of ownership and work led to the effective imposition of a tax on labor of 50 percent. It is simply not the case that one can separate out issues of equity and efficiency.

Moreover, the notion that one could separate out issues of equity and efficiency also rested on the ability to engage in lump-sum redistributions. If one did not like the distribution of income, one could achieve any distribution one wanted by such redistributions – leaving the competitive market processes in place. But as J. A. Mirrlees had pointed out, with imperfect information, this was not possible; all redistributive taxation was distortionary. But this had important implications for a wider range of policies beyond simply the design of tax structures. It meant that interventions in the market which changed the before-tax distribution of income could be desirable, because they lessened the burden on redistributive taxation. Again, the conclusion: the second welfare theorem, effectively asserting the ability to separate issues of distribution and efficiency, was not true.

In effect, the Arrow-Debreu model had identified the single set of assumptions under which markets were (Pareto) efficient. There had to be perfect information, or, more accurately, information (beliefs) could not be *endogenous*, they could not change either as a result of the actions of any individual or firm, including investments in information. But in an information economy, a model which assumes that information is *fixed* seems increasingly irrelevant.

Dysfunctional Institutions

As the theoretical case that markets in which information was imperfect were not efficient became increasingly clear, several arguments were put forward against government intervention. One we have already dealt with: the government too faces informational imperfections. But our analysis had shown that the incentives and constraints facing government differed from those facing the private sector, so that even when government faced exactly the same *informational* constraints, welfare could be improved upon.

There was another argument which held up no better. The existence of market failures – absent or imperfect markets – gives rise to non-market institutions. The absence of death insurance gave rise to burial societies. Families provide insurance to their members against a host of risks for which they either cannot buy insurance, or for which the insurance premium is viewed as too high. But in what I call the *functionalist fallacy*, it is easy to go from the observation that an institution arises to fulfill a function to the conclusion that actually, *in equilibrium*, it serves that function. Those who succumbed to this fallacy seemed to argue that there was no need for government intervention because these nonmarket institutions would "solve" the market failure, or at least do as well as any government. Arnott and I showed that, to the contrary, nonmarket institutions could actually make matters worse. Insurance provided by the family could crowd out market insurance; insurance companies would recognize that the insured would take more risk because they had obtained insurance from others, and accordingly cut back on the amount of insurance that they offered. But since the nonmarket (family) institutions did a poor job of divesting risk, welfare was decreased.

The Arnott-Stiglitz analysis reemphasized the basic point made at the end of the last subsection: it was only under very special circumstances that markets could be shown to be efficient. Why then should we expect an equilibrium involving non-market institutions and markets to be efficient?

APPLICATIONS OF THE NEW PARADIGM

The New Theory of the Firm and the Foundations
of Modern Macroeconomics

The construction of a macroeconomic model that embraces the consequences of imperfections of information in labor, product, and capital markets has become one of my major preoccupations over the past fifteen years. Given the complexity of *each* of these markets, creating a general equilibrium model has not proven an easy task. At the heart of that model lies a new theory of the firm, for which the theory of asymmetric information provides the foundation. The modern theory of the firm in turn rests on three pillars: the theory of corporate finance, the theory of corporate governance, and the theory of organizational design.

The Theory of Corporate Finance

Under the older, perfect information theory, it made no real difference whether firms raised capital by debt or equity, in the absence of tax distortions. This was the central insight of the Modigliani-Miller theorem. We have noted how the willingness to hold (or to sell) shares conveys information, so that how firms raise capital does make a difference. Firms rely heavily on debt finance, and bankruptcy, resulting from the failure to meet debt obligations, matters. Both because of the cost of bankruptcies and limitations in the design of managerial incentive schemes, firms typically act in a risk averse manner – with risk being more than just correlation with the business cycle.

Moreover, with credit rationing (or the potential of credit rationing) not only does the firm's net worth (the market value of its assets) matter, but so too does its asset structure, including its liquidity. In traditional neoclassical investment theory, investment depends on the real interest rate and the firm's perception of expected returns. The firm's cash flow or its net worth should make no difference. The earliest econometric studies of investment, by E. Kuh and J. Meyer, suggested that that was not the case. But under the strength of the theoretical strictures that these variables could not matter, they were excluded from econometric analysis for two decades following the work of R. Hall and D. W. Jorgenson. It was not until work on asymmetric information had restored theoretical respectability to introducing such variables in investment regressions that it was acceptable to do so; and when that was done, it was shown that, especially for small-and medium-sized enterprises, these variables were crucial.

Moreover, in the traditional theory, there is no corporate veil: individuals can see perfectly what is going on inside the firm, and it makes no difference whether the firm distributes or retains its profits (other than for taxes). But if there is imperfect information about what is going on inside the firm, then there is a corporate veil, which cannot be easily pierced.

Corporate Governance

That there were important consequences for the theory of the firm of the separation of ownership and control had earlier been noted by A. A. Berle and G. C. Means, but it was not until information economics that we had a coherent way of thinking about the implications. The fact that outsiders could not see perfectly what was going on inside the firm provided managers with discretion, which they could use to their advantage.

In the simple neoclassical model, there was no question about what firms should do, and in particular what was entailed by profit maximization. But there *are* disagreements about what the firm should do – partly motivated by differences in judgments, partly motivated by differences in objectives. Managers can take actions which advance their interests at the expense of that of shareholders, and majority shareholders can advance their interests at the expense of minority shareholders.

The owners (who, in the language of S. Ross came to be called the principal) not only could not monitor their workers and managers (the agents), but because of asymmetries of information, they also typically did not even know what these people who were supposed to be acting on their behalf *should* do.

The problem of corporate governance, of course, arises both from the problems of information imperfections *and* the public good nature of management/oversight: if a shareholder engages in expenditures on oversight, and succeeds in improving the firm's performance, all shareholders benefit equally (similarly with creditors).

Early on in this debate, I raised questions on theoretical grounds about the efficacy of the takeover mechanism, which some argued ensured that managers would have to maximize shareholder value. The most forceful set of arguments were subsequently put forward by Grossman and O. Hart, who observed that any small shareholder who believed that the takeover would subsequently increase the market value would not be willing to sell his or her shares. Only takeovers that were expected to be value decreasing would be successful. Moreover, the subsequent work by Edlin and Stiglitz showed how existing managers could take actions to reduce the effectiveness of competition for management, that is, the threat of takeovers, by increasing asymmetries of information.

Organization Design

In a world with perfect information, organizational design too is of little moment. In practice, it is of central concern to businesses. We have already extensively discussed the issue of incentives: how, on the one hand, information imperfections limit the extent of efficient decentralizability, and how, on the other, organizational design – by having alternative units perform comparable tasks – can enable a firm to glean information on the basis of which better incentive systems can be based.

To err is human. Raj Sah and I explored in a series of papers the consequences of alternative organizational design and decision-making structures for organizational mistakes, for instance, where good projects get rejected or bad projects get accepted. We suggested that in a variety of circumstances, especially when there is a scarcity of good projects, decentralized polyarchical organizational structures have distinct advantages.

Macroeconomics

In joint work with Greenwald and Weiss, we have shown how the theories of asymmetric information can help provide explanations of macroeconomic phenomena. The imperfections of capital markets are key. They lead to risk averse behavior of firms and to households and firms being affected by cash flow constraints.

The new macroeconomic theories not only explained the slowness of wage and price adjustments; they also explained why even if wages and prices adjusted more rapidly, shocks to the economy could have long-lasting effects.

The Greenwald-Stiglitz theory of adjustment argued that, at least for commodities for which inventory costs were reasonably low, the risks arising from informational imperfections were greater for price and wage adjustments than from quantity adjustments. Risk averse firms would make smaller adjustments to variables, the consequences of which were more uncertain. We went on to explain why in many cases the uncertainty associated with wage and price adjustments was greater than with quantity adjustments – implying that there would be some degree of wage and price rigidity.

But Greenwald and I were also concerned about the consequences of the wage and price adjustments that did occur. In debt contracts, typically not indexed (or fully indexed) for changes in prices, whenever prices fell below the level expected (or in variable interest rate contracts, when real interest rates rose above the level expected) there were transfers from debtors to creditors. In these circumstances, excessive downward price flexibility (not just price rigidities) could give rise to problems. Large shocks could lead to bankruptcy, and with bankruptcy (especially when it results in firm liquidation) there was a loss of organizational and informational capital.

Because all production is risky, shocks affect aggregate supply, as well as the demand for investment. Firm net worth could only be restored over time, so the effects of a shock persisted. By the same token, there were hysteresis effects associated with policy: an increase in interest rates that depleted firm net worth had impacts even after the interest rates were reduced. If firms were credit rationed, then reductions in liquidity could have particularly marked effects.

Theory of Money

The new information paradigm not only lead to a reformulation of macroeconomics in general, but also of monetary theory in particular. In modern economies, credit, not money, is required (and used) for most transactions, and most transactions are simply exchanges of assets, and therefore not directly related to income generation. Moreover, today, most money is interest bearing, with the difference between the interest rate paid, say on a money market account and T bill rates, having little to do with monetary policy, and related solely to the bank's transaction costs. Credit is at the heart of understanding monetary economics; ascertaining creditworthiness – determining the supply of credit – is a matter of information. In short, *information* is at the heart of monetary economics. The theory shows how not only traditional monetary instruments but also regulatory instruments can be used to affect the supply of credit, interest rates charged, and the bank's risk portfolio. The analysis also showed how excessive reliance on capital adequacy requirements could be counterproductive. It provides a new basis for a "liquidity trap"; explains some of the recent policy failures, both in the inability of the Fed to forestall the 1991 recession and the failures of the IMF in East Asia in 1997; and shifts the prevailing emphasis from looking at the Fed Funds rate, or the money supply, to variables of more direct relevance to economic activity, such as the level of credit and the interest rates charged to firms (and it explains the movement in the spread between that rate and the Federal Funds rate). The theory predicts that there is scope for monetary policy even in the presence of dollarization. We also analyzed the importance of credit interlinkages among firms, and between trade credit and bank credit.

Growth and Development

The importance of capital markets for growth had long been recognized; without capital markets, firms have to rely on retained earnings. But how firms raise capital is important for growth. In particular, "equity rationing" – especially important in developing countries, where informational problems are even greater – impedes firms' willingness to invest and undertake risks, and thus slows down growth. Changes in economic policy that enable firms to bear more risk enhance economic growth. Conversely, policies such as those associated with IMF interventions – in which interest rates are raised to very high levels – discourage the use of debt, and in developing countries where equity markets do not function, this forces firms to rely more heavily on retained earnings. Again, not only have these interventions had adverse effects in the short run; they are also likely to have long-term effects on countries' growth performance.

Research

One of the most important determinants of the pace of growth is, for developed countries, the investment in research, and for less developed countries, efforts at closing the knowledge gap between themselves and more developed countries. Knowledge is, of course, a particular *form* of information. Two conclusions (related to the general results on the economics of information) stand out: that market economies in which research and innovation play an important role are not well described by the standard competitive model, and that the market equilibrium, without government intervention, is not in general efficient.

POLICY FRAMEWORKS

As we have seen, asymmetries of information give rise to a host of other market failures – such as missing markets, and especially capital market imperfections, leading to firms that are risk averse and cash constrained – and policy has to deal with these indirect consequences as well. But beyond this, the new information paradigm helps us to think about policy from a new perspective, one which recognizes the pervasiveness of imperfections of information.

Pareto Efficient Taxation

Here, I want to briefly note the problems posed to government in the conduct of its "business" that arise from information asymmetries in three key areas: taxation, regulation, and production.

One of the functions of government is to redistribute income; even if it did not wish to redistribute actively, it has to raise revenues to finance public goods, and there is a concern that the revenue be raised in an equitable manner, that is, that those who are more able to contribute (or who benefit more) do so. But government has a problem of identifying these individuals. The critical question for the design of a tax system thus becomes *what is observable*. If ability is not directly observable, the government had to rely on other observables – like income – to make inferences; but, as in all such models, market participants, as they recognize that inferences are being made, alter their behavior. Mirrlees showed how, if income alone were observable (and not the underlying ability of individuals), the optimal income tax system would distort incentives. But in different circumstances, either more or less information might be available. It might be possible to observe hours worked, in which case wages would be observable. It might be possible to observe the quantity of each good purchased by *any particular individual*, or it might be possible to observe only the aggregate quantity of goods produced.

For each information structure, there is a *Pareto efficient tax structure*, that is, a tax structure such that no one (group) can be made better off without making some other group worse off. The choice among such tax structures depends on the social welfare function (attitudes toward inequality.) Although this is not the occasion to provide a complete description of the results, two are worth noting: what had been thought of as optimal commodity tax structures by F. P. Ramsey were shown to be part of a Pareto efficient tax system only under highly restricted conditions, for example, if there was no income tax. On the other hand, it was shown that in a central benchmark case, it was not optimal to tax interest income.

Theory of Regulation and Privatization

The government faced the same problem posed by information asymmetries in regulation that it faced in taxation. It cannot ensure, for instance, that a natural monopoly in a public utility behave as it would like – investing the right amount and not overcharging, partly because it does not know fully their technology. Over the past quarter century, a huge literature has developed making use of self-selection mechanisms, allowing far better and more effective systems of regulation than had existed in the past.

In the 1980s, there was a strong movement toward privatizing state enterprises. The theories of imperfect information made it clear that even the best-designed regulatory systems would work imperfectly. In 1991 H. Simon emphasized that there was no compelling theoretical argument for why large private organizations would solve these incentive problems better. In work with D. Sappington, we showed that the conditions under which privatization would necessarily be welfare enhancing were extremely restrictive, and closely akin to those under which competitive markets would yield Pareto efficient outcomes.

KEY POLICY DEBATES: APPLYING BASIC IDEAS

The perspectives provided by the new information paradigm not only shaped theoretical approaches to policy, but in innumerable concrete issues also led to markedly different policy stances from those taken by those wedded to the old paradigm.

Development and the Washington Consensus

Elsewhere, I have documented the failures of policies in development, as well as in managing the transition from communism to a market economy and in managing crises. Ideas matters, and it is not surprising that policies based on models that depart as far from reality as those underlying the Washington Consensus so often led to failure.

Bankruptcy, Aggregate Supply, and the East Asia Crisis

Perhaps the most dramatic policy failure at those wedded to the old paradigm occurred in the management of economic crises. Poorly designed policies can lead to an unnecessarily large reduction in credit availability and unnecessary large increases in bankruptcy, both leading to large adverse effects on aggregate supply, exacerbating the economic downturn. But this is precisely what the IMF did: by raising interest rates to extremely high levels in countries where firms were already highly leveraged, it forced massive bankruptcy, and the economies were thus plunged into deep recession and depression. The policies were defended by saying that they were necessary to stabilize the economies and attract capital. They did neither. Capital was not attracted to the country, but rather fled. As capital fled, the exchange rate plummeted further. Thus, the policies even failed to stabilize the exchange rate. There were alternative policies available, debt standstills followed by corporate financial restructurings, which, while they might not have avoided a downturn, would have resulted in the downturns being shallower and shorter. Malaysia, whose economic policies conformed much more closely to those than our theories would have suggested, not only recovered more quickly, but also was left with less of a legacy of debt to impair its future growth, than did neighboring Thailand, which conformed more closely to the IMF's recommendation.

Corporate Governance, Open Capital Markets, and the Transition to a Market Economy

The transition from communism to a market economy represents one of the most important economic experiments of all time, and the failure (so far) in Russia, and the successes in China, shed considerable light on many of the issues that I have been discussing. The full dimension of Russia's failure is hard to fathom. Communism, with its central planning (requiring more information gathering, processing, and dissemination capacity than could be managed with *any* technology), its lack of incentives, and its system rife with distortions, was viewed as highly inefficient. The movement to a market, it was assumed, would bring enormous increases in incomes. Instead, incomes plummeted, a decline confirmed not only by GDP statistics and household surveys, but also by social indicators. The numbers in poverty soared, from 2 percent to upward of 50 percent (depending on the year and measure used). Although there were many dimensions to these failures, one stands out: the privatization strategy, which paid little attention to the issues of corporate governance that we stressed earlier. Empirical work confirms that countries that privatized rapidly but lacked "good" corporate governance did not grow more rapidly. As Sappington and my paper warned, privatization might not lead to an increase in social welfare; rather than providing a basis for wealth creation, it led to asset stripping and wealth destruction.

BEYOND INFORMATION ECONOMICS

As time evolved, it became clear that the imperfect information paradigm itself was highly robust; there were some quite general principles, while the working out of the models in detail in different situations might well differ. We succeeded in showing that an alternative robust paradigm with great explanatory power could be constructed. The new information economics – extended to incorporate changes in knowledge – at last began to address systematically the foundations of a market economy. As J. Schumpeter had argued long ago, the strength of the market economy rested not so much on the efficiency with which resources were allocated within a static framework as on its innovativeness. But the standard competitive paradigm had assumed that technology was fixed.

There was thus more wrong with the standard model than its assumptions concerning information. In a way, I had focused my attention on the one deficiency that was easiest to address. Everyone could agree that information was imperfect; no one could really deny the existence of the problems of adverse selection and incentive. The other deficiencies raised, perhaps, problems that were harder to address.

With my increased attention to the problems of development, I became, for instance, increasingly convinced of the inappropriateness of the assumption of fixed preferences. Development was, above all, concerned with changing people's mind-sets. I also became increasedly disturbed by the attempt to separate out economics from broader social and political concerns. A major impediment to development in Africa has been the civil strife that has been endemic there, itself in part a consequence of the economic circumstances.

It seemed to me that policies based on an excessively narrow view of society – focusing exclusively on economics, and too often on a "wrong" economic model – were doomed to failure. Many of the policies of the IMF – including the manner in which it interacted with governments, basing loans on conditionality – were counterproductive. The IMF policies in Indonesia, including the elimination of food and fuel subsidies for the very poor just as the country was plunging into depression, with wages plummeting and unemployment soaring, predictably led to riots; the economic consequences are still being felt. At the World Bank (where I was then serving as Chief Economist and Senior Vice President), there began fundamental changes in development strategy toward one that embraced a more comprehensive approach to development.

Finally, I have become convinced that the dynamics of change may not be well described by the equilibrium models that have long been at the center of economic analysis. Information economics has alerted us to the fact that history matters; there are important hysteresis effects. Random events – the black plague – have consequences that are irreversible. Dynamics may be better described by evolutionary processes and models than by equilibrium processes. And although it may be difficult to describe fully these evolutionary processes, this much is already clear: there is no reason to believe that they are, in any general sense, "optimal."

Many of the same themes that emerged from our simpler work in information economics applied here. For instance, repeatedly in the information theoretic models discussed above, we showed that multiple equilibria (some of which Pareto dominated others) could easily arise. So too here. This in turn has several important consequences, beyond the observation already made that history matters. First, it means that one cannot simply predict where the economy will be by knowing preferences and technology (and initial endowments). There can be a high level of indeterminacy. Second, as in Darwinian ecological models, the major determinant of one's environment is the behavior of others, and their behavior may in turn depend on their beliefs about others' behavior. Third, government intervention can sometimes move the economy from one equilibrium to another; and having done that, continued intervention might not be required.

THE POLITICAL ECONOMY OF INFORMATION

My earlier work had shown how imperfections of information affected economic processes. My years in Washington had given me the opportunity to study closely, at first hand, political processes. Information was no less imperfect, and I began to reflect on the questions of how these information imperfections affected political processes, and whether some of the insights from the economics of information might be of relevance to an understanding of political processes.

Here, I have time only to note some of the ways in which information affects political processes. Perhaps most importantly, the "information rules of the game," both for the economy and for political processes, can become a subject of intense political debate. The United States and the IMF argued strongly that lack of transparency was at the root of the 1997 financial crisis, and said that the East Asian countries had to become more transparent. The recognition that quantitative data concerning capital flows (outstanding loans) by the IMF and the U.S. Treasury could have been taken as a concession of the inappropriateness of the competitive paradigm (in which *prices* convey all the relevant information); but the more appropriate way of viewing the debate was *political*, a point which became clear when it was noted that partial disclosures could be of only limited value, and could possibly be counterproductive, as capital would be induced to move through channels involving less disclosure, channels like offshore banking centers that were also less well regulated. The U.S. Treasury opposed the OECD initiative to combat money laundering through greater transparency of offshore banking centers until it became clear that terrorists might be using them to help finance their operations; at that point, the balance of American interests changed, and the U.S. Treasury changed its position.

Political processes inevitably entail asymmetries of information: our political leaders are *supposed* to know more about threats to defense, about our economic situation, and so on, than ordinary citizens. There has been a delegation of responsibility for day-to-day decision making, just as there is within a firm. The problem is to provide incentives for those so entrusted to act on behalf of those who they are supposed to be serving – the standard principle agent problem. Just as we recognize that current management has an incentive to *increase* asymmetries of information in order to enhance its market power, increase its discretion, so too in public life. And just as we recognize that disclosure requirements – greater transparency – and specific rules of the game (for example, related to corporate governance) can affect the effectiveness of the takeover mechanism and the overall quality of corporate governance, so too the same factors can affect political contestability and the quality of public governance.

In the context of political processes, where "exit" options are limited, one needs to be particularly concerned about abuses. If a firm is mismanaged – if the managers attempt to enrich themselves at the expense of shareholders and customers and entrench themselves against competition – the damage is limited: customers at least can switch. But in political processes, those who see the quality of public services deteriorate cannot do so as easily. If all individuals were as mean-spirited and selfish as economists have traditionally modeled them, matters would indeed be bleak: as I have put it elsewhere, ensuring the public good (public management) is itself a public good. But there is a wealth of evidence that the economists' traditional model of the individual is too narrow – and that indeed intrinsic rewards, for example, public service, can be even more effective than extrinsic rewards, for example, monetary compensation (which is not to say that compensation is not of some importance). This public-spiritedness (even if blended with a modicum of self-interest) is manifested in a variety of civil society organizations, through which *voluntarily* individuals work *collectively* to advance their perception of the collective interests.

There are strong forces on the part of those in government to reduce transparency. More transparency reduces their scope for action – it not only exposes mistakes, but also corruption (as the expression goes, sunshine is the strongest antiseptic). Government officials may try to enhance their power, by trying to advance specious arguments for secrecy, and then say, in effect, to justify their otherwise inexplicable or self-serving behavior, "Trust me . . . if you only knew what I knew."

There is a further rationale for secrecy: secrecy is an artificially created scarcity of information, and like most artificially created scarcities, it gives rise to rents, rents which in some countries are appropriated through outright corruption (selling information), but in others are part of a "gift exchange" in which reporters not only provide "puff" pieces praising the government official who has given the reporter privileged access to information, particularly in ways which are designed to enhance the official's influence and power, but also distort news coverage. I was in the unfortunate position of watching closely this process work, and work quite effectively. Without unbiased information, the effectiveness of the check that can be provided by the citizenry is limited; without good information, the contestability of the political processes can be undermined.

CONCLUDING REMARKS

In this essay I have traced the replacement of one paradigm with another. The underlying forces of supply and demand are still important, although in the new paradigm, they become only part of the analysis; they are not the whole analysis. It has been a revolution in economics, in which the most sacred, long-standing results have been overturned. In the three decades since the revolution began, it has affected virtually every branch of economics – industrial and rural organization, finance and accounting, taxation and regulation, development and growth, labor economics and organizational theory, macroeconomics and monetary theory. In some circles, the old theories still predominate, and policies based on those old theories are still pushed. The progress made in three decades has been enormous. But we are still at the beginning.

© The Nobel Foundation

SELECTED REFERENCES

Caprio, G., P. Honohan, and J. E. Stiglitz (eds.) (2001). *Financial Liberalization: How Far, How Fast?* Cambridge: Cambridge University Press.

Hoff, E., A. Braverman, and J. E. Stiglitz (eds.) (1993). *The Economics of Rural Organization: Theory, Practice, and Policy.* New York: Oxford University Press for the World Bank.

Meier, Gerald and Joseph E. Stiglitz (eds.) (2000). *The Future in Perspective.* London: Oxford University Press.

Stiglitz, Joseph. (2001). *Economics of the Public Sector*, Third Edition. New York: Norton.

2

Behavioral Economics

Matthew Rabin

INTRODUCTION

The formal neoclassical paradigm that has dominated economics for decades draws out the implications of a narrow conception of human nature – that we are entirely rational, time-consistent pursuers of our material self-interest. Although there have always been economists who have called for greater realism, only recently has the more narrow conception clearly begun to lose its grip within mainstream economics.

In the last twenty years, more and more economists have attempted to integrate findings from psychology and other fields into economics, using experiments, surveys, and more traditional methods to identify some basic patterns of human preferences, cognition, and behavior that have been traditionally ignored by economists. With a boost from such innovators as Thomas Schelling and George Akerlof, economists have begun to accept that there is merit to exploring such alternatives, while psychologists Daniel Kahneman and Amos Tversky and economist Richard Thaler have been articulating some core psychological principles that economists should pay attention to. Many of the principles proposed by these and other researchers that were perceived ten years ago as ill-conceived, implausible, or unusable by economists are now far more widely accepted. Today, many young researchers have begun to pursue research in behavioral economics; increasingly, they are being hired by top economics departments and published in top economics journals.

This essay reviews some of the psychological principles that have been emphasized in this line of research, which has come to be labeled *behavioral economics*. The range of topics I discuss is necessarily restricted and somewhat arbitrary, and the exposition of those topics is necessarily abbreviated. For space considerations, I will place little emphasis on the methods used to establish these facts, on attempts to formalize them within the paradigm of mainstream economics, or even on economic applications. Rather, this essay is meant to provide a sense for the most important challenges raised, and insights supplied, by behavioral economics.[1]

My perspective on this material is that of a mainstream economist who believes that the insights of behavioral economics should and will be integrated into our current general framework, substantially reforming mainstream economics rather than presenting an alternative paradigm. (This view of the current course of behavioral economics is not particularly idiosyncratic, but nor is it universal.)

Whereas some of the challenges posed by behavioral economics are seen by many as a radical shift in perspective, there are two senses in which I believe the shift we are witnessing is decidedly nonradical.

First, as many of us perceive the program, it has developed to be rather conservative in its methods and its perspective about how we should go about studying economic behavior. Mainstream economics employs a powerful combination of methods: methodological individualism, mathematical formalization of assumptions, logical analysis of the consequences of those assumptions, and sophisticated empirical field testing. These methods are tremendously useful, and we should strive to understand psychological findings in light of these methods. Yet these methods raise problems for doing full justice to behavioral reality: Because of the high premium economics places on the logic and precision of arguments and the quantification of evidence, attending to all facets of human nature is neither feasible nor desirable. This problem has led many economists who are in principle sympathetic to pushing for greater realism to nonetheless resist engaging such behavioral evidence for the sake of the "tractability" and "parsimony" of our models. Yet more and more economists have come to conclude that the realization that many details of human behavior must be ignored does not license institutionalized complacency about the behavioral validity of our assumptions. In this new perspective, tractability and parsimony are guiding principles in our efforts to make our research more realistic, not pretexts for avoiding this task.

---

[1] For more detailed overviews, see Thaler (1992), Camerer (1995), Laibson and Zeckhauser (1998), and especially Kahneman and Tversky (2000). This essay draws heavily on Rabin (1998), Rabin (in press), and on work for a book I am currently writing.

The second way that behavioral economics is nonradical is in its acceptance of the tremendous insight of current economic assumptions. To say that the assumptions of "100 percent " rationality and "100 percent" self-interest are invalid and misleading is obviously not equivalent to saying that people are 0 percent rational or 0 percent self-interested (whatever that might mean). The assumptions that economists have come to accept are tremendously useful base cases because they represent substantial truths and capture important insights about economic behavior. People are, especially in their economic realms, very largely self-interested and it would be ridiculous for economics to ignore that fact. The findings of behavioral research, however, are that there are nontrivial ways in which people sacrifice their material self-interest to treat others fairly or (more often) to retaliate against those who have mistreated them. Similarly, the fact that people are also substantially purposive and intelligent in pursuing their wants is not to be questioned; behavioral research does not in the least suggest that people behave randomly or (except in a few domains) the opposite of what they are trying to achieve; it is that in our reasonably intelligent pursuit of our wants there are some identifiable, systematic departures from full rationality.

The organization of my presentation reflects the view that behavioral economics ought play off the existing standard model as an important base case. By focusing on evidence consistent with rational choice – basically positing that preferences are different than economists have supposed – the first several topics involve relatively small modifications of the familiar economic framework. I then present a few topics in biases in judgment under uncertainty which, by assuming that people fail to maximize their preferences, pose a more radical challenge to the economics model. The final few topics point to an even more radical critique of the economics model: Even if we are willing to modify our standard assumptions about preferences, or allow that people make systematic errors in judgment when attempting to maximize utility, it is sometimes misleading to conceptualize people as attempting to maximize a coherent, stable, and accurately perceived set of preferences.

This essay mostly reviews the core findings of recent behavioral research. It therefore ignores the most recent trend in behavioral economics: To fold these findings into mainstream economics by proposing modifications to the formal assumptions of economics, developing empirical tests of this in the field, and (most importantly) applying the findings to core areas of study in economics. This "second wave" of behavioral economics is expanding rapidly, but is still essentially in its infancy. In a concluding section, I very briefly discuss some of these trends and offer a prognosis for the field of behavioral economics.

Reference Levels, Adaptation, and Losses

Overwhelming evidence shows that humans are often more sensitive to how their current situation differs from some reference level than to the absolute characteristics of the situation (Helson 1964). For instance, the same temperature that feels cold when we are adapted to hot temperatures may appear hot when we are adapted to cold temperatures. Understanding that people are often more sensitive to changes than to absolute levels suggests that we ought incorporate into utility analysis such factors as habitual levels of consumption. Instead of utility at time t depending solely on present consumption, c_t, it may also depend on a "reference level," r_t, determined by factors like past consumption or expectations of future consumption. Hence, instead of a utility function of the form $u_t(c_t)$, utility should be written in a more general form, $u_t(r_t); c_t$. Although some economists have over the years incorporated reference dependence into their economic analysis, it is fair to say that the ways and degrees to which reference points influence behavior have not fully been appreciated by economists.

Researchers have identified a pervasive feature of reference dependence: In a wide variety of domains, people are significantly more averse to losses than they are attracted to same-sized gains (Kahneman, Knetsch, and Thaler 1990). One realm where such *loss aversion* plays out is in preferences over wealth levels. Tversky and Kahneman (1991) suggest that in the domain of money, (and in others where the sizes of losses and gains can be measured), people value modest losses roughly twice as much as equal-sized gains. That the displeasure from a monetary loss is greater than the pleasure from a same-sized gain is also implied by a concave utility function, which economists typically use as the explanation for risk aversion. But loss aversion says that the value function abruptly changes slope at the reference level, so that people dislike even small-scale risk. For instance, most people prefer their status quo to a 50/50 bet of losing $10 or gaining $11. The standard concave-utility-function explanation for risk aversion is simply not a plausible explanation of such risk attitudes. Epstein and Zin (1990) have, for instance, observed that the expected-utility framework using standard utility functions cannot simultaneously explain both the small-scale and large-scale risk attitudes implied by macroeconomic data, and Rabin (2000) provides a "calibration theorem" that shows that *no* concave utility function can simultaneously explain plausible small-scale and large-scale risk attitudes. A reference-based kink in the utility function is required to explain such risk attitudes within the expected-utility framework. I return to this issue below in discussing research on risk aversion.

Loss aversion is related to the *endowment effect* identified by Thaler (1980): Once a person comes to possess a good, he or she immediately values it more than before he or she possessed it. Kahneman, Knetsch, and Thaler (1990) nicely illustrate this phenomenon. They randomly gave mugs worth about $5 each to one group of students. Minimal selling prices were elicited from those given the mugs (with an incentive-compatible procedure that ensured honest reports). Minimal "prices" – sums of money such that they would choose that sum rather than the mug – were elicited from another group of subjects not given mugs. These two groups – "sellers" and "choosers" – faced precisely the same choice between money and mugs, but their reference points differed: Those who were randomly given mugs treated the mugs as part of their reference levels or endowments, and considered leaving without a mug to be a loss, whereas individuals not given mugs considered leaving without a mug as remaining at their reference point. In one experiment, the median value placed on the mug was $3.50 by choosers but $7.00 by sellers. Such results have been replicated repeatedly by many researchers in many contexts.

In addition to loss aversion, another important reference-level effect is *diminishing sensitivity*: The marginal effects in perceived well-being are greater for changes close to one's reference level than for changes further away. As Kahneman and Tversky (1979) note, diminishing sensitivity is a pervasive pattern of human perception, where our perceptions are a concave function of the magnitudes of change. For instance, we are more likely to discriminate between 3° and 6° changes in room temperature than between 23° and 26° changes. This applies to both increases and decreases in temperature. In the context of preferences over uncertain monetary outcomes, diminishing sensitivity implies that the slope of a person's utility function over wealth becomes flatter as his or her wealth gets further away from his or her reference level. Because for losses relative to the reference level "further away" implies lower wealth levels, diminishing sensitivity has a provocative implication: Whereas people are likely to be risk averse over gains, they are often risk-*loving* over losses. Kahneman and Tversky (1979) found that 70 percent of subjects report that they would prefer a 3/4 chance of losing nothing and 1/4 chance of losing $6,000 to a 2/4 chance of losing nothing and 1/4 chance each of losing $4,000 or

$2,000. Because the preferred lottery here is a mean-preserving spread of the less-preferred lottery, the responses of 70 percent of the subjects are inconsistent with the standard concavity assumption.

In order to study the effects of reference points in a dynamic utility-maximization framework, we need to take into account how people feel about the effects their current choices have on their future reference points. To maximize their long-run utilities when reference points matter, people must determine two things beyond how they feel about departures from reference points: how current behavior affects future reference points and how they feel about changes in their reference points. Economists Ryder and Heal (1973) model the process by which reference points change with the formula $r_t \equiv \alpha c_{t-1} + (1 - \alpha) r_{t-1}$, where $\alpha \in (0,1)$ is a parameter measuring how quickly people adjust their reference points. In a rational-expectations model, people will take this formula into account when maximizing their long-run well-being. Such an account of how reference levels are determined seems intuitive, although there seems to be little evidence on this topic.[2] Evidence is similarly sparse about how people's preferences depend on changes in reference points. Without assumptions about these relationships, there will be a relatively small set of circumstances where loss aversion and diminishing sensitivity can be integrated into models of dynamic utility maximization.

There have been some initial attempts to study loss aversion, the endowment effect, and the status quo bias in economic contexts. For instance, Shea (1995a, 1995b) and Bowman, Minehart, and Rabin (1999) show that consumers are more averse to lowering consumption in response to bad news about income than they are to increasing consumption in response to good news, and argue that this behavior is a natural implication of loss aversion.

Social Preferences and Fair Allocations

Perhaps the most famous passage in economics, a staple of introductory lectures of introductory economics courses, is the following quote from Adam Smith's *The Wealth of Nations* (1776, 26–7):

[2] Bowman, Minehart, and Rabin (1999) combine the Ryder and Heal approach of rational-expectations, reference-dependent utilities with a utility function that incorporates loss aversion and diminishing sensitivity. Duesenberry (1949) implicitly posited a reference function closer to $r_t \equiv \text{Max} \{c_\tau : \tau < t\}$ – that is, a person's reference level was his or her highest past consumption level.

It is not from the benevolence of the butcher, the brewer, or the baker that we expect our dinner, but from their regard for their own interest. We address ourselves not to their humanity, but to their self-love, and never talk to them of our necessities, but of their advantage.

There is not much to disagree with in Smith's poetic analysis of the motivations driving most market behavior, and probably no other two-word description of human motives comes close to "self-interest" in explaining economic behavior. Yet pure self-interest is far from a complete description of human motivation, and realism suggests that economists should move away from the presumption that people are *solely* self-interested. Dawes and Thaler (1988, 195) eloquently set parameters for this endeavor:

In the rural areas around Ithaca it is common for farmers to put some fresh produce on the table by the road. There is a cash box on the table, and customers are expected to put money in the box in return for the vegetables they take. The box has just a small slit, so money can only be put in, not taken out. Also, the box is attached to the table, so no one can (easily) make off with the money. We think that the farmers have just about the right model of human nature. They feel that enough people will volunteer to pay for the fresh corn to make it worthwhile to put it out there. The farmers also know that if it were easy enough to take the money, someone would do so.

Experimental research makes clear that preferences depart from pure self-interest in nontrivial ways: Subjects contribute to public goods more than can be explained by pure self-interest; they often share money when they could readily grab it for themselves; and they often sacrifice money to retaliate against unfair treatment. The literature identifying the nature of such "social preferences" is among the most active and rapidly developing areas of research in experimental economics.

A simple hypothesis for how people care about others' well-being is natural for economists, and has the longest history in economics: altruism – a positive concern for others as well as yourself. Altruism can be either "general" or "targeted"; you may care about all others' well-being, or maybe selected others' (friends, family) well-being. Most often, *ceteris paribus*, the more a sacrifice helps somebody the more likely you are to be willing to make this sacrifice. This is as predicted by simple altruistic preferences that assume people weight others' utility positively in their own utility function. In this sense, assuming simple altruism provides insight into departures from self-interest.

But such simple altruism is not adequate for understanding many behaviors. Other aspects of social preferences show up prominently in psychological and recent experimental–economic evidence. For one thing, people care about the fairness and equity of the distribution of resources, beyond ways that it increases total direct well-being. Let me quickly illustrate with some examples.[3] All of these decisions involve decisions as to how much money (either pennies in Berkeley, California, or pesetas in Barcelona, Spain) to allocate two anonymous parties. The first example involves Party C choosing between two different allocations for two other anonymous parties, A and B:

C chooses between (A,B) allocations: ($7.50, $3.75) vs. ($4.00, $4.00)
Approximate findings: 50%   50%

A natural interpretation of these findings (consistent with other experimental evidence) is that C may want to help these parties, but cares about both social efficiency and "equality" – producing a sort of "Rawlsian" desire to help the worse off. Those who care relatively more about social efficiency choose the higher total-surplus outcome ($7.50, $3.75), while those caring more about helping the worse off choose ($4.00, $4.00).

Now let us consider the same situation, except that B – one of the two interested parties – is making the choice. He or she may choose differently than does the disinterested Party C because of self-interest, or because he or she would be envious if he or she comes out behind, or for other reasons. The findings are as follows:

B chooses between (A,B) allocations: ($7.50, $3.75) vs. ($4.00, $4.00)
Approximate findings: 40%   60%

B does indeed seem to have similar preferences as neutral party C, though is a bit less willing to choose the allocation that is good for A and bad for him- or herself. This difference (which in these cases and by replication is small but statistically significant) may be because B is self-interested, or because he or she is envious of coming out behind A.

While the laboratory investigation of social preferences has been a tremendous advance, the eventual goal is to apply the insights to economic phenomena outside the laboratory. In moving from abstract, context-free allocation problems to everyday economic fairness judgments, things become significantly more complicated. Notably, as everywhere, reference levels are crucial. Thaler (1985) and Kahneman, Knetsch, and Thaler (1986a, 1986b) demonstrate that loss aversion plays a very strong role in people's notion of fairness; firms have more of an obligation not to hurt

---

[3] The games and findings are from Charness and Rabin (in press), but they are similar to many of the findings in this literature.

workers or customers relative to reference transactions than they have to improve the terms of trade.

Reciprocity and Attribution

The previous subsection considered evidence about social preferences defined over the allocations of goods. Psychological evidence indicates, however, that social preferences are not merely a function of consumption levels, or even changes in consumption levels. Rather, social preferences over other people's consumption depend on the behavior, motivations, and intentions of those other people. The same people who are altruistic toward deserving people are often indifferent to the plight of undeserving people, and motivated to hurt those whom they believe to have misbehaved. If somebody is being nice to you or others, you are inclined to be nice to him or her; if somebody is being mean to you or others, you are inclined to be mean to him or her.

Reciprocity motives manifest themselves in people's refusal to cooperate with others who are being uncooperative. But evidence indicates the strongest form of reciprocal motivation is the willingness to sacrifice to hurt others who are being unfair. A consumer may refuse to buy a product sold by a monopolist at an "unfair" price, even if he or she hurts herself by foregoing the product. An employee who feels he or she has been mistreated by a firm may engage in costly acts of sabotage, perhaps to the point of violently retaliating against his or her employers. Members of a striking labor union may strike longer than is in their material interests because they want to punish a firm for being unfair.

A crucial feature of the psychology of reciprocity is that people determine their dispositions toward others according to motives attributed to these others, not solely according to actions taken. When motivated by reciprocal altruism, for instance, people differentiate between those who take a generous action by choice and those who are forced to do so. Demonstrating both the basic principle of reciprocity and the role of volition, Goranson and Berkowitz (1966, 229) conducted an experiment in which confederates posing as subjects were in a position to help real subjects fill out some worksheets. One-third of the subjects were told that the confederate had voluntarily offered to help; one-third were told that the experimenter had *instructed* the confederate to help; and one-third were told that the confederate *might* be willing to help, but the confederate was instructed to refuse to help. When the subjects were later given an opportunity to assist the confederates, they reciprocated earlier help, but did so significantly more when it was voluntary than when it was involuntary.

To see more concretely how reciprocation of the behavior of others might affect choice, I return to the examples discussed above. These examples illustrated how parties might assess the attractiveness of different allocations in what might be termed a "reciprocity-free" context. That is, one party is making a decision that affects one or more other parties who have not themselves behaved nobly. But now suppose that B makes the same choice as in the previous example, but chooses *after A has created this choice by rejecting ($5.50, $5.50)*. A's decision to forego an allocation of ($5.50, $5.50) in favor of trying to get B to choose ($7.50, $3.75) is clearly selfish and unfair behavior, as it involves a miniscule increase in total surplus while leading to an unequal allocation. The findings are as follows:

Following a choice by A to forego the allocation ($5.50, $5.50) to give B this choice, B chooses between (A,B) allocations: ($7.50, $3.75) vs. ($4.00, $4.00)
Approximate findings: **10%**   **90%**

Compared to the behavior by B in nonreciprocal settings, we see that B is much less likely to want to sacrifice to give the good allocation to A following this obnoxious choice by A. Note that B's choice in the previous two examples is identical in terms of outcomes. And yet here, and in many related examples, players in games behave systematically differently as a function of previous behavior by other players. This shows that people care not only about outcomes, but also how they arrived at those outcomes. The fact that preferences cannot be defined solely over outcomes can be reconciled with preference theory, but requires an expansion of the notion of what enters the utility function. But the extra complications appear necessary to do justice in economic models to such issues as employee and citizen concerns for procedural justice, and the complications are crucial for understanding the nature of retaliation and reciprocal altruism.

Volition is also central to the propensity to retaliate against negative actions. Blount (1995) asked subjects about their willingness to accept take-it-or-leave-it offers made by anonymous other parties on how to split $10.[4] One group of subjects was told that the "ultimatum" was coming from anonymous other students, and that their responses would determine the division between them and these anonymous other students.

---

[4] The "ultimatum game" of the sort studied by Blount was first developed by Güth, Schmittberger, and Schwarze (1982). For reviews of the (massive) literature developed since, see Thaler (1988), Güth and Tietz (1990), and Camerer and Thaler (1995).

Another group was told that *a third party* (also an anonymous student) was to determine the offer made. In this variant, the person who would be hurt by a subject's decision to reject an offer did not participate in the offer, and the third party who made the offers would not be affected by the subject's decision. A final group of subjects were told that the offer would be generated *randomly* by a computer-simulated roulette wheel. In one study, the average acceptable offers for those groups were $2.91, $2.08, and $1.20. That is, people did reject very low offers even if computer- or third-party generated, but were less keen to reject offers that were not the result of volition by the person who would be hurt by the rejections.

Such examples indicate that interpreting other peoples' motives depend on what we believe *their beliefs* about the consequences of their actions are. Another example of the importance of beliefs is if you think somebody has been generous to you solely to get a bigger favor from you in the future, then you do not view his or her generosity to be as pure as if he or she had expected no reciprocity from you. For example, Kahn and Tice (1973) found that subjects' reactions to others' statements of intentions depended on whether they thought those making statements knew that their intentions would be made known to the subjects.[5]

The role of reciprocity and volition appears in some important economic contexts. Akerlof (1982) posits that firms and workers can be thought of as engaging in "gift exchange," a view of social exchange emphasized in sociology and especially anthropology. If a firm pays a higher wage to an employee, that employee is likely to reciprocate with higher quality work. Consequently, firms may give higher wages hoping workers will reciprocate with higher effort. Similarly, Akerlof (1982, 1984) and Akerlof and Yellen (1990) propose that "efficiency wages," above the market-clearing wages, will be paid to workers to induce higher effort by those workers. Fehr, Kirchsteiger, and Riedl (1993) tested this hypothesis in laboratory models of labor markets. Subjects were assigned roles as "firms" or "workers." Firms offered a wage – involving a real monetary transfer from firm to worker – and workers responded by choosing an "effort" level, where this effort was monetarily costly to workers. The results were that most workers chose effort levels higher than their money-maximizing levels. Moreover, whereas low wages induced little or

[5] To formalize the role of intentions in fairness judgments, Rabin (1993) adopts the framework developed by Geanakoplos, Pearce, and Stacchetti (1989), who modify conventional game theory by allowing payoffs to depend on players' beliefs as well as their actions. By positing that my beliefs about your beliefs are arguments in my utility function, we can model my beliefs about your motives as directly influencing my fairness judgments.

no effort by workers, workers rewarded firms for setting high wages by providing high effort.

What is the source of high effort levels by workers in response to high wages by firms? Although workers may simply be choosing to share some of their additional wealth from higher wages with the firm, they may also be reciprocating the volitional generosity of firms. Charness (1996) conducts experiments that helps us differentiate these hypotheses. In Fehr, Kirchler, and Weichbold (1994), it is clear to the worker–subjects that the firms choose wages of their own volition. Charness (1996) replicates this condition, but also conducts variants of the experiment in which wages are either chosen randomly, or by a "third party" (the experimenter). In these conditions, a high wage is not an act of kindness by a firm, and a low wage is not act of meanness; both are beyond a firm's control. Results indicated that the high-wages-yields-high-effort reaction has both a "share-the-wealth" and an attribution element: Workers were substantially more likely to reward high wages with high effort and punish low wages with low effort when the wages reflected the volition of the firm.

Biases in Judgment

Economists have traditionally assumed that, when faced with uncertainty, people correctly form their subjective probabilistic assessments according to the laws of probability. But researchers have documented many systematic departures from rationality in judgment under uncertainty. Tversky and Kahneman (1974, 1124) help conceptualize observed departures from perfect rationality by noting that people rely on "heuristic principles which reduce the complex tasks of assessing probabilities and predicting values to simpler judgmental operations. In general, these heuristics are quite useful, but sometimes they lead to severe and systematic errors." As the quote clearly suggests, the research described here does not at all suggest economists should abandon the assumption that people are intelligent and purposive in their decision making. Rather the research explores how people depart from *perfect* rationality, positing biases that represent specific and systematic ways that judgment departs from perfect rationality.

I briefly outline some biases that might interest economists.[6] The first is *anchoring and adjustment*. Slovic and Sarah Lichtenstein (1971)

---

[6] For a more thorough introduction to this literature, see Kahneman, Slovic, and Tversky (1982), or, for an outstanding review of this material, and of individual decision making more generally, see Camerer (1995).

demonstrate that, in forming numerical estimates of uncertain quantities, adjustments in assessments away from (possibly arbitrary) initial values are typically insufficient. Tversky and Kahneman (1974) provide the following example:

[S]ubjects were asked to estimate various quantities, stated in percentages (for example, the percentage of African countries in the United Nations). For each quantity, a number between 0 and 100 was determined by spinning a wheel of fortune in the subjects' presence. The subjects were instructed to indicate first whether that number was higher or lower than the value of the quantity, and then to estimate the value of the quantity by moving upward or downward from the given number. Different groups were given different numbers for each quantity, and these arbitrary numbers had a marked effect on estimates. For example, the median estimates of the percentage of African countries in the United Nations were 25 and 45 for groups that received 10 and 65, respectively, as starting points. Payoffs for accuracy did not reduce the anchoring effect.

Although this example is somewhat artificial, Tversky and Kahneman point out that anchoring can occur as a natural part of the assessment process itself. If we ask an individual to construct a probability distribution for the level of the Dow Jones, his or her likely beginning point would be to estimate a median level. This value would likely then serve as an anchor for his or her further probability assessments. By contrast, if he or she were asked by somebody to construct the probability assessments by stating the likelihood of the Dow Jones exceeding a prespecified value, he or she would likely anchor on this value. The two procedures, therefore, are likely to lead to different predictions, with the first procedure yielding a probability distribution more concentrated around the median than the second.

One of the most widely studied biases in the judgment literature is the *hindsight bias*. Fischhoff (1975, 288) first proposed this bias by observing that "(a) Reporting an outcome's occurrence increases its perceived probability of occurrence; and (b) people who have received outcome knowledge are largely unaware of its having changed their perceptions [along the lines of (a)]." Combining these, the literature on the hindsight bias shows that people exaggerate the degree to which their beliefs before an informative event would be similar to their current beliefs. We tend to think we "knew it would happen all along." After a politician wins an election, people label it as inevitable – and believe that they *always* thought it was inevitable.

One example of Fischhoff's (1975) original demonstration of this effect was to give subjects a historical passage regarding British intrusion into

India and military interaction with the Gurkas of Nepal. Without being told the outcome of this interaction, some subjects were asked to predict the likelihood of each of four possible outcomes: (1) British victory, (2) Gurka victory, (3) military stalemate with a peace settlement, (4) military stalemate without a peace settlement. Four other sets of subjects were each *told* a different one of the four outcomes was the true one (the *real* true outcome is that the two sides fought to a stalemate without reaching a peace settlement). For each reported outcome, when compared to a control group not told any outcome, subjects' average *ex post* guesses of their hypothetical *ex ante* estimates were 15 percent higher than those of the control group. People do not sufficiently "subtract" information they currently have about an outcome in imagining what they would have thought without that information.

A pervasive fact about human judgment is that people disproportionately weight *salient, memorable,* or *vivid* evidence even when they have better sources of information.[7] For instance, our assessment of a given city's crime rate is likely to be too influenced by whether we personally know somebody who has been assaulted, even if we are familiar with much more relevant general statistics. Likewise, dramatic stories by people we know about difficulties with a brand of car are likely to be overly influential even if we are familiar, via *Consumer Reports*, with general statistics of the reliability of different brands. In both these cases, and in many others, the more salient information should have virtually no influence on our beliefs in the face of much more pertinent statistical information. Tversky and Kahneman (1973) discuss, for example, how salience may distort clinicians' assessments of the relationship between severe depression and suicide. Incidents in which patients commit suicide are much more likely to be remembered than are instances where patients do not commit suicide. This is likely to lead to an exaggerated assessment of the probability that depressed patients will commit suicide.

Finally, there is a mass of psychological research that finds people are prone toward overconfidence in their judgments. The vast majority of researchers argue that such overconfidence is pervasive, and most of the research concerns possible explanations (of which confirmatory bias discussed above is one).

---

[7] In Tversky and Kahneman's (1973) formulation: "[A] person is said to employ the *availability heuristic* whenever he estimates frequency or probability by the ease with which instances or associations could be brought to mind." For more general reviews of the role of salience and vividness, see Fiske and Taylor (1991, Chapters 5 and 7).

I now turn to a discussion of two more biases in more detail, followed by a discussion of the hypothesis that learning and expertise pervasively eliminate hypotheses.

The Law of Small Numbers

Tversky and Kahneman (1974) provide evidence for the *representativeness heuristic*. Bayes's Law tells us that our assessment of likelihoods should combine representativeness with base rates (the percentage of the population falling into various groups). Yet people underuse base-rate information in forming their judgments. If we see somebody who looks like a criminal, our assessment of the probability that he or she is a criminal tends to underuse knowledge about the percentage of people who are criminals. Similarly, if a certain medical test always comes out positive among people with a rare disease, and only occasionally among people without the disease, people will tend to exaggerate the likelihood of having the disease given a positive result. Given the rarity of the disease, the total number of false positives may be far greater than the number of true positives. According to a bias called "the law of small numbers" (Tversky and Kahneman 1971), people exaggerate how closely a small sample will resemble the parent population from which the sample is drawn. We expect even small classes of students to contain very close to the typical distribution of smart ones and personable ones. Likewise, we underestimate how often a good financial analyst will be wrong a few times in a row, and how often a clueless analyst will be right a few times in a row. Because we expect close to the same probability distribution of types in small groups as in large groups, for example, we tend to view it as comparably likely that at least 80 percent of twenty coin flips will come up heads than that at least 80 percent of five coin flips will come up heads; in fact, the probabilities are about 1 percent and 19 percent, respectively. Kahneman and Tversky (1982a, 44) asked undergraduates the following question:

A certain town is served by two hospitals. In the larger hospital about 45 babies are born each day, and in the smaller hospital about 15 babies are born each day. As you know, about 50 percent of all babies are boys. However, the exact percentage varies from day to day. Sometimes it may be higher than 50 percent, sometimes lower.

For a period of 1 year, each hospital recorded the days on which more than 60 percent of the babies born were boys. Which hospital do you think recorded more such days?

Twenty-two percent of the subjects said that they thought that it was more likely that the larger hospital recorded more such days, and 56 percent said that they thought the number of days would be about the same. Only 22 percent of subjects correctly answered that the smaller hospital would report more such days. This is the same fraction as guessed exactly wrong. Apparently, the subjects simply did not see the relevance of the number of childbirths per day. Although people believe in the law of small numbers, they apparently do not believe in the law of large numbers: We *underestimate* the resemblance that large samples will have to the overall population. Kahneman and Tversky (1982a), for instance, found that subjects on average thought that there was a more than 1/10 chance that more than 750 of 1,000 babies born on a given day would be male. The actual likelihood is far less than 1 percent. To overstate it a bit, people seem to have a universal probability distribution over sample means that is insensitive to the sample size.

The law of small numbers implies that people exaggerate the likelihood that a short sequence of flips of a fair coin will yield roughly the same number of heads as tails. What is commonly known as "the gambler's fallacy" is a manifestation of this bias: If a fair coin has not (say) come up tails for a while, then on the next flip it is "due" for a tails, because a sequence of flips of a fair coin ought to include about as many tails as heads.

When the underlying probability distribution generating observed sequences is uncertain, the gambler's fallacy leads people to overinfer the probability distribution from short sequences. Because we underestimate the frequency of a mediocre financial analyst making lucky guesses three times in a row, we exaggerate the likelihood that an analyst is good if he or she is right three times in a row. This tendency to overinfer from short sequences, in turn, leads to misperception of *regression to the mean*. Because we read too much into patterns that depart from the norm, we do not expect that further observations will look more normal. As teachers, we exaggerate the extent to which one good or bad performance on a test is a sign of good or bad aptitude, so we do not expect exceptional performances to be followed by unexceptional performances as often as they are.

Misunderstanding regression to the mean gives rise to spurious explanations for observed regression. When a student performs poorly on the midterm but well on the final, teachers infer that the student has worked harder; if the student performs well on a midterm but poorly on the final, teachers infer that the student has slacked off. Tversky and Kahneman (1974) give another example. Flight-training instructors observed that when they praised pilots for smooth landings, performance usually deteriorated on the next landing, but when they criticized pilots for poor landings, performance improved the next time. But *random* performance will lead to "deterioration" following a good landing and "improvement" following a poor landing. These flight instructors developed a wrong theory of incentives based on erroneous statistical reasoning.

Another implication of the law of small numbers is that people expect too few lengthy streaks in sequences of random events. As with regression to the mean, therefore, people tend to generate spurious explanations for long streaks that are determined by chance. For instance, there is widespread belief in the "hot hand" in basketball – that particular basketball players are streak shooters who have "on" nights and "off" nights which cannot be explained by randomness. Thomas Gilovich, Robert Vallone, and Tversky (1985) and Tversky and Gilovich (1989a, 1989b) have argued that the almost universally accepted phenomenon of the hot hand is nonexistent in basketball. The exaggerated belief in hot hands seems partly explained by the misperception that purely random streaks are too long to be purely random.

Belief Perseverance and Confirmatory Bias

A range of research suggests that once having formed strong hypotheses, people are often too inattentive to new information contradicting their hypotheses. Once you become convinced that one investment strategy is more lucrative than another, you may not sufficiently attend to evidence suggesting the strategy is flawed. A particularly elegant demonstration of such "anchoring" is found in Jerome Bruner and Mary Potter (1964). About ninety subjects were shown blurred pictures that were gradually brought into sharper focus. Different subjects began viewing the pictures at different points in the focusing process, but the pace and final degree of focus were identical for all subjects. Of those subjects who began their viewing at a severe-blur stage, less than a quarter eventually identified the pictures correctly, whereas over half of those who began viewing at a light-blur stage were able to correctly identify the pictures. Bruner and Potter (1964, 424) conclude that "Interference may be accounted for partly by the difficulty of rejecting incorrect hypotheses based on substandard cues." That is, people who use weak evidence to form initial hypotheses have difficulty correctly interpreting subsequent, better information that contradicts those initial hypotheses. Perkins (1981) argues that such experiments provide support for the perspective that "fresh" thinkers may be better at seeing solutions to problems than people who have meditated at length on the problems, because the fresh thinkers are not overwhelmed by the "interference" of old hypotheses.

This form of anchoring does not necessarily imply that people *misinterpret* additional evidence, only that they ignore additional evidence. Psychological evidence reveals a stronger and more provocative phenomenon: People tend to *misread* evidence as *additional* support for initial hypotheses. If a teacher initially believes that one student is smarter than another, he or she has the propensity to confirm that hypothesis when interpreting later performance.

Some evidence for confirmatory bias is a series of experiments demonstrating how providing the *same* ambiguous information to people who differ in their initial beliefs on some topic can move their beliefs *further apart*. To illustrate such polarization, Lord, Ross, and Lepper (1979) asked 151 undergraduates to complete a questionnaire that included three questions on capital punishment. Later, forty-eight of these students were recruited to participate in another experiment. Twenty-four of them were selected because their answers to the earlier questionnaire indicated that they were "'proponents' who favored capital punishment, believed it to have a deterrent effect, and thought most of the relevant research supported their own beliefs. Twenty-four were opponents of capital punishment, doubted its deterrent effect and thought that the relevant research supported *their* views." These subjects were then asked to judge the merits of randomly selected studies on the deterrent efficacy of the death penalty, and to state whether a given study (along with criticisms of that study) provided evidence for or against the deterrence hypothesis. Subjects were then asked to rate, on sixteen point scales ranging from -8 to $+8$, how the studies they had read moved their attitudes toward the death penalty, and how they had changed their beliefs regarding its deterrent efficacy. At confidence levels of $p < 0.01$ or stronger, Lord, Ross, and Lepper found that proponents of the death penalty became on average more in favor of the death penalty and believed more in its deterrent efficacy, while opponents became even *less* in favor of the death penalty and believed even *less* in its deterrent efficacy. Scott Plous (1991) replicates the Lord, Ross, and Lepper results in the context of judgment about the safety of nuclear technology.

Darley and Gross (1983) demonstrate a related and similarly striking form of polarization. Seventy undergraduates were asked to assess a nine-year-old girl's academic skills in several different academic areas. Before completing this task, the students received information about the girl and her family and viewed a videotape of the girl playing in a play-ground. One group of subjects was given a fact sheet that described the girl's parents as college graduates who held white-collar jobs; these students viewed a video of the girl playing in what appeared to be a well-to-do suburban neighborhood. The other group of subjects was given a fact sheet that described the girl's parents as high school graduates who held blue-collar jobs; these students viewed a video of the same girl playing in what appeared to be an impoverished inner-city neighborhood. With-out being supplied any more information, half of each group of subjects was then asked to evaluate the girl's reading level, measured in terms of equivalent grade level. There was a small difference in the two groups' estimates – those subjects who had viewed the "inner-city" video rated the girl's skill level at an average of 3.90 (that is, 9/10 through third grade) whereas those who had viewed the "suburban" video rated the girl's skill level at an average of 4.29. The remaining subjects in each group were shown a second video of the girl answering (with mixed success) a series of questions. Afterward, they were asked to evaluate the girl's reading level. The inner-city video group rated the girl's skill level at an average of 3.71, significantly *below* the 3.90 estimate of the inner-city subjects who did not view the question–answer video. Meanwhile, the suburban video group rated the girl's skill level at an average of 4.67, significantly *above* the 4.29 estimate of the suburban subjects who did not view the second video. Even though the two groups viewed the *identical* question-and-answer video, the additional information further polarized their assess-ments of the girl's skill level. Darley and Gross (1983) interpret this result as evidence of confirmatory bias – subjects were influenced by the girl's background in their initial judgments, but their beliefs were evidently in-fluenced even more strongly by the effect their initial hypotheses had on their interpretation of further evidence.

Certain types of evidence flows seem to be most conducive to confirma-tory bias. Ambiguity of evidence is widely recognized to be an important mediating factor in both confirmatory bias and overconfidence (see, for example, Keren 1987 and Griffin and Tversky 1992). Keren (1988) notes the lack of confirmatory bias in visual perceptions, and concludes that confirmatory tendency depends on some degree of abstraction and the need for interpretation not present in simple visual tasks. Lord, Ross, and Lepper (1979, 2099) posit that when faced with complex and ambigu-ous evidence, we emphasize the strength and reliability of confirming evidence but the weaknesses and unreliability of disconfirming evidence. Even when each individual datum is unambiguous, confirmatory bias can be generated when people must statistically assess correlations extended over time. Nisbett and Ross (1980) argue that the inability to accurately perceive correlation is one of the most robust shortcomings in human reasoning, and people often imagine correlations between events when no such correlation exists. Jennings, Amabile, and Ross (1982) argue that illusory correlation can play an important role in the confirmation of false hypotheses, finding that people underestimate correlation when they have no theory of the correlation, but exaggerate correlation and see it where it is not when they have a preconceived theory of it.

Do We Know What Makes Us Happy?

The research on judgmental biases reviewed above indicates that people misjudge the probabilistic consequences of their decisions. But other research suggests that, even when they correctly perceive the *physical* consequences of their decisions, people systematically misperceive the well-being they derive from such outcomes. We often systematically mispredict our future experienced utility, even when those predictions rely only on accurate assessments of our past experienced utility (Kahneman 1994 and Kahneman, Peter Wakker, and Rakesh Sarin 1997). As Kahneman (1994, 21) puts it, "These considerations suggest an explicit distinction between two notions of utility. The *experienced utility* of an outcome is the measure of the hedonic experience of that outcome. . . . The *decision utility* of an outcome . . . is the weight assigned to that outcome in a decision." The realization that decision and experienced utility may be systematically different cuts to the core of our models of choice. It also cuts to the core of our methods of research, requiring us to formulate ways of inferring and eliciting preferences that go beyond a "revealed preference" method to attempt to infer people's hedonic experiences through such methods as self-reports of satisfaction and even psychological measurements.

How do people misperceive their utilities? One pattern is that we tend to underestimate how quickly and how fully we will adjust to changes, not foreseeing that our reference points will change. In a classic study, when Brickman, Coates, and Janoff-Bulman (1978) interviewed both lottery winners (with average winnings of about $479,545) and a control group, they found virtually no difference in rated happiness of lottery nonwinners and winners. While such interview evidence is inconclusive, the researchers controlled for alternative explanations (such as selection bias or biased presentation by interviewers). Two effects seemed to explain why lottery winners would be less happy than the winners had presumably anticipated. First, mundane experiences become less satisfying by contrast to the "peak" experience of winning the lottery. Second, we become habituated to our circumstances: Along the lines of the material presented earlier, eventually the main carriers of utility become not the absolute levels of consumption, but departures from our (new) reference level.

People do not anticipate the degree of such adaptation, and hence exaggerate expected changes in utility caused by changes in their lives. In the simple model of reference-point adjustment discussed earlier, this can be translated as saying that people systematically underestimate the parameter α. This suggests that the "decision-utility" aversion people have to losses is *not* consonant with "experienced utility." This realization, in turn, calls for a reexamination of an earlier topic: Are loss aversion, the endowment effect, and other reference effects rational or irrational? If people experience losses relative to a status quo as quite unpleasant, then loss-averse behavior is rational, because people are correctly anticipating and avoiding unpleasant sensations. And, the remembered "loss" of an owned mug may carry over time, or in any event be substantial relative to the long-term utility consequences of owning the mug.

Yet loss aversion often seems to be a judgmental bias: In decisions with significant long-run consequences, people should put less weight than they do on their initial experience of losses. Indeed, some researchers invoke loss aversion more as an irrational rule of thumb than as a rational utility function. Benartzi and Thaler (1995) argue that the equity-premium puzzle can be explained by investors' aversion to short-term financial losses, even though they will not be spending their investment in the short term. Camerer et al. (1997) argue that New York taxi drivers decide when to quit driving for the day by a rule of thumb that says they should make sure to match their usual take for the day. In some more extreme examples of loss aversion, it is hard to believe that the "transition utility" can rationally rank high relative to long-term utility. For instance, Thaler (1980) compared subjects' willingness to pay for a cure for a disease that leads to a quick and painless death with probability 0.001 versus the minimum price you would accept to voluntarily subject yourself to the same disease. Subjects often required more money to expose themselves to the disease than they would pay for a cure. People charge heavy premiums for losses relative to their status quo, even when it is hard to imagine that any experienced "transition utility" is significant relative to long-term utility consequences.

A major way people predict the utility they will derive from future experiences is to recollect utility from comparable past experiences. Whereas we might presume that people accurately recollect their utility from familiar experiences, research on the endowment effect hints that this presumption may not be accurate: If we systematically misperceive the long-run consequences of giving up minor consumer items such as mugs, we may not have learned to assess correctly the utility consequences of even our everyday choices. Additional research even more dramatically demonstrates systematic differences between people's experienced utility of episodes and their recollections of those episodes. Several recent experiments compare recollected utility to experienced utility for episodes extended over time, by collecting periodic hedonic reports by subjects of their current well-being. In evaluating the overall utility from such an extended episode, one must formulate criteria for adding up flows of experienced well-being. Kahneman (1994) posits that an uncontroversial criterion for comparing episodes is *temporal monotonicity* – that adding moments of pain to an otherwise unchanged experience decreases overall well-being, and that adding episodes of pleasure increase overall well-being.

Kahneman (1994) argues that experiments suggest biases in how people's own retrospective evaluations of episodes compare to their experienced well-being. First, in evaluating past episodes, people tend to remember the extremes of pain and pleasure more than the average. Second, when an "episode" is well-defined (for example, a vacation), people tend to put too much weight on the end of the episode (for example, the last night of the vacation) in assessing their overall experience of the episode. Finally, we tend to neglect the duration of an episode. In assessing the dissatisfaction of an extremely unpleasant medical procedure (colonoscopy), for instance, patients seems to all but neglect the duration of the procedure – which ranged from four to sixty-nine minutes. Of course, one must carefully consider the pain and pleasure associated with an episode before and after the actual episode; anticipation and recollection of pain, for instance, are clearly important influences on long-run utility, just as anticipation and recollection of a vacation are very significant in evaluating the overall well-being associated with vacations. Such an interpretation of most of the experimental evidence, however, seems tenuous.

The fact that we do not always correctly predict experienced utility is obviously important for welfare implications of choice, and it prescribes caution in reliance on revealed preference-based welfare economics. But there may be important behavioral implications of a related phenomenon whereby people misperceive their future *behavior*. Loewenstein and Adler (1995) performed an experiment based on the endowment-effect experiments of Kahneman, Knetsch, and Thaler (1991) discussed earlier. Some subjects were first asked to "imagine that we gave you a mug exactly like the one you can see, and that we gave you the opportunity to keep it or trade it for some money." All subjects were then given a mug, and their minimal selling prices were elicited. Before receiving the mugs, subjects on average predicted their own minimal selling price at $3.73. Once they had the mugs, however, their actual minimal selling price averaged $4.89. That is, subjects systematically underestimated the endowment effect, and behaved significantly differently than they had predicted about themselves *moments* earlier.

Framing Effects

People often lack stable preferences that are robust to different ways of eliciting those preferences. The most prominent set of research that points to such an interpretation of choice behavior concerns *framing effects*: Two logically equivalent (but not *transparently* equivalent) statements of a problem lead decision makers to choose different options. An important and predictable influence of framing on choice relates to loss aversion and diminishing sensitivity, as outlined above. Because losses resonate with people more than gains, a frame that highlights the losses associated with a choice makes that choice less attractive. Similarly, a frame that exploits diminishing sensitivity by making losses appear small relative to the scales involved makes that choice more attractive. Tversky and Kahneman (1986, S254–5) give the following example of framing effects, taken from a study of medical decisions by McNeil et al. (1982):

Respondents were given statistical information about the outcomes of two treatments of lung cancer. The same statistics were presented to some respondents in terms of mortality rates and to others in terms of survival rates. The respondents then indicated their preferred treatment. The information was presented [exactly] as follows.

Problem 1 (Survival frame)

Surgery: Of 100 people having surgery 90 live through the post-operative period, 68 are alive at the end of the first year and 34 are alive at the end of five years.

Radiation Therapy: Of 100 people having radiation therapy all live through the treatment, 77 are alive at the end of one year and 22 are alive at the end of five years.

Problem 1 (Mortality frame)

Surgery: Of 100 people having surgery 10 die during surgery or the post-operative period, 32 die by the end of the first year and 58 die by the end of five years.

Radiation Therapy: Of 100 people having radiation therapy, none die during treatment, 23 die by the end of one year and 77 die by the end of five years.

The inconsequential difference in formulation produced a marked effect. The overall percentage of respondents who favored radiation therapy rose from 18% in the survival frame ($N = 247$) to 44% in the mortality frame ($N = 336$). The advantage of radiation therapy over surgery evidently looms larger when stated as a reduction of the risk of immediate death from 10% to 0% rather than as an increase from 90% to 100% in the rate of survival. The framing effect was not smaller for experienced physicians or for statistically sophisticated business students than for a group of clinic patients.

This question is hypothetical, but similar framing effects were found in choices over lotteries with small monetary stakes, and Tversky and Kahneman (1986) cite some important real-world examples of framing effects. For instance, people react differently to firms charging different prices for different services (or the same service at different times) depending on whether the lower price is called a discount or the higher price is called a surcharge. Similarly, Schelling (1981) noticed huge differences in his students' attitudes toward tax deductions for children depending on how the deductions were framed. Money illusion provides perhaps the best example of the importance of framing effects for economics. Kahneman, Knetsch, and Thaler (1986a) provide survey evidence that people are very attentive to nominal rather than real changes in wages and prices in assessing the fairness of firm behavior. A nominal wage increase of 5 percent in a period of 12 percent inflation offends people's sense of fairness less than a 7 percent decrease in a time of no inflation. More generally, people react more to decreases in real wages when they are also nominal decreases, and react negatively to nominal price increases even if they represent no increase in real prices (Shafir, Diamond, and Tversky 1997).

Framing effects can often be viewed as heuristic errors – people are boundedly rational, and the presentation of a choice may draw our attention to different aspects of a problem, leading us to make mistakes in pursuing our true, underlying preferences. But sometimes framing effects cut more deeply to economists' model of choice: More than confusing people in pursuit of stable underlying preferences, the "frames" may in fact partially *determine* a person's preferences.

Related phenomena even more strongly call into doubt the view that choices reflect stable, well-defined preferences. *Preference reversals* have been studied widely by economists and psychologists over the years: When confronted with certain pairs of gambles with roughly the same expected value, people often choose one of the pair over the other, while *pricing* the other more highly. To use an example from Tversky and Thaler (1990), consider an H bet that with 8/9 chance yields $4 and with 1/9 chance yields $0, and an L bet with a 1/9 chance to win $40 and 8/9 chance of $0. Most subjects choose the H bet over the L bet when asked to choose between the two. But when asked to state the lowest price at which they would be willing to sell each gamble, most subjects put a higher price on the L bet. More generally, people choose bets with a high chance of winning small amounts, but put a higher price on bets with a low chance of winning big amounts; economic theory predicts these two different elicitation procedures should yield the same preferences.

Simonson and Tversky (1992) provide examples of *context effects*, where the addition of a new option to a menu of choices may actually increase the proportion of consumers who choose one of the existing options. For example, the proportion of consumers who chose a particular model of microwave oven increased when a second, more expensive model was added to their choice set. (Subjects were first asked to look at a catalog containing the prices and descriptions of all the relevant choices from which their eventual choice sets were drawn, so the results seem unlikely to be due to any information revealed by the choice sets.) As another example, Simonson and Tversky (1992) ran an experiment that illustrates elicited subjects' preference for an elegant Cross pen versus receiving $6. While only 36 percent of subjects choosing only between the Cross pen and the $6 chose the Cross pen, 46 percent of subjects who were also given the choice of a less attractive pen chose the Cross pen. In both these examples, the addition of an option that compared unfavorably (as more expensive or lower quality) to an existing option enhanced the perceived attractiveness of the existing option.

Although people are often unaware that the menu of choices influences their decisions, Simonson and Tversky note that at other times decision makers explicitly *rationalize* their choices with references to their choice sets. For instance, people may state explicitly that a given choice is a compromise between two other choices. Indeed, such findings suggest an alternative to the utility-maximization framework that may help explain framing effects, preference reversals, and context effects: People may make choices in part by asking themselves whether they have a "reason" to choose one option over another (Shafir, Simonson, and Tversky 1993).

Present-Biased Preferences

People have a taste for immediate gratification. We procrastinate on tasks such as mowing the lawn that involve immediate costs and delayed rewards and do soon things such as seeing a movie that involve immediate rewards and delayed costs. Economists traditionally model such tastes by assuming that people discount streams of utility over time exponentially. An important qualitative feature of exponential discounting is that it implies that a person's intertemporal preferences are time-consistent: A person feels the same about a given intertemporal tradeoff no matter when he or she is asked.

Casual observation, introspection, and psychological research all suggest that the assumption of time consistency is importantly wrong. Our short-term tendency to pursue immediate gratification is inconsistent with our long-term preferences. Whereas today we feel that it is best that we not overeat tomorrow, tomorrow we tend to overeat; although today we feel we should write a referee report tomorrow, tomorrow we tend to put it off. More generally, when considering tradeoffs between two future moments, we give stronger relative weight to the earlier moment as it gets closer. Kris Kirby and Herrnstein (1995), for instance, asked subjects to state their preferences among a series of pairs, in each case choosing between a smaller, earlier reward and a larger, later reward. Subjects were (truthfully) told that one of their choices would be implemented. In two experiments with monetary rewards, twenty-three of twenty-four subjects "consistently reversed their choices from the smaller, earlier reward to the later, larger reward as the delay to both rewards increased." Both the monetary stakes and the delays were substantial – subjects received an average of about $21.50, with an average delay of about $2\frac{1}{2}$ weeks.[8]

Hence, a person's preferences today over his or her future delays in rewards are different than his or her future preferences over those same

---

[8] These numbers are calculated from the data presented by Kirby and Herrnstein (1995, 85–6). Other psychological research showing that preferences are not time-consistent includes Ainslie (1991), Thaler (1981), and Loewenstein and Prelec (1992).

delays, so that preferences are *not* time-consistent. Formal models of such time-*variant* preferences have been developed.[9] Laibson (1994, 1997) adopts the model Phelps and Pollak (1968) developed in an intergenerational context to capture the taste for immediate gratification with a simple two-parameter model that slightly modifies exponential discounting. Let u_t be the instantaneous utility a person gets in period t. Then her intertemporal preferences at time t, U^t, can be represented by the following utility function, where both β and δ lie between 0 and 1:

$$\text{For all } t, \ U^t(u_t, u_{t+1}, \cdots, u_T) \equiv (\delta)^t \cdot u_t + \beta \cdot \sum_{\tau=t+1}^{T} (\delta)^\tau \cdot u_\tau$$

The parameter δ determines how "time-consistently patient" a person is, just as in exponential discounting. If $\beta = 1$, then these preferences are simply exponential discounting. But for $\beta < 1$, these preferences capture in a parsimonious way the type of time-inconsistent preferences so widely observed. To see how these preferences capture the preference for immediate gratification, suppose that you had a choice between doing ten hours of an unpleasant task on April 14, versus spending eleven hours to complete the same task on April 15. Assume that your instantaneous disutility from doing work is simply the number of hours of work: $u_t(10) = -10$ and $u_t(11) = -11$ for all t. Suppose that $\delta = 1$, but that $\beta = 0.8$ for a one-day delay: You are willing to suffer a given loss in utility tomorrow for a gain in utility today that is 80 percent as large.

Suppose that April 14 has arrived and you are considering whether or not to work. You can experience a disutility of -10 by working today, or experience a discounted utility of $0.8 \cdot (-11) = -8.8$ by delaying the work until tomorrow. You will, therefore, delay work. Contrast this with what your decision would be if, instead of choosing when to work on April 14, you are told by your boss that you must decide on February 1. Because from February 1 you discount *both* dates by β, you will choose to work ten hours on April 14 rather than eleven hours on April 15. From the February 1 point of view, you find procrastinating in April an undesirable thing. For the exact same problem, your choice on February 1 is different than your choice on April 14. Irrespective of its specific prediction, exponential discounting would predict that your choice would be the same whether you made that choice on February 1 or April 14. This example

---

[9] For economics papers on time-inconsistent discounting, see, e.g., Strotz (1955), Goldman (1979, 1980), Schelling (1978), Thaler and Shefrin (1981), Laibson (1994, 1997), and O'Donoghue and Rabin (1999).

seems well-calibrated: On April 14, most of us are apt to put off the work until April 15, even if it means a little more work. Absent a substantive difference between the two dates, virtually no one would choose the delay if asked on February 1.

To examine dynamic choice given time-variant preferences, for each point in time, a person is modeled as a separate "agent" who chooses his or her current behavior to maximize his or her current long-run preferences, whereas each of his or her future selves, with his or her own preferences, will choose his or her future behavior to maximize *his or her* preferences. On one level, this idea of multiple selves – that a single human does not have unified preferences that are stable over time – is a radical departure from the utility-maximization framework. But because this conceptualization of intertemporal choice uses a familiar tool – dynamic game theory – it is ready-made for adoption by economists interested in improving the behavioral realism of our models.

The behavior predicted by models of time-variant preferences often differs dramatically from the behavior predicted by the exponential model. The most notorious examples are efforts at *self-control*: Because you may not like the way you will behave in the future, you may scheme to manipulate your future options. Consider again the work example. Instead of your boss telling you that you *must* choose on February 1 when to work, suppose now she gives you three options: You commit to do the task on April 14; you commit to do the task on April 15; or you *wait* until April 14 and *then* choose on which day to do the task. Which would you choose? The advantage of waiting is manifest: By not precluding either of your options, if there are *any* uncertainties that may be resolved between now and April, the flexibility you have retained may be valuable. Yet we sometimes engage in behavior precisely *to* restrict our own future flexibility. If there were few uncertainties, you might want to commit on February 1 to the April 14 date. Given your current preference to do the task earlier, you wish to restrict your future self from procrastinating. More generally, researchers have explored many *self-commitment* devices we employ to limit our future choices. Such self-commitment devices include alcohol clinics and fat farms from which you cannot check out, not owning a television, contributing to a "Christmas Club" from which you are not allowed to withdraw money until Christmas, or buying only small packages of enticing foods so that you would not overeat when you get home. More subtly, you may try to control yourself through a variety of internal "rules" (for example, never drink alcohol), even if you have no external mechanisms of self-control.

Attempts to control our own future behavior indicate an awareness that we may not behave as we would wish to behave. This raises the question of how aware people are of their time inconsistency. You may have expectations about your propensity to misbehave, or you may naively believe that your preferences in the future will match your current preferences. If today you prefer not to overeat tomorrow, you may naively believe that you will feel the same way when facing an enticing bowl of ice cream tomorrow. If on February 1 you prefer less work on April 14 to more work on April 15, you may believe you will feel the same way in April.

Strotz (1955) labels people who are fully aware of their future self-control problems as *sophisticated*, and people who are fully unaware that they will have a self-control problem as *naïve*. Although some degree of sophistication is implied by the existence of some of the self-commitment devices illustrated above, it does appear that people underestimate the degree to which their future behavior will not match their current preferences over future behavior. This accords with the evidence discussed earlier, that people often incorrectly predict their own future preferences: As with predicting the effects of changes in reference points, here too knowing your future preferences means that you know your preferences *would not* accord with your current preferences. For example, people may repeatedly not have the "willpower" to forego tempting foods or quit smoking while predicting that *tomorrow* they will have this willpower. Although behavioral evidence that calibrates the degree of sophistication seems sparse, Loewenstein (1996, 281–2) reaches the conclusion that people may be naïve indirectly from psychological findings such as the evidence of people mispredicting changes in utility.

Whether they are sophisticated or naïve, people's time-inconsistent propensity for immediate gratification is important in a variety of economic realms. As investigated by several researchers (see, for example, Thaler and Shefrin 1981 and Laibson 1997), such preferences may be important to savings behavior because the benefits of current consumption are immediate, whereas the increased future consumption that saving allows is delayed. Self-control problems are also clearly important in the demand for addictive goods and fatty foods. Similarly, the role of self-control in purchasing decisions is well known among marketing experts (Stephen Hoch and Loewenstein 1991). Naughty goods are sold in small packages because people tend to avoid large packages of such goods to prevent overconsumption.

Prognosis

Research of the sort described above provides the foundation for developing a psychologically more realistic discipline of economics. Happily, this has begun to happen, as research has recently been evolving to what I call "second-wave" behavioral economics – which moves beyond pointing out problems with current economic assumptions, and even beyond articulating alternatives, and on to the task of systematically and formally exploring the alternatives with much the same sensibility and mostly the same methods that economists are familiar with. David Laibson addresses mainstream macro issues with mainstream tools, but adds an additional, psychologically motivated parameter. Ernst Fehr addresses important core issues in labor economics without assuming 100 percent self-interest *a priori*. Theorists such as myself use mostly the standard tools of microeconomics in exploring the implications of these alternative assumptions. All said, this second wave of research continues to employ mainstream economic methods, construed broadly. But it shows that addressing standard economic questions with standard economic methods need not be based solely on the particular set of assumptions – such as 100 percent self-interest, 100 percent rationality, 100 percent self-control, and many ancillary assumptions – typically made in economic models but not supported by behavioral evidence.

This research program is not only built on the premise that mainstream economic *methods* are great, but also that most mainstream economic *assumptions* are great. It does not abandon the correct insights of neoclassical economics, but supplements these insights with the insights to be had from realistic new assumptions. For instance, rational analysis predicts that people care about the future, and hence save, and are more likely to save the longer their planned retirement. But psychologically inspired models that allow the possibility of less-than-100-percent self-control *also* make the above predictions *and* allow us to investigate the possibility that people undersave, and overborrow, and more nuanced and important predictions such as simultaneous high savings on illiquid assets and low savings on liquid assets. Rational analysis predicts that employees are more likely to quit the lower their real wages and the higher the wages available elsewhere. But psychologically inspired models that allow the possibility of some money illusion and loss aversion and fairness concerns *also* make the above predictions *and* allow us to investigate the possibility that people are more sensitive to recent cuts in nominal wages than can be explained purely in terms of concerns for relative real wages. Rational analysis predicts that the demand for addictive products is decreasing in current and expected future prices and that people are more likely to consume substances they find enjoyable, and less likely to consume substances with bad effects. But psychologically inspired models that allow the possibility of less-than-100-percent time-consistency and less-than-100-percent foresight *also* make the above predictions *and* allow us to investigate the possibility that people overconsume addictive substances.

All said, efforts to improve the psychological realism of economics while maintaining the best of current economics assumptions and methods is an approach whose time has come.

REFERENCES

Ainslie, George W. "Derivation of 'Rational' Economic Behavior from Hyperbolic Discount Curves," *American Economic Review*, May 1991, *81*(2), pp. 334–40.

Akerlof, George. "Labor Contracts as Partial Gift Exchange," *Quarterly Journal of Economics*, Nov. 1982, *97*(4), pp. 543–69.

Akerlof, George. "Gift Exchange and Efficiency-Wage Theory: Four Views," *American Economic Review*, May 1984, *74*(2), pp. 79–83.

Akerlof, George and Yellen, Janet. "The Fair Wage-Effort Hypothesis and Unemployment," *Quarterly Journal of Economics*, May 1990, *105*(2), pp. 255–83.

Benartzi, Shlomo and Thaler, Richard. "Myopic Loss Aversion and the Equity Premium Puzzle," *Quarterly Journal of Economics*, Feb. 1995, *110*(1), pp. 73–92.

Blount, Sally. "When Social Outcomes Aren't Fair: The Effect of Causal Attributions on Preferences," *Organizational Behavior and Human Decision Processes*, Aug. 1995, *63*(2), pp. 131–44.

Bowman, David, Minehart, Deborah, and Rabin, Matthew. "Loss aversion in a consumption-savings model," *Journal of Economic Behavior & Organization* *38*(2), Feb. 1999, pp. 155–78.

Brickman, Philip, Coates, Dan, and Janoff-Bulman, Ronnie. "Lottery Winners and Accident Victims: Is Happiness Relative?" *Journal of Personality & Social Psychology*, Aug. 1978, *36*(8), pp. 917–27.

Bruner, Jerome S. and Potter, Mary C. "Interference in Visual Recognition," *Science*, Apr. 24, 1964, *144*(3,617), pp. 424–5.

Camerer, Colin F. "Individual Decision Making," in John Kagel and Alvin E. Roth, *Handbook of Experimental Economics*. Princeton: Princeton Univ. Press, 1995, pp. 587–703.

Camerer, Colin, Babcock, Linda, Loewenstein, George, and Thaler, Richard. "Labor Supply of New York City Cabdrivers: One Day at a Time," *Quarterly Journal of Economics*, May 1997, *112*(2), pp. 407–41.

Camerer, Colin F. and Thaler, Richard. "Anomalies: Ultimatums, Dictators and Manners," *Journal of Economic Perspectives*, Spring 1995, *9*(2), pp. 209–19.

Charness, Gary. "Attribution and Reciprocity in a Simulated Labor Market: An Experimental Investigation." Mimeo, U. California – Berkeley, 1996.

Charness, Gary and Rabin, Matthew. "Understanding Social Preferences with Simple Tests," *Quarterly Journal of Economics*, August 2001.

Darley, John M. and Gross, Paget H. "A Hypothesis-Confirming Bias in Labeling Effects," *Journal of Personality & Social Psychology*, Jan. 1983, *44*(1), pp. 20–33.

Dawes, Robyn and Thaler, Richard H. "Anomalies: Cooperation," *Journal of Economic Perspectives*, Summer 1988, *2*(3), pp. 187–97.

Duesenberry, James S. *Income, saving and the theory of consumer behavior*. Cambridge: Harvard University Press, 1949.

Epstein, Larry G. and Zin, Stanley E. " 'First-Order' Risk Aversion and the Equity Premium Puzzle," *Journal of Monetary Economics*, Dec. 1990, *26*(3), pp. 387–407.

Fehr, Ernst, Kirchler, Erich, and Weichbold, Andreas. "When Social Forces Remove the Impact of Competition: An Experimental Investigation." Mimeo, Department of Economics, U. Technology, Vienna, 1994.

Fehr, Ernst, Kirchsteiger, Georg, and Riedl, Arno. "Does Fairness Prevent Market Clearing? An Experimental Investigation," *Quarterly Journal of Economics*, May 1993, *108*(2), pp. 437–59.

Fischhoff, Baruch. "Hindsight Is Not Equal to Foresight: The Effect of Outcome Knowledge on Judgment Under Uncertainty," *Journal of Experimental Psychology: Human Perception & Performance*, Aug. 1975, *104*(1), pp. 288–99.

Fiske, Susan T. and Taylor, Shelley E. *Social cognition*. New York: McGraw-Hill, 1991.

Geanakoplos, John, Pearce, David, and Stacchetti, Ennio. "Psychological Games," *Games and Economic Behavior*, Mar. 1989, *1*(1), pp. 60–79.

Gilovich, Thomas, Vallone, Robert, and Tversky, Amos. "The Hot Hand in Basketball: On the Misperception of Random Sequences," *Cognitive Psychology*, July 1985, *17*(3), pp. 295–314.

Goldman, Steven M. "Intertemporally Inconsistent Preferences and the Rate of Consumption," *Econometrica*, May 1979, *47*(3), pp. 621–6.

Goldman, Steven M. "Consistent Plans," *Review of Economic Studies*, Apr. 1980, *47*(3), pp. 533–7.

Goranson, Richard E. and Berkowitz, Leonard. "Reciprocity and Responsibility Reactions to Prior Help," *Journal of Personality & Social Psychology*, 1966, *3*(2), pp. 227–32.

Griffin, Dale and Tversky, Amos. "The Weighing of Evidence and the Determinants of Confidence," *Cognitive Psychology*, July 1992, *24*(3), pp. 411–35.

Güth, Werner, Schmittberger, Rolf, and Schwarze, Bernd. "An Experimental Analysis of Ultimatum Bargaining," *Journal of Economic Behavior and Organization*, 1982, *3*, pp. 367–88.

Güth, Werner and Tietz, Reinhard. "Ultimatum Bargaining Behavior: A Survey and Comparison of Experimental Results," *Journal of Economic Psychology*, Sept. 1990, *11*(3), pp. 417–49.

Helson, Harry. *Adaptation level theory: An experimental and systematic approach to behavior*. New York: Harper & Row, 1964.

Hoch, Steven J. and Loewenstein, George. "Time-Inconsistent Preferences and Consumer Self-Control," *Journal of Consumer Research*, Mar. 1991, *17*(4), pp. 492–507.

Jennings, Dennis L., Amabile, Teresa M., and Ross, Lee. "Informal Covariation Assessment: Data-Based versus Theory-Based Judgments," in Daniel Kahneman, Paul Slovic, and Amos Tversky 1982, pp. 211–30.

Kahn, Arnold and Tice, Thomas E. "Returning a Favor and Retaliating Harm: The Effects of Stated Intentions and Actual Behavior," *Journal of Experimental Social Psychology*, Jan. 1973, *9*(1), pp. 43–56.

Kahneman, Daniel. "New Challenges to the Rationality Assumption," *Journal of Institutional and Theoretical Economics*, 1994, *150*(1), pp. 18–36.

Kahneman, Daniel, Knetsch, Jack, and Thaler, Richard. "Fairness as a Constraint on Profit Seeking: Entitlements in the Market," *American Economic Review*, Sept. 1986a, *76*(4), pp. 728–41.

Kahneman, Daniel, Knetsch, Jack, and Thaler, Richard. "Fairness and the Assumptions of Economics," *J. Business*, Oct. 1986b, *59*(4), pp. S285–S300.

Kahneman, Daniel, Knetsch, Jack, and Thaler, Richard. "Experimental Tests of the Endowment Effect and the Coase Theorem," *Journal of Political Economy*, Dec. 1990, *98*(6), pp. 1325–48.

Kahneman, Daniel, Knetsch, Jack, and Thaler, Richard. "Anomalies: The Endowment Effect, Loss Aversion, and Status Quo Bias," *Journal of Economic Perspectives*, Winter 1991, *5*(1), pp. 193–206.

Kahneman, Daniel, Slovic, Paul, and Tversky, Amos, eds. *Judgment under uncertainty: Heuristic and biases*. Cambridge: Cambridge University Press, 1982.

Kahneman, Daniel and Tversky, Amos. "Prospect Theory: An Analysis of Decision under Risk," *Econometrica*, Mar. 1979, *47*(2), pp. 263–91.

Kahneman, Daniel and Tversky, Amos. "Subjective Probability: A Judgment of Representativeness," in Daniel Kahneman, Paul Slovic, and Amos Tversky 1982a, pp. 32–47.

Kahneman, Daniel and Tversky, Amos, eds. *Choices, values, and frames*, New York: Russell Sage Foundation; Cambridge, UK: Cambridge University Press, 2000.

Keren, Gideon. "Facing Uncertainty in the Game of Bridge: A Calibration Study," *Org. Behavior & Human Decision Processes*, Feb. 1987, *39*(1), pp. 98–114.

Keren, Gideon. "On the Ability of Monitoring Non-Veridical Perceptions and Uncertain Knowledge: Some Calibration Studies," *Acta Psychologica*, May 1988, *67*(2), pp. 95–119.

Kirby, Kris N. and Herrnstein, Richard J. "Preference Reversals Due to Myopic Discounting of Delayed Reward," *Psychological Science*, Mar. 1995, *6*(2), pp. 83–9.

Laibson, David. "Essays in Hyperbolic Discounting." Mimeo, M.I.T., 1994.

Laibson, David. "Golden Eggs and Hyperbolic Discounting," *Quarterly Journal of Economics*, May 1997, *112*(2), pp. 443–78.

Laibson, David and Zeckhauser, Richard. "Amos Tversky and the Ascent of Behavioral Economics," *Journal of Risk and Uncertainty*, 1998, *16*, pp. 7–47.

Loewenstein, George. "Out of Control: Visceral Influences on Behavior," *Organizational Behavior and Human Decision Processes*, Mar. 1996, *65*(3), pp. 272–92.

Loewenstein, George and Adler, Daniel. "A Bias in the Prediction of Tastes," *Economic Journal*, July 1995, *105*(431), pp. 929–37.

Loewenstein, George and Prelec, Drazen. "Anomalies in Intertemporal Choice: Evidence and an Interpretation," *Quarterly Journal of Economics*, May 1992, *107*(2), pp. 573–97.

Lord, Charles G., Ross, Lee, and Lepper, Mark R. "Biased Assimilation and Attitude Polarization: The Effects of Prior Theories on Subsequently Considered Evidence," *Journal of Personality & Social Psychology*, Nov. 1979, *37*(11), pp. 2098–109.

McNeil, Barbara J., Pauker, Stephen G., Sox, Harold C. Jr., and Tversky, Amos. "On the Elicitation of Preferences for Alternative Therapies," *New England Journal of Medicine*, May 27, 1982, *306*, pp. 1259–62.

Nisbett, Richard E. and Ross, Lee. *Human inference: Strategies and shortcomings of social judgment*. Englewood Cliffs, NJ: Prentice Hall, 1980.

O'Donoghue, Ted and Rabin, Matthew. "Doing It Now or Later," *American Economic Review 89(1)*, Mar. 1999, pp. 103–24.

Perkins, David N. *The mind's best work*. Cambridge: Harvard University Press, 1981.

Phelps, Edmund S. and Pollak, Robert A. "On Second-Best National Saving and Game-Equilibrium Growth," *Review of Economic Studies*, Apr. 1968, *35*(2), pp. 185–99.

Plous, Scott. "Biases in the Assimilation of Technological Breakdowns: Do Accidents Make Us Safer?" *Journal of Applied Social Psychology*, July 1991, *21*(13), pp. 1058–82.

Rabin, Matthew. "Incorporating Fairness into Game Theory and Economics," *American Economic Review*, Dec. 1993, *83*(5), pp. 1,281–1,302.

Rabin, Matthew. "Psychology and Economics," *Journal of Economic Literature* *36*(1), Mar. 1998, pp. 11–46.

Rabin, Matthew. "Risk Aversion and Expected-Utility Theory: A Calibration Theorem," *Econometrica 68*(5), Sept. 2000, pp. 1281–92.

Rabin, Matthew. "A Perspective on Psychology and Economics," *European Economic Review*, May 2002.

Ryder, Harl E. Jr. and Heal, Geoffrey M. "Optimal Growth with Intertemporally Dependent Preferences," *Review of Economic Studies*, Jan. 1973, *40*(1), pp. 1–33.

Schelling, Thomas C. "Egonomics, or the Art of Self-Management," *American Economic Review*, May 1978, *68*(2), pp. 290–4.

Schelling, Thomas C. "Economic Reasoning and the Ethics of Policy," *Public Interest*, Spring 1981, *63*, pp. 37–61.

Shafir, Eldar, Diamond, Peter, and Tversky, Amos. "Money Illusion," *Quarterly Journal of Economics*, May 1997, *112*(2), pp. 341–74.

Shafir, Eldar, Simonson, Itamar, and Tversky, Amos. "Reason-Based Choice. Special Issue: Reasoning and Decision Making," *Cognition*, Oct.-Nov. 1993, *49*(1–2), pp. 11–36.

Shea, John. "Union Contracts and the Life-Cycle/Permanent-Income Hypothesis," *American Economic Review*, Mar. 1995a, *85*(1), pp. 186–200.

Shea, John. "Myopia, Liquidity Constraints, and Aggregate Consumption: A Simple Test," *Journal of Money, Credit & Banking*, Aug. 1995b, *27*(3), pp. 798–805.

Simonson, Itamar and Tversky, Amos. "Choice in Context: Tradeoff Contrast and Extremeness Aversion," *Journal of Marketing Research*, Aug. 1992, *29*(3), pp. 281–95.

Slovic, Paul and Lichtenstein, Sarah (1971). "Comparison of Bayesian and Regression Approaches to the Study of Information Processing in Judgment," *Organizational Behavior & Human Performance*, Nov. 1971, *6*(6), pp. 649–744.

Smith, Adam. *An inquiry into the nature and causes of the wealth of nations*. Reprinted, Roy H. Campbell and Andrew S. Skinner, eds. Oxford: Clarendon Press, 1976. Original publication, 1776.

Strotz, Robert H. "Myopia and Inconsistency in Dynamic Utility Maximization," *Review of Economic Studies*, 1955, *23*(3), pp. 165–80.

Thaler, Richard H. "Toward a Positive Theory of Consumer Choice," *Journal of Economic Behavior and Organization*, 1980, *1*, pp. 39–60.

Thaler, Richard H. "Some Empirical Evidence of Dynamic Inconsistency," *Econ. Letters*, 1981, *81*, pp. 201–7.

Thaler, Richard H. "Mental Accounting and Consumer Choice," *Marketing Science*, Summer 1985, *4*(3), pp. 199–214.

Thaler, Richard H. "Anomalies: The Ultimatum Game," *Journal of Economic Perspectives*, Fall 1988, *2*(4), pp. 195–206.

Thaler, Richard H. and Shefrin, Hersh M. "An Economic Theory of Self-Control," *Journal of Political Economy*, Apr. 1981, *89*(2), pp. 392–406.

Thaler, Richard H. *The winner's curse: paradoxes and anomalies of economic life*, New York: Free Press, 1992.

Tversky, Amos and Gilovich, Thomas. "The Cold Facts about the 'Hot Hand' in Basketball," *Chance*, 1989a, *2*(1), pp. 16–21.

Tversky, Amos and Gilovich, Thomas. "The Hot Hand: Statistical Reality or Cognitive Illusion," *Chance*, 1989b, *2*(4), pp. 31–4.

Tversky, Amos and Kahneman, Daniel. "Belief in the Law of Small Numbers," *Psych. Bulletin*, Aug. 1971, *76*(2), pp. 105–10.

Tversky, Amos and Kahneman, Daniel. "Availability: A Heuristic for Judging Frequency and Probability," *Cognitive Psychology*, Sept. 1973, *5*(2), pp. 207–32.

Tversky, Amos and Kahneman, Daniel. "Judgment under Uncertainty: Heuristics and Biases," *Science*, Sept. 1974, *185*(4157), pp. 1124–31.

Tversky, Amos and Kahneman, Daniel. "Judgement under Uncertainty: Heuristics and Biases" in Daniel Kahneman, Paul Slovic, and Amos Tversky 1982, pp. 84–98.

Tversky, Amos and Kahneman, Daniel. "Rational Choice and the Framing of Decisions," *Journal of Business*, Oct. 1986, *59*(4), pp. S251-78.

Tversky, Amos and Kahneman, Daniel. "Loss Aversion in Riskless Choice: A Reference-Dependent Model," *Quarterly Journal of Economics*, Nov. 1991, *106*(4), pp. 1039–61.

Tversky, Amos and Thaler, Richard H. "Anomalies: Preference Reversals," *Journal of Economic Perspectives*, Spring 1990, *4*(2), pp. 201–11.

3

Experiments with Financial Markets: Implications for Asset Pricing Theory

Peter Bossaerts

1. INTRODUCTION

This essay surveys experiments of financial markets that were designed with the competitive paradigm in mind. The results will be analyzed from a particular theoretical angle, namely, asset pricing theory. That is, we discuss to what extent a given financial markets experiment can shed light on the validity of asset pricing theory.

Modern asset pricing theory has strong roots in economics and probability theory. Its models are logically compelling, and the derivations elegant. Many models are widely used in industry and government, in applications of capital budgeting, industry rate regulation, and performance evaluation, among others. Yet, there is surprisingly little evidence in support of the theory, and what has come forth is controversial. But tests of asset pricing models have almost exclusively been based on econometric analysis of historical data from naturally occurring markets. That type of empirical analysis is very difficult, because many auxiliary assumptions (homogeneous, correct ex ante beliefs, stationarity, unbiased samples, and so on) have to be added to the theory for it to become testable.

Experimentation would provide an alternative means to verify the principles of asset pricing theory, because many auxiliary assumptions are under the control of the experimenter. That is, experimentation provides one way to gauge the validity of what would otherwise remain mere elegant mathematics. This essay reports on what has been accomplished so far.

Not all experiments on financial markets were designed with the idea that they should verify theoretical principles. Often, the link with the theory is vague. Sometimes, the outcomes of loosely designed experiments were ambiguous and, because of the absence of a solid theoretical foundation, difficult to interpret. As it turns out, this will include some widely cited experiments and, consequently, our analysis will be provocative. But that is meant to generate renewed interest in experimentation with financial markets. Indeed, after much activity in the eighties, interest in financial markets experiments disappeared almost entirely. Only recently have experiments reappeared, and the successes may be attributed to their solid asset pricing theoretic foundation.

Asset pricing theory studies the pricing and allocation of risk in competitive financial markets. (Although it could widen its scope to other mechanisms, the competitive market is studied almost exclusively.) At the outset is the presumption that there are risk averse agents who invest, to smooth consumption over time, and to diversify risk. The latter implies that portfolio analysis (allocation of wealth across several securities) take a core position.

Asset pricing theory also studies the ability of competitive financial markets to aggregate diverse information about uncertain future events. This led to the development of new equilibrium concepts that go beyond the neoclassical Walrasian equilibrium that is generally appealed to in the study of goods markets. We should mention here, in particular, the perfect foresight equilibrium or PFE (see Radner 1972), and the rational expectations equilibrium (REE) – with its two variations: the fully revealing REE or FRREE (see, for example, Green 1977, Radner 1979, and Lucas 1972), and the partially revealing REE or PRREE (Admati 1985 and Grossman and Stiglitz 1980).

The existence of several equilibrium concepts obviously makes aggregation analysis difficult and controversial. Perhaps because of the controversies, it was aggregation that first caught the attention of experimenters. But it is also the more difficult part of asset pricing theory. So, asset pricing theorists would be surprised to see this historical development. The interest in aggregation may be explained by experimenters' (then unproven) conviction that risk aversion cannot possibly play a role in experimental financial markets, because of the size of typical risks that subjects take on. Recent experiments demonstrate convincingly that risk aversion (or something that has the same features) clearly plays a role in financial markets.

Of the many predictions of asset pricing theory, we are going to focus on two. We already mentioned one, namely, that financial markets can aggregate (partially or fully) dispersed information. The other prediction is: financial markets equilibrate, to the point that expected excess returns are proportional to covariance with aggregate risk.[1] The latter statement encompasses virtually all homogeneous-information asset pricing models, including the Capital Asset Pricing Model (CAPM) (where aggregate risk is measured by the return on the market portfolio[2]) as well as consumption-based models (in which aggregate risk is proportional to the marginal rate of substitution of consumption over time). It is this second prediction that has occupied empiricists who study historical pricing data.

To test either prediction, experiments are in a certain sense necessary. That is, it is in principle impossible to test them on historical data. For the second prediction, we cannot observe aggregate risk, and proxies may give misleading information. In the case of the CAPM, Roll (1977) showed that there will always be a proxy for which the CAPM prediction holds, whether the CAPM really determines prices or not. Likewise, to test aggregation, the empiricist faces the impossible task of collecting data on the (dispersed) information in the marketplace. In contrast, both aggregate risk and individual information can be controlled in an experimental setting.

As a matter of fact, careful control of aggregate risk and information can dramatically enhance the significance of the experimental results. Below, we will discuss two experiments with a large number of subjects. The first one was meant to test the CAPM. The experiment was designed such that no subject knew what the composition of the market portfolio was. Yet, the CAPM emerged (prices were set such that expected excess returns were proportional to covariance with the return on the market portfolio). Only the experimenter could verify this. Subjects could neither deliberately invest according to the CAPM (by purchasing the market portfolio), nor set prices correspondingly. In the second experiment, each subject was given a tiny bit of information about future payoffs. Only when aggregated across subjects did this give a clear prediction. Only the experimenter could verify to what extent the dispersed information was aggregated.

We will interpret the experiments that the literature reports on, not as attempts to mimic the naturally occurring markets like the NYSE or NASDAQ, but as tests of the basic principles of asset pricing theory. For

---

[1] One should be more precise. Asset pricing theory says nothing about the process by which an economy reaches equilibrium. Instead, the focus is on the equilibrium itself.

[2] The market portfolio is to be understood as the net aggregate supply of risky securities in the marketplace.

the latter to be universal, they must work in simple laboratory settings. Otherwise, its scientific value should be questioned. (The CAPM, for instance, was not meant to be applicable solely to the NYSE.) By the same token, one ought to be careful when extrapolating conclusions from experiments to naturally occurring markets. Instead, the experiments are meant to verify whether the empirical rejections on historical data came about because there is something fundamentally wrong with asset pricing theory (for example, markets do not equilibrate).

The experiments that are discussed in this essay have often been tightly designed with a particular theory in mind (e.g., Arrow and Debreu's complete-markets model). One may object that it would not be surprising if such experiments confirm the theory. This is not necessarily true. We already mentioned that the right design can enhance the significance of the results. When testing Arrow and Debreu's model, for instance, it should not be made obvious to the subjects what the aggregate wealth in each of the future states is. In Arrow and Debreu's model, prices for (Arrow-Debreu) securities that pay off in equally likely states are ranked inversely to the aggregate wealth across those states. When the experimenter detects that prices align accordingly, the result is forceful, because only the experimenter could possibly have verified this. Similarly, equilibration of financial markets is far from a foregone conclusion. This question has preoccupied general equilibrium theorists for a long time, and we know that the answers can easily be negative. (See, for example, Arrow and Hahn 1971, Negishi 1962, and Scarf 1960.)

Recent experiments have demonstrated that markets must be thick in order to facilitate equilibration in accordance with competitive theory. That is, the number of subjects has to be sufficiently large, often far above the typical numbers of goods markets experiments. At present, we do not know how the number of subjects relates to the number of securities. We do know, however, that thick markets translate into small and stable bid-ask spreads, enabling subjects to rebalance their portfolios at minimum cost. This could be the reason why thick markets experiments have been far more successful.

A last general remark is necessary before we discuss individual experiments. There is one important dimension in which financial markets experiments differ from the more traditional and better known goods markets experiments. In the latter, equilibrium prices can generally be computed directly, and equilibration measured in a straightforward way. Because of lack of knowledge of subjects' risk aversion, equilibration in financial markets experiments has to be verified indirectly. Asset pricing theory provides the means, though. Generally, the theory characterizes equilibrium independent of not only risk aversion, but also endowments. This provides an opportunity, because, even if we were to know subjects' risk preferences, and, hence, were to compute equilibrium prices, the inevitable off-equilibrium trading leads to changes in endowments that may well invalidate the equilibrium based on initial allocations. Off-equilibrium trading has plagued the interpretation of many goods experiments. Asset pricing theory makes it possible to measure the distance from equilibrium in experimental financial markets without concern for off-equilibrium asset reallocations.

The remainder of this article is organized as follows. In the next section, we discuss the design of a typical financial markets experiment. In Section 3, we present the results of experiments aimed at testing theoretical predictions about the pricing of risk. Section 4 elaborates on information aggregation experiments. Section 5 concludes with a list of open questions.

2. ANATOMY OF A TYPICAL (LARGE-SCALE) EXPERIMENT

Imagine the following situation. A number of subjects are endowed with a set of securities whose liquidation values depend on the realization of a state, randomly drawn with commonly known probabilities (usually equal likelihood). The subjects are allowed to trade the securities during a certain period before the state is drawn and liquidation values are determined. They are also given some cash, because the securities are to be traded in markets where settlement occurs in terms of currency, to be called francs (F).[3] After liquidation values are determined, subjects are paid based on their final holdings of securities and cash, minus a preset minimum threshold, to be thought of as the payment for the loan of securities.

---

[3] The presence of cash may at first seem puzzling. There is no cash in standard asset pricing theory. Still, cash is an integral part of realistic trading systems. The theory assumes perfect competition and equilibrium, yet is silent about how these two can be implemented. Experimental design is concerned with creating the conditions in the laboratory that come close to emulating the environment that is needed for perfect competition and equilibrium to emerge. This may involve a central medium of exchange (cash). The introduction of cash at the same time may introduce off-equilibrium phenomena that are not part of the standard theory, such as binding cash-in-advance constraints. These constraints have to be designed carefully, because if they bind too frequently, they may inhibit equilibration, as observed in early experiments reported in Bossaerts and Plott (2001).

Table 1. *Typical Payoff Matrix.*

Security	State		
	X	Y	Z
A	170	370	150
B	160	190	250
Notes	100	100	100

Let there be three securities, two that are risky ("A" and "B"), and one that is risk-free ("Notes"). Their payoffs are determined by a matrix like the one displayed in Table 1. Securities A and B cannot be sold short, but the Notes can, up to a certain level (say, 8).[4]

Trade takes place in web-based electronic open-book markets for each security. Subjects submit limit orders, which are either crossed against opposing orders (at the price of the latter), or displayed in a book. The market setup is very much like the one found in the Paris Bourse or the Tel Aviv Stock Exchange. Subjects have access to the entire book. Identities are not revealed (each subject is assigned an individual ID number, which is the only identification that ever appears in the public records). Subjects also have access to the entire history of transactions (graphically and numerically). The trading interface is referred to as Marketscape.

The main webpage of Marketscape is reproduced in Figure 1. For each market, this core webpage displays (i) individual holdings, (ii) best standing bid and ask, (iii) last transaction price, (iv) personal best bid and ask,

---

[4] In the experiments to be reported below, only a few subjects were ever bound by the shortsale constraints. The shortsale constraints were added to avoid subjects exploiting the limited-liability feature of the experimental setting (subjects outside Caltech could at most lose the money they had earned in earlier rounds of an experiment). Like cash, shortsale constraints are a feature of the experimental design. The theory only deals with equilibrium. In the equilibrium theory to be presented shortly, the shortsale constraints do not bind. To the extent that they bind on the way toward equilibrium, however, shortsale constraints may inhibit equilibration. That is, theoretical predictions may fail to emerge not because the theory is "wrong," but because the specific laboratory environment does not facilitate equilibration. A simple analogy with physics experiments may be useful here. One physics prediction is that objects on the face of the earth are attracted by the force of gravity at a constant acceleration equal to 9.5 m/s^2. The prediction obtains only in a vacuum. On the face of the earth, there is no vacuum. Yet physicists create in the laboratory an environment that emulates a vacuum. In this artificial vacuum, the theoretical prediction is readily verified.

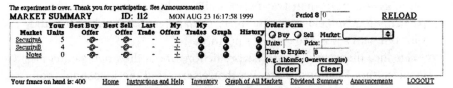

The experiment is over. Thank you for participating. See Announcements

MARKET SUMMARY   ID: 112   MON AUG 23 16:17:58 1999   Period 8 |0   RELOAD

Market	Your Units	Best Buy Offer	Best Sell Offer	Last Trade	My Offers	My Trades	Graph	History
SecurityA	5	-◎-	-◎-	-	±	●	●	●
SecurityB	4	-◎-	-◎-	-	±	●	●	●
Notes	0	-◎-	-◎-	-	±	●	●	●

Order Form
○ Buy ○ Sell Market: [   ] [≑]
Units: [   ] Price: [   ]
Time to Expire: [8]
(e.g. 1h6m5s; 0=never expire)
[Order]   [Clear]

Your francs on hand is: 400   Home   Instructions and Help   Inventory   Graph of All Markets   Dividend Summary   Announcements   LOGOUT

Figure 1. Caltech's Marketscape trading interface.

(v) access to historical data (individual and public), and (vi) an order form. Inspection of the latter reveals that subjects can submit limit orders for multiple units, and can attach a deadline. The core webpage has links to many other webpages, including instructions, help, payout (dividend) history, and so on. Announcements are displayed on the main webpage and logged in an announcements webpage.

At the beginning of each (trading) period, subjects are endowed with a certain number of each security – for example, 5 of A, 4 of B, and no Notes. It is important to understand that these endowments are private information only, so that nobody really knows what the aggregate endowment is. In addition, since the trading is web-based and, therefore, usually physically decentralized (subjects log in from any place that they find convenient), subjects can only get a rough idea of how many participants there are, by looking at the open book or the history of transactions.

Nobody is given superior information about the likelihood of the states that are to be drawn at the end of each period. In other words, information is symmetric.

The endowment of cash is typically F400. Subjects cannot submit bids if they have insufficient cash to execute them. So, there is a cash-in-advance constraint that will noticeably affect the interest rate in the experiments. A typical loan repayment is F1900. This amounts to a relatively high level of leverage,[5] meant to amplify risk. The franc earnings are exchanged for U.S. dollars at a preannounced exchange rate (for example, $0.02 per franc).

Experiments usually last for three or four hours, with periods of twenty-five minutes of trading followed by a five minute break (to determine payouts, and to refresh the allocations of securities and cash). Subjects take home the cumulative earnings. If a subject has negative cumulative

---

[5] With an initial allocation of 5 of A and 4 of B, and the payoff matrix in Table 1, the expected payment per period is only F450 (−400 + 5 * 230 + 4 * 200−1900).

earnings for more than two periods, he or she is barred from further participation. Subjects are sometimes given a signup reward, so that they start out with a positive earnings position.

Finance theory makes precise predictions about the pricing outcomes in this setting. Foremost, it predicts that, each period, markets should equilibrate. Second, in equilibrium, expected returns in excess of the risk-free rate will be proportional to aggregate risk. Translating this prediction into two specific asset pricing models, the CAPM and the Arrow-Debreu complete-markets model (notice that the number of securities with independent payoffs equals the number of states, so that markets are indeed complete), this means:

1. Expected excess returns are proportional to market "beta" or, equivalently, the market portfolio is mean-variance optimal.
2. The ranking of the state prices should be inverse to the ranking of the aggregate payout across the states.

The CAPM is more restrictive, as it assumes quadratic utility. But its prediction is more specific than that of the Arrow-Debreu model. Hopefully, a quadratic function approximates subjects' risk attitudes well enough for mean-variance analysis to obtain. This may be reasonable, given the size of a typical stake in a financial markets experiment.

One aspect of these predictions deserves emphasis. It is possible to characterize equilibrium without having to know subjects' attitudes toward risk. They only have to be risk averse. No matter what the level of risk aversion is, the distance from equilibrium can be measured by how far the market portfolio is from mean-variance optimality (CAPM) or whether the ranking of state prices is inverse to the ranking of aggregate wealth (Arrow-Debreu model).

This is important, as mentioned before, not only because experimenters do not know subjects' risk attitudes, but also because these attitudes may change through inevitable wealth changes in the trading toward, equilibrium. The prices that support (instantaneous) equilibrium at the original endowments may no longer be valid after a few off-equilibrium trades. Still, the prices that support equilibrium at the new wealth levels must be such that the market portfolio is mean-variance optimal (CAPM) or they must imply state prices that are ranked inversely to aggregate payout (Arrow-Debreu model).

If the above predictions are confirmed in the data, the results are powerful, because subjects themselves do not have the necessary information to verify or exploit them, as pointed out earlier. In particular, subjects are not told what other subjects' endowments are. Moreover, the decentralized nature of these web-based markets makes it hard to estimate the size (number of subjects) of the market. Hence, subjects do not know the nature of aggregate risk (aggregate payoff across states), or, in CAPM language, the composition of the market portfolio.

3. EXPERIMENTAL EVIDENCE ON THE PRICING OF RISK

The first large-scale[6] financial markets experiment was organized on October 7, 1998. It will be referred to as the "Yale 1" experiment. Participants were students in the MSIA program at the Yale School of Management, who traded over the Internet using the interface of Figure 1. Thirty subjects took part in this experiment, and each was given an equal number of each of the risky securities (A and B), but none of the notes. This information was not common knowledge. (In later experiments, the allocations were changed, in order to verify that the CAPM and Arrow-Debreu equilibria come about even with very asymmetric allocations of risky securities.) The remainder of the situation is as described in the previous section.

Figure 2 provides a plot of the evolution of the transaction prices of the three securities in "Yale 1." Each point corresponds to a transaction in one of the securities (the prices of the other securities are taken from their respective last transactions). Vertical lines delineate periods. The figure leads to the following observations. Prices of risky securities generally deviate from their expected payoff (indicated by the horizontal lines). This is clear proof of risk aversion. Still, it is not clear whether the values in Figure 2 are equilibrium prices. At first, one would doubt this, because there is a trend in the prices.

Notice that the price of the Notes invariably starts below the payout of F100, implying a positive interest rate (its payoff is F100), only to increase to F100 by the end of each period. Because there is no time value to money (cash earns zero interest, and the time horizon is really small), the equilibrium interest rate is zero. At the end of each period, the pricing of the Notes does reflect a zero interest rate. Earlier on, however,

---

[6] Results from similar, small-scale financial markets experiments are reported in Bossaerts and Plott (2001). Because of thin market problems, small-scale markets do not generate results that are as sharp as the ones reported here. Small-scale experiments can also be found in Levy (1997), which reports only tests of linearity in the relationship between expected returns and beta, however, and not full mean-variance optimality of the market portfolio.

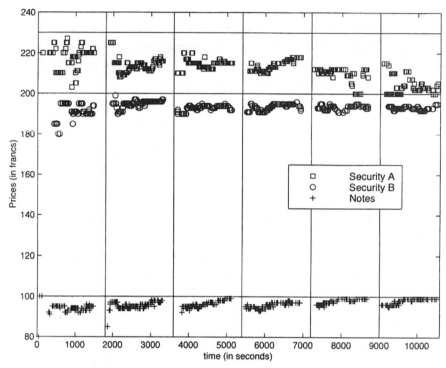

Figure 2. Transaction prices in experiment "Yale 1." Vertical bars delineate periods.

the positive interest rate suggests a binding cash-in-advance constraint: subjects borrow money in order to purchase one type of risky security without having to first procure the necessary cash by selling the other type. Cash-in-advance constraints have been appealed to in macroeconomics to explain the role of money and risk-free bonds (see, for example, Glower 1967 and Lucas 1982), but have usually been associated with the purchase of goods, and not with portfolio rebalancing. It is the latter that drives the interest rate in the experiments.

Figure 3 plots the distance from the CAPM equilibrium for each transaction point. The distance is measured as the difference between the Sharpe ratio of the market portfolio (which the experimenters obviously knew, even if subjects did not) and the maximum Sharpe ratio. The Sharpe ratio is the ratio of the mean excess return divided by the volatility.

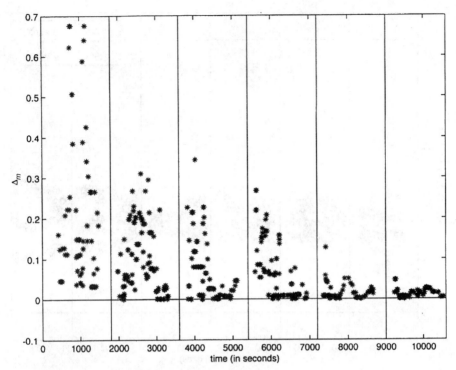

Figure 3. Distance from CAPM equilibrium (Δ_m) in experiment "Yale 1." Vertical bars delineate periods.

In the CAPM equilibrium, expected excess returns ought to be proportional to covariance with the market portfolio. As mentioned in the previous section, this means that the market portfolio is mean-variance efficient: it offers the highest mean excess return for its volatility. The Sharpe ratio provides a simple measure of a portfolio's mean excess return against its volatility. In the CAPM equilibrium, the Sharpe ratio of the market portfolio should be maximal, that is, it generates maximum mean excess return for a given volatility. Figure 3 verifies that the market moved toward the CAPM equilibrium by plotting the difference between the market Sharpe ratio and the maximal Sharpe ratio. This difference is referred to as Δ_m. For the CAPM equilibrium,

$$\Delta_m = 0.$$

The plot in Figure 3 is remarkable. While it does take a substantial amount of time, the market in "Yale 1" eventually reaches the CAPM equilibrium.

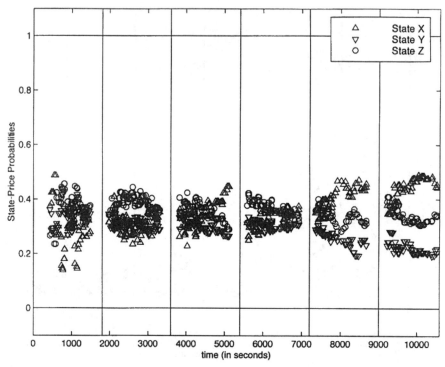

Figure 4. State-price probabilities (normalized AD security prices), experiment "Yale 1." Vertical bars delineate periods.

This is solid support in favor of the CAPM. It implies that the CAPM is not merely a nice mathematical model, but also that it predicts the eventual pricing of risky securities in experimental financial markets. In other words, it has scientific value.

It should be emphasized that the CAPM obtains despite the fact that subjects did not know what the market portfolio was. One may think that this is not compelling evidence, because, in "Yale 1," subjects were given the same initial allocations of risky securities, and, hence, could rightly assume that the composition of the market portfolio was like their own. In the other experiments, however, the initial allocations varied across subjects, and, hence, if subjects really thought that their own portfolio mirrored the market portfolio, they would have been very wrong.

Figure 4 plots the evolution of the Arrow-Debreu state contingent securities prices (called AD securities prices) implied by the transaction prices of securities A, B, and the Notes. The AD securities prices were normalized to add up to one. The resulting prices are known in mathematical finance as state-price probabilities or equivalent martingale probabilities. The Arrow-Debreu model predicts that the state prices, and, hence, the state-price probabilities, will rank inversely to the aggregate payout (in this case, the payout on the market portfolio) across states. (Again, this is an implication of the general prediction that expected excess returns will be proportional to covariance with aggregate risk.) From Table 1 and the fact that an equal number of securities A and B were in the market, it follows that the aggregate payout is highest in state Y, followed by states Z and X. Consequently, the state-price probability for state X should be highest, and that for state Y lowest.

Figure 4 shows that the prediction from the Arrow-Debreu model eventually obtains. In fact, already early on, the state-price probability for X tends to increase, and that for Y tends to decrease, whereas that for Z attempts to position itself in the middle.

Again, this is remarkable support for asset pricing theory. Subjects did not know the distribution of the aggregate payout across states, so did not price the Arrow-Debreu claims deliberately in accordance with the theory. In fact, it is doubtful whether subjects cared about state contingent securities at all. These were not directly traded. They could not even have been created artificially as a portfolio of A, B, and the Notes, because that would require one to shortsell at least one of the risky securities, which was not allowed. Also, only a minority of subjects were familiar with the notion of a state security, or state-price probabilities.

The picture one forms of "Yale 1" was easily replicated in other experiments. (See Bossaerts and Plott 1999 for further details.) This illustrates one important advantage of experimental work over empirical analysis of historical data: replicability. Overall, the experiments demonstrated the validity of the cornerstone of modern asset pricing theory, namely, that markets tend to price assets such that expected returns are proportional to covariance with aggregate risk.

Of course, it is a leap of faith to deduce from this evidence that the CAPM or Arrow-Debreu equilibrium must somehow be the driving force in markets such as the NYSE or NASDAQ. The experimental financial markets are very simple, and successes emerge only when their scale is sufficiently large. In contrast, the NYSE and NASDAQ are far more complex, the stakes involved much bigger, and trade is very heterogeneous. But the experiments demonstrate that the basic propositions of modern asset pricing theory are not only a nice example of applied mathematics, but also predict the outcomes in simple market environments. This success is the beginning of a long journey that hopefully will lead to a better understanding of far more complex financial markets such as the NYSE and NASDAQ.

4. EXPERIMENTS ON INFORMATION AGGREGATION

Much to the surprise of empiricists who have studied historical data from naturally occurring financial markets, experiments have in fact mostly focused on what would seem to be the more difficult of the two branches of asset pricing theory, namely, information aggregation. This may be because of a widely held belief that risk aversion does not play a role at the scale of standard experimental financial markets, and, hence, that the theory of risk allocation cannot be studied experimentally. Because trade may become thin or nonexistent if subjects are indeed risk neutral, experimenters have often resorted to paying different dividends across subjects, thereby giving them a serious reason to trade. Unfortunately, this design does make it hard to interpret the experiments, because asset pricing theory does not allow for differentiation of dividends across investors (nor is it allowed in naturally occurring financial markets such as the NYSE[7]). Examples of experiments on information aggregation are Ang and Schwarz 1985, Camerer and Weigelt 1993, Copeland and Friedman 1987, Copeland and Friedman 1991, Dejong et al. 1992, Forsythe and Lundholm 1990, Liu 1996, O'Brien and Srivastava 1991, Plott and Sunder 1988, Sunder 1992, and Watts 1992.[8]

Thinking about information aggregation led to the (fairly loose) Efficient Markets Hypothesis or EMH (see Fama 1970, 1991), followed by

---

[7] But after-tax dividends generally vary across investors. Still, asset pricing under differential taxation continues to raise ample unresolved issues. See Constantinides and Dammon (1983), Spatt and Zhang (1999) (theory) and Bossaerts and Dammon (1994) (empirics).

[8] There is a related class of experiments, namely, those that study the Perfect Foresight Equilibrium (PFE; it can also be considered to be a Fully Revealing Rational Expectations Equilibrium – FRREE, which is what the experimenters have generally called them). These experiments demonstrate that futures markets speed up convergence to PFE, by providing unambiguous signals about future equilibrium prices. Among others, see Forsythe, Palfrey, and Plott (1982), Forsythe, Palfrey, and Plott (1984), Friedman, Harrison, and Salmon (1983), Friedman, Harrison, and Salmon (1984), Harrison (1986), and Porter and Smith (1995). The focus is on the mechanics of price discovery, attempting to discover the catalyzers that accelerate equilibration. There is not a unified theoretical framework that inspires the conjectures behind the experiments, but the regularities that are discovered do indicate that there must be one. A related study is Forsythe and Lundholm (1990), where the impact of common knowledge of the market parameters on the speed of convergence to FRREE is gauged experimentally. More recently, Biais and Pouget (1999) have used pretrade (preopening) communication schemes to accelerate equilibration.

extensions of equilibrium notions aimed at understanding EMH; namely, FRREE (Green 1977, Lucas 1972, and Radner 1979) as well as PRREE (Grossman and Stiglitz 1980).

Experiments meant to verify information aggregation have generated mixed support. One only infrequently observes FRREE, and the frequency appears to depend on the design specifics. In particular, when the payoff structure is unknown (except one's own), financial markets are generally not capable of fully aggregating the information that is out there.

While the analogy is not watertight, absence of common knowledge of the payoff structure is akin to absence of common knowledge of the aggregate supply of risk. Asset pricing theory does make precise predictions about the impact of absence of common knowledge of aggregate risk on information aggregation. Problems are known to arise and led to the development of the notion of PRREE. (See Admati 1985 and Grossman and Stiglitz 1980.) So, one sensible conjecture is that the right equilibrium that explains the outcomes in these experiments is PRREE, and not FRREE. In other words, experimenters wanted to verify FRREE in their markets, whereas they should have looked for PRREE.[9]

The problem with PRREE is that the precise amount of aggregation of information depends on the level and distribution of risk aversion, both of which are hard to control in an experimental setting, or cannot be measured without knowledge of the PRREE that is to be determined. See, for example, the model in Admati (1985), in which equilibrium prices are noisy signals of the aggregate information in the marketplace, and the noise depends not only on the precision of individuals' signals, but also on risk aversion.

Consequently, experimental verification of PRREE seems impossible. One can only test whether prices aggregate any information at all, that is, reject the null of no information aggregation, which experimentalists have been referring to as private information equilibrium (PIE). Likewise, one can reject the null of full information aggregation (FRREE). Both equilibria are rejected in the experiments. So, the truth of aggregation lies in between no and full aggregation. But that does not imply markets settle at the theoretical PRREE. Markets may as well remain in an unsettled state of partial revelation but no equilibrium.

---

[9] PRREE was used to evaluate experimental results in Copeland and Friedman (1991), but the risk aversion that is crucial to the theory was not part of the analysis.

As mentioned before, however, certain experimental designs did produce unambiguous evidence of full information aggregation when aggregate risk was fully knowable. These include experiments with a single risky security with common payoff for everybody, or with a complete, uniform (same number for each subject/state) set of state contingent claims. Both designs are studied in, for example, the seminal paper by Plott and Sunder (1988). Theory predicts that FRREE would obtain, and indeed, these experimental designs do generate the best support of full information aggregation.

In Plott and Sunder (1988), one design involved a complete set of contingent claims, though with different payoffs depending on the holder. Hence, the aggregate risk could not possibly have been common knowledge at the outset, because the experimenters did not preannounce all possible payoff structures. Still, one can plausibly assume that the aggregate risk became quickly transparent from the aggressive bids of the subjects who would receive the highest dividend in a given state. This would explain the relative success of the experimental design.

In summary, experiments of information aggregation have produced ample evidence that financial markets do not always fully aggregate information. It can be argued that this confirms asset pricing theory, because aggregate risk was generally unknown, and, hence, theory would predict that information would only be partially revealed in equilibrium prices (PRREE). Unfortunately, we cannot determine precisely whether prices settled at a PRREE, absent control and knowledge of subjects' risk aversion. We only know that prices did aggregate some information. Experimental designs with transparent aggregate risk do produce better evidence in favor of full information aggregation. Again, this confirms asset pricing theory.

5. INFORMATION MIRAGES

Even in experiments that provide the best support for full information aggregation, failures do occur. That is, information sometimes does not aggregate, or markets become convinced that the wrong state is drawn. This phenomenon has become known in the literature as "information mirages," and were investigated extensively in Camerer and Weigelt (1991).

Asset pricing theory predicts that, if the conditions are right (common knowledge of aggregate risk, and so on), markets should be capable of aggregating information 100 percent of the time. But this conclusion is based on the implausible assumption that investors know the mapping from states to prices. Because experiments invariably are limited in time, markets may not be able to fully learn this mapping. Because they are in a learning process, mistakes are bound to occur, no matter how rational markets are.

To put this differently: even the best Bayesian learner makes mistakes. But then an interesting question emerges: are the number of mistakes we observe in the laboratory consistent with Bayesian learning? Methodology has recently been developed to answer this question. This methodology was originally aimed at testing asset pricing theory on historical data. Analysis of such data is rendered extremely difficult because they may display subtle biases, either because the market happened to have mistaken expectations over the history at hand (for example, investors were too optimistic), or the empiricist is forced to work with a biased sample (investors' optimism was warranted when taking a longer-term view, or based on a larger cross-section of assets). In both cases, the market's prior belief cannot be readily estimated from the frequency distribution of actual outcomes, unlike what has been implicitly assumed in virtually the entire empirical literature on asset pricing. (See Bossaerts 1996, 2004.) The empirical success of the technique was demonstrated in Bondarenko (1997), Bondarenko and Bossaerts (2000), Bossaerts (2004), and Bossaerts and Hillion (2001).

The methodology lends itself also to verifying whether mirages in experiments on information aggregation are consistent with the theoretical tendency of even the most rational learner to make mistakes. In this context, the methodology works as follows. At the beginning of every period, the market starts with a (potentially arbitrary or time-varying) prior over the possible states of nature. As orders come to the market and trades take place, the market updates its beliefs (as reflected in the transaction prices) in a Bayesian way. When implementing Bayes' law, it is assumed that the market reads the information correctly, namely, that it knows the likelihood of the signals (which come out of the "book," that is, the list of bids and asks, as well as recent trades) given the eventual state. These assumptions lead to rather simple restrictions on the dynamics of securities prices, which can readily be verified on experimental data.

Among other things, one can prove the following:

$$E\left[\frac{1}{R_t^i}|I_{t-1}, s = i\right] = 1, \tag{1}$$

where R_t^i denotes the return on security i over the period $(t-1, t)$, I_{t-1} is the information that the market had (state of the "book"), and the state (indexed s) equals i. Security i is a state contingent security that pays one dollar when the state is i and zero otherwise. In words, the inverse return on winning state contingent security must be one on average. (See Bossaerts 1996.)

The restriction in (1) provides the basis for an indirect test of the conjecture that the number of "mirages" (false price developments) corresponds to what one would expect to happen by chance if markets learn in a rational way.

To illustrate this, consider pricing data from a recent (May 25, 1999) pilot thick-market information aggregation experiment ran at Caltech. Like the experiments in Camerer and Weigelt (1991), they generally showed support for the notion that financial markets are capable of aggregating even weak signals, and that traders are unable to consistently manipulate the outcome. Still, a certain number of failures occurred.

The market technology was the same as the one described in Section 2. Now, however, a complete set of state contingent claims was traded, covering all ten possible states, labeled Q through Z. Every subject received an equal number of each of the state contingent claims, in addition to cash. When a state was drawn, say R, state claim R paid 200 francs. If another state was drawn, claim R paid zero.

Private information ("clues") was given to each of the subjects, in the following form. At the beginning of a period, three letters were randomly drawn (with replacement) from an urn for each subject. The urn contained twelve letters. Three of these letters equaled the actual state that had been selected for that period, while the other nine letters in the urn would correspond to the nine other states. The subjects were told the recalculated (conditional) probabilities as well, in order to facilitate inference. Of course, they were free to ignore that information.

Notice how limited this private information was. While the prior probability of any state was one out of ten, the updated probability for any state would change little. For instance, if a subject was given the sequence "RUS," then she would infer that the chances of states R, U, and S would have increased to 0.19 only. But over sixty subjects participated in this experiment. Combining sixty three-letter signals provides one with almost certainty of the actual state.

The market prices did not always fully aggregate the available information, as one can infer from Figure 5, which plots the evolution of the transaction prices of the winning contingent claim (only) in each period. Under full aggregation, we would expect the prices of the winning contract to rise to its payoff, namely, 200 francs. Figure 5 demonstrates that

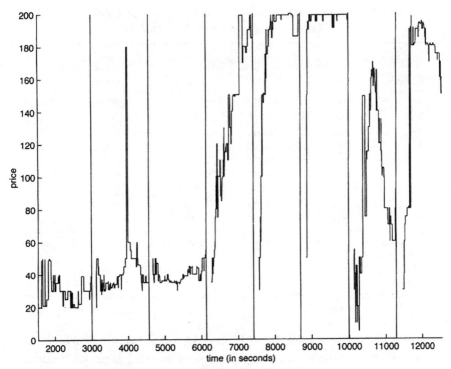

Figure 5. Evolution of the transaction prices of winning contingent claims in the large-scale Caltech 5/25/99 aggregation experiment. Vertical bars delineate periods.

this is often not the case, even if the price almost invariably increases above its unconditional expected payoff of 20 francs ($=0.10 * 200$).

With the restriction in (1), however, one can test whether the dynamics of the transaction prices of winner contracts are consistent with the null that the market read the information (in the book) correctly, as explained above. Table 2 lists, across all periods and for each period separately, (i) the average inverse return on winning contingent claims, (ii) the corresponding z-statistic. Returns were computed from one transaction to the next. That is, time is implicitly measured as transaction time. Across all periods, the inverse return equals 1.0015. The corresponding z-statistic, at 1.16, indicates that this is not significantly different from one (two-sided test). Hence, we fail to reject the null behind the restriction in Equation (1). The same conclusion obtains for each period, except period 6, where the z-statistic is -1.65, which is just significant at the 10 percent level (two-sided test).

Table 2. *Returns ($R_{i,t}$) on Contingent Claims, Caltech Large-Scale*
Aggregation Experiment, May 25, 1999.

| Period | Sample Size | $1/R_{i,t}$ | | $R_{i,t}$ | |
		Average[a]	z-stat[b]	Average[c]	z-stat[d]
All	4,994	1.0015	1.16	1.0047	3.50**
1	579	1.0039	0.88	1.0061	1.28*
2	882	1.0017	0.62	1.0030	1.08
3	803	1.0002	0.20	1.0007	0.66
4	645	0.9982	−1.11	1.0034	2.03*
5	625	0.9990	−0.51	1.0036	1.56*
6	498	0.9979	−1.65*	1.0036	1.56*
7	446	1.0151	1.46	1.0162	1.57*
8	516	0.9991	−0.28	1.0061	1.48*

[a] Average inverse return, where return is measured from the price change between two transactions.
[b] Heteroscedasticity-adjusted; * = significant at the 10% level (two-sided).
[c] Average return, where return is measured from the price change between two transactions.
[d] Heteroscedasticity-adjusted; * = significant at the 10% level (one-sided); ** = significant at the 1% level (one-sided).

For comparison, Table 2 also displays the average of the returns themselves (not the inverse returns) and the corresponding z-statistics. Because only the returns on winning securities are measured, one expects the average to be above one. This is the result of selection bias. Across all periods, the effect is strong: the average return on winning contracts is 1.0047, which, with a z-statistic of 3.5, is significant even at the 0.1 percent level. The period results are less pronounced, with six averages that are significantly positive only at the 10 percent level. One can compute, however, the probability of obtaining six or more rejections (at the 10 percent level) of the null that the average is nonpositive: it is less than 0.1 percent, confirming the overall image.

Hence, the results in Table 2 support the hypothesis that the market read correctly whatever information was revealed through trading activity and entries in the book. The market did make mistakes (it often failed to completely aggregate the available information), but these are to be expected even from a rational Bayesian learner who knows how to interpret signals from the book. That is, the "information mirages" are no indication of irrationality.

There may be a problem with this experiment (and others organized like this one), however. All subjects start out with the same number of each contingent claim, and this is common knowledge. That implies: there is no aggregate risk, and this is known. Not only does this mean that there will be no risk premium (prices equal expected payoffs, which is assumed behind [1]), but it also means that nobody should trade, because nobody has a risky endowment, even if prices are not fully revealing.

This is an awkward situation: subjects are invited to trade, but the experiment is designed such that there would be no trade. Why do subjects trade? Are they confused?

The second column of Table 2 indicates that there was a fair amount of trade. Per period, up to 882 transactions took place in the winning security only. This amounts to more than ten transactions per subject. Trading volume does decline later in the experiment, but is still high in the last period.

Disagreement about how to interpret the information in the book may explain the trading activity. Unfortunately, there is not much theory to support such an explanation. Virtually all asset pricing theory (as well as most of game theory) is based on a common prior assumption, which means that investors essentially hold the same unconditional beliefs and interpret signals alike, even if signals may differ across investors. An exception is Biais and Bossaerts (1998). (In game theory, this common prior assumption is referred to as the Harsanyi doctrine; in dynamic asset pricing theory, an even more extreme position is taken, namely that the prior belief is correct – see Lucas 1978.)

Absent a well-developed theory of asset pricing with disagreeing investors ("beauty contests"), it is hard to interpret the experimental results in Figure 5 and Table 2, just like it was not possible to fully understand the failure of information aggregation in older experiments such as those reported in Plott and Sunder (1988), where payouts depended on the identity of the holder, a situation that has not been thoroughly investigated in asset pricing theory.

To give subjects a reason to trade, one could have allocated a different number of contingent claims to different subjects. That is, a minor change in the experimental design would make the experiment easier to understand from a theoretical point of view.

6. CONCLUSION

This article discussed recent experiments involving financial markets in light of asset pricing theory. That is, it studied to what extent these experiments provided support of the basic tenets of modern asset pricing theory. These are: (i) markets equilibrate to the point that only covariance with aggregate risk is priced, and (ii) markets aggregate dispersed information.

The support for the first prediction seems to be solid, at least from large-scale experiments. The significance of this finding cannot be understated, because the evidence comes from experiments where subjects could not possibly have used the theory to deliberately set prices accordingly.

What conclusion can one draw from these experiments with respect to pricing in markets outside the laboratory? As discussed in the article, it would be premature to claim that asset pricing theory explains the workings of complex institutions such as the NYSE or NASDAQ. The experiments are only a first step: they demonstrated that asset pricing theory has scientific value. Far more work will have to be done before the experimental results shed light on workings of the NYSE and NASDAQ.[10]

The article argued that there is less evidence on prediction (ii), namely, that financial markets aggregate dispersed information. However, experiments that were meant to test aggregation are harder to interpret from a theoretical point of view, because their design often deviated in important respects from the theoretical modeling. Most significantly, payoffs generally depended on the identity of the holder. Or the design led to situations where theory predicted that there would be no trade, yet substantial trading occurred. This calls for new experiments, designed closer to the most important theoretical models and building on the successes of the first set of experiments (those involving risk sharing only). Preliminary evidence from Caltech experiments have proven promising in this respect, recovering the very (noisy) rational expectations equilibria that have been the focus of the theoretical literature (see Admati 1985 and Grossman and Stiglitz 1980).

The article did provide a formal test that the "information mirages" that one observes in successful aggregation experiments – instances where the market did fail to aggregate the information – are to be explained as the natural mistakes that even the most rational (Bayesian) learner would make. In particular, even if one knows the likelihood of the state of the trading book given each possible final outcome, one would not have been able to do better than the market.

The general conclusion that this article conveys, then, is that experimentation with financial markets should be solidly founded on the theory.

---

[10] The situation is similar in the physical sciences. Being able to prove in the laboratory that gravity attracts objects in a vacuum with a constant acceleration seems to be utterly irrelevant in designing large aircraft. Yet, the finding that the acceleration caused by gravity was indeed constant eventually did lead to enough understanding of physics to build jumbo jets.

Grossman, Sanford and Joseph E. Stiglitz. 1980. "On the Impossibility of Informationally Efficient Markets," *American Economic Review* 70, 393–408.

Harrison, Glenn W. 1986. "Experimental Futures Markets," in *Futures Markets: Their Establishment and Performance*, edited by Barry A. Goss. New York University Press, 43–76.

Levy, Haim. 1997. "Risk and Return: An Experimental Analysis," *International Economic Review* 38, 119–49.

Liu, Yu-Jane. 1996. "Auction Mechanisms and Information Structure: An Experimental Study of Information Aggregation in Securities Markets," *Research in Experimental Economics* 6, 165–211.

Lucas, R. 1972. "Expectations and the Neutrality of Money," *Journal of Economic Theory* 4, 103–24.

Lucas, R. 1978. "Asset Prices in an Exchange Economy," *Econometrica* 46, 1429–45.

Lucas, R. 1982. "Interest Rates and Currency Prices in a Two-Country World," *Journal of Monetary Economics* 10, 335–59.

Negishi, Takashi. 1962. "The Stability of a Competitive Economy: A Survey Article," *Econometrica* 30, 635–69.

O'Brien, John and Sanjay Srivastava. 1991. "Dynamic Stock Markets with Multiple Assets: An Experimental Analysis," *The Journal of Finance* 46, 1811–38.

Plott, Charles R. and Shyam Sunder. 1982. "Efficiency of Experimental Security Markets with Insider Information," *Journal of Political Economy* 90, 663–98.

Plott, Charles R. and Shyam Sunder. 1988. "Rational Expectations and the Aggregation of Diverse Information in Laboratory Security Markets," *Econometrica* 56, 1085–8.

Porter, David P. and Vernon L. Smith. 1992. "Price Expectations in Experimental Asset Markets with Futures Contracting," Social Science Working Paper 827, California Institute of Technology.

Porter, David P. and Vernon L. Smith. 1995. "Futures Contracting and Dividend Uncertainty in Experimental Asset Markets," *Journal of Business* 68, 509–41.

Radner, Roy. 1972. "Existence of Equilibrium of Plans, Prices, and Price Expectations in a Sequence of Markets," *Econometrica* 40, 289–303.

Radner, Roy. 1979. "Rational Expectations Equilibrium: Generic Existence and the Information Revealed by Prices," *Econometrica* 47, 655–78.

Roll, R. 1977. "A Critique of the Asset Pricing Theory's Tests, Part I: On the Past and Potential Testability of the Theory," *Journal of Financial Economics* 4, 129–76.

Scarf, H. 1960. "Some Examples of Global Instability of the Competitive Equilibrium," *International Economic Review* 1, 157–72.

Sunder, Shyam. 1992. "Market for Information: Experimental Evidence," *Econometrica* 60, 667–95.

Watts, Susan G. 1992. "Private Information, Prices, Asset Allocation, and Profits: Further Experimental Evidence," *Research in Experimental Economics* 5, 81–117.

4

Two Puzzles of Asset Pricing and Their Implications for Investors[*]

John Y. Campbell

1. INTRODUCTION

The tradeoff of risk and return is becoming ever more important for individuals, institutions, and public policy. In fact, Bernstein (1996) suggests that the rational analysis of risk is a defining characteristic of the modern age.

This essay explores risk and return in aggregate stock market investment. It is based on several earlier expositional and research pieces, notably Campbell (1999, 2000, 2003), Campbell and Cochrane (1999), Campbell and Shiller (2001), and Campbell and Viceira (2002).

The comparison of the stock market with the money market is startling. For example, if we look at log real returns on U.S. stocks and Treasury bills over the period 1947.2–1998.4, we find, first, that the average stock return is 8.1 percent, while the average bill return is 0.9 percent; and second, that the volatility of the stock return is 15.6 percent, while the volatility of the ex post real bill return is only 1.8 percent.[1]

These facts lead to two puzzles of asset pricing. The first was christened the *equity premium puzzle* by Mehra and Prescott (1985): Why is the *average* real stock return so high (in relation to the average short-term

---

[*] This paper was developed from the author's 2001 Marshall Lectures, University of Cambridge.

[1] The gap between average stock and bill returns is even higher if one computes an average of simple returns (an arithmetic return average) rather than an average of log returns (a geometric return average). In this essay I work with log returns throughout, but I adjust average log returns as required by the theoretical models I explore. In practice this means adding one-half the variance to the difference of average log returns, in effect converting from geometric to arithmetic average returns.

real interest rate)? The second might be called the *equity volatility puzzle*: Why is the *volatility* of stock returns so high (in relation to the volatility of the short-term real interest rate)? The classic reference to this second puzzle is Shiller (1981).

Economists have tried to resolve these puzzles by linking asset prices to aggregate consumption. This is a natural approach because consumption is the most obvious determinant of marginal utility (in simple models, the only determinant). Hence, covariance with consumption measures risk. Also, consumption can be thought of as the dividend on the portfolio of aggregate wealth. It is natural to model stocks as claims to the stream of consumption.

Unfortunately, aggregate consumption has several properties that deepen the puzzles of asset pricing. First, real consumption growth is very stable, with an annualized standard deviation of 1.1 percent. Second, the correlation of consumption growth and stock returns is weak (0.23 at a quarterly frequency, and 0.34 at an annual frequency). Third, stock prices have very little ability to forecast consumption growth. The R^2 statistic of a regression of consumption growth on the log dividend-price ratio is never greater than 4 percent at horizons from one to four years.

Economists also try to link stock prices to the behavior of dividends, without assuming that dividends equal consumption. Here too, there are puzzles. Quarterly dividend volatility is high (28 percent), but this is due to strong seasonality in dividends. Annual dividend volatility is only about 6 percent. This volatility is much larger than consumption growth (1 percent), but much smaller than stock returns (16 percent). Stock returns are somewhat more strongly correlated with dividends than with consumption, but the maximum correlation at any horizon up to four years is only 0.34 at a one-year horizon. Finally, the dividend-price ratio has little ability to forecast dividend growth. The R^2 statistic of a regression of dividend growth on the log dividend-price ratio is never greater than 8 percent at horizons from one to four years.

These features of U.S. financial data are also apparent in other countries. Campbell (2003) summarizes stock market data from Morgan Stanley Capital International (MSCI) and macroeconomic data from the International Financial Statistics (IFS) of the International Monetary Fund for eleven developed countries. He also reports results for long-term annual data from Sweden (starting in 1920), the UK (starting in 1919), and the United States (starting in 1891). He shows that stock markets have delivered average real returns of 5 percent or better in almost every country and time period. The exceptions to this occur in short-term quarterly data, and are concentrated in markets that are particularly small relative to GDP (Italy) or that predominantly represent claims on natural resources (Australia). Short-term debt, on the other hand, has rarely delivered an average real return above 3 percent. Stock markets are volatile in every country, while aggregate consumption is smooth and aggregate dividends have an intermediate volatility.

These numbers show that the equity premium and equity volatility puzzles are not unique to the United States, but characterize many other countries as well. Recently, a number of authors have suggested that average excess returns in the United States may be overstated by sample selection or survivorship bias. If economists study the United States because it has had an unusually successful economy, then sample average U.S. stock returns may overstate the true mean U.S. stock return. The international data suggest that this is not a serious problem.[2]

The organization of this paper is as follows. Section 2 presents the equity premium and equity volatility puzzles. Section 3 argues that the equity volatility puzzle is the harder of the two to resolve, and presents several possible explanations. Section 4 discusses implications for investors.

2. THE EQUITY PREMIUM PUZZLE AND THE EQUITY VOLATILITY PUZZLE

I now state the equity premium puzzle using the stochastic discount factor (SDF) paradigm. This approach to asset pricing, which has its roots in the work of Rubinstein (1976), Breeden (1979), Grossman and Shiller (1981), and Shiller (1982), has become increasingly influential since the work of Hansen and Jagannathan (1991). Cochrane (2001) provides a unified textbook treatment of asset pricing in these terms.

Consider the intertemporal choice problem of an investor, indexed by k, who can trade freely in some asset i and can obtain a gross simple rate of return $(1 + R_{i,t+1})$ on the asset held from time t to time $t + 1$. If the investor consumes C_{kt} at time t and has time-separable utility with discount

---

[2] Jorion and Goetzmann (1999) consider international stock-price data from earlier in the twentieth century and argue that the long-term average real growth rate of stock prices has been higher in the United States than elsewhere. However, they do not have data on dividend yields, which are an important component of total return and were particularly important in Europe during the troubled interwar period. Dimson, Marsh, and Staunton (2002) do measure dividend yields and find that total returns in the United States did not exceed returns in all other countries in the early twentieth century.

factor δ and period utility $U(C_{kt})$, then his first-order condition is

$$U'(C_{kt}) = \delta E_t \left[(1 + R_{i,t+1}) U'(C_{k,t+1}) \right]. \tag{1}$$

The left-hand side of (1) is the marginal utility cost of consuming one real dollar less at time t; the right-hand side is the expected marginal utility benefit from investing the dollar in asset i at time t, selling it at time $t + 1$, and consuming the proceeds. The investor equates marginal cost and marginal benefit, so (1) must describe the optimum. Dividing (1) by $U'(C_{kt})$ yields

$$1 = E_t \left[(1 + R_{i,t+1}) \delta \frac{U'(C_{k,t+1})}{U'(C_{kt})} \right] = E_t \left[(1 + R_{i,t+1}) M_{k,t+1} \right], \tag{2}$$

where $M_{k,t+1} = \delta U'(C_{k,t+1})/U'(C_{kt})$ is the intertemporal marginal rate of substitution of the investor, also known as the stochastic discount factor or SDF. As marginal utility must always be positive, the SDF must always be positive.

The derivation just given for Equation (2) assumes the existence of an investor maximizing a time-separable utility function, but in fact the equation holds more generally. The existence of a positive stochastic discount factor is guaranteed by the absence of arbitrage in markets in which nonsatiated investors can trade freely without transactions costs. In general there can be many such stochastic discount factors – for example, different investors k whose marginal utilities follow different stochastic processes will have different $M_{k,t+1}$ – but each stochastic discount factor must satisfy Equation (2). It is common practice to drop the subscript k from this equation and simply write $1 = E_t[(1 + R_{i,t+1})M_{t+1}]$. In complete markets, the stochastic discount factor M_{t+1} is unique because investors can trade with one another to eliminate any idiosyncratic variation in their marginal utilities.

To understand the implications of (2) in a simple way, I follow Hansen and Singleton (1983) and assume that the joint conditional distribution of asset returns and the stochastic discount factor is lognormal and homoskedastic. While these assumptions are not literally realistic – stock returns in particular have fat-tailed distributions with variances that change over time – they do make it easier to discuss the main forces that should determine the equity premium.

The assumption of lognormality implies that the log riskless interest rate satisfies

$$r_{f,t+1} = - E_t m_{t+1} - \frac{\sigma_m^2}{2}. \tag{3}$$

The log riskless interest rate is negatively related to the conditional expectation of the log SDF. When the SDF is expected to be high, marginal utility in the future is expected to be high relative to the present; the investor has an incentive to save, and this depresses the equilibrium riskless interest rate. The log riskless interest rate also depends negatively on the conditional volatility of the log SDF. Volatility produces a precautionary savings motive, which depresses the riskless interest rate.

Also, the expected excess return on risky assets over the riskless rate satisfies

$$E_t\left[r_{i,t+1} - r_{f,t+1}\right] + \frac{\sigma_i^2}{2} = -\sigma_{im}. \tag{4}$$

The variance term on the left-hand side of (4) is a Jensen's Inequality adjustment arising from the fact that we are describing expectations of log returns. This term effectively converts the return difference from a geometric average to an arithmetic average. It would disappear if we rewrote the equation in terms of the log expectation of the ratio of gross simple returns: $\log E_t[(1 + R_{i,t+1})/(1 + R_{f,t+1})] = -\sigma_{im}$.

The right-hand side of (4) says that the risk premium is the negative of the covariance of the asset with the SDF. An asset with a high expected return must have a low covariance with the SDF. Such an asset tends to have low returns when investors have high marginal utility. It is risky in that it fails to deliver wealth precisely when wealth is most valuable to investors. Investors therefore demand a large risk premium to hold it.

The covariance σ_{im} can be written as the product of the standard deviation of the asset return σ_i, the standard deviation of the SDF σ_m, and the correlation between the asset return and the SDF ρ_{im}. Since $\rho_{im} \geq -1$, $-\sigma_{im} \leq \sigma_i \sigma_m$. Substituting into (4),

$$\sigma_m \geq \frac{E_t\left[r_{i,t+1} - r_{f,t+1}\right] + \sigma_i^2/2}{\sigma_i}. \tag{5}$$

This inequality was first derived by Shiller (1982); a multiasset version was derived by Hansen and Jagannathan (1991). The right-hand side of (5) is the excess return on an asset, adjusted for Jensen's Inequality, divided by the standard deviation of the asset's return – a logarithmic Sharpe ratio for the asset. Equation (5) says that the standard deviation of the log SDF must be greater than this Sharpe ratio for all assets i; that is, it must be greater than the maximum possible Sharpe ratio obtainable in asset markets.

Table 1 uses the data of Campbell (2003) and Equation (5) to illustrate the equity premium puzzle. For each country and sample period, the first column of the table reports the average excess return on stock over short-term debt, adjusted for Jensen's Inequality by adding one-half the sample variance of the excess log return to get a sample estimate of the numerator in (5). This adjusted average excess return is multiplied by 400 to express it in annualized percentage points. The second column of the table gives the annualized standard deviation of the excess log stock return, a sample estimate of the denominator in (5). The third column gives the ratio of the first two columns, multiplied by 100; this is a sample estimate of the lower bound on the standard deviation of the log SDF, expressed in annualized percentage points. In the postwar U.S. data, the estimated lower bound is a standard deviation greater than 50 percent a year; in the other quarterly data sets, it is below 10 percent for Italy, between 15 percent and 20 percent for Australia and Canada, and above 30 percent for all the other countries. In the long-run annual data sets, the lower bound on the standard deviation exceeds 30 percent for all three countries. These are extraordinarily high volatilities considering that the SDF M_{t+1} is a random variable with a mean close to one that must always be positive.

2.1. The Equity Premium Puzzle and Consumption-Based Asset Pricing

To understand why these numbers are disturbing, I now follow Rubinstein (1976), Lucas (1978), Breeden (1979), Grossman and Shiller (1979), Mehra and Prescott (1985), and other classic papers on the equity premium puzzle and assume that there is a representative agent who maximizes a time-separable power utility function defined over aggregate consumption C_t:

$$U(C) = \frac{C_t^{1-\gamma} - 1}{1 - \gamma} \tag{6}$$

where γ is the coefficient of relative risk aversion.

The assumption of power utility is not an arbitrary one. A scale-independent utility function is required to explain the fact that over the past two centuries, as wealth and consumption have grown manyfold,

Table 1. *The Equity Premium Puzzle*

Country	Sample Period	$\overline{aer_e}$	$\sigma(er_e)$	$\sigma(m)$	$\sigma(\Delta c)$	$\rho(er_e, \Delta c)$	$cov(er_e, \Delta C)$	RRA(1)	RRA(2)
USA	1947.2–1998.3	8.071	15.271	52.853	1.071	0.205	3.354	240.647	49.326
AUL	1970.1–1998.4	3.885	22.403	17.342	2.059	0.144	6.640	58.511	8.421
CAN	1970.1–1999.1	3.968	17.266	22.979	1.920	0.202	6.694	59.266	11.966
FR	1973.2–1998.3	8.308	23.175	35.848	2.922	−0.093	−6.315	<0	12.270
GER	1978.4–1997.3	8.669	20.196	42.922	2.447	0.029	1.446	599.468	17.542
ITA	1971.2–1998.1	4.687	27.068	17.314	1.665	−0.006	−0.252	<0	10.400
JAP	1970.2–1998.4	5.098	21.498	23.715	2.561	0.112	6.171	82.620	9.260
NTH	1977.2–1998.3	11.421	16.901	67.576	2.510	0.032	1.344	849.991	9.260
SWD	1970.1–1999.2	11.539	23.518	49.066	1.851	0.015	0.674	1713.197	26.501
SWT	1982.2–1998.4	14.898	21.878	68.098	2.123	−0.112	−5.181	<0	32.076
UK	1970.1–1999.1	9.169	21.198	43.253	2.511	0.093	4.930	185.977	17.222
USA	1970.1–1998.3	6.353	16.976	37.425	0.909	0.274	4.233	150.100	41.178
SWD	1920–1997	6.540	18.763	34.855	5.622	0.167	8.830	74.062	12.400
UK	1919–1997	8.674	21.277	40.767	5.630	0.351	21.042	41.223	14.483
USA	1891–1997	6.723	18.496	36.345	6.437	0.495	29.450	22.827	11.293

134

riskless interest rates and risk premia do not seem to have trended up or down. Power utility is one of the few utility functions that have this property.[3] Related to this, if different investors in the economy have different wealth levels but the same power utility function, then they can be aggregated into a single representative investor with the same utility function as the individual investors.

Power utility implies that marginal utility $U'(C_t) = C_t^{-\gamma}$, and the SDF $M_{t+1} = \delta(C_{t+1}/C_t)^{-\gamma}$. The assumption made previously that the SDF is conditionally lognormal will be implied by the assumption that aggregate consumption is conditionally lognormal (Hansen and Singleton 1983). Making this assumption for expositional convenience, the log SDF is $m_{t+1} = \log(\delta) - \gamma \Delta c_{t+1}$, where $c_t = \log(C_t)$.

Equation (3) now becomes

$$r_{f,t+1} = -\log \delta + \gamma E_t \Delta C_{t+1} - \frac{\gamma^2 \sigma_c^2}{2}. \qquad (7)$$

where σ_c^2 denotes the unconditional variance of log consumption innovations $Var(c_{t+1} - E_t c_{t+1})$. This equation says that the riskless real rate is linear in expected consumption growth, with slope coefficient equal to the coefficient of relative risk aversion. The conditional variance of consumption growth has a negative effect on the riskless rate by stimulating precautionary savings.

Equation (4) becomes

$$E_t [r_{i,t+1} - r_{f,t+1}] + \frac{\sigma_i^2}{2} = \gamma \sigma_{ic}, \qquad (8)$$

where σ_{ic} denotes the unconditional covariance of innovations $Cov(r_{i,t+1} - E_t r_{i,t+1}, c_{t+1} - E_t c_{t+1})$. The log risk premium on any asset is the coefficient of relative risk aversion times the covariance of the asset return with consumption growth. Intuitively, an asset with a high consumption covariance tends to have low returns when consumption is low, that is, when the marginal utility of consumption is high. Such an asset is risky and commands a large risk premium.

---

[3] A few other utility functions also have this property. Epstein and Zin (1991) and Weil (1989) have proposed a recursive utility specification that preserves the scale-invariance of power utility, but relaxes the restriction of power utility that the coefficient of relative risk aversion is the reciprocal of the elasticity of intertemporal substitution. Models of habit formation make relative risk aversion constant in the long run but variable in the short run.

Table 1 uses (8) to illustrate the equity premium puzzle. As already discussed, the first column of the table reports a sample estimate of the left-hand side of (8), multiplied by 400 to express it in annualized percentage points. The second column reports the annualized standard deviation of the excess log stock return, the fourth column reports the annualized standard deviation of consumption growth, the fifth column reports the correlation between the excess log stock return and consumption growth, and the sixth column gives the product of these three variables – which is the annualized covariance σ_{ic} between the log stock return and consumption growth.

Finally, the table gives two columns with implied risk aversion coefficients. The column headed RRA(1) uses (8) directly, dividing the adjusted average excess return by the estimated covariance to get estimated risk aversion.[4] The column headed RRA(2) sets the correlation of stock returns and consumption growth equal to one before calculating risk aversion. Although this is of course a counterfactual exercise, it is a valuable diagnostic because it indicates the extent to which the equity premium puzzle arises from the *smoothness* of consumption rather than the *low correlation* between consumption and stock returns. The correlation is hard to measure accurately because it is easily distorted by short-term measurement errors in consumption, and Campbell (2003) shows that empirically it is quite sensitive to the measurement horizon. By setting the correlation to one, the RRA(2) column indicates the extent to which the equity premium puzzle is robust to such issues. A correlation of one is also implicitly assumed in the volatility bound for the SDF (5), and in many calibration exercises such as Mehra and Prescott (1985) or Campbell and Cochrane (1999).

Table 1 shows that the equity premium puzzle is a robust phenomenon in international data. The coefficients of relative risk aversion in the RRA(1) column are generally extremely large. They are usually many times greater than ten, the maximum level considered plausible by Mehra and Prescott (1985). In a few cases, the risk aversion coefficients are negative because the estimated covariance of stock returns with consumption growth is negative, but in these cases the covariance is extremely close to zero. Even when one ignores the low correlation between stock returns and consumption growth and gives the model its best chance by setting the

---

[4] The calculation is done correctly, in natural units, even though the table reports average excess returns and covariances in percentage point units. Equivalently, the ratio of the quantities given in the table is multiplied by 100.

correlation to one, the RRA(2) column still has risk aversion coefficients above ten in most cases.

2.2. Could the Equity Premium Puzzle Be Spurious?

The risk aversion estimates in Table 1 are point estimates and are subject to sampling error. No standard errors are reported for these estimates. However, authors such as Cecchetti, Lam, and Mark (1993) and Kocherlakota (1996), studying the long-run annual U.S. data, have found small enough standard errors that they can reject risk aversion coefficients below about eight at conventional significance levels.

Of course, the validity of these tests depends on the characteristics of the data set in which they are used. Rietz (1988) has argued that there may be a peso problem in these data. A peso problem arises when there is a small positive probability of an important event, and investors take this probability into account when setting market prices. If the event does not occur in a particular sample period, investors will appear irrational in the sample and economists will misestimate their preferences. While it may seem unlikely that this could be an important problem in 100 years of annual data, Rietz (1988) argues that an economic catastrophe that would destroy almost all stock market value can be extremely unlikely and yet have a major depressing effect on stock prices.

One difficulty with this argument is that it requires not only a potential catastrophe, but also one which affects stock market investors more seriously than investors in short-term debt instruments. Many countries that have experienced catastrophes, such as Russia or Germany, have seen very low returns on short-term government debt as well as on equity. A peso problem that affects both asset returns equally will affect estimates of the average levels of returns, but not estimates of the equity premium. The major example of a disaster for stockholders that did not negatively affect bondholders is the Great Depression of the early 1930s, but of course this is included in the long-run annual data for Sweden, the UK, and the United States, all of which display an equity premium puzzle.

Also, the consistency of the results across countries requires investors in all countries to be concerned about catastrophes. If the potential catastrophes are uncorrelated across countries, then it becomes less likely that the data set includes no catastrophes; thus the argument seems to require a potential international catastrophe that affects all countries simultaneously.

Even if the equity premium puzzle is not entirely spurious, there are several reasons to think that stock returns exceeded their true long-run mean in the late twentieth century. Dimson, Marsh, and Staunton (2002) present comprehensive international data for the whole twentieth century and find that returns were generally higher in the later part of the century. Siegel (1998) reports similar results for U.S. data going back to the early nineteenth century. Fama and French (2002) point out that average U.S. stock returns in the late twentieth century were considerably higher than accountants' estimates of the return on equity for U.S. corporations. Thus if óne uses average returns as an estimate of the true cost of capital, one is forced to the implausible conclusion that corporations destroyed stockholder value by retaining and reinvesting earnings rather than paying them out.

Unusually high stock returns in the late twentieth century could have resulted from unexpectedly favorable conditions for economic growth. But they could also have resulted from a correction of historical mispricing, a one-time decline in the equity premium. Several economists have recently argued that the equity premium is now far lower than it was in the early twentieth century (Jagannathan, McGrattan, and Scherbina 2000; McGrattan and Prescott 2000).[5]

2.3. Could Risk Aversion Be Higher Than We Thought?

It is possible that the equity premium puzzle has an extremely simple solution, namely that the coefficient of relative risk aversion γ is higher than economists traditionally thought. After all, it is hard to get evidence about risk aversion from any other source than asset markets. Experimental evidence is of very little use because it is almost impossible to design experiments involving significant stakes, and people should be almost indifferent with respect to small gambles.[6] One might think that "thought experiments," or introspection, would be sufficient to rule out very large values of γ, but Kandel and Stambaugh (1991) point out that introspection can deliver very different estimates of risk aversion depending on

---

[5] Glassman and Hassett (1999) take this argument to an extreme. They argue that the equity premium should be zero, and that U.S. stock prices will rise threefold from 1999 levels as the transition continues. Events since 1999 have not been kind to this view, but it is certainly possible that the equity premium remains lower today than it was for most of the twentieth century.

[6] Experimental evidence is well described by the prospect theory of Kahneman and Tversky (1979), but it is not at all clear that this theory can be used to describe people's responses to the significant lifetime risks involved in financial markets.

the size of the gamble considered. This suggests that introspection can be misleading or that some more general model of utility is needed.

The assumption of a high γ, however, leads to a second puzzle. Equation (7) implies that the unconditional mean riskless interest rate is

$$Er_{f,t+1} = - \log \delta + \gamma g - \frac{\gamma^2 \delta_c^2}{2}, \tag{9}$$

where g is the mean growth rate of consumption. Since g is positive, as shown in Table 2, high values of γ imply high values of γg. Ignoring the term $-\gamma^2 \sigma_c^2/2$ for the moment, this can be reconciled with low average short-term real interest rates, shown in Table 2, only if the discount factor δ is close to or even greater than one, corresponding to a low or even negative rate of time preference. This is the risk-free rate puzzle emphasized by Weil (1989).

Intuitively, the risk-free rate puzzle is that if investors are risk averse, then with power utility they must also be extremely unwilling to substitute intertemporally. Given positive average consumption growth, a low riskless interest rate and a high rate of time preference, such investors would have a strong desire to borrow from the future to reduce their average consumption growth rate. A low riskless interest rate is possible in equilibrium only if investors have a low or negative rate of time preference that reduces their desire to borrow.[7]

Of course, if the risk aversion coefficient γ is high enough, then the negative quadratic term $-\gamma^2 \sigma_c^2/2$ in Equation (9) dominates the linear term and pushes the riskless interest rate down again. The quadratic term reflects precautionary savings; risk averse agents with uncertain consumption streams have a precautionary desire to save, which can work against their desire to borrow. But a reasonable rate of time preference is obtained only as a knife-edge case.

Table 2 illustrates the risk-free rate puzzle in international data. The table first shows the average risk-free rate, the mean consumption growth rate, and the standard deviation of consumption growth. These moments and the risk aversion coefficients calculated in Table 1 are substituted into Equation (9), and the equation is solved for an implied time preference rate. The time preference rate is reported in percentage points per year; it can be interpreted as the riskless real interest rate that would

---

[7] As Abel (1996) and Kocherlakota (1996) point out, negative time preference is consistent with finite utility in a time-separable model provided that consumption is growing, and marginal utility shrinking, sufficiently rapidly. The question is whether negative time preference is plausible.

Table 2. *The Risk-Free Rate Puzzle*

Country	Sample Period	$\overline{r}_f$	$\overline{\Delta c}$	$\sigma(\Delta c)$	RRA(1)	TPR(1)	RRA(2)	TPR(2)
USA	1947.2–1998.3	0.896	1.951	1.071	240.647	−136.270	49.326	−81.393
AUL	1970.1–1998.4	2.054	2.071	2.059	58.511	−46.512	8.421	−13.880
CAN	1970.1–1999.1	2.713	2.170	1.920	59.266	−61.154	11.966	−20.618
FR	1973.2–1998.3	2.715	1.212	2.922	<0	N/A	12.270	−5.735
GER	1978.4–1997.3	3.219	1.673	2.447	599.468	9757.265	17.542	−16.910
ITA	1971.2–1998.1	2.371	2.273	1.665	<0	N/A	10.400	−19.765
JAP	1970.2–1998.4	1.388	3.233	2.561	82.620	−41.841	9.260	−25.735
NTH	1977.2–1998.3	3.377	1.671	2.510	849.991	21349.249	26.918	−18.769
SWD	1970.1–1999.2	1.995	1.001	1.851	1713.197	48590.956	26.501	−12.506
SWT	1982.2–1998.4	1.393	0.559	2.123	<0	N/A	32.076	6.636
UK	1970.1–1999.1	1.301	2.235	2.511	185.977	676.439	17.222	−27.838
USA	1970.1–1998.3	1.494	1.802	0.909	150.100	−175.916	41.178	−65.701
SWD	1920–1997	2.209	1.730	2.811	74.062	90.793	12.400	−13.165
UK	1919–1997	1.255	1.472	2.815	41.223	7.913	14.483	−11.749
USA	1891–1997	2.020	1.760	3.218	22.827	−11.162	11.293	−11.247

prevail if consumption were known to be constant forever at its current level, with no growth and no volatility. Risk aversion coefficients in the RRA(2) range imply negative time preference rates in every country except Switzerland, whereas larger risk aversion coefficients in the RRA(1) range imply time preference rates that are often positive but always implausible and vary wildly across countries.

The risk-free rate puzzle can be mitigated by use of the recursive preferences suggested by Epstein and Zin (1991) and Weil (1989). These preferences allow the elasticity of intertemporal substitution to be a free parameter, independent of the coefficient of relative risk aversion, whereas power utility forces one to be the reciprocal of the other. The risk-free rate puzzle is caused by a low elasticity of intertemporal substitution rather than a high coefficient of relative risk aversion. Direct evidence on the elasticity of intertemporal substitution (Hall 1988; Campbell and Mankiw 1989) suggests that it is fairly low, certainly well below one, although possibly higher than the reciprocal of risk aversion.

2.4. The Equity Volatility Puzzle

So far I have asked why average stock returns are so high, given their volatility (and the behavior of aggregate consumption). Now I ask where the volatility itself comes from.

In order to understand the second moments of stock returns, it is essential to have a framework relating movements in stock prices to movements in expected future dividends and discount rates. The present value model of stock prices is intractably nonlinear when expected stock returns are time-varying, and this has forced researchers to use one of several available simplifying assumptions. The most common approach is to assume a discrete-state Markov process either for dividend growth (Mehra and Prescott 1985) or, following Hamilton (1989), for conditionally expected dividend growth. The Markov structure makes it possible to solve the present value model, but the derived expressions for returns tend to be extremely complicated and so these papers usually emphasize numerical results derived under specific numerical assumptions about parameter values.

An alternative framework, which produces simpler closed-form expressions and hence is better suited for an overview of the literature, is the loglinear approximation to the exact present value model suggested by Campbell and Shiller (1988). Campbell and Shiller's loglinear relation between prices, dividends, and returns provides an accounting framework: High prices must eventually be followed by high future dividends or low future returns, and high prices must be associated with high expected future dividends or low expected future returns. Similarly, high returns must be associated with upward revisions in expected future dividends or downward revisions in expected future returns.

The loglinear approximation starts with the definition of the log return on some asset i, $r_{i,t+1} = \log(P_{it+1} + D_{i,t+1}) - \log(P_{it})$. The log return is a nonlinear function of log prices p_{it} and p_{it+1} and and log dividends $d_{i,t+1}$, but it can be approximated around the mean log dividend-price ratio, $\overline{d_{it} - p_{it}}$, using a first-order Taylor expansion. The resulting approximation is a stochastic difference equation that can be solved forward to an infinite horizon if one is willing to impose the terminal condition that $\lim_{j\to\infty} \rho^j p_{i,t+j} = 0$, effectively ruling out explosive behavior of stock prices relative to dividends (the "rational bubbles" of Blanchard and Watson [1982]).[8]

Finally, Campbell and Shiller take expectations to find that

$$d_{it} - p_{it} = \frac{-k}{1-\rho} + E_t \sum_{j=0}^{\infty} \rho^j \left[r_{i,t+1+j} - \Delta d_{i,t+1+j} \right]. \tag{10}$$

This equation says that the log dividend-price ratio is high when dividends are expected to grow slowly, or when stock returns are expected to be high. The equation should be thought of as an accounting identity rather than a behavioral model; it has been obtained merely by approximating an identity, solving forward subject to a terminal condition, and taking expectations. Intuitively, if the stock price is high today, then from the definition of the return and the terminal condition that the stock price is nonexplosive, there must either be high dividends or low stock returns in the future. Investors must then expect some combination of high dividends and low stock returns if their expectations are to be consistent with the observed price.

Equation (10) describes the log dividend-price ratio rather than the log price itself. This is a useful way to write the model because in many

---

[8] There are, however, several reasons to rule out such bubbles. The theoretical circumstances under which bubbles can exist are quite restrictive; Tirole (1985), for example, uses an overlapping generations framework and finds that bubbles can only exist if the economy is dynamically inefficient, a condition that seems unlikely on prior grounds and that is hard to reconcile with the empirical evidence of Abel et al. (1989). Santos and Woodford (1997) also conclude that the conditions under which bubbles can exist are fragile. Empirically, bubbles imply explosive behavior of prices in relation to dividends and other measures of fundamentals; there is no evidence of this, although nonlinear bubble models are hard to reject using standard linear econometric methods.

data sets dividends appear to follow a loglinear unit root process, so that log dividends and log prices are nonstationary. In this case changes in log dividends are stationary, so from (10) the log price-dividend ratio is stationary provided that the expected stock return is stationary. Thus, log stock prices and dividends are cointegrated, and the stationary linear combination of these variables involves no unknown parameters since it is just the log ratio.

Equation (10) can also be understood as a dynamic generalization of the famous formula, usually attributed to Myron Gordon (1962) but probably due originally to John Burr Williams (1938), that applies when the discount rate is a constant R and the expected dividend growth rate is a constant G:

$$\frac{D}{P} = R - G. \tag{11}$$

So far I have written asset prices as linear combinations of expected future dividends and returns. Campbell (1991) shows that it is also possible to write asset returns as linear combinations of *revisions* in expected future dividends and returns, but I do not pursue this approach further here.

I now use this accounting framework to illustrate the stock market volatility puzzle. The intertemporal budget constraint for a representative agent, $W_{t+1} = (1 + R_{p,t+1})(W_t - C_t)$, implies that aggregate consumption is the dividend on the portfolio of all invested wealth, denoted by subscript w:

$$d_{wt} = c_t. \tag{12}$$

Many authors, including Grossman and Shiller (1981), Lucas (1978), and Mehra and Prescott (1985), have assumed that the aggregate stock market, denoted by subscript e for equity, is equivalent to the wealth portfolio and thus pays consumption as its dividend. Here I follow Campbell (1986) and Abel (1999) and make the slightly more general assumption that the dividend on equity equals aggregate consumption raised to a power. In logs, we have

$$d_{et} = \lambda c_t. \tag{13}$$

The coefficient λ can be interpreted as a measure of leverage. When $\lambda > 1$, dividends and stock returns are more volatile than the returns on the aggregate wealth portfolio. This framework has the additional advantage that a riskless real bond with infinite maturity – an inflation-indexed consol, denoted by subscript b – can be priced merely by setting

$\lambda = 0$. The relative volatility of dividends and consumption suggests that $\lambda = 5$ or 6 might be a reasonable assumption.

The representative-agent asset pricing model with power utility, conditional log-normality, and homoskedasticity implies that

$$E_t r_{e,t+1} = \mu_e + \gamma E_t \Delta c_{t+1}, \tag{14}$$

where μ_e is an asset-specific constant term. The expected log return on equity, like the expected log return on any other asset, is just a constant plus relative risk aversion times expected consumption growth.[9]

Substituting Equations (13) and (14) into Equation (10), I find that

$$d_{et} - p_{et} = \frac{-k_e}{1-p} + (\gamma - \lambda) E_t \sum_{j=0}^{\infty} \rho^j \Delta c_{t+1+j}. \tag{15}$$

Expected future consumption growth has offsetting effects on stock prices. It has a direct positive effect by increasing expected future dividends γ-for-one, but it has an indirect negative effect by increasing expected future real interest rates λ-for-one.

These offsetting effects make it almost impossible for the standard power utility model to explain the volatility of stock returns and their positive correlation with consumption growth. We already know that the coefficient of relative risk aversion must be large to explain the equity premium puzzle. If $\lambda < \gamma$, then good news about future consumption drives down stock prices because the interest-rate effect overwhelms the dividend effect. In this case positively autocorrelated consumption growth implies that stock returns are *negatively* correlated with consumption. If $\lambda = \gamma$, then the dividend-price ratio is constant and the volatility of stock returns is just λ times the volatility of consumption growth. Only if $\lambda > \gamma$ can we get stock returns to be positively correlated with consumption growth, and an implausibly large λ is required to match the observed volatility of stock returns.

2.5. Do Stock Prices Forecast Dividend or Earnings Growth?

Of course, all these calculations are dependent on the assumption made at the beginning of this subsection, that the log dividend on stocks is a multiple of log aggregate consumption. More general models, allowing

---

[9] Campbell (1999) analyzes the more general Epstein-Zin-Weil model, where relative risk aversion need not equal the reciprocal of the elasticity of intertemporal substitution ψ. In that model the coefficient on expected consumption growth is actually the reciprocal $1/\psi$.

separate variation in dividends and consumption, can in principle generate volatile stock returns from predictable variation in dividend growth
without creating offsetting variation in real interest rates. But this explanation for stock market volatility requires that the stock market forecasts
dividend growth.

Campbell and Shiller (2003) present a simple graphical analysis that
makes it clear that stock prices have very little forecasting power for
future dividend growth. They point out that if a valuation ratio, such as
the dividend-price ratio, is stationary, then when the ratio is at an extreme
level either the numerator or the denominator of the ratio must move in a
direction that restores the ratio to a more normal level. *Something* must be
forecastable based on the ratio, either the numerator or the denominator.
In the case of the dividend-price ratio, a high ratio must forecast either
slow dividend growth or rapid price growth.[10]

Does the dividend-price ratio forecast future dividend movements or
future price movements? To answer this question, Campbell and Shiller
use annual U.S. data from 1872 to 2000, and present a pair of scatterplots
shown in Figure 1. Each scatterplot has the dividend-price ratio, measured
as the previous year's dividend divided by the January stock price, on the
horizontal axis. (The horizontal axis scale is logarithmic, but the axis is
labeled in levels for ease of reference.) Over this period, the historical
mean value for the dividend-price ratio was 4.65 percent.

In the top part of the figure, the vertical axis is the growth rate of
real dividends (measured logarithmically as the change in the natural log
of real dividends) over a time interval sufficient to bring the dividend-
price ratio back to its historical mean of 4.65 percent. More precisely, the
dividend growth rate is measured from the year preceding the year shown
until the year before the dividend-price ratio again crossed 4.65 percent.
Because dividends enter the dividend-price ratio with a one-year lag, this
is the appropriate way to measure growth in dividends from the base level
embodied in a given year's dividend-price ratio to the level that prevailed
when the dividend-price ratio next crossed its historical mean.

Since 1872, the dividend-price ratio has crossed its mean value twenty-
nine times, with intervals between crossings ranging from one year to

---

[10] A similar point can be understood by looking at Equation (15). If the dividend-price
ratio varies, then either the expected rate of dividend growth or the expected rate of
return must vary. Note, however, that this is a slightly different point. The total rate of
return includes both the dividend yield and the rate of price appreciation. This is why
the argument based on Equation (15) does not rely on stationarity of the dividend-price
ratio. Earlier work on the ability of stock prices to predict dividends includes Shiller
(1981) and Campbell and Shiller (1988).

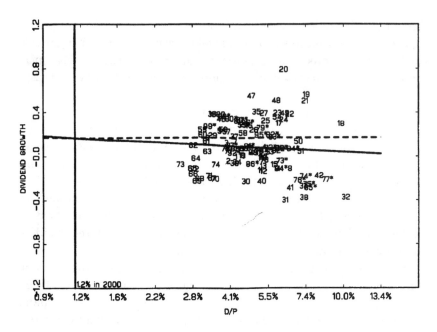

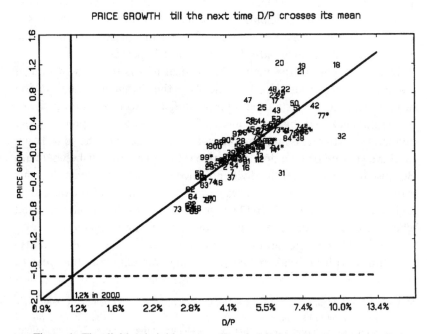

Figure 1. The dividend yield as a predictor of dividend and price growth.

twenty years (the twenty-year interval being between 1955 and 1975). The different years are indicated on the scatter diagram by two-digit numbers; a star after a number denotes a nineteenth-century date. The last year shown is 1983, as this is the last year that was followed by the dividend-price ratio crossing its mean. (The ratio has been below its mean ever since.) A regression line is fit through these data points, and a vertical line is drawn to indicate the dividend-price ratio at the start of the year 2000. The implied forecast for dividend growth, starting in the year 2000, is the horizontal dashed line marked where the vertical line intersects the regression line.

It is obvious from the top part of Figure 1 that the dividend-price ratio has done a poor job as a forecaster of future dividend growth to the date when the ratio is again borne back to its mean value. The regression line is nearly horizontal, implying that the forecast for future dividend growth is almost the same regardless of the dividend-price ratio. The R^2 statistic for the regression is 0.25 percent, indicating that only one-quarter of 1 percent of the variation of dividend growth is explained by the initial dividend-price ratio.

It must follow, therefore, that the dividend-price ratio forecasts movements in its denominator – the stock price – and that it is the stock price that has moved to restore the ratio to its mean value. In the lower part of Figure 1, the vertical axis shows the growth rate of real stock prices (measured logarithmically as the change in log real stock prices) between the year shown and the next year when the dividend-price ratio crossed its mean value. The scatterplot shows a strong tendency for the dividend-price ratio to predict future price changes. The regression line has a strongly positive slope, and the R^2 statistic for the regression is 63 percent. This answers the question: It is clearly the denominator of the dividend-price ratio that brings the ratio back to its mean, not the numerator.

There are several reasons to be cautious in interpreting the results of Figure 1. First, the behavior of the dividend-price ratio can be altered by shifts in corporate financial policy. A permanent shift toward the use of share repurchases, for example, can reduce current dividends but permanently increase the growth rate of dividends per share by creating a steady decline in the number of shares outstanding. This may have happened in recent years, in which case the low current dividend-price ratio does not necessarily forecast low returns. To address this concern, Campbell and Shiller (2001) look at earnings as well as dividends. To eliminate the effects of short-run cyclical variation in earnings, they average earnings over ten years as recommended in the classic investment text of Graham and Dodd (1934). They find that the ratio of prices to smoothed earnings predicts price variation rather than earnings variation, consistent with the results just reported for dividends.

Second, the different points in the scatter diagram are not independent of one another. There are not 120 independent observations over 120 years; rather, there are only twenty-nine independent observations corresponding to the twenty-nine occasions on which the dividend-price ratio crossed its mean. If one uses a fixed horizon of ten years, as Campbell and Shiller do elsewhere in their study, there are only twelve independent observations. Even allowing for this fact, however, the results appear statistically significant in a Monte Carlo study reported by Campbell and Shiller.

Third, the movements of the dividend-price and price-earnings ratio are extremely persistent. This can create serious statistical problems with standard tests for predictability of returns. Campbell and Yogo (2002) and Lewellen (2003), however, present modified tests that are appropriate when predictor variables have near unit roots, and find that these tests still deliver some evidence for predictability of returns.

Finally, the runup in stock prices in the late 1990s diminished the statistical evidence that valuation ratios predict stock returns. For several years in the late 1990s, the stock market delivered high returns despite record low dividend-price ratios. This evidence is not reflected in Figure 1 because the dividend-price ratio has not yet returned to its mean. On the other hand, it is extremely hard to rationalize the runup in prices using a model with a fixed discount rate, because the implied dividend growth forecasts appear wildly optimistic (Heaton and Lucas 1999); also the predictability of dividend growth from the dividend-price ratio does not seem to have increased. For these reasons I believe that the experience of the late 1990s is either an extreme version of previous swings in the stock market, or possibly a one-time structural change to a permanently lower equity premium; in either case it does not alter the overall message of Figure 1. In the next part of this essay, I will discuss alternative explanations of equity volatility, and their implications for portfolio management.

3. EXPLAINING EQUITY VOLATILITY

In the previous part of this essay, I discussed two puzzles of asset pricing, the equity premium puzzle and the equity volatility puzzle. Several solutions to the equity premium puzzle are potentially available. For example, investors may have higher risk aversion than economists used to think; returns may have been unusually high in the late twentieth century; and these high returns may have been caused in part by a one-time correction of historical equity mispricing. In this case future returns will tend to be lower than historical returns, and the equity premium will diminish as a focus of academic attention.

The situation is not so favorable with respect to the equity volatility puzzle. This puzzle raises fundamental questions about the relationship between aggregate consumption and aggregate wealth. Because consumption is ultimately financed by wealth (broadly defined to include human wealth), any model with stationary asset returns implies that the ratio of consumption to wealth must be stationary. As consumption and wealth appear individually to have unit roots, this implies that consumption and wealth are cointegrated. In the very long run, then, the annualized growth rates of consumption and wealth must be almost identical; in particular, they must have identical volatilities. The difficulty is that in the short run, the volatility of consumption growth is far smaller than the volatility of wealth growth.[11] Consumption is very smooth, whereas wealth is very volatile.

How can we reconcile the observed short-run properties of consumption and wealth with the properties we know they must have in the long run? There are only two possibilities. First, it may be that the annualized volatility of consumption growth increases with the horizon over which it is measured, so that ultimately it reaches the high volatility of wealth growth. This would require that consumption is not a random walk, but has positive serial correlation in growth rates. Second, it may be that the annualized volatility of wealth growth decreases with the horizon over which it is measured, so that ultimately it reaches the low volatility of consumption growth. This would require that wealth is not a random walk, but has negative serial correlation in growth rates. These two possibilities represent fundamentally different views of the world. Is the world safe as suggested by consumption, or risky as suggested by the stock market?

Recent work of Lettau and Ludvigson (2001) suggests that consumption – not wealth – accurately represents long-term risk. Lettau and

---

[11] In Table 1, we saw that consumption is far less volatile than stock returns. While equities are not the only component of wealth, other components are not smooth enough to compensate for the volatility of stock returns (Campbell 1996; Lettau and Ludvigson 2001).

Ludvigson use U.S. Flow of Funds data to construct a proxy for total asset wealth, including not only equities but also other assets such as real estate. They use labor income to proxy for human wealth, arguing that labor income and human wealth should be cointegrated. They analyze the three aggregate time series for consumption, labor income, and asset wealth, and find that the three are cointegrated (even though no two of them are cointegrated). The stationary linear combination of these variables forecasts wealth, not consumption or labor income. In their data, consumption is extremely close to a random walk. Thus Lettau and Ludvigson find that wealth is mean-reverting and adjusts over long horizons to match the smoothness of consumption. A satisfactory model of equity volatility must be consistent with this finding.

The loglinear asset pricing framework of Campbell and Shiller (1988) and Campbell (1991) allows us to divide explanations for equity volatility into several categories. First, equity volatility might be caused by predictable variation in dividend growth (equivalent to predictable variation in consumption growth if equities are modeled as consumption claims, that is, as proxies for aggregate wealth). The empirical difficulty with this explanation is that stock prices are not good forecasters of consumption or dividend growth. There is also a theoretical difficulty that predictable variation in consumption growth should cause offsetting movements in real interest rates that dampen the effect on stock prices.

If equity volatility is not caused by predictable variation in cash flows, then it must be caused by variation in discount rates. The first and most obvious component of the equity discount rate is the riskless real interest rate. Although there is some variation in the real interest rate, unfortunately it is not large enough to cause big swings in the stock market, as pointed out by Campbell (1991). Also, the timing of real interest rate movements seems to be quite different from the timing of stock market movements. The 1970s, for example, saw low real rates and a depressed stock market, whereas the 1980s saw much higher real rates and a buoyant stock market. For this reason stock prices are not good forecasters of real interest rates (Campbell 2003).

The remaining component of the equity discount rate is the equity premium, the expected excess return on stocks over short-term debt. Stock market valuation ratios have historically predicted stock returns over long horizons, consistent with the view that stock market movements are driven by movements in the equity premium itself.

The equity premium can be thought of as volatility times the reward for bearing volatility, or the quantity of risk times the price of risk. Equity volatility does move over time, and does correlate positively with return forecasts, rising during recessions and stock market declines. However these movements of volatility are not proportional to movements in returns, as pointed out by Campbell (1987) and Harvey (1989). Thus we are forced inexorably to the conclusion that the price of risk itself must be moving over time. As stock prices tend to increase when the economy is strong and consumption is growing rapidly, the price of risk must be countercyclical, moving opposite to consumption growth. I now explore alternative structural models that can generate countercyclical time-variation in the price of risk.

One class of models works within a representative-investor framework and asks what preferences might generate countercyclical risk aversion. Models of habit formation, such as Constantinides (1990) and Campbell and Cochrane (1999), have this property, and I discuss these models in detail in the next section. Countercyclical risk aversion also arises naturally in behavioral finance models that combine the prospect theory of Kahneman and Tversky (1979) with the "house money effect" of Thaler and Johnson (1990), that is, the tendency of investors to worry less about losses that offset prior gains (Barberis, Huang, and Santos 2001).

A second class of models emphasizes the aggregation of heterogeneous agents. Each individual agent might have constant risk aversion, yet they might interact in such a way that the representative agent has time-varying risk aversion. Different models emphasize different types of heterogeneity. There might be heterogeneous constraints, so that some investors are constrained from stock market participation or are prevented from diversifying their stock portfolios (Constantinides, Donaldson, and Mehra 2002; Heaton and Lucas 1999; Vissing-Jorgensen 2002). A relaxation of such constraints allows equity risk to be shared more broadly, driving down the equilibrium price of risk. This story might explain a one-time decline in the equity premium in the late twentieth century, but is less suitable for explaining recurring cyclical variation in the price of risk.[12]

Investors might also have heterogeneous uninsurable labor income (Constantinides and Duffie 1996). Variation in the degree of idiosyncratic risk can cause a high and possibly time-varying equity premium. Heterogeneous risk aversion may also be important (Wang 1996; Chan and Kogan 2002). In this case high stock returns would tend to increase the

---

[12] Even on a one-time basis, it is hard to get large effects of expanding participation because new participants tend to be much poorer than old participants, so the wealth-weighted expansion in participation is relatively small.

wealth of risk-tolerant investors, increasing their weight in the aggregate and driving down the risk aversion of the representative investor.

A third class of models emphasizes irrational expectations on the part of at least some investors. Hansen, Sargent, and Tallarini (1999) have emphasized that pessimism about long-run growth prospects can explain both the equity premium and risk-free rate puzzles.[13] The extrapolation of shocks to growth rates ("irrational exuberance" if the shocks are positive and irrational gloom if they are negative) can generate a time-varying and countercyclical price of risk (Barsky and De Long 1993; Barberis, Shleifer, and Vishny 1998; Cecchetti, Lam, and Mark 2000; Shiller 2000).

3.1. Habit Formation

Sundaresan (1989) and Constantinides (1990) have argued for the importance of habit formation, a positive effect of today's consumption on tomorrow's marginal utility of consumption.

Two modeling issues arise at the outset. Writing the period utility function as $U(C_t, X_t)$, where X_t is the time-varying habit or subsistence level, the first issue is the functional form for U. Abel (1990) has proposed that U should be a power function of the ratio C_t/X_t, while most other researchers have used a power function of the difference $C_t - X_t$. The second issue is the effect of an agent's own decisions on future levels of habit. In standard "internal habit" models such as those in Constantinides (1990) and Sundaresan (1989), habit depends on an agent's own consumption and the agent takes account of this when choosing how much to consume. In "external habit" models such as those in Abel (1990) and Campbell and Cochrane (1999), habit depends on aggregate consumption that is unaffected by any one agent's decisions. Abel calls this "catching up with the Joneses." Similar results can be obtained in either class of model, but external habit models are generally easier to work with.

The choice between ratio models and difference models of habit is important because ratio models have constant risk aversion, whereas difference models have time-varying risk aversion. In Abel's (1990) ratio model, external habit adds a term to the equation describing the riskless interest rate, but does not change the equation that describes the excess return of risky assets over the riskless interest rate. The effect on the riskless interest rate has to do with intertemporal substitution. Holding

---

[13] This is similar to the peso problem story of Rietz (1988), except that investor fears are no longer required to be rational.

consumption today and expected consumption tomorrow constant, an increase in consumption yesterday increases the marginal utility of consumption today. This makes the representative agent want to borrow from the future, driving up the real interest rate.

This instability of the riskless real interest rate is a fundamental problem for habit formation models. Time-nonseparable preferences make marginal utility volatile even when consumption is smooth, because consumers derive utility from consumption relative to its recent history rather than from the absolute level of consumption. But unless the consumption and habit processes take particular forms, time-nonseparability also creates large swings in expected marginal utility at successive dates, and this implies large movements in the real interest rate. I now present an alternative specification in which it is possible to solve this problem, and in which risk aversion varies over time.

Campbell and Cochrane (1999) build a model with external habit formation in which a representative agent derives utility from the difference between consumption and a time-varying subsistence or habit level. They assume that log consumption follows a random walk with mean g and innovation ϵ_{t+1}. This is a fairly good approximation for U.S. data. The utility function of the representative agent is a time-separable power utility function, with curvature γ, of the difference between consumption C_t and habit X_t. Utility is only defined when consumption exceeds habit.

It is convenient to capture the relation between consumption and habit by the surplus consumption ratio S_t, defined by

$$S_t \equiv \frac{C_t - X_t}{C_t}. \tag{16}$$

The surplus consumption ratio is the fraction of consumption that exceeds habit and is therefore available to generate utility. The SDF in this model is given by

$$M_{t+1} = \delta \left(\frac{S_{t+1}}{S_t} \right)^{-\gamma} \left(\frac{C_{t+1}}{C_t} \right)^{-\gamma}. \tag{17}$$

The SDF is driven by proportional innovations in the surplus consumption ratio, as well as by proportional innovations in consumption. If the surplus consumption ratio is only a small fraction of consumption, then small shocks to consumption can be large shocks to the surplus consumption ratio; thus, the SDF can be highly volatile even when consumption is smooth.

Even more important, the volatility of the SDF is itself time-varying since it depends on the level of the surplus consumption ratio. Shocks to consumption have a larger proportional effect on S_t when S_t is small than when it is large:

$$\frac{C}{S}\frac{dS}{dC} = \frac{1-S}{S}. \tag{18}$$

Hence investors are more averse to consumption risk when S_t is small. If habit X_t is held fixed as consumption C_t varies, the local coefficient of relative risk aversion is

$$\frac{-CU_{cc}}{U_c} = \frac{\gamma}{S_t}, \tag{19}$$

where U_c and U_{cc} are the first and second derivatives of utility with respect to consumption. Risk aversion rises as the surplus consumption ratio S_t declines, that is, as consumption approaches the habit level. Note that γ, the curvature parameter in utility, is no longer the coefficient of relative risk aversion in this model.

To complete the description of preferences, one must specify how the habit X_t evolves over time in response to aggregate consumption. Campbell and Cochrane suggest an AR(1) model for the log surplus consumption ratio, $s_t \equiv \log(S_t)$:

$$s_{t+1} = (1 - \phi)\bar{s} + \phi s_t + \lambda(s_t)\,\epsilon_{t+1} \tag{20}$$

The parameter ϕ governs the persistence of the log surplus consumption ratio, while the "sensitivity function" $\lambda(s_t)$ controls the sensitivity of s_{t+1} and thus of log habit x_{t+1} to innovations in consumption growth ϵ_{t+1}. This modelling strategy ensures that the habit process implied by a process for s_{t+1} always lies below consumption.

The logic of Hansen and Jagannathan (1991) implies that the largest possible Sharpe ratio is given by the conditional standard deviation of the log SDF. This is proportional to $(1 + \lambda[s_t])$, so a sensitivity function that varies inversely with s_t delivers a time-varying, countercyclical Sharpe ratio.

The same mechanism helps to stabilize the riskless real interest rate. When the surplus consumption ratio falls, investors have an intertemporal-substitution motive to borrow from the future, but this is offset by an increased precautionary savings motive created by the volatility of the SDF. Campbell and Cochrane parameterize the model so that these two effects exactly cancel. This makes the riskless real interest rate constant, a knife-edge case that helps to reveal the pure effects of time-varying risk aversion on asset prices. With a constant riskless rate, real bonds of all maturities are also riskless and there are no real term premia. Thus the equity premium is also a premium of stocks over long-term bonds.

When this model is calibrated to fit the first two moments of consumption growth, the average riskless interest rate, and the Sharpe ratio on the stock market, it also roughly fits the volatility, predictability, and cyclicality of stock returns. The model does not resolve the equity premium puzzle, since it relies on high average risk aversion, but it does resolve the stock market volatility puzzle. The Campbell-Cochrane model assumes random walk consumption and implies negative autocorrelation of stock returns. The Constantinides (1990) model of habit formation, by contrast, assumes IID asset returns and implies positive autocorrelation of consumption growth. Thus these two models take different stands on the question of whether wealth or consumption accurately represents long-run risk. The Constantinides model fits the equity premium with low risk aversion, but it achieves this success at the cost of a positively serially correlated consumption process that contradicts the empirical findings of Lettau and Ludvigson (2001).

3.2. Heterogeneous Labor Income

The heterogeneity of utility-maximizing stock market investors may have important effects. For example, if investors are subject to large idiosyncratic risks in their labor income and can share these risks only indirectly by trading a few assets such as stocks and Treasury bills, their individual consumption paths may be much more volatile than aggregate consumption. Even if individual investors have the same power utility function, so that any individual's consumption growth rate raised to the power $-\gamma$ would be a valid SDF, the aggregate consumption growth rate raised to the power $-\gamma$ may not be a valid SDF.

This problem is an example of Jensen's Inequality. Since marginal utility is nonlinear, the average of investors' marginal utilities of consumption is not generally the same as the marginal utility of average consumption. The problem disappears when investors' individual consumption streams are perfectly correlated with one another, as they will be in a complete markets setting. Grossman and Shiller (1982) point out that it also disappears in a continuous-time model when the processes for individual consumption streams and asset prices are diffusions.

Constantinides and Duffie (1996) have provided a simple framework within which the effects of heterogeneity can be understood. Constantinides and Duffie postulate an economy in which individual investors k have different consumption levels C_{kt}. The cross-sectional distribution of individual consumption is lognormal, and the change from time t to time $t + 1$ in individual log consumption is cross-sectionally uncorrelated with the level of individual log consumption at time t. All investors have the same power utility function with time discount factor δ and coefficient of relative risk aversion γ.

In this economy each investor's own intertemporal marginal rate of substitution is a valid SDF. Hence the cross-sectional average of investors' intertemporal marginal rates of substitution is a valid SDF, I write this as

$$M_{t+1}^* \equiv \delta E_{t+1}^* \left[\left(\frac{C_{k,t+1}}{C_{kt}} \right)^{-\gamma} \right], \tag{21}$$

where E_t^* denotes an expectation taken over the cross-sectional distribution at time t. That is, for any cross-sectionally random variable X_{kt}, $E_t^* X_{kt} \equiv \lim_{k \to \infty} (1/K) \sum_{k=1}^K X_{kt}$, the limit as the number of cross-sectional units increases of the cross-sectional sample average of X_{kt}. Note that $E_t^* X_{kt}$ will in general vary over time and need not be lognormally distributed conditional on past information.

An economist who knows the underlying preference parameters of investors but does not understand the heterogeneity in this economy might attempt to construct a representative-agent SDF, M_{t+1}^{RA}, using aggregate consumption:

$$M_{t+1}^{RA} \equiv \delta \left(\frac{E_{t+1}^*[C_{k,t+1}]}{E_t^*[C_{kt}]} \right)^{-\gamma}. \tag{22}$$

Using the assumptions on the cross-sectional distribution of consumption, the difference between the valid log SDF m_{t+1}^* and the invalid log representative-agent SDF m_{t+1}^{RA} can be written as

$$m_{t+1}^* - m_{t+1}^{RA} = \frac{\gamma(\gamma + 1)}{2} Var_{t+1}^* \Delta c_{k,t+1}, \tag{23}$$

where Var_{t+1}^* is defined analogously to E_t^* as $Var_t^* X_{kt} = \lim_{k \to \infty} (1/K)$ $\sum_{k=1}^K (X_{kt} - E_t^* X_{kt})^2$, and like E_t^* will in general vary over time.

The time series of this difference can have a nonzero mean, helping to explain the risk-free rate puzzle, and a nonzero variance, helping to explain the equity premium puzzle. If the cross-sectional variance of log consumption growth is negatively correlated with the level of aggregate consumption, so that idiosyncratic risk increases in economic downturns, then the true SDF m^*_{t+1} will be more strongly countercyclical than the representative-agent SDF constructed using the same preference parameters; this has the potential to explain the high price of risk without assuming that individual investors have high risk aversion. Mankiw (1986) makes a similar point in a two-period model. It is also possible that the correlation between idiosyncratic risk and aggregate consumption itself moves over time in such a way that the price of risk is time-varying.

An important unresolved question is whether the heterogeneity we can measure has the characteristics that are needed to help resolve the asset pricing puzzles. In the Constantinides-Duffie model the heterogeneity must be large to have important effects on the SDF; a cross-sectional standard deviation of log consumption growth of 20 percent, for example, is a cross-sectional variance of only 0.04, and it is variation in this number over time that is needed to explain the equity premium puzzle. Interestingly, the effect of heterogeneity is strongly increasing in risk aversion since $Var^*_{t+1}\Delta c_{k,t+1}$ is multiplied by $\gamma(\gamma + 1)/2$ in (23). This suggests that heterogeneity may supplement high risk aversion, but cannot altogether replace it as an explanation for the equity premium puzzle.

Cogley (1998) looks at consumption data and finds that measured heterogeneity has only small effects on the SDF. Lettau (2002) reaches a similar conclusion by assuming that individuals consume their income, and calculating the risk aversion coefficients needed to put model-based SDFs inside the Hansen-Jagannathan volatility bounds. This procedure is conservative in that individuals trading in financial markets are normally able to achieve some smoothing of consumption relative to income. Nevertheless, Lettau finds that high individual risk aversion is still needed to satisfy the Hansen-Jagannathan bounds.

These conclusions may not be surprising given the Grossman-Shiller (1982) result that the aggregation problem disappears in a continuous-time diffusion model. In such a model, the cross-sectional variance of consumption is locally deterministic and hence the false SDF M^{RA}_{t+1} correctly fits risk premia. In a discrete-time model, the cross-sectional variance of consumption can change randomly from one period to the next, but in practice these changes are likely to be small. This limits the effects of consumption heterogeneity on asset pricing.

It is also important to note that idiosyncratic shocks are assumed to be permanent in the Constantinides-Duffie model. Heaton and Lucas (1996) calibrate individual income processes to micro data from the Panel Study of Income Dynamics (PSID). Because the PSID data show that idiosyncratic income variation is largely transitory, Heaton and Lucas find that investors can minimize its effects on their consumption by borrowing and lending. This prevents heterogeneity from having any large effects on aggregate asset prices.

To get around this problem, several recent papers have combined heterogeneity with constraints on borrowing. Heaton and Lucas (1996) and Krusell and Smith (1997) find that borrowing constraints or large costs of trading equities are needed to explain the equity premium. Constantinides, Donaldson, and Mehra (2002) focus on heterogeneity across generations. In a stylized three-period overlapping generations model, young agents have the strongest desire to hold equities because they have the largest ratio of labor income to financial wealth. If these agents are prevented from borrowing to buy equities, the equilibrium equity premium is large.

Heterogeneity in preferences may also be important. Several authors have recently argued that trading between investors with different degrees of risk aversion or time preference, possibly in the presence of market frictions or portfolio insurance constraints, can lead to time-variation in the market price of risk (Dumas 1989; Grossman and Zhou 1996; Wang 1996; Chan and Kogan 2002). Intuitively, risk-tolerant agents hold more risky assets so they control a greater share of wealth in good states than in bad states; aggregate risk aversion therefore falls in good states, producing effects similar to those of habit formation.

3.3. Irrational Expectations

A number of papers have explored the consequences of relaxing the assumption that investors have rational expectations and understand the behavior of dividend and consumption growth. In the absence of arbitrage, there exist positive state prices that can rationalize the prices of traded financial assets. These state prices equal subjective state probabilities multiplied by ratios of marginal utilities in different states. Thus given any model of utility, there exist subjective probabilities that produce the necessary state prices and in this sense explain the observed prices of traded financial assets. The interesting question is whether these subjective probabilities are sufficiently close to objective probabilities, and sufficiently related to known psychological biases in behavior, to be plausible.

Many of the papers in this area work in partial equilibrium and assume that stocks are priced by discounting expected future dividends at a constant rate. This assumption makes it easy to derive any desired behavior of stock prices directly from assumptions on dividend expectations. Barsky and De Long (1993), for example, assume that investors believe dividends to be generated by a doubly integrated process, so that the dividend growth rate has a unit root. These expectations imply that rapid dividend growth increases stock prices more than proportionally, so that the price-dividend ratio rises when dividends are growing strongly. If dividend growth is in fact stationary, then the high price-dividend ratio is typically followed by dividend disappointments, low stock returns, and reversion to the long-run mean price-dividend ratio. Under this assumption of stationary dividend growth, Barsky and DeLong's model produces overreaction of stock prices to dividend news, and this accounts for the equity volatility puzzle and the predictability of stock returns.[14]

Another potentially important form of irrationality is a failure to understand the difference between real and nominal magnitudes. Modigliani and Cohn (1979) argued that investors suffer from inflation illusion, in effect discounting real cash flows at nominal interest rates. Ritter and Warr (2002) and Sharpe (1999) argue that inflation illusion may have led investors to bid up stock prices, as inflation has declined since the early 1980s. An interesting issue raised by this literature is whether misvaluation is caused by a high *level* of inflation (in which case it is unlikely to be important today) or whether it is caused by *changes* in inflation from historical benchmark levels (in which case it may contribute to high current levels of stock prices).

A limitation of these models is that they do not consider general equilibrium issues, in particular the implication of irrational beliefs for aggregate consumption. Using for simplicity the fiction that dividends equal consumption, investors' irrational expectations about dividend growth should be linked to their irrational expectations about consumption growth. Interest rates are not exogenous, but like stock prices, are determined by investors' expectations. Thus it is significantly harder to build a general equilibrium model with irrational expectations.

---

[14] Shiller (2000) discusses psychological factors that contribute to the formation of extrapolative expectations, with special reference to the runup in stock prices during the 1990s. Barberis, Shleifer, and Vishny (1998) present a related model.

To see how irrationality can affect asset prices in general equilibrium, consider first a static model in which log consumption follows a random walk with drift. Investors understand that consumption is a random walk, but they underestimate its drift. Such irrational pessimism lowers the average risk-free rate, increases the equity premium, and has an ambiguous effect on the price-dividend ratio. Thus pessimism has the same effects on asset prices as a low rate of time preference and a high coefficient of risk aversion, and it can help to explain both the risk-free rate puzzle and the equity premium puzzle (Hansen, Sargent, and Tallarini 1999).

To explain the volatility puzzle, a more complicated model of irrationality is needed. Suppose now that log consumption growth follows an AR(1) process, but that investors overestimate the persistence of this process. In this model the equity premium falls when consumption growth has been rapid, and rises when consumption growth has been weak. This model, which can be seen as a general equilibrium version of Barsky and De Long (1993) or Shiller (2000), fits the apparent cyclical variation in the market price of risk. One difficulty with this story is that it has strong implications for bond market behavior. When investors become irrationally exuberant, their optimism should lead to a strong desire to borrow from the future, which should drive up the riskless interest rate even while it drives down the equity premium. Cecchetti, Lam, and Mark (2000) handle this problem by allowing the degree of investors' irrationality itself to be stochastic and time-varying.

4. IMPLICATIONS FOR PORTFOLIO CHOICE

I have argued that the price of risk is time-varying. It follows that a rational investor, who lives entirely off financial wealth without idiosyncratic labor income, must have time-varying risk aversion in order to buy and hold an aggregate equity index. This leads naturally to the question, what should a rational investor do if he or she lives off financial wealth and has constant risk aversion?

This topic of portfolio choice is the original subject of modern financial economics. Mean-variance analysis, developed almost fifty years ago by Markowitz (1952), has provided a basic paradigm for portfolio choice. This approach usefully emphasizes the ability of diversification to reduce risk, but it ignores several critically important factors. Most notably, the analysis is static; it assumes that investors care only about risks to wealth one period ahead. However many investors, both individuals and institutions such as charitable foundations or universities, seek to finance a stream of consumption over a long lifetime.

Merton (1969, 1971, 1973) showed thirty years ago that the solution to a long-term portfolio choice problem can be very different from the solution to a short-term problem. In particular, if investment opportunities are varying over time, then long-term investors care about shocks to investment opportunities – the productivity of wealth – as well as shocks to wealth itself. They may seek to hedge their exposures to wealth productivity shocks, and this gives rise to intertemporal hedging demands for financial assets. Brennan, Schwartz, and Lagnado (1997) have coined the phrase "strategic asset allocation" to describe this far-sighted response to time-varying investment opportunities.

Unfortunately Merton's intertemporal model is hard to solve. Until recently solutions to the model were only available in those trivial cases where it reduces to the static model. Therefore the Merton model has not become a usable empirical paradigm, has not displaced the Markowitz model, and has had only limited influence on investment practice. Recently this situation has begun to change as a result of advances in both analytical and numerical methods. A new empirical paradigm is emerging. Interestingly, this paradigm both supports and qualifies traditional rules of thumb used by financial planners. Campbell and Viceira (1999, 2001, 2002) present an integrated empirical approach to the recent portfolio choice literature.

Time-variation of the equity premium has two effects on optimal portfolio choice for investors with constant risk aversion. First, it implies that investors should "time the market," increasing their equity allocations at times when the equity premium is high and reducing them at times when the equity premium is low.[15]

A second effect on portfolio choice arises from the fact that the equity premium tends to fall when stock prices rise, because valuation ratios such as D/P move inversely with prices. This implies mean-reversion in stock returns, that is, a tendency for the annualized volatility of returns to fall with the investment horizon. Direct evidence for reduction in volatility at long horizons is presented by Siegel (1998). Campbell and Viceira (2002) use a simple time-series model, related to the evidence presented

---

[15] Note that these adjustments take place gradually, since the variables that predict the equity premium move relatively slowly. Thus they are nothing like the rapid moves that are sometimes recommended by commercial market timing or tactical asset allocation models.

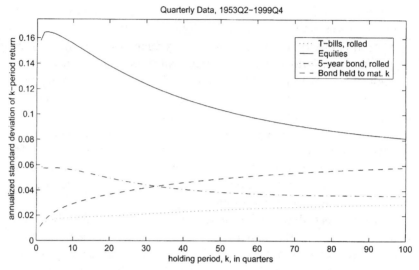

Figure 2. Asset risk in relation to holding period, postwar quarterly data.

earlier on stock return predictability, to generate implied volatilities of returns on stocks, bonds, and Treasury bills at all horizons. Their results are summarized graphically in Figures 2 and 3 for quarterly postwar and long-term annual U.S. data. In both data sets equity volatility is in the range 16 percent to 18 percent over one year, but it falls to 9 percent in the quarterly data and 13 percent in the annual data over longer holding periods. The volatility of Treasury bill investments, by contrast, increases with the holding period because real interest rates vary over time in a persistent fashion.

Mean-reversion in stock returns creates a horizon effect on portfolio choice: Long-term investors may invest differently from short-term investors. The reduction in long-term stock market risk is directly relevant for long-term buy-and-hold investors (Barberis 2000). These investors will increase their equity holdings, relative to the holdings of otherwise identical short-term investors, because they perceive equities as having lower risk.

Long-term investors who can rebalance their portfolios each period have intertemporal hedging demand (Merton 1973). They may wish to hedge the risk that future investment opportunities will deteriorate. If their risk aversion is greater than one, they wish to hold assets that increase in value when investment opportunities deteriorate. The most obvious example of such an asset is an inflation-indexed bond, whose value increases when real interest rates fall. But stocks also have this property,

Annual Data, 1892–1998

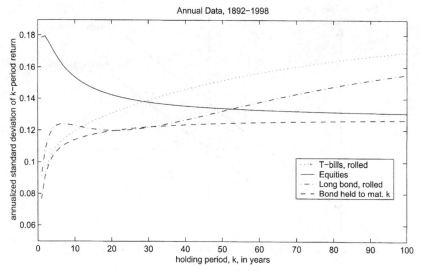

Figure 3. Asset risk in relation to holding period, long-term annual data.

because an increase in stock prices signals a decrease in future stock returns and thus a deterioration in investment opportunities (Campbell and Viceira 1999).

Figure 4 illustrates alternative portfolio rules. The horizontal axis shows the equity premium, with its long-run average marked by a vertical dashed line. In the presence of mean-reversion, the equity premium will fall if stock prices have risen (one will move to the left in the diagram) and will rise if stock prices have fallen (one will move to the right). The vertical axis shows the portfolio allocation to stocks, assuming that the alternative is to hold cash at a constant riskless interest rate and that there are no constraints on leverage or short sales.

The three lines in the figure are three alternative portfolio rules. The horizontal line marked "Myopic Investor" is the traditional buy-and-hold allocation that would come out of a single-period mean-variance analysis, ignoring time-variation in the equity premium. The sloped line marked "Tactical Investor" is the allocation that would be recommended by single-period mean-variance analysis that takes account of time-variation in the equity premium, in the manner of commercial tactical asset allocation strategies. This line passes through the origin, because an equity premium of zero would imply zero allocation to stocks. The sloped line marked "Strategic Investor" is the optimal portfolio rule derived by Campbell and Viceira (1999) for long-term investors with constant

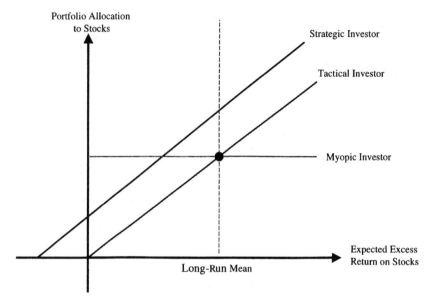

Figure 4. Alternative portfolio allocation values.

relative risk aversion greater than one. It has almost the same slope as the tactical portfolio rule (if anything it is slightly steeper), but it is shifted upward by positive intertemporal hedging demand. A strategic investor should hold some equities even if the equity premium temporarily dips to zero, in order to hedge against further deterioration in investment opportunities.

It is interesting to relate these results to recent discussions of stock market risk. Equities have traditionally been regarded as risky assets. They may be attractive because of their high average returns, but these returns represent compensation for risk; thus, equities should be treated with caution by all but the most aggressive investors. In recent years, however, authors such as Siegel (1998) and Glassman and Hassett (1999) have argued that equities are actually relatively safe assets for investors who are able to hold for the long term.

The revisionist view that stocks are safe assets is based on the evidence that excess stock returns are less volatile when they are measured over long holding periods. Mathematically, such a reduction in stock market risk at long horizons can only be due to mean-reversion in excess stock returns, which is equivalent to time-variation in the equity premium. Yet revisionist investment advice typically ignores the implications of a time-varying equity premium. Siegel (1998) recommends an aggressive buy-and-hold strategy, like the horizontal line in Figure 4 but shifted upward to reflect the reduced risk of stocks for long-term investors. The optimal policy is instead the sloped line marked "Strategic Investor" in Figure 4.

The difference between the optimal strategy and the strategy recommended by Siegel is particularly dramatic in the aftermath of a bull market in equities. At such a time, the optimal equity allocation may be no higher – it may even be lower – than the allocation implied by a traditional short-term portfolio analysis. To put it another way, investors who are attracted to the stock market by the prospect of high returns combined with low long-term risk are trying to have their cake and eat it too. If expected stock returns are constant over time, then one can hope to earn high stock returns in the future similar to the high returns of the past; but in this case stocks are much riskier than bonds in the long term, just as they are in the short term. If instead stocks mean-revert, then they are relatively safe assets for long-term investors; but in this case future returns are likely to be meagre as mean-reversion unwinds the spectacular stock market runup of the last two decades of the twentieth century.

It is important to keep in mind two limitations of this portfolio analysis. First, it ignores constraints that might prevent investors from short-selling or from borrowing to invest in risky assets. The Siegel strategy of buying and holding stocks might be much closer to optimal for an aggressive investor who cannot borrow to leverage a stock market position, and who therefore normally holds the maximum 100 percent weight in equities.

Second, I have solved the microeconomic portfolio choice problem of a rational investor with constant relative risk aversion and no human wealth, but such an investor cannot be the representative investor. As I discussed earlier on, the representative investor must have different preferences, constraints, or beliefs in order to be content to hold the aggregate wealth portfolio. Thus, the portfolio advice of Figure 4 can only be used by atypical investors.

5. CONCLUSION

In this essay I have described two puzzles of asset pricing, the equity premium puzzle and the equity volatility puzzle. The equity premium puzzle may in the end be explained by a combination of factors, including both high risk aversion of investors and unexpectedly high returns in the late twentieth century (possibly caused by a one-time correction of historical equity mispricing). The equity volatility puzzle is more fundamental. The data suggest that historical variations in stock prices have been driven primarily by changes in expected stock returns, rather than changes in expected future dividends.

In the second part of this essay I have argued that the stock market moves as if risk aversion is volatile and countercyclical. This behavior could be caused by habit formation, countercyclical idiosyncratic labor income risk, heterogeneity in risk aversion, or irrational expectations.

These findings have interesting implications for the optimal portfolio choice of investors with constant risk aversion and no labor income risk. Such investors should invest more aggressively when consumption and stock prices are low than when they are high. Also, long-term investors with constant risk aversion greater than one should invest more aggressively on average than short-term investors with the same risk aversion. This last result supports the view, sometimes expressed by financial planners, that investors can afford to take greater stock market risk if they have a long investment horizon.

REFERENCES

Abel, Andrew B. 1990. "Asset Prices under Habit Formation and Catching Up with the Joneses," *American Economic Review Papers and Proceedings* 80, 38–42.

Abel, Andrew B. 1999. "Risk Premia and Term Premia in General Equilibrium," *Journal of Monetary Economics* 43, 3–33.

Abel, Andrew B., M. Gregory Mankiw, Lawrence H. Summers, and Richard J. Zeckhauser. 1989. "Assessing Dynamic Efficiency: Theory and Evidence," *Review of Economic Studies* 56, 1–20.

Barberis, Nicholas. 2000. "Investing for the Long Run When Returns Are Predictable," *Journal of Finance* 55, 225–64.

Barberis, Nicholas, Ming Huang, and Tano Santos. 2001. "Prospect Theory and Asset Prices," *Quarterly Journal of Economics* 116, 1–53.

Barberis, Nicholas, Andrei Shleifer, and Robert Vishny. 1998. "A Model of Investor Sentiment," *Journal of Financial Economics* 49, 307–43.

Barsky, Robert B. and J. Bradford De Long. 1993. "Why Does the Stock Market Fluctuate?" *Quarterly Journal of Economics* 107, 291–311.

Bernstein, Peter. 1996. *Against the Gods: The Remarkable Story of Risk.* Wiley.

Blanchard, Olivier J. and Mark Watson. 1982. "Bubbles, Rational Expectations, and Financial Markets." In *Crises in the Economic and Financial Structure: Bubbles, Bursts, and Shocks,* edited by P. Wachtel. Lexington, MA: Lexington.

Breeden, Douglas T. 1979. "An Intertemporal Asset Pricing Model with Stochastic Consumption and Investment Opportunities," *Journal of Financial Economics* 7, 265–96.

Brennan, Michael J., Eduardo S. Schwartz, and Ronald Lagnado. 1997. "Strategic Asset Allocation," *Journal of Economic Dynamics and Control* 21, 1377–1403.

Campbell, John Y. 1987. "Stock Returns and the Term Structure," *Journal of Financial Economics* 18, 373–99.

Campbell, John Y. 1991. "A Variance Decomposition for Stock Returns," *Economic Journal* 101, 157–79.

Campbell, John Y. 1996. "Understanding Risk and Return," *Journal of Political Economy* 104, 298–345.

Campbell, John Y. 1999. "Asset Prices, Consumption, and the Business Cycle." Chapter 19 in *Handbook of Macroeconomics Vol. 1*, 1231–1303, edited by John Taylor and Michael Woodford. Amsterdam: North-Holland.

Campbell, John Y. 2000. "Asset Pricing at the Millennium," *Journal of Finance* 55, 1515–67.

Campbell, John Y. 2003. "Consumption-Based Asset Pricing." Chapter 13 in *Handbook of the Economics of Finance* 801–885, edited by George Constantinides, Milton Harris, and Rene Stulz. Amsterdam: North-Holland.

Campbell, John Y. and John H. Cochrane. 1999. "By Force of Habit: A Consumption-Based Explanation of Aggregate Stock Market Behavior," *Journal of Political Economy* 107, 205–51.

Campbell, John Y. and N. Gregory Mankiw. 1989. "Consumption, Income, and Interest Rates: Reinterpreting the Time Series Evidence." In Olivier J. Blanchard and Stanley Fischer, eds., *National Bureau of Economic Research Macroeconomics Annual* 4, 185–216.

Campbell, John Y. and Robert J. Shiller. 1988. "The Dividend-Price Ratio and Expectations of Future Dividends and Discount Factors," *Review of Financial Studies* 1, 195–228.

Campbell, John Y. and Robert J. Shiller. 2003. "Valuation Ratios and the Long-Run Stock Market Outlook: An Update." Forthcoming in *Advances in Behavioral Finance, Vol. II*, edited by Richard Thaler. Russell Sage Foundation.

Campbell, John Y. and Luis M. Viceira. 1999. "Consumption and Portfolio Decisions When Expected Returns Are Time Varying," *Quarterly Journal of Economics* 114, 433–95.

Campbell, John Y. and Luis M. Viceira. 2001. "Who Should Buy Long-Term Bonds?" *American Economic Review* 91, 99–127.

Campbell, John Y. and Luis M. Viceira. 2002. *Strategic Asset Allocation: Portfolio Choice for Long-Term Investors.* Oxford: Oxford University Press.

Campbell, John Y. and Motohiro Yogo. 2002. "Efficient Tests of Stock Return Predictability," unpublished paper, Harvard University.

Cecchetti, Stephen G., Pok-sang Lam, and Nelson C. Mark. 1993. "The Equity Premium and the Risk-Free Rate: Matching the Moments," *Journal of Monetary Economics* 31, 21–45.

Cecchetti, Stephen G, Pok-sang Lam, and Nelson C. Mark. 2000. "Asset Pricing with Distorted Beliefs: Are Equity Returns Too Good to Be True?" *American Economic Review* 90, 787–805.

Chan, Y. Lewis and Leonid Kogan. 2002. "Catching Up with the Joneses: Heterogeneous Preferences and the Dynamics of Asset Prices," *Journal of Political Economy* 110, 1255–85.

Cochrane, John H. 2001. *Asset Pricing*. Princeton, NJ: Princeton University Press.

Cogley, Timothy. 1998. "Idiosyncratic Risk and the Equity Premium: Evidence from the Consumer Expenditure Survey," working paper, Federal Reserve Bank of San Francisco.

Constantinides, George M. 1990. "Habit Formation: Resolution of the Equity Premium Puzzle," *Journal of Political Economy* 98, 519–43.

Constantinides, George M., John B. Donaldson, and Rajnish Mehra. 2002. "Junior Can't Borrow: A New Perspective on the Equity Premium Puzzle," *Quarterly Journal of Economics* 117, 269–96.

Constantinides, George M. and Darrell Duffie. 1996. "Asset Pricing with Heterogeneous Consumers," *Journal of Political Economy* 104, 219–40.

Dimson, Elroy, Paul Marsh, and Mike Staunton. 2002. *Triumph of the Optimists*. Princeton, NJ: Princeton University Press.

Dumas, Bernard. 1989. "Two-Person Dynamic Equilibrium in the Capital Market, *Review of Financial Studies* 2, 157–88.

Epstein, Lawrence and Stanley Zin. 1991. "Substitution, Risk Aversion, and the Temporal Behavior of Consumption and Asset Returns: An Empirical Investigation," *Journal of Political Economy* 99, 263–86.

Fama, Eugene and Kenneth R. French. 2002. "The Equity Premium," *Journal of Finance* 57, 637–59.

Glassman, James K. and Kevin A. Hassett. 1999. *Dow 36,000*. New York: Times Books.

Gordon, Myron. 1962. *The Investment, Financing, and Valuation of the Corporation*. Homewood, IL: Irwin.

Graham, Benjamin and David L. Dodd. 1934. *Security Analysis*. New York: McGraw-Hill.

Grossman, Sanford J. and Robert J. Shiller. 1981. "The Determinants of the Variability of Stock Market Prices," *American Economic Review* 71, 222–7.

Grossman, Sanford J. and Robert J. Shiller. 1982. "Consumption Correlatedness and Risk Measurement in Economies with Non-Traded Assets and Heterogeneous Information," *Journal of Financial Economics* 10, 195–210.

Grossman, Sanford J. and Z. Zhou. 1996. "Equilibrium Analysis of Portfolio Insurance," *Journal of Finance* 51, 1379–1403.

Hall, Robert E. 1988. "Intertemporal Substitution in Consumption," *Journal of Political Economy* 96, 221–73.

Hamilton, James D. 1989. "A New Approach to the Analysis of Nonstationary Returns and the Business Cycle," *Econometrica* 57, 357–84.

Hansen, Lars P. and Ravi Jagannathan. 1991. "Restrictions on Intertemporal Marginal Rates of Substitution Implied by Asset Returns," *Journal of Political Economy* 99, 225–62.

Hansen, Lars P., Thomas J. Sargent, and Thomas Tallarini. 1999. "Robust Permanent Income and Pricing," *Review of Economic Studies* 66, 873–907.

Harvey, Campbell R. 1989. "Time-Varying Conditional Covariances in Tests of Asset Pricing Models," *Journal of Financial Economics* 24, 289–317.

Heaton, John and Deborah Lucas. 1996. "Evaluating the Effects of Incomplete Markets on Risk Sharing and Asset Pricing," *Journal of Political Economy* 104, 668–712.

Heaton, John and Deborah Lucas. 1999. "Stock Prices and Fundamentals," *NBER Macroeconomics Annual* 213–42. Cambridge, MA: MIT Press.

Jagannathan, Ravi, Ellen R. McGrattan, and Anna Scherbina. 2000. "The Declining U.S. Equity Premium," *Federal Reserve Bank of Minneapolis Quarterly Review* 24(4), 3–19.

Jorion, Philippe and William N. Goetzmann. 1999. "Global Stock Markets in the Twentieth Century," *Journal of Finance* 54, 953–80.

Kandel, Shmuel and Robert F. Stambaugh. 1991. "Asset Returns and Intertemporal Preferences," *Journal of Monetary Economics* 27, 39–71.

Kocherlakota, Narayana. 1996. "The Equity Premium: It's Still A Puzzle," *Journal of Economic Literature* 34, 42–71.

Krusell, Per and A. A. Smith, Jr. 1997. "Income and Wealth Heterogeneity, Portfolio Choice, and Equilibrium Asset Returns," *Macroeconomic Dynamics* 1, 387–422.

Lettau, Martin. 2002. "Idiosyncratic Risk and Volatility Bounds, or Can Models with Idiosyncratic Risk Solve the Equity Premium Puzzle?" *Review of Economics and Statistics* 84, 376–80.

Lettau, Martin and Sydney Ludvigson. 2001. "Consumption, Aggregate Wealth, and Expected Stock Returns," *Journal of Finance* 56, 815–49.

Lewellen, Jonathan. 2003. "Predicting Returns with Financial Ratios," Aug 2002, *Journal of Financial Economics*.

Lucas, Robert E. Jr. 1978. "Asset Prices in an Exchange Economy," *Econometrica* 46, 1429–46.

Mankiw, N. Gregory. 1986. "The Equity Premium and the Concentration of Aggregate Shocks," *Journal of Financial Economics* 17, 211–19.

Markowitz, Harry. 1952. "Portfolio Selection," *Journal of Finance* 7, 77–91.

McGrattan, Ellen R., and Edward C. Prescott. 2000. "Is the Stock Market Overvalued?" *Federal Reserve Bank of Minneapolis Quarterly Review* 24(4), 20–40.

Mehra, Rajnish and Edward C. Prescott. 1985. "The Equity Premium: A Puzzle," *Journal of Monetary Economics* 15, 145–61.

Merton, Robert C. 1969. "Lifetime Portfolio Selection under Uncertainty: The Continuous Time Case," *Review of Economics and Statistics* 51, 247–57.

Merton, Robert C. 1971. "Optimum Consumption and Portfolio Rules in a Continuous-Time Model," *Journal of Economic Theory* 3, 373–413.

Merton, Robert C. 1973. "An Intertemporal Capital Asset Pricing Model," *Econometrica* 41, 867–87.

Modigliani, Franco and Richard A. Cohn. 1979. "Inflation and the Stock Market," *Financial Analysts Journal* 35, 24–44.

Rietz, Thomas. 1988. "The Equity Premium Puzzle: A Solution?" *Journal of Monetary Economics* 21, 117–32.

Ritter, Jay R. and Richard S. Warr. 2002. "The Decline of Inflation and the Bull Market of 1982 to 1997," *Journal of Financial and Quantitative Analysis* 37, 29–61.

Rubinstein, Mark. 1976. "The Valuation of Uncertain Income Streams and the Pricing of Options," *Bell Journal of Economics* 7, 407–25.

Santos, Manuel S. and Michael Woodford. 1997. "Rational Asset Pricing Bubbles," *Econometrica* 65, 19–57.

Sharpe, Steven A. 1999. "Reexamining Stock Valuation and Inflation: The Implications of Analysts' Earnings Forecasts," *Review of Economics and Statistics* 84, 632–48.

Shiller, Robert J. 1981. "Do Stock Prices Move Too Much to Be Justified by Subsequent Changes in Dividends?" *American Economic Review* 71, 421–36.

Shiller, Robert J. 1982. "Consumption, Asset Markets, and Macroeconomic Fluctuations," *Carnegie-Rochester Conference Series on Public Policy* 17, 203–38.

Shiller, Robert J. 2000. *Irrational Exuberance*. Princeton, NJ: Princeton University Press.

Siegel, Jeremy. 1998. *Stocks for the Long Run*, 2nd ed. New York: McGraw-Hill.

Sundaresan, Suresh M. 1989. "Intertemporally Dependent Preferences and the Volatility of Consumption and Wealth," *Review of Financial Studies* 2, 73–88.

Thaler, Richard H. and Eric J. Johnson. 1990. "Gambling with the House Money and Trying to Break Even: The Effects of Prior Outcomes on Risky Choice," *Management Science* 36, 643–60.

Tirole, Jean. 1985. "Asset Bubbles and Overlapping Generations," *Econometrica* 53, 1499–1527.

Vissing-Jorgensen, Annette. 2002. "Limited Stock Market Participation and the Elasticity of Intertemporat Substitution," *Journal of Political Economy* 110, 825–53.

Wang, Jiang. 1996. "The Term Structure of Interest Rates in a Pure Exchange Economy with Heterogeneous Investors," *Journal of Financial Economics* 41, 75–110.

Weil, Philippe. 1989. "The Equity Premium Puzzle and the Risk-Free Rate Puzzle," *Journal of Monetary Economics* 24, 401–21.

Williams, John Burr. 1938. *The Theory of Investment Value*. Cambridge, MA: Harvard University Press.

PART II

MACROECONOMICS AND PUBLIC POLICIES

5

Whither Macro?

Perry Mehrling

I

When I first began serious study of macroeconomics, twenty years ago at the London School of Economics, the field was in serious disarray. (Me being who I was, that was part of the attraction.) The Keynesian consensus of the 1960s was long gone, eroded equally by pressure from inside and from outside academia. Inside, the New Classical alternative of Robert E. Lucas and his collaborators had already replaced Milton Friedman's loyal monetarist opposition as the most significant challenger, and the Real Business Cycle initiative of Ed Prescott and others was in the air. Outside, the dismal economic performance of the 1970s had eroded confidence that economists knew how the economy worked, much less how to employ available policy tools to make it work better. Unthinkably drastic measures were being undertaken (Paul Volcker's tight money disinflation in the United States, and Margaret Thatcher's attempt to dismantle the welfare state in Britain), and no one knew how it would all turn out.

Twenty years later, the field has been put back in some order. There is, we are told, a central "core of usable macroeconomics" (Solow 1997), consisting of an updated version of the Hicksian IS-LM as a model of demand-driven business fluctuation. This central core is apparently most firmly embraced by those academics who have the most regular interactions with the practical worlds of government and business. In notable contrast, *The Handbook of Macroeconomics*, produced for a more narrowly academic target audience, is more cautious: "the area of common ground is considerable, though we cannot yet announce a 'new synthesis' that could be endorsed by most scholars working in the field" (Taylor and Woodford 1999, xi).[1] One suspects that the current practical consensus owes more than a little to the 1990s expansion, much as the previous disarray owed a lot to the 1970s slump, but the contrast is nonetheless striking.

Some have gone so far as to claim that the emerging new consensus is just a more analytically solid version of the old consensus (Mankiw and Romer 1991, 15), but this goes too far. The shift from fiscal to monetary policy as the preferred tool for economic stabilization is one measure of the distance we have traveled. Another measure is the shift from optimism to pessimism about the degree of stabilization we can reasonably hope to achieve. But even these measures underestimate. What is most remarkable about the current consensus is not how different it is from the consensus during the heyday of Keynesianism, but rather how similar it is to the pre-Keynesian central banker's view of the world. The core of modern usable macroeconomics would, I think, have been recognizable to a man like Ralph Hawtrey, whose *Currency and Credit* (1919) sought to theorize the role of monetary policy for his own times.

This is a strong claim, and not very obviously supportable, if only because Hawtrey was writing about a gold standard world very different from our own. But was Hawtrey's world actually so different? Certainly so if the standard of comparison is the immediate postwar period, a time of separate nation states, largely unintegrated into any larger world commercial system, and still suffering the legacy of Depression and World War. But if we move the clock forward, and especially if we project into the future the evident trends toward globalization and market integration, then Hawtrey's world is not so obviously different. Nor is Hawtrey's economics so obviously different from the current consensus, once we look at the details. Let's look at the details.

Current practical consensus has converged on "inflation targeting" as the appropriate long-run goal for monetary policy, and on the Federal Funds rate of interest (not the money supply) as the appropriate instrument for achieving that and other short-run policy goals (McCallum 1999; Bernanke 1999). The consensus is organized around the empirical success of the Taylor Rule equation for fitting aggregate data:

$$R_t = a + b(\pi_t - \pi^*) + c(y_t - y^*),$$

---

[1] A technically gentler introduction to the range of views in modern macroeconomics can be obtained from Snowdon and Vane (1999) and Ibanez (1999). See also Backhouse and Salanti (1999) and Goodfriend and King (1997).

where R_t is the rate of interest, π_t inflation, π^* the inflation target, y_t aggregate income, and y^* the income target. Whatever academic economists may say, the Taylor Rule is what central bankers apparently do. Macroeconomists who seek to influence policy are accordingly well-advised to place their arguments within this frame. Note how the Taylor Rule framework permits a clear distinction between long-run goals (moving π^* toward zero at some optimal pace) and short-run goals (selecting parameters b and c in some optimal fashion). As the optimal policy will depend on the assumed underlying structural model, there is room enough in the Taylor Rule framework for everyone.

Increasingly the Taylor Rule is the framework of monetary policy discussion not only in the United States but also around the world, so we can speak of an emerging "inflation targeting" monetary system. The important point is that an inflation-targeting system is quite similar to a gold standard. To see this, express purchasing power parity in rates of change as $\pi_t = \Delta e/e_t + \pi_t'$; domestic inflation equals foreign inflation plus exchange rate appreciation. Take long-term expectations and substitute in the inflation targets for long-term inflation expectations to get $\pi^* = E(\Delta e/e) + \pi^{*\prime}$; long-run expected exchange rate appreciation is just the difference between domestic and foreign inflation targets. Unlike the gold standard, exchange rates are not fixed, and of course targets are not the same thing as firm commitments. But like the gold standard, there is a firm basis for expectations about long-run exchange rates, a basis for stabilizing rather than destabilizing speculation.

It will be objected that, unlike the gold standard system with its fixation on stabilizing the exchange rate, the inflation targeting framework leaves room for monetary policy to address the broader goals of stabilizing inflation and income. But this too is arguably more a difference of degree than of kind. Under the gold standard, central bankers could and did choose whether to respond to a gold drain by raising bank rate in order to reverse the drain, or by expanding central bank credit in order to accommodate it. They had, in effect, their own implicit Taylor Rule, albeit without benefit of our modern statistical capability to calculate price indices and to measure aggregate income.

One could go even further, to make the case that the old literature of central banking is the true origin of macroeconomics as a distinct field of inquiry, and to interpret Keynes' 1936 *General Theory of Employment, Interest, and Money* as an adaptation of that traditional literature for the unusual conditions of his own time. But this would be a longer argument, and also unnecessary for the issue at hand. For our purposes, it is enough simply to point out that modern macroeconomics has in a sense come full circle back to pre-Keynesian discourse, and that the fundamental reason for that recurrence has to do with the fact that the organization of the macroeconomy has also in a sense come full circle.

We are not, however, right back where we started. First, the economic role of the state has in the meantime tremendously enlarged, now encompassing between one-quarter and one-third of GDP in most developed countries. Obviously, the fiscal effects of what such a large entity decides to do remain important for macroeconomic aggregates, even if those decisions are not directed by stabilization goals. Second, the integration of financial markets has also advanced tremendously. This is partly because of technology (computers and telecommunications), but also partly because of new financial theory that suggests efficiency gains (a free lunch) from the integration of risk bearing. The modern nation state is large, but the modern financial market is larger still. These are the significant changes in material fact with which a modern-day Hawtrey must grapple.

From this point of view, the current practical consensus strikes me as living too much in the past. To be sure, the enlarged role of the nation state is obvious to everyone. The decreased attention to fiscal stabilization policy has therefore been matched by increased attention to other aggregative consequences of state spending. The literature on the macroeconomics of Social Security is one example, and I predict we will soon see similar literatures on the macroeconomics of our health care and education systems. That is where the money goes. The burgeoning literature on endogenous growth is another example of an attempt to grapple with the macroeconomic consequences of an enlarged role for government.

What is missing is adequate engagement with the second defining fact of our age, the worldwide integration of markets in general and of financial markets in particular. The dialogue of macro with finance has so far been mainly a dialogue with corporate finance, one directed mainly toward improving our understanding of the determinants of investment spending, and that is about it. For the most part, our stories about the monetary transmission mechanism (credit channel, net worth channel) theorize a world of quantitatively significant inefficient credit rationing, ignoring the revolutionary changes that the financial industry has by now effected. Even more troubling, our stories about central bankers who set monetary policy in order to maximize some domestic welfare function largely abstract from the private bankers who seek profit in any deviation of asset prices from their equilibrium levels.

In this latter regard, the Taylor Rule might usefully be contrasted with the classic Fisher equation, which explains the nominal interest rate as the sum of the equilibrium real interest rate and future inflation as expected by private creditors and debtors: $R = \rho + E\pi$. The problem is this: If the Fisher equation tells us the nominal interest rate that clears private credit markets, then the rate implied by the Taylor Rule must be a disequilibrium rate. But, in a financially developed world like ours, we generally expect disequilibrium asset prices to attract arbitrageurs. Why is monetary policy an exception? We have no very satisfactory answer to the question.

The consensus model simply asserts that the central bank sets the rate of interest, and focuses analytical attention instead on the consequences for aggregate demand and, through sticky prices, the consequences also for real output and income. We have developed elaborate theories and models of all these consequences. Indeed, the sum and substance of postwar macroeconomics consists of little else. Money moves, and income and prices follow. "This story feels simple and natural. Indeed, it is not very different from the account given by quantity theorists of the nineteenth century. What the recent research has done has been to clarify various parts of the argument and to point to a number of unresolved issues" (Blanchard 2000, 1389). Quite so. But the biggest unresolved issue is why asset prices can be assumed to adjust to central bank policy rather than vice versa, as might seem most simple and natural in today's financial world.

Living and teaching in New York City, as I do, it is entirely possible that I am oversensitive to the importance of financial developments for understanding the modern macroeconomy. If I lived in Europe, likely I would be placing much more emphasis on the challenge rather than the reality of market integration, and focusing more attention on labor market imperfection than on financial market integration. But if a New York address blinds one to some things, it opens one's eyes to others.

Most important, one begins to suspect that the foundational presumption of postwar macroeconomics – that the nation state can control its own macroeconomic destiny by using available aggregative policy tools – may seriously misjudge the nature of the world in which we now live. Because the United States is the largest and most powerful of nation states, that postwar presumption has persisted here longer than elsewhere. And because the world economics profession yet finds its center in the United States, the same postwar presumption has persisted in academia longer than in government and business circles. But persistence does not make it right.

II

One reason academic discourse has fallen behind the curve is that the world has changed out from under us. Another reason is that the language we use to understand our current world remains the language we developed to understand the rather different world of yesterday. One way of stating the problem is that our principal theoretical framework for system-level thinking, general equilibrium theory in the mode of Arrow and Debreu, has no place in it for money (Hahn 1965). This was perhaps not such a problem when macroeconomics was about fiscal policy, and when general equilibrium was considered an idealization of little practical interest for problems of the disequilibrium short run. It is much more of a problem when macroeconomics is about monetary policy, and when general equilibrium is being promoted as a model of short-run business fluctuation. Just when we need it most, we find ourselves without much in the way of fundamental monetary theory to guide us.

Given the practical consensus around the Taylor Rule with inflation targeting, the question naturally arises whether this set of practical policy rules has any deeper theoretical basis. Woodford (2001) is perhaps the most successful attempt so far to provide such a basis, but there remains a long way to go. His reliance on the ad hoc assumption of a cash-in-advance constraint to produce a demand for money does little to address the fundamental theoretical issue at stake. In his defense, he is only following the theoretical strategy that characterizes the work of all New Keynesians, a strategy that seeks essentially to support the core of usable macroeconomics, by fundamental models if possible but also by ad hoc models if necessary. Given the Hahn problem, ad hoc models are all we can hope for if we insist on staying within the framework of general equilibrium theory.

Roger Farmer (1993, 189) frames the problem of monetary economics as it is seen by most economists (see also Wallace 2001):

There are two puzzles that form the core of monetary theory. The first is the question of why a piece of paper that has no intrinsic value can come to be exchanged for commodities that yield utility. The second is why apparently identical pieces of paper that have identical risk characteristics can trade at different prices. Otherwise stated, the first is the question of why the price of money in terms of commodities is positive, and the second is the question of why the money rate of interest is positive.

This formulation is so familiar to us that it is hard to imagine monetary theory being organized in any different way, but nonetheless that is just what I want to suggest lies in our future. Observe that neither of Farmer's puzzles poses any problem in a gold standard world. In such a world, the price of money in terms of commodities is positive because money is convertible into gold that has a positive price. In such a world, the money rate of interest is not driven to zero by intermediaries issuing zero-yield monetary liabilities against Treasury bill assets because such monetary liabilities would also have to be convertible in order to be money. Put another way, no one finds it puzzling that, in a gold standard world, people are willing simultaneously to hold zero-yielding gold and positive-yielding inside credit. Farmer's puzzles are puzzles only in a world of fiat money, not in a world where money is a promise to pay gold. I have already argued that the emerging inflation targeting monetary system has many of the properties of a gold standard system. One of the consequences for monetary theory is that we need to start thinking of money as a promise to pay, and that will inevitably change the way we conceptualize the central problems of monetary economics.

Forty years ago, Gurley and Shaw (1960) drew our attention to the distinction between outside and inside money. For whatever reasons (maybe the Depression-era collapse of the gold standard, maybe postwar generalization from special wartime practice), postwar economics had got into the habit of thinking about government-issued currency as outside money. Gurley and Shaw did not deviate from orthodoxy in this respect, but they did attempt to shift emphasis to the inside credit character of all other forms of money. What I propose for the future of monetary economics is that we go beyond the program of Gurley and Shaw by starting to think of even government-issued currency as a promise to pay.

But what is it that money promises to pay? It must be admitted that the answer is not so clear, but the inflation targeting framework does suggest at least the outlines of a possible answer. Since long-run inflation targets imply long-run exchange rate targets, in effect an inflation-targeting central bank commits to defend the international value of domestic currency in terms of other currencies. In this sense domestic currency is a promise to pay international reserves. The value of such a promise depends on the ability and willingness of the promisor (the central bank) to attract reserves by influencing the pattern of trade on the current and capital accounts. (The large literature on central bank "credibility" is relevant here, even though it typically conflates willingness to pay with ability to pay.)

One reason that economists have historically been reluctant to view currency as a promise to pay is that we feel the need to distinguish government issue from bank deposits. In the older literature, the former is called money and the latter is called credit. In the more recent literature, the former is high-powered (fiat) money and the latter is simply (inside credit) money. If we begin to treat government money as a promise to pay, don't we risk losing analytical sight of the apparent fact about the world that government money is better than bank money? Quite the contrary. Indeed, by embracing the credit character of government money as well as private money, we are forced to confront the question *why* government money is better, rather than treating that question as solved by definition. This is the puzzle, if you will, around which a future monetary economics is likely to be organized.

The similarity of this puzzle to Farmer's second may suggest that the answer to the puzzle is similar as well, namely legal restrictions that give special status to government money. No. There are many such legal restrictions, but I tend to think they are not the cause of money's special status but rather merely the codification of that status. Put another way, I am sufficiently impressed by the ability of bankers and financiers to evade legal restrictions in their search for profit that I would not want to build a monetary theory on the assumption that their attempts to evade are always unsuccessful.

Instead, embracing the credit character of government money forces us to confront the question why monetary systems tend naturally to be organized hierarchically. We see this natural hierarchy clearly in the correspondent banking system that preceded central banking in the United States, a system in which the deposit liabilities of money center banks were better money than the deposit liabilities of correspondents. The superiority of central bank liabilities over member bank liabilities seems to be much the same kind of phenomenon, and by extension so too the superiority of government issue over private issue. What kind of theory can explain such a phenomenon? We need, it appears, a model of an inside credit payment system in which patterns of payment, across heterogeneous agents and across time, give rise endogenously to hierarchy as an efficient institutional arrangement. The key agents in such a model will be banks, conceived as payment intermediaries using their own balance sheets to span the gap between payer and payee, and conceived also as market makers in their own monetary liabilities. In this latter role banks play a crucial role, knitting together adjacent layers in the hierarchy of credit.

The kind of thing I have in mind would build on Hicks' sketch in his last book *A Market Theory of Money* (1989). In terms of formal modeling, the conception of banks as market makers suggests that we might start from the finance literature on "market microstructure." The big difference, of course, is that in the stock market you cannot sell what you do not own, at least not in the cash market (derivatives markets are another matter). Banks, by contrast, make markets in their own liabilities precisely by expanding and contracting their balance sheets. In the language of finance, bank deposits are nothing more than the open interest in cash.

The potential payoff from such an effort of theory construction will be a more solid basis for monetary theory, and hence also for monetary policy, than that currently provided by the ad hoc cash-in-advance constraint models. The payoff will also be a true integration of macroeconomics with finance that will bring our theoretical constructs into line with the significant facts of our day.

III

So far I have told a story in which the development of macroeconomics is driven by the development of the macroeconomy, but with a lag. And I have used that lag to forecast the future of macroeconomics as being about the integration of finance and macroeconomics in order to produce a new, more adequate, theoretical foundation for monetary economics. That is what I think will happen, and it is also what I think should happen, but it is probably going to take a long time.

In the meanwhile, we are likely to see development following a more internal and professionally driven logic. Existing models will be refined, expanded, confronted with data, and all the usual business of normal science. We will continue living, as we have done these last forty years, in the shadow of the Keynesian consensus of the 1960s. In the past, much of the energy of macroeconomists has been absorbed either attacking IS-LM for its presumed theoretical inadequacy or coming to its defense with one ad hoc theoretical justification or another. This past is likely to be our future as well, at least in the short run, if only because (as noted above) the practical consensus around a core of usable macroeconomics has been cast in IS-LM terms. It is worth revisiting some of that past history, if only to avoid being condemned to repeat it.

Because IS-LM was understood as a model of fixed-price equilibrium, much of its defense has involved explanations of why prices may fail to be sufficiently flexible to clear markets. And so we got the spectacle of academic economists working hard to explain rigidities even as the actual economy was becoming ever more flexible and competitive, union membership was on the decline, and American companies were facing ever more competitive international markets. Whatever one might think about the policy implications of New Classical or Real Business Cycle models, their insistence on price flexibility and competitive behavior does seem more in line with essential features of the real world, while the New Keynesians seem to be stuck explaining the rigidities of a bygone age.

Put another way, the main positive contribution of New Keynesians seems to have been to our understanding of information problems in individual markets (efficiency wages, menu costs, and the like). But it is by no means clear that the New Keynesian microeconomic imperfections add up to a convincing positive story of macroeconomic fluctuation. Blanchard admits as much when he calls for "an integrated macro model, based on only a few central imperfections" (p. 1402) as the first task for the immediate future of macroeconomics. But can it be done that way? Up to now, these microeconomic imperfection stories have played the smaller, and largely defensive, role of justifying a supplementary assumption of sticky prices in our macro models.

I would guess that this pattern of discourse will continue into the future as it has in the past, and will probably also continue to absorb the attention of most of the profession. From the point of view of the development of macroeconomics, the main positive result will be to increase sophistication of technique both theoretical and econometric. Already the real business cycle program has evolved to embrace multiple equilibria, sunspot equilibria, and complex dynamics. The impact on econometric practice has been equally transformative. Looking forward, agent heterogeneity seems likely to be the next big technical hurdle, its importance mooted by the theoretical dissonance between representative agent modeling and assumptions of market imperfection. Importantly, the embrace of heterogeneity looks like being an important hurdle from the standpoint of the longer run development of macroeconomic theory as well. Simply put, heterogeneity is of the essence for understanding credit and payments systems. The problem is to find a mathematical structure that is both general and tractable. (See Bewley 1983, and Mehrling 1995, 1998 for one possibility.)

IV

The practical world will of course not wait for economists to sort out their foundational problems, or to develop tools adequate to the task. Practical macroeconomics is therefore likely to continue following its own course, responding to practical developments without much immediate influence on or influence by deeper theoretical developments. That means we will likely see continued refinement and elaboration of the Taylor Rule, but there may be room in the practical literature for other things as well.

If I am right that the current period represents a return to the pre-Keynesian era of central bank dominance, then it stands to reason that the preoccupations of that earlier literature may be expected to reemerge. Already the Taylor Rule discourse has revived the Wicksellian distinction between the natural rate of interest and the money rate of interest, and there is more down that road. Wicksell, and Hawtrey even more so, developed a sophisticated explanation for how credit expansion and contraction serve as the mechanism through which deviations of the money rate from the natural rate translate into fluctuations in aggregate income. Perhaps some such elaboration will be the next step in developing the Taylor Rule framework.

Such elaboration can also be expected to widen the audience involved in macroeconomic discussion, and that would be a good thing. Currently the Taylor Rule discourse involves mainly a subset of academics and central bank economists. There is room to expand that discourse, but doing so will require economists to engage the facts and language of the practical world of banking and finance. In this regard, we badly need a modern-day analogue to that venerable nineteenth-century best seller *Lombard Street: a description of the money market* by Walter Bagehot (1873). The closest thing available is Marcia Stigum's *The Money Market* (1990), unfortunately now somewhat outdated, but still the most useful desk reference on how the money markets actually work.

In fall 1998, I started using Stigum as the main textbook for my undergraduate class on the Economics of Money and Banking. The students found it tough going, and so did I since it forced me to produce entirely new lecture material. Ultimately, however, they found the experience worthwhile, and so did I. With Stigum's help, and using the *Financial Times* as an update, we had begun to educate our sense of what should feel simple and natural for a monetary economics of the twenty-first century.

REFERENCES

Backhouse, Roger E. and Andrea Salanti. 1999. *Macroeconomics and the Real World*. Volume 1: Econometric Techniques and Macroeconomics. Volume 2: Keynesian Economics, Unemployment, and Policy. Oxford, UK: Oxford University Press.

Bagehot, Walter. 1873. *Lombard Street, a description of the money market.* London: H. S. King.

Bernanke, Ben S. 1999. *Inflation targeting: lessons from the international experience.* Princeton, NJ: Princeton University Press.

Bewley, Truman. 1983. "A Difficulty with the Optimum Quantity of Money." *Econometrica* 51: 1485–504.

Blanchard, Olivier. 2000. "What Do We Know About Macroeconomics That Fisher and Wicksell Did Not?" *Quarterly Journal of Economics* 115 No. 4 (November): 1375–409.

Farmer, Roger E. A. 1993. *The Macroeconomics of Self-Fulfilling Prophecies.* Cambridge, MA: MIT Press.

Goodfriend, M. and R. E. King. 1997. "The New Neoclassical Synthesis and the Role of Monetary Policy." Pages 231–82 in *NBER Macroeconomics Annual 1997.*

Gurley, John G. and Edward Stone Shaw. 1960. *Money in a Theory of Finance.* Washington, DC: Brookings Institution.

Hahn, Frank H. 1965. "On some problems of proving the existence of equilibrium in a monetary economy." In F. H. Hahn and F. P. R. Brechling, eds., *The Theory of Interest Rates.* London: Macmillan, 126–35.

Hawtrey, Ralph George. 1919. *Currency and Credit.* London: Longmans, Green.

Hicks, John Richard, Sir. 1989. *A Market Theory of Money.* Oxford: Clarendon Press.

Ibanez, Carlos Usabiaga. 1999. *The Current State of Macroeconomics, Leading Thinkers in Conversation.* New York: St. Martin's.

Mankiw, N. Gregory and Paul Romer, eds. 1991. *New Keynesian Economics.* 2 vols. Cambridge, MA: MIT Press.

McCallum, Bennett T. 1999. "Recent Developments in Monetary Policy Analysis: the Roles of Theory and Evidence." Pages 115–39 in Backhouse and Salanti (1999).

Mehrling, Perry. 1995. "A Note on the Optimum Quantity of Money." *Journal of Mathematical Economics* 24: 249–58.

———. 1998. "Idiosyncratic Risk, Borrowing Constraints, and Asset Prices." *Metroeconomica* 49 No. 3 (October): 261–83.

Snowdon, Brian and Howard Vane. 1999. *Conversations with Leading Economists: Interpreting Modern Macroeconomics.* Cheltenham, UK: Edward Elgar.

Solow, Robert M. 1997. "Is There a Core of Usable Macroeconomics We Should All Believe In?" *American Economic Review* 87 No. 2 (May): 230–2.

Stigum, Marcia. 1990. *The Money Market,* 3rd ed. Homewood, IL: Dow Jones-Irwin.

Taylor, John B. and Michael Woodford. 1999. *Handbook of Macroeconomics.* 3 vols. New York: Elsevier.

Wallace, Neil. 2001. "Whither Monetary Economics?" *International Economic Review* 42 (November): 847–69.

Woodford, Michael. 2001. "The Taylor Rule and Optimal Monetary Policy." *American Economic Review* 91 No. 2 (May): 232–7.

6

Recent Developments in and Future Prospects for Public Economics

James M. Poterba

Public economics is the study of the government's role in the economy. Because that role is constantly changing, public economics is a constantly evolving field. Some of the field's core questions – such as how the tax rates on different goods should be set – transcend generations, whereas others, such as how best to reform the aging Social Security systems in many developed nations, have recently emerged as central topics. New insights from theoretical and empirical advances in many other subfields of economics help to inform long-standing issues in public economics. In turn, the emerging issues within the field often provide the stimulus for new theoretical and applied research.

The last few decades have been a period of very rapid advancement in public economics. Important new theoretical and empirical discoveries have substantially advanced our understanding of the efficiency and incidence of various taxes, as well as the economic effects and optimal design of social insurance programs. There has been substantial progress in both the economic theory that relates to public economics, and in the empirical analysis that supports detailed policy evaluations.

Different parts of public economics have advanced at different rates. In the early 1970s, the major research advances involved the application of economic theory to the second-best problems of tax design. In the late 1970s and 1980s, the advent of household-level and firm-level databases permitted new exploration of how tax incentives and other factors affected the behavior of economic agents. This ushered in a period of rapid growth in empirical public economics, and many applied econometricians turned their interests to public finance issues. The 1990s were marked by rapid expansion in positive political economy and related fields.

The increasing sophistication of much of the applied research within public economics has led to the creation of several subspecialties within the field, such as the "economics of aging" and the "economics of school finance." The ongoing work in these fields is concerned with issues that are broadly within the purview of public economics, but that also draw upon insights and methodologies that have been developed in health economics, demography, and labor economics.

This short essay summarizes some of the key advances in public economics during the last few decades and sketches several areas that seem well positioned for substantial research progress in the near future. Some of the past advances have been the direct result of progress in other subfields of economics, such as the econometric analysis of panel data on households and firms. Others have been the result of new research stimulated by emerging issues in the public sector. One of the most important skills that researchers in the field of public economics must master is spotting topics that are likely to become important issues of public policy, and on which economic analysis can provide important insights, *before* they have attracted substantial policy attention. In this way, researchers can help to provide an economic framework for subsequent policy discussions.

1. IMPORTANT ADVANCES IN PUBLIC ECONOMICS: THE LAST THREE DECADES

This section describes several topics on which there has been substantial research progress during the last three decades. Many other topics have witnessed at least as much progress, and they are omitted only in the interest of space. This summary is probably tilted toward advances in empirical work, since I am most familiar with that strand of research. I have chosen to discuss a few topics in some detail because that provides an opportunity to explain the evolving nature of public economics research.[1]

The Effect of Income Taxation on Household Behavior

Since the mid-1970s, three forces have combined to dramatically advance our understanding of how income taxation affects the behavior of

---

[1] The April 2002 issue of the *Journal of Public Economics* includes a symposium in which several of the leading scholars who contributed to the advance of public economics during the last three decades review both recent research accomplishments and suggest directions for future work. Auerbach and Feldstein (2002) provide an excellent introduction to the current state of research in public economics.

taxpayers. The first is the increased availability of public use data sets that provide information on choices such as labor supply, saving, and charitable giving that may be affected by taxation. These data sets include the Current Population Survey, the Survey of Consumer Finances, the Panel Survey of Income Dynamics, and the Statistics of Individual Income Tax Model files.

The second force is the rapid advance of econometric methods for the analysis of both cross-sectional and panel data on household behavior. Many of the early applications of new econometric methods focused on the analysis of how taxes and social insurance programs affect household labor supply and other behaviors. This was true of panel data methods in the 1970s and 1980s, as well as of nonparametric methods in the 1990s.

The third factor is the presence of several substantial tax reforms during the 1980s and 1990s that generate substantial variation in household marginal tax rates. The Economic Recovery Tax Act of 1981 reduced marginal tax rates for most households, and the Tax Reform Act of 1986 provided even sharper rate reductions for those at the top of the income distribution. Some of the changes that were enacted in the 1986 Act were reversed in 1993, when the Omnibus Budget and Reconciliation Act raised marginal tax rates for high-income households. For some types of income, notably capital gains, the Taxpayer Relief Act of 1997 provided a substantial change in marginal tax rates. The most recent tax reforms, the Economic Growth and Recovery Tax Act of 2001 and the Job Growth and Taxpayer Relief Reconciliation Act (JGTRRA) of 2003, promise further substantial changes in the marginal tax rates facing many households.

Taken together, these tax changes resulted in substantial changes in marginal tax rates, with a very erratic time series pattern. The weighted average marginal income tax rate on dividend income, for example, fell by almost twenty percentage points between 1980 and 1990, but then rose by several percentage points during the first half of the 1990s. It declined sharply after JGTRRA took effect. The average tax rate on wages fell by more than eight percentage points during the 1980s, and then rose again in the 1990s. The tax rate on realized capital gains nearly doubled between 1985 and the mid-1990s, but then declined in the late 1990s. These tax changes have provided a wealth of opportunity for public finance researchers to investigate how taxation affects household behavior.

What have we learned? First, there is much evidence that taxpayers take advantage of short-term reallocations of income or other financial flows that will substantially reduce their tax liability. The surge in capital gains realizations around the Tax Reform Act of 1986 testifies to this sensitivity, as does the retiming of income receipts in late 1992 and early 1993, when increases in top marginal income tax rates were widely expected. In general, it appears that reported taxable income is quite sensitive to the marginal tax rates that households face, particularly for households at the top of the income distribution.

Second, a growing body of research suggests that hours of work and labor force participation are sensitive to marginal tax rates. Evidence on the response of secondary earners to marginal tax rate reductions in the Tax Reform Act of 1986, and on the response of lower-income households to changes in the incentives embodied in the Earned Income Tax Credit, is particularly revealing in this regard.

Third, we have learned that it is essential to adopt a comprehensive view in analyzing tax incentives, and not just to focus on the incentives in a particular part of the tax system. Both the estate tax and the individual income tax appear to affect the level of lifetime charitable giving as well as the division of charitable giving between lifetime gifts and charitable bequests. The corporate income tax and the individual income tax interact to determine the mix of income between subchapter S and subchapter C corporations, and the behavior of entrepreneurs who may consider starting a new firm.

In spite of these advances, much remains to be done. For example, there is little consensus on how sensitive the labor supply of primary earners is with respect to the after-tax wage, or on how the level of such labor supply would change after the general equilibrium effects of a major tax reform were fully recognized. Hours of work are only one dimension of labor supply for such workers, and it is not clear whether there is substantial elasticity on other margins, such as the difficulty of the job or the need for business travel. There is also a growing recognition that many aspects of household behavior may be affected not just by current tax rates but by past and expected future tax rates, although few empirical studies have incorporated this insight.

The Incentive Effects of Social Insurance Programs

The availability of household-level data sets beginning in the mid-1970s made it possible for public finance researchers to study the effect of social insurance programs such as unemployment insurance (UI), workers compensation, Medicaid, and Social Security on household behavior. Nearly three decades of research has now yielded a convincing body of evidence on how these programs affect labor supply, retirement, job search, the utilization of medical care, and a range of other behaviors.

Researchers have exploited many different sources of variation in program rules and the availability of social insurance benefits. Some research uses cross-national differences in programs. Recent studies of how labor supply rates of older men are related to Social Security and disability programs show much higher rates of labor force withdrawal in countries that offer generous program benefits to workers who are no longer in the labor force than in countries without such benefits. Other research uses cross-state differences in program rules. There are many studies based on administrative record data for the U.S. states that explore how the availability of unemployment insurance benefits affects the duration of unemployment spells. These studies generally find substantial effects of changes both in benefit generosity and in the length of benefit availability on the length of unemployment spells.

Still other studies have used detailed aspects of program variation within states or other administrative jurisdictions. The Medicaid program, for example, was substantially expanded in the 1980s and 1990s, but the expansions were targeted to particular types of households, and in some cases to children of particular ages. Researchers have compared the behavior of households that have children of very similar ages, but which because of the arbitrary nature of age-cutoffs in program eligibility have different eligibility status with respect to Medicare. The results show that access to Medicaid not only affects health care utilization, but also changes the labor supply behavior of the eligible households.

The analysis of social insurance programs and household behavior has offered a rich base for the application of new econometric tools that have been developed for "program evaluation." The most refined research in this spirit has devoted careful attention to the question of why policies in some states changed, while policies in other states remained the same. It has tried to identify genuinely exogenous shocks to the policy environment. Such shocks provide the best opportunity to learn about the link between program characteristics and household behavior.

Research suggesting that social insurance programs affect household behavior has begun to affect the way policymakers view program design. There is growing recognition that behavioral changes may affect the cost of program reforms, and a realization that behavioral distortions associated with these programs may have substantial efficiency effects.

The Efficiency and Incidence of Taxes on Capital Income

The economic analysis of taxes on capital income, and particularly corporate capital income, has been one of the most active research areas in public economics for the last few decades. This is also an area where one can identify a clear link between research findings and public policy. My discussion will focus on four distinct advances.

The first was the use of computable general equilibrium models, along with careful analysis of the institutional structure of the corporate income tax, to evaluate the cost of capital and the "effective tax rate" for a range of different capital assets. In the late 1970s, inflation combined with a nominal tax code, one that provided depreciation allowances based on the historical cost of acquiring assets, to substantially raise the tax burden on corporate capital income. This was an important factor behind the enactment of the Economic Recovery Tax Act (ERTA) of 1981, which provided accelerated depreciation for many asset types. After ERTA, the effective tax burdens on different assets varied quite substantially. Documenting this, and quantifying the potential efficiency costs from large differences in the effective tax rates on different assets, was one of the major research accomplishments of the early 1980s. This research featured prominently in the policy debate leading up to the Tax Reform Act of 1986, which "leveled the playing field" across different assets.

A second important development in the analysis of capital income taxation was the introduction of the asset price approach to tax incidence. Prior to the early 1980s, most discussions of the incidence of the corporate income tax were carried out in the context of multisector models that assumed that capital could flow freely between different uses, while the total supply of capital was fixed. The asset price approach, in contrast, recognized the short-run inability to reallocate capital from one use to another. The accumulated capital assets that are deployed in residential real estate cannot be easily transformed to industrial plant and equipment when the tax burden on those assets declines. Raising the tax burden on one class of assets, and lowering it on another, will therefore lead to changes in the market price of existing assets. These price changes will in turn provide signals for new investment to flow to sectors in which the after-tax return is highest. The insights of the asset price approach called attention to the difference between tax burdens on new capital and the tax burdens on old capital, and also illustrated how the asset price changes associated with tax reforms could feature prominently in understanding the distributional effects of these reforms.

A third development in recent decades, linked to research advances in corporate finance, has been the recognition that the average tax burden on corporations, as well as the marginal tax burdens on new projects, may affect investment incentives. Previous research stressed the cost of capital as the channel linking tax parameters to the incentives for undertaking new investment. More recent research has also recognized that factors that affect the return on existing assets – and thereby the cash flow that firms have available for investment – may also affect the flow of new investment. This research has led to a better understanding both of the differences between the internal and external capital markets facing corporations, and to a clearer evaluation of policy changes that might not affect marginal investment incentives but might affect total corporate tax burdens.

Finally, theoretical research has generated new insights on the optimal design of capital income taxes. Researchers have discovered that in infinite horizon models, the optimal steady-state capital tax rate is zero. To the extent that capital income taxes are featured in the efficient tax program, it is because they offer an opportunity for a "taking" from those who hold capital at the time when the tax is enacted – such taxes are taxes on old capital, not on new investment. Of course, one-time levies on capital are difficult if not impossible to implement in practice, as governments face well-known problems of dynamic inconsistency. Even if *today's* government promises not to tax capital in the future, *tomorrow's* government may find it optimal to tax capital and thereby to renege on the earlier policy. The risk of such expropriation of some of the returns to capital discourages investment by those who are considering new long-term projects. The efficiency arguments against taxing capital income represent a counterweight to the arguments that some make for taxing capital income on distributional grounds.

Deficits and Intertemporal Fiscal Policy

Musgrave (1959) divided the study of public economics into three strands: one concerned with the allocation of economic resources, another concerned with the distribution of economic resources, and a third concerned with the stabilization of economic fluctuations. In recent years, however, much of the research on stabilization issues has shifted to macroeconomics and monetary economics, as public finance economists have concentrated on the analysis of the microeconomic effects of tax and expenditure programs. A notable exception to this statement involves recent advances in

methods for measuring deficits and defining the intergenerational consequences of fiscal policy.

One line of inquiry has drawn attention to the need for careful accounting, beyond that provided in standard government accounts, to fully
describe the impact of the government sector on the economy. The 1970s
brought an awareness of how inflation affects reported budget magnitudes. The real value of nominal government debt shrinks during infla-
tionary periods, making standard budget statistics quite misleading. The
savings and loan crisis of the 1980s reminded policy makers and public economists that it is important to account for contingent liabilities
in considering any measure of fiscal stance. Government insurance programs may commit future resources, and thereby tighten the government
budget constraint, even though they do not have any immediate effect
on reported budget statistics. There has similarly been progress in the
recognition that governments own capital assets that may appreciate or
depreciate over time.

The second advance with respect to analyzing the effects of budget rules
is motivated by the limitations of standard budget statistics. It recognizes
that the budget we observe in any single year is really just a part of a
larger intertemporal fiscal program, which provides benefits to and levies
taxes on many different cohorts of citizens. A number of studies have
risen to the challenge of documenting the net effect of the fiscal system
on a lifetime basis. Recent research has suggested that the "generational
accounts" that arise from current fiscal rules may look very different for
those who are old and those who are young. In particular, the need to
finance large, ongoing social insurance programs, such as Social Security
and Medicare in the United States, places heavy fiscal burdens on the
workers who will be in the labor force and paying taxes several decades
from now. This is not revealed by traditional budget measures, but it
does reflect an important feature of current fiscal policy. "Experimental"
budget accounts, recognizing these factors, are now being prepared with
increasing levels of detail regarding prospective fiscal policy.

Positive Political Economy Models of Fiscal Outcomes

One of the most active areas of recent research progress has been at the
interface between formal political science and economics. Models of voter
behavior and of the nature of equilibrium in political systems have been
used to provide new insight on the types of tax and expenditure policies that may emerge in representative democracies, and on the potential

impact of fiscal and political institutions on policy outcomes. This line of inquiry parallels a related research program in international trade, in which the central question is what explains the nature of tariff policies chosen by different nations.

Within public economics, the link between a jurisdiction's fiscal constitution and its fiscal policy has attracted substantial attention. During the 1970s and 1980s, researchers explored the link between electoral institutions, such as the four-year cycle in presidential elections in the United States, and macroeconomic policy (the "political business cycle"). More recent work has shifted from an interest in cycles to a focus on how various political institutions and constitutional constraints may affect budget deficits. This was very relevant in the United States in the late 1980s, when there was active policy debate about a balanced budget amendment.

More generally, there has been substantial interest in understanding how fiscal institutions affect budget outcomes. Researchers working in the tradition of the median voter model were poorly equipped to address questions about the potential effects of new fiscal rules that were designed to reduce the likelihood of budget deficits, as institutions play no role in that model. They were also unable to address questions like the possible bias toward deficit finance in some types of legislative systems. Yet important progress has been made on these questions by drawing upon recent advances in the formal analysis of voting and electoral choice. The result has been a substantial body of research on topics such as the effect of line-item veto power for a governor or a president on the level and composition of spending, and the effect of parliamentary as opposed to presidential government on the average level of budget deficits.

Optimal Income Taxation and the Design of Tax and Transfer Programs

A final dimension along which public economics has progressed in recent decades concerns the theory of optimal taxation and optimal policy design. Path-breaking theoretical work in the early 1970s provided a range of new insights on the economic analysis of distortions associated with income taxation. One critical insight is the importance of "self-selection constraints" in determining the structure of optimal tax and transfer policies. In designing a subsidy program, government planners must recognize that some households who are not part of their notional target population may try to qualify for program benefits. Households that currently have jobs may decide to enter the pool of the unemployed if unemployment insurance benefits are sufficiently generous. Similarly, behavior may change in response to taxes. Workers who have the potential to earn substantial amounts at high wages may decide to work less, and pay less in taxes while consuming more leisure, if marginal tax rates are high.

The focus on ways to design transfer programs that will not be too attractive to households outside the target group has led to new insights. For example, we now recognize that it is at least possible that distributing aid in-kind rather than in cash, and making it somewhat difficult to apply for and to receive particular transfer programs, may be part of the optimal transfer policy. This represents a substantial turnabout relative to the emphasis on negative income taxes and cash transfers in prior economic research.

A second important insight involves the link between consumer preferences and the structure of optimal income tax and optimal commodity tax rates. Early work on both income taxation and commodity taxation did not consider the interplay between the two taxes. Some researchers tried to characterize the vector of optimal commodity taxes, whereas others tried to describe the shape of the optimal income tax. Yet recent research suggests that the two are intimately connected. For many classes of consumer preferences, including the preferences that are associated with many utility functions that are popular for pedagogical purposes, if the government has access to an optimal nonlinear income tax, it will never choose to utilize commodity taxes. Moreover, there is a growing recognition that the detailed structure of optimal commodity taxes depends on information about the derivatives of compensated demands with respect to many different prices, and that this information may be impossible to estimate with any precision. This development has generated some doubt about the general usefulness of the optimal commodity tax framework, at least when efficiency considerations are the primary factor underlying the design of the taxes.

2. PROMISING RESEARCH DIRECTIONS FOR THE FUTURE

The rising volume of research in public economics during the last few decades testifies to the research community's belief that there are widespread opportunities for interesting and informative study. There are still many topics that offer promising avenues for future work. This section offers an idiosyncratic perspective on some of the issues that may represent the most fruitful directions for future research. Some are areas of long-standing interest, where the returns to further work appear to be substantial. Others are emerging topics, where growing public policy attention suggests substantial benefits from economic analysis.

Environmental Economics and Optimal Second-Best Policy

Growing interest in environmental policies, particularly in nations other than the United States, has raised many interesting public economics issues. Many of these topics were addressed during the wave of interest in environmental economics during the early 1970s, but warrant reinvestigation using more recent advances both in applied economic theory and in empirical methods. The central issues include the measurement of environmental costs, which is a precondition for designing optimal Pigouvian taxes, and the integration of Pigouvian taxes with other elements of the revenue structure. Proposals for carbon taxes that could collect substantial amounts of revenue led to an active public economics debate in the late 1990s on the subject of the "double dividend" associated with environmental taxes. This is the notion that by taxing pollutants, and thereby correcting an externality, a nation might raise enough revenue to be able to improve the efficiency of other aspects of its tax system, thereby generating a double increase in economic efficiency. The most careful research suggests that the double dividend is likely to be illusory, but further analysis is in order.

The pervasive nature of cross-border pollution concerns also makes environmental economics an interesting setting in which to develop models of intergovernmental policy competition and coordination. This is an issue with a long history in public economics: whether competition between governments leads to inefficiently low levels of taxes and consequently public spending is an unresolved issue. Studying how environmental as well as tax policies are set in nations of different sizes, and with different degrees of cross-border spillovers in their policy benefits, should provide a wealth of opportunities to enrich what we know about intergovernmental interaction.

The Economics of Aging

The demographic shift that is already underway in the United States and many other developed nations has first-order implications for the public sector. In future years, there will be an increased need for spending on cash transfers to the elderly, as well as increased need for the provision of in-kind services such as medical care. The prospective revenue costs of such programs are so substantial that they may lead to changes in existing programs before the largest age groups reach retirement. The recent policy debate in the United States on Social Security privatization testifies to the importance of evaluating the impact of population aging. Similar debates are taking place in many other nations.

Public economics researchers have recently begun to study alternative options for ensuring an adequate supply of retirement resources when the largest cohorts leave the labor force. These include modifying the investment policies of government trust funds; changing the structure of current old-age benefit programs; and using new revenue sources, such as income tax, to finance transfers to elderly households.

The research needs for developing a coherent analysis of policy choices in the face of population aging are daunting. They include the impact of population aging on the rate of economic growth – and consequently the growth of the government's revenue base – as well as on the prospective returns to various financial assets. Other issues center on how changes in policy parameters would affect household behavior. For example, the impact of current Social Security and Medicare programs on retirement and saving behavior, and the potential impact of program reforms such as means-testing or raising the age of eligibility, is a topic of substantial interest both within economics and in policy circles. The government's role in regulating the private pension system is also likely to attract increased attention as a rising fraction of the population enters the age groups when pension payouts feature prominently in household income.

The next decade may be a golden age for research on the economics of aging. Databases that have only become available in the last few years, such as the Health and Retirement Survey and AHEAD surveys in the United States, provide panel data on the elderly population. These surveys are far more detailed than most previous studies of this population group, so they hold the potential for newly enriched analysis. They are particularly valuable because they offer some insight on the links between economic decisions, such as labor supply and wealth accumulation, health outcomes, and the availability of government programs.

"Privatization" and the Scope of Government

Around the globe, "privatization" has become one of the most discussed issues concerning the government sector. The former Soviet republics and many other nations in Eastern Europe have privatized what were once state-owned enterprises, while states and cities in the United States have sold assets and outsourced activities ranging from prison management to the collection of parking tickets. Understanding the consequences of such changes is critical. What rules should guide the government's role in the economy? The central issue is how one trades off the potential benefits of government intervention designed to correct market failures, or affect the distribution of resources, with the "government failures" associated with government involvement in various market activities. There are many aspects of economic activity where there is an active debate on the role of government in providing goods and services. The provision of airport security services, currently a topic of active interest, is one example. Another is the role of vouchers or other methods of introducing competition in the provision of elementary and secondary education.

One very important area where the role of government is likely to be a continuing subject of debate, and where there are very promising opportunities for research, concerns health care. Health care costs have grown so rapidly in recent years, and the government's share of these costs is so substantial, that projections of current trends imply dire budgetary consequences in just a decade or two. Although much of the research in health economics focuses on the health production function and related issues that lie outside public economics, a great deal of health economics research does bear on issues involving the public sector. This is because a whole range of issues in government program design hinge on behavioral parameters such as the price elasticity of demand for medical care and the elasticity of nursing home supply with respect to Medicaid reimbursement rates. Some of the empirical work that is needed to measure this broad range of elasticities has been done, but far more remains to be done. Even more importantly, public sector analysts need a framework for analyzing the source of rapid health care cost growth. How much of the growth is due to technical progress, and how much of that is the result of government policies? Which policies are most important in affecting spending growth? Framing and answering these issues will help set the stage for a national policy debate on the nature of government involvement in the health care and health insurance industries.

Important issues about the role of the government sector in the private economy arise in both developed and developing nations. Many of the most interesting applications are in Third World nations. The government's role in financial markets is one example. A number of studies have documented market failures in both credit and insurance markets in developing nations. Yet in some nations, government incentives have created credit cooperatives or risk-sharing pools that offer substantial benefits for the households that participate. Evaluating the net benefits of such government interventions is a substantial research priority.

Tax and Expenditure Policies in Open Economies

One of the notable trends of the last few decades is the increasing openness of the world economy. Transportation and communication costs have fallen, and the mobility of firms and factors of production seems to have increased. These developments suggest several new subjects for research in public economics.

One set of issues concerns the effects of tax policy on the behavior of multijurisdictional actors. This can involve trying to identify the effect of tax policy differences on the location and financing choices of multinational firms, or the analysis of household mobility across national or state boundaries in response to tax and benefit differences. There is a small literature on optimal income taxation in the presence of international labor mobility. A larger literature explores the empirical evidence on Tiebout sorting and the degree of household specialization within jurisdictions. Whether it is possible to tax highly mobile capital at all is an open question, and one that some of the OECD's recent policy deliberations about tax havens underscore.

A second set of issues concerns the strategic interaction of jurisdictions in setting tax policy. If one country decides to become a tax haven, part of the revenue it collects will come at the expense of other countries that have not chosen the tax haven route. Estimating the magnitude of such effects and the welfare effects of designing policies that might mitigate policy competition, and using the tools of game theory to model such strategic interactions, is a promising avenue for further work.

Optimal Social Insurance Program Design

The outpouring of empirical research on the effects of social insurance programs has run ahead of theoretical work establishing the principles of optimal program design. What are the central second-best considerations? There is a need for further research designed to describe the insurance that is provided by the wide range of existing programs, and to quantify the importance of such insurance. Some important research has begun to provide insight on how social insurance programs reduce the volatility of household consumption. Yet there is still relatively little discussion of the precise operation of private insurance markets, and of the nature of the market failures that create a case for government action. Because the government rarely offers complete insurance for the various risks that households face, there is also an important question about how private insurance markets insure the *residual* risk that remains after government insurance programs.

One aspect of social insurance program design concerns financing, particularly the role of mandated benefits in delivering insurance protection. Mandated benefits arise when a government requires other actors to provide a given set of insurance benefits. When governments face tight revenue constraints, requiring private firms to provide benefits or requiring individuals to purchase insurance policies, this can appear to be an attractive way of achieving policy objectives without spending government resources. These requirements may burden subfederal governments, or firms, or households. The economic analysis of mandated benefits is still at an early stage, in part because it is difficult to find credible sources of variation in mandate policy. The incidence of mandated benefits, and more generally the choice between such mandates and other methods of implementing social insurance program objectives, is a fruitful avenue for further work.

Taxation and the Behavior of Households and Firms

Much has been learned in the last few decades about how households respond to tax incentives, and about how the tax system distorts the decisions of corporations. Yet this is such a central topic for public economics, and so much new data becomes available each year, that it is both an area of great recent progress and an area where the future prospects are very bright. The research community has not yet had an opportunity to analyze any of the effects of the 1997 Taxpayer Relief Act on household behavior, and even more substantial tax changes were enacted in 2001 and 2003. There are also substantial potential changes underway in state and local tax policy, thereby offering still further opportunities for exploring how taxes affect behavior.

The questions that require further attention include many "usual suspects." These include the effects of taxes on labor supply, the link between tax policy and saving behavior, and the effect of the tax treatment of housing, charitable giving, and state and local taxes on household behavior. Other important issues include the impact of the tax system on household insurance purchases and the link between taxation and investment in various types of plant and equipment.

With respect to the corporate tax, controversy still runs high on the choice between marginal incentives – such as accelerated depreciation allowances – and "average" incentives – such as reductions in the statutory tax rate on corporate income. The effect of taxation on corporate financial policies is also an issue that has attracted relatively little attention from public finance economists and corporate finance economists in recent years, but where reinvestigation seems overdue. Long-standing puzzles, such as "why do firms pay dividends?" have become less puzzling over time as corporate financial policy has moved away from high payout rates and many young firms have decided not to pay dividends. The 2003 tax reform will provide a new opportunity to evaluate how the tax system affects corporate payout policy. More generally, the impact of the tax system on the choice between debt and equity, and on the form of compensation, particularly the choice between stock option-based compensation and traditional wage income, remains an open issue. There is a clear need for a conceptual framework that would make it possible to evaluate the efficiency costs of different tax-related distortions in the corporate finance area.

Tax and Expenditure Programs in a Life Cycle Perspective

There is a growing dissatisfaction with the traditional "snapshot" incidence models for analyzing tax and expenditure policies. There has already been some progress toward analyzing such policies in a life cycle context, with explicit recognition that households that are in low income positions at one point in time may be in more favorable positions at other times, and vice versa. Moreover, analyzing the incidence of programs such as Medicare or Social Security that combine taxes during one part of the life cycle with transfers during another part requires a life cycle rather than a static setting. Part of the required research involves the measurement of transition rates across income positions as households age. Another part involves measuring the impact of policies on households of different ages and income circumstances. As longitudinal data sets increasingly provide the wherewithal for studying incidence issues in long-term frameworks, life cycle methods of policy analysis are sure to grow in interest and sophistication.

Medicare illustrates how the life cycle perspective can generate novel insights on the distributional burden of expenditure programs. At any age, the beneficiaries of Medicare in lower income ranges consume more medical care per capita than the better-off participants. But, if one stratifies households by lifetime income and asks how the total value of Medicare benefits varies with income, it appears that higher income households, who live longer and receive Medicare benefits for more years, may receive a larger total benefit package than their lower-income counterparts.

Economics of National Security

Since the early 1960s, the share of government expenditure devoted to national defense has declined sharply. The end of the Cold War provided an important opportunity to reduce the share of national resources devoted to the military, and this reduction in defense outlays contributed to the shift from federal deficits to federal surpluses in the late 1990s. Recent world events suggest that we are likely to see rising expenditures on defense and other security programs. This will raise new issues for researchers in public economics. How should the costs of reducing the likelihood of terrorist attacks be divided between the government and the private sector? How should the costs of a global initiative be divided across countries? What, if anything, can economists offer to help guide the cost–benefit calculations that are likely to be central to formulating policy in these areas?

3. CONCLUSION

Public economics is timeless, yet dynamic. Many of the basic principles of optimal tax design were enunciated in Adam Smith's *Wealth of Nations*, and they were surely recognized much earlier by thoughtful monarchs and finance ministers. Yet research advances in the last few decades have provided new insights on many aspects of how the tax system affects household and firm behavior. These insights have implications for optimal tax design. Similarly, although large-scale government spending has been evident in various regimes since antiquity, we are still discovering interesting new perspectives on the optimal design of both exhaustive expenditure programs and transfer programs.

Public economics offers exciting opportunities to investigate current issues in public policy with the most recent innovations in both economic theory and econometric method. Much of the research progress of the last few decades – and many of the challenges ahead – involve empirical research on how tax policies and expenditure programs affect household and firm behavior.

One must not lose sight, however, of the critical role that economic theory plays in advancing the field of public economics. Public economics is fundamentally a "general equilibrium" field. It is concerned not only with the first-round effects of government policies on economic behavior, but also with the ultimate effects that operate through general equilibrium changes in prices and behavior. As such, analyzing most questions in public economics requires more than simply a partial equilibrium model of households or firms. Notions of market equilibrium – whether in broad markets for factors such as labor and capital, or in specific markets like those for tobacco or gasoline – play a central role in policy analysis. Economic theory provides the grammar that we use to discuss both the effects of existing policies and the design of future policies. Part of the dynamism of public economics derives from the wonderful opportunity it offers for theory to influence empirical work, and vice versa.

REFERENCES

Auerbach, Alan and Martin Feldstein, eds. 1985/87. *Handbook of Public Economics: Volumes 1 and 2*. Amsterdam: North Holland.
Auerbach, Alan and Martin Feldstein, eds. 2002. *Handbook of Public Economics, Volumes 3 and 4*. Amsterdam: North Holland.
Musgrave, Richard. 1959. *The Theory of Public Finance*. New York: McGraw-Hill.
Myles, Gareth. 1995. *Public Economics*. New York: Cambridge University Press.
Slemrod, Joel, ed. 2000. *Does Atlas Shrug? The Economic Consequences of Taxing the Rich*. New York: Russell Sage Foundation.
Stiglitz, Joseph. 2001. *Economics of the Public Sector*, Third Edition. New York: Norton.

PART III

INTERNATIONAL TRADE AND DEVELOPMENT

7

Economic Theory and the Interpretation of GATT/WTO

Kyle Bagwell and Robert W. Staiger

1. INTRODUCTION

Over the postwar period, the General Agreement on Tariffs and Trade (GATT) has sponsored eight rounds of trade-policy negotiations. The most recent round of negotiations, which was completed in 1994, resulted in the creation of the World Trade Organization (WTO). The WTO includes the text of GATT, but it also goes further and embodies a set of agreements that build on and extend GATT principles to new areas. The central role played in the world economy by GATT/WTO is widely accepted. Indeed, through the eight rounds of GATT negotiations, the average ad valorem tariff on industrial goods has fallen from over 40 percent to below 4 percent. Over this period, GATT/WTO membership has also grown in number from twenty-three to now over 140 countries.

Given the significant influence of GATT/WTO on the world economy, it is of special importance to assess the progress that economists have made in providing a theoretical interpretation of GATT/WTO. This is the focus of the present essay.[1] Our discussion proceeds in three broad steps. First, we consider the theory of trade agreements. We organize our discussion here around a simple but fundamental question: What is the problem that a trade agreement might solve? Second, we briefly describe the history and institutional design of GATT/WTO. Finally, we draw on the recent theoretical literature and interpret the design of GATT/WTO. Our discussion examines two key features of GATT/WTO: reciprocity and enforcement.

---

[1] This essay draws heavily from our book (Bagwell and Staiger, 2002).

The work described here cuts across two fields of economics. The first is international trade. In this field, there is the famous result that unilateral free trade is optimal, whenever a government maximizes national income and presides over a small country. For an economist seeking a theoretical interpretation of GATT/WTO, this result is initially discouraging. Apparently, in some circumstances, governments have no reason to pursue reciprocal tariff liberalization through GATT/WTO negotiations, as each already has the unilateral incentive to eliminate its own tariff. But in fact, this result has important constructive value. It suggests that a trade agreement might solve a problem that arises because the negotiating governments (i) have political motivations and do not maximize national income, or (ii) preside over large countries.

Of course, there is little doubt that real-world governments have political motivations. Actual governments are interested not just in the size of national income but also in its distribution. As a consequence, the optimal unilateral policy for a government with political motivations may not be free trade. A positive tariff, for example, may be the means through which such a government steers surplus toward its import-competing firms. But it is quite another matter to say that political considerations constitute a problem that two governments might solve with a trade agreement. As we explain, in the leading political-economy models of trade policy, if the negotiating governments preside over small countries, then the governments can do no better with a trade agreement than without one. In these models, at least, politics itself fails to explain the appeal of a trade agreement.

The other possibility is that governments preside over large countries. What does this mean? In a standard general equilibrium model of trade in two goods, a country is said to be large if a change in its trade policy alters the terms on the world market at which its export good is traded for its import good. For example, if the government of a large country were to depart from free trade and select a positive import tariff, then the import good would become more plentiful on the world market, and so the world price of this good would drop. The government has then engineered a terms-of-trade gain for its country: a unit of its export good can be exchanged on world markets for a greater volume of its import good. By the same logic, the trading partner then experiences a terms-of-trade loss. Because a government does not internalize the terms-of-trade externality that its import tariff imposes upon its trading partner, the optimal unilateral tariff for a national income-maximizing government of a large country is positive. If both governments behave this way and set positive import tariffs, a Prisoners' Dilemma situation is created. In the Nash equilibrium, tariffs are too high and trade volumes are too low; hence, a trade agreement that facilitates a reciprocal reduction in tariffs could be mutually beneficial.

Governments of large countries thus may gain from a trade agreement. This insight is hardly new. The terms-of-trade theory of trade agreements was identified by Mill (1844) and Torrens (1844), and Johnson (1953–4) provides a famous and elegant formalization. Nevertheless, many trade economists have objected to this theory as a foundation from which to interpret actual trade agreements. One objection is that this theory leaves out the important political constraints under which real-world governments labor. A second objection is simply that real-world governments just do not think this way. It is difficult, for example, to find any mention of the "terms of trade" in actual policy disputes. As we show, these objections are less worrisome than they might initially appear. The terms-of-trade theory is easily generalized to include political considerations, and it may be directly interpreted in the context of the market-access language that trade policy negotiators use.

This theoretical perspective offers a means by which to interpret the rules of GATT/WTO. For instance, it suggests that a government may hesitate to liberalize unilaterally, as it does not want to face the terms-of-trade loss that such behavior would imply. If the governments were to liberalize reciprocally, however, then the terms of trade could be preserved, and the impediment to liberalization thereby would be removed. An interpretation of reciprocity is thereby facilitated. Likewise, a government would hesitate to liberalize as part of a reciprocal negotiation, if it were concerned that its negotiating partner might later "cheat" and raise its tariff. We argue that the GATT/WTO enforcement provisions can be interpreted in this light.

The second field to which this essay contributes is applied game theory. Within this field, there is a rich theoretical literature that examines how players that interact repeatedly might construct self-enforcing agreements, so as to overcome a Prisoners' Dilemma problem and achieve a more efficient outcome. The theory of collusion among firms, for example, falls into this category. As there are no GATT/WTO police, agreements between governments achieved through GATT/WTO negotiations must be self-enforcing. Indeed, the rules of GATT/WTO may be interpreted as a codification of supergame strategies. This essay thus may also be of interest to applied game theorists, as it describes the creation and interprets the design of a successful self-enforcing agreement.

The essay proceeds as follows: In Section 2, we discuss the theory of trade agreements. Next, in Section 3, we discuss the history and design of GATT/WTO. Section 4 contains our interpretation of GATT/WTO's reciprocity and enforcement features. Concluding thoughts are offered in Section 5.

2. THE THEORY OF TRADE AGREEMENTS

A theory of trade agreements must explain the purpose of a trade agreement. To this end, we first present a standard two-good general equilibrium model of trade between two countries. Next, we specify a general family of government preferences. Our representation follows the political-economy literature and allows that governments are concerned with the distributional consequences of their trade-policy decisions. With these ingredients, we then identify and discuss the problem that a trade agreement can solve.

2.1. The General Equilibrium Model

We consider a standard general equilibrium model of trade. There are two countries – home and foreign – that trade two goods, where these goods are normal goods in consumption and produced in perfectly competitive markets under conditions of increasing opportunity costs.[2] With x (y) denoting the natural import good of the home (foreign) country, we define $p \equiv p_x/p_y$ ($p^* \equiv p_x^*/p_y^*$) as the local relative price facing home (foreign) producers and consumers. We denote the home (foreign) ad valorem import tariff as t (t^*), and we assume that this tariff is not prohibitive. Letting $\tau \equiv (1+t)$ and $\tau^* = (1+t^*)$, we then have the following relationships among prices: $p = \tau p^w \equiv p(\tau, p^w)$ and $p^* = p^w/\tau^* \equiv p^*(\tau, p^w)$, where $p^w = p_x^*/p_y$ is the "world" (that is, untaxed) relative price.[3] The foreign (domestic) terms of trade is given by p^w ($1/p^w$). We interpret $\tau > 1$ ($\tau < 1$) as an import tax (import subsidy) and similarly for τ^*.[4]

---

[2] Throughout, we follow convention and distinguish domestic and foreign variables by placing an asterisk on the latter.

[3] Henceforth, p denotes the function $p(\tau, p^w)$, and p^* indicates the function $p^*(\tau^*, p^w)$.

[4] In this two-sector general equilibrium setting, the Lerner symmetry theorem ensures that trade taxes and subsidies can be equivalently depicted as applying to exports or imports.

How are production and consumption determined? Within a given country, production is given by the point on the production possibilities frontier at which the marginal rate of transformation between x and y is equal to the local relative price. We may thus represent domestic and foreign production functions as $Q_i = Q_i(p)$ and $Q_i^* = Q_i^*(p^*)$ for $i = \{x, y\}$.

Consumption is also influenced by the local relative price, as this price defines the tradeoff faced by consumers and implies the level and distribution of factor income in the economy. In addition, consumption is dependent upon tariff revenue $R(R^*)$, which is distributed lump-sum to domestic (foreign) consumers and measured in units of the local export good at local prices. Therefore, we may represent domestic and foreign consumption as $D_i = D_i(p, R)$ and $D_i^* = D_i^*(p^*, R^*)$ for $i = \{x, y\}$. Next, we observe that tariff revenue is implicitly defined by $R = [D_x(p, R) - Q_x(p)][p - p^w]$ or $R = R(p, p^w)$ for the domestic country and by $R^* = [D_y^*(p^*, R^*) - Q_y^*(p^*)][1/p^* - 1/p^w]$ or $R^* = R^*(p^*, p^w)$ for the foreign country. Under the assumption that goods are normal, each country's tariff revenue increases with its terms of trade. Having now expressed tariff revenue as a function of local and world prices, we may also express national consumption as a function of local and world prices: $C_i(p, p^w) \equiv D_i(p, R(p, p^w))$ and $C_i^*(p^*, p^w) \equiv D_i^*(p^*, R^*(p^*, p^w))$ for $i = \{x, y\}$.

We consider next the determination of imports and exports. For the home country, imports of x and exports of y are respectively defined by $M_x(p, p^w) \equiv C_x(p, p^w) - Q_x(p)$ and $E_y(p, p^w) \equiv Q_y(p) - C_y(p, p^w)$. Likewise, for the foreign country, we represent imports of y and exports of x as $M_y^*(p^*, p^w)$ and $E_x^*(p^*, p^w)$, respectively. For any prices, home and foreign budget constraints imply that

$$p^w M_x(p, p^w) = E_y(p, p^w), \text{ and} \qquad (2.1)$$
$$M_y^*(p^*, p^w) = p^w E_x^*(p^*, p^w) \qquad (2.2)$$

Making explicit the dependence of the local price upon the tariff and the world price, we may now determine the equilibrium world price, $\tilde{p}^w(\tau, \tau^*)$, by the requirement of market clearing for good y:

$$E_y(p(\tau, \tilde{p}^w), \tilde{p}^w) = M_y^*(p^*(\tau^*, \tilde{p}^w), \tilde{p}^w). \qquad (2.3)$$

Market clearing for good x is then implied by (2.1), (2.2), and (2.3).

We place some modest structure on the equilibrium prices. Specifically, we assume that the Metzler and Lerner paradoxes are ruled out, so that $dp/d\tau > 0 > dp^*/d\tau^*$ and $\partial \tilde{p}^w/\partial \tau < 0 < \partial \tilde{p}^w/\partial \tau^*$. The latter inequalities ensure that each country is "large," as a country can improve its terms of trade by increasing its tariff.

In summary, equilibrium values are implied by a given pair of tariffs in the following manner. First, given the tariffs, the equilibrium world price is determined by (2.3). Second, the equilibrium world price and the given tariffs determine the local prices. Third, the world and local prices imply values for the production, consumption, import, export, and tariff revenue levels.

2.2. Government Preferences

In representing government preferences, the traditional approach is to impose the assumption that governments maximize national income. By contrast, the political-economy approach emphasizes that governments are motivated by distributional concerns. Here, we follow Bagwell and Staiger (1999, 2002) and adopt a general representation for government preferences that (i) allows for both the terms-of-trade externality and political motivations, and (ii) facilitates the identification of the respective roles played by the terms-of-trade externality and political motivations in explaining the purpose of a trade agreement.

Formally, we represent the objectives of the home and foreign governments with the general functions $W(p, \tilde{p}^w)$ and $W^*(p^*, \tilde{p}^w)$, respectively. In expressing the welfare functions in this way, we break with the usual game-theoretic custom, under which payoffs (welfare values) are expressed directly in terms of actions (tariffs). Instead, we find it convenient to represent welfare in terms of the prices that the tariffs induce. As will become clear, this representation enables us to disentangle the separate roles played by the terms-of-trade externality and political motivations.

Allowing for a wide range of political motivations, we place no restrictions on government preferences over local prices. In fact, we impose only one assumption on the welfare functions (aside from standard assumptions to ensure that second-order conditions are globally met in each of the optimization problems considered below). We assume that, holding its local price fixed, each government achieves higher welfare when its terms of trade improve:

$$W_{\tilde{p}^w} < 0 \text{ and } W^*_{\tilde{p}^w} > 0. \tag{2.4}$$

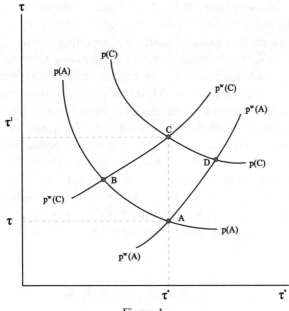

Figure 1.

This assumption can be understood using Figure 1. Point $A \equiv (\tau, \tau^*)$ represents an initial tariff pair. This pair is associated with a domestic iso-local-price locus, $p(A) \to p(A)$, and an iso-world-price locus, $p^w(A) \to p^w(A)$.[5] Point $C \equiv (\tau^1, \tau^*)$ denotes the tariff pair that obtains following an increase in the home tariff. This pair is associated with a second set of prices, corresponding to the domestic iso-local-price locus, $p(C) \to p(C)$, and the iso-world-price locus, $p^w(C) \to p^w(C)$. The world price is lower at C than at A, reflecting an improved terms-of-trade for the domestic country. A reduction in the world price that maintains the domestic local price is thus achieved with the movement from A to B. This movement corresponds to a higher (lower) domestic (foreign) import tariff. The meaning of condition (2.4) is thus simply that the domestic government values the international income transfer that is implied by the movement from A to B.

In both the traditional and the leading political-economy approaches to trade policy, governments maximize a welfare function of this form.

---

[5] Given our assumption that the Metzler and Lerner Paradoxes are ruled out, the iso-world-price locus takes a positive slope while the iso-local-price locus takes a negative slope.

Important formalizations of the traditional approach are offered by Dixit (1987), Johnson (1953–4), Kennan and Reizman (1988), and Mayer (1981). These models proceed under the assumption that the national welfare of a country improves when it experiences a terms-of-trade improvement. Within the political-economy literature, several specific models are entertained. As Mayer (1984) shows, if the government arises from a representative democracy, then the government sets its trade policy to promote the interests of the median voter, whose utility can be represented as a function of this form. Other major approaches to the political economy of trade policy are explored by Olson (1965), Caves (1976), Brock and Magee (1978), Feenstra and Bhagwati (1982), Findlay and Wellisz (1982), and Hillman (1982). As Baldwin (1987) observes, all of these approaches can also be represented in this form. Finally, the framework presented here also includes the lobbying models of Grossman and Helpman (1994, 1995).

2.3. Unilateral Trade Policies

In order to determine the problem that a trade agreement might solve, we must first characterize the unilateral trade policies that would arise in the absence of a trade agreement. We therefore derive the home and foreign tariff reaction functions. To this end, we suppose that each government sets its tariff policy to maximize its welfare, taking as given the tariff choices of its trading partner. These optimization problems determine the reaction functions, which are defined implicitly by

$$W_p[dp/d\tau] + W_{\tilde{p}^w}[\partial \tilde{p}^w/\partial \tau] = 0 \tag{2.5}$$

$$W_{p^*}^*[dp^*/d\tau^*] + W_{\tilde{p}^w}^*[\partial \tilde{p}^w/\partial \tau^*] = 0. \tag{2.6}$$

Let $\lambda \equiv [\partial \tilde{p}^w/\partial \tau]/[dp/d\tau] < 0$ and $\lambda^* \equiv [\partial \tilde{p}^w/\partial \tau^*]/[dp^*/d\tau^*] < 0$. We may rewrite (2.5) and (2.6) as

$$W_p + \lambda W_{\tilde{p}^w} = 0. \tag{2.7}$$

$$W_{p^*}^* + \lambda^* W_{\tilde{p}^w}^* = 0. \tag{2.8}$$

As these expressions make clear, the best-response tariff of each government reflects the combined effect on welfare of the induced local- and world-price movements.

Figure 1 offers further insight. Beginning at the initial tariff pair $A \equiv (\tau, \tau^*)$, suppose that the domestic government unilaterally increases its tariff and thus induces the new pair $C \equiv (\tau^1, \tau^*)$. As (2.7) suggests, we can disentangle the overall movement from A to C into separate movements in the local and world prices. The movement from A to B isolates the change in the world price, and the corresponding welfare effect for the domestic government is captured in (2.7) with the term $\lambda W_{\tilde{p}^w}$. This term is strictly positive by (2.4). The movement from B to C isolates the induced increase in the local price, holding fixed the world price, and the associated change in the domestic government's welfare is represented in (2.7) with the term W_p.

The welfare implications of the local-price movement from B to C are domestic in nature: they reflect the balance for the domestic government between the costs of the associated economic distortions and the benefits of any induced political support. By contrast, the welfare implications of the world-price movement from A to B are international in kind: they reflect the benefits to the domestic government of shifting the costs of its policy onto the foreign government. The cost shifting occurs, as this movement corresponds to an improvement (deterioration) in the domestic (foreign) country's terms of trade. Due to this terms-of-trade externality, if the domestic government seeks to implement a local price corresponding to the iso-local-price locus $p(C) \to p(C)$, then a unilateral increase in the domestic import tariff serves to shift a portion of the costs of this outcome onto the foreign government.

In a Nash equilibrium, both governments are on their reaction curves. A Nash equilibrium tariff pair, (τ^N, τ^{*N}), thus satisfies (2.7) and (2.8). We assume that this equilibrium represents the trade-policy decisions that governments would make if there were no trade agreement.

2.4. The Value of a Trade Agreement

Governments seek a trade agreement in order to achieve mutually beneficial changes in trade policy. If governments set Nash tariffs in the absence of a trade agreement, it follows that a trade agreement is valuable to governments if it results in tariff changes that generate Pareto improvements in government welfare beyond that achieved in the Nash equilibrium. This is possible, of course, if and only if the Nash equilibrium is inefficient (relative to government preferences). We therefore next discuss the efficiency frontier and its relationship to the Nash equilibrium.

We make three observations.[6] The first observation is that the Nash equilibrium is inefficient. This is intuitive. When a government sets its

---

[6] For formal proofs of these observations, see Bagwell and Staiger (1999, 2002).

trade policy unilaterally, it is able to shift some of the costs of its policy onto its trading partner, through the change in the terms of trade that its policy implies. In the absence of a trade agreement, therefore, governments do not have the incentive to set trade policies in an efficient manner. The second observation is that both governments can experience welfare gains relative to the Nash equilibrium only if they both agree to set tariffs below their Nash levels. The necessity of reciprocal trade liberalization is intuitive, too. In a Nash equilibrium, governments set tariffs that are higher than is efficient, because they each recognize that some of the costs of a higher tariff can be passed on to the trading partner. Not surprisingly, then, if both governments are to benefit from a trade agreement, then each must lower its tariff below its Nash level. Evidently, governments are attracted to trade agreements that result in reciprocal trade liberalization, whether or not the governments maximize national welfare.

The terms-of-trade externality is clearly one reason that the Nash equilibrium is inefficient. But are there also political externalities that create an additional reason for a trade agreement? To answer this question, we consider a hypothetical world in which governments are not motivated by the terms-of-trade implications of their trade-policy choices.[7] If unilateral tariff choices would be efficient in such a world, then it follows that the terms-of-trade externality is the only rationale for a trade agreement. We therefore define politically optimal tariffs as any tariff pair (τ^{PO}, τ^{*PO}) that satisfies the following two conditions:

$$W_p = 0 \text{ and } W_{p*}^* = 0.$$

In the special case where governments maximize national welfare, politically optimal tariffs correspond to reciprocal free trade. More generally, government objectives may also reflect political considerations, and then there is no expectation that politically optimal tariffs correspond to reciprocal free trade.

We come now to our third observation: politically optimal tariffs are efficient. To gain some intuition, suppose that each government sets its trade policy in order to achieve its preferred local price, so that tariffs are

---

[7] Our assumption here is not that governments fail to understand the terms-of-trade effects of their tariff choices. Instead, we consider a hypothetical situation in which governments are not motivated by these effects. In the context of (2.7), we allow that governments understand that $\lambda < 0$, but we now suppose that their welfare functions are such that $W_{\tilde{p}^w} \equiv 0$. After identifying the tariffs that would be selected by governments with these hypothetical preferences, we evaluate the efficiency of these tariffs with respect to actual government preferences.

set at their politically optimal levels, and consider a small increase in the domestic tariff. The tariff increase has three effects. First, it causes a small increase in the local price in the domestic country. Given that the domestic government initially has its preferred local price, however, this effect has no first-order impact on the domestic government's welfare. Second, the domestic tariff increase generates a small decrease in the local price of the foreign country. The foreign government, however, also initially has its preferred local price, and so this effect has no first-order impact on the foreign government's welfare. Third, the small increase in the domestic tariff induces a decrease in the world price. This terms-of-trade change, however, represents a pure international transfer in tariff revenue and thus cannot generate an efficiency gain. We may conclude that, if the terms-of-trade motivation is eliminated from the trade-policy choices of governments, then there is no potential for further Pareto improvements.

We pause now to remark on our large-country assumption. For the moment, suppose that the politically motivated governments preside over small countries. In this case, the terms-of-trade motivation would be eliminated from the trade-policy decisions of each government, simply because each government would recognize that it is unable to alter the terms of trade with its tariff selection. The governments of small countries would thus select the politically optimal tariffs, and their policies thus would be efficient. Consequently, in the leading political economy models of trade policy, there is no reason for the governments of small countries to form a trade agreement among themselves, regardless of the political motivations that these governments may possess. The value of trade agreements thus stems not from political motivations but rather from the terms-of-trade externality that is associated with the trade-policy choices of large countries.

To gain additional intuition, we return to Figure 1. Once again, suppose that tariffs are initially at point A and that the domestic government evaluates a tariff increase that would generate the point C. Consider first the possibility that the domestic government is motivated by the terms-of-trade consequences (that is, the movement from D to C) of its tariff policy. The domestic government then recognizes that some of the costs of achieving the higher local price at C are shifted onto its foreign trading partner, through the reduced world price, and this makes the tariff increase especially attractive. For this reason, Nash tariffs are always inefficient, with tariffs (trade volumes) that are too high (low). Consider second the possibility that the domestic government is not motivated by the terms-of-trade implications of its trade policy. In this case, it would

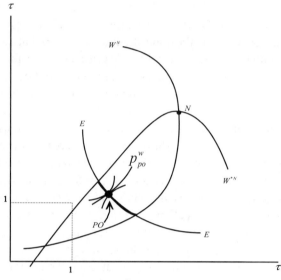

Figure 2.

prefer point C to point A if and only if it also prefers point D to point A. The potential appeal of point C is now separate from any cost-shifting benefits that derive from the consequent world price change; therefore, the domestic government now has the "right" incentives when evaluating the tariff increase.[8] When both governments reason in this manner, the resulting consistent set of tariffs is politically optimal and efficient.

Figure 2 offers a compact summary of the observations.[9] In agreement with the first observation, the Nash tariffs (point N) lie off of the efficiency locus (depicted by the curve $E \rightarrow E$). The figure also represents the Nash iso-welfare curves and thereby illustrates the second observation: a trade agreement can give both governments greater-than-Nash welfare only if the agreement results in a reduction in both tariffs. Finally, as the third observation requires, the politically optimal tariffs (point PO) rest on the efficiency locus. Of course, the iso-welfare curves are tangent at every

---

[8] A movement from A to D in Figure 1 induces no externality through the terms of trade. It does cause a change in the foreign local price; however, if the foreign government also selects politically optimal tariffs, then a small change of this kind has no first-order effect on foreign welfare.

[9] In this figure, we assume that a unique Nash equilibrium exists, a unique political optimum exists, and that the political optimum lies on the contract curve (i.e., it is on that portion of the efficiency locus at which each government obtains greater-than-Nash welfare). The political optimum rests on the contract curve, provided that countries are sufficiently symmetric.

point along the efficiency locus. At the politically optimal tariffs, however, the iso-welfare curves are also tangent to the iso-world-price locus (the locus $p_{po}^w \rightarrow p_{po}^w$). The contract curve is represented by the bold portion of the efficiency locus.

Figure 2 illustrates the basic task facing governments that seek to design a trade agreement. Noncooperative governments would set trade policies unilaterally and obtain the Nash outcome N. A trade agreement is then appealing to governments as a means to facilitate cooperation, so that tariffs may be moved from the inefficient Nash point to some alternative point on the contract curve. Among the tariffs on the contract curve, the politically optimal tariffs are focal: these tariffs remedy the terms-of-trade inefficiency in a direct way. As Figure 2 illustrates, the efficiency locus need not pass through the free-trade point, when governments have political concerns. But although governments' political motivations affect their preferences over tariffs (for example, the location of the efficiency locus), it is the terms-of-trade externality that creates a problem that a trade agreement might solve.

2.5. The Interpretation of the Terms-of-Trade Externality

The discussion above confirms a simple idea: governments can gain from a cooperative trade agreement, if otherwise each would attempt to shift costs onto the other and thus adopt inefficient unilateral policies. In this context, the terms-of-trade externality is simply the means through which such cost shifting would occur.

As explained in the Introduction, however, many economists are skeptical of the practical relevance of the terms-of-trade argument for trade agreements. One objection to this argument is that it is traditionally advanced in the company of the counterfactual assumption that governments maximize national income. We have just established, however, that the essential elements of the terms-of-trade argument are maintained whether or not governments have political motivations. A second objection is that the argument is based on abstract general equilibrium reasoning that seems to emphasize a logic that would not likely weigh heavily in the practical minds of policy makers.

We now address this second objection. The key point is that the terms-of-trade argument also may be interpreted in other ways, which are less abstract and thus suggest greater practical relevance. First, the theory may be developed in a partial-equilibrium framework. Cost shifting then occurs via the terms-of-trade externality if foreign exporters bear some of the incidence of the import tariff. Unilateral tariffs are now inefficient for an immediately plausible reason: the domestic government fails to internalize the harm to foreign exporters that its import tariff implies.[10] Second, the terms-of-trade theory is easily translated into the market-access language that dominates real-world trade policy negotiations. To see the point, suppose that the home government raises its import tariff and thereby shifts in its import demand curve. Notice that the resulting "price effect" (that is, the home country's terms-of-trade improvement) then has a corresponding "volume effect" (that is, the foreign country's reduction in access to the home market). Viewed in this light, it is natural that trade-policy negotiators emphasize the market-access implications of trade policy.

2.6. Rules versus Power

Our discussion to this point indicates that the purpose of a trade agreement is to provide an escape from a terms-of-trade driven Prisoners' Dilemma. In essence, we have supposed that a trade agreement enables governments to move from the inefficient Nash equilibrium, as depicted by the point N in Figure 2, to a point on the contract curve. This discussion, however, leaves open two important questions. First, how might governments best structure their negotiations in order to successfully navigate their way from the Nash equilibrium to the contract curve? Second, once governments leave the Nash equilibrium, each has some incentive to cheat (deviate to its reaction curve), and it therefore becomes important to ask: How is a trade agreement enforced? We begin our discussion of the first question here, and we consider both questions in some detail in Section 4.

A broad distinction can be made between two approaches to the structure of trade-policy negotiations. In particular, following Jackson (1997, 109–12), we draw a distinction between "power-based" and "rules-based" approaches to negotiation. Under a power-based approach, governments would bargain over tariffs in a direct fashion that is not constrained by agreed-upon principles of negotiation. For example, the negotiation between governments might be characterized by the Nash Bargaining

---

[10] This interpretation is developed further in Bagwell and Staiger (2001), where we use a partial equilibrium model and derive the three observations mentioned above. In Bagwell and Staiger (2002), we refer to empirical studies and argue for the presumption that foreign exporters are unable to completely "pass through" an import tariff.

Solution. Such a negotiation would deliver a point on the contract curve; however, the exact location of the negotiated outcome would depend upon the Nash payoffs (that is, the "threat point"). Consequently, the negotiated outcome would reflect existing "power asymmetries" across negotiation partners.

By contrast, under the approach to negotiations embodied in GATT/WTO, governments identify and agree upon certain principles by which subsequent negotiations must abide. The negotiation approach used in GATT/WTO is thus better described as a rules-based approach. Of course, to gain some understanding of the trade-policy negotiated outcome that might be induced by GATT/WTO rules, it is first necessary to identify the specific rules by which member governments must abide. We may then consider whether these rules can serve to reduce, or even eliminate, existing power asymmetries across negotiating partners. From the perspective of the terms-of-trade theory, if these rules induce large countries to behave as if they were small countries, and thereby guide the outcome of trade negotiations toward the political optimum, then we may conclude that GATT/WTO rules indeed do reduce power asymmetries.

3. THE HISTORY AND DESIGN OF GATT/WTO

Having discussed the theory of trade agreements, we now present a brief overview of the history and design of GATT/WTO. This overview provides an institutional context that guides our discussion in the next section.

3.1. The Origin of GATT and the WTO

GATT arose in response to the protectionist trade policies of the 1920s and 1930s. As is well known, trade barriers became increasingly restrictive following World War I. The situation worsened when the United States enacted the Smoot-Hawley Tariff Act in 1930. Average U.S. tariffs then increased from 38 percent to 52 percent. U.S. trading partners were, of course, not pleased, and a spate of retaliatory tariffs were imposed. Ultimately, the major powers imposed tariff rates that were generally on the order of 50 percent.

As Hudec (1990, 5) explains, "the postwar design for international trade policy was animated by a single-minded concern to avoid repeating the disastrous errors of the 1920's and 1930's." In terms of Figure 2, we may think of the Nash point N as corresponding to the "tariff war" that is associated with the Smoot-Hawley tariffs. The challenge before governments was then to find some means by which to implement a more cooperative trade-policy relationship, such as represented in Figure 2 by the efficiency locus.

During the 1920s and 1930s, there were, in fact, many multilateral attempts to achieve such a cooperative trade-policy relationship. The World Economic Conference of 1927 is one prominent example. These attempts were not successful, however. The interesting point here is that a general awareness among governments that mutual gains from cooperation were possible did not, by itself, result in the spontaneous emergence of cooperative behavior. In this regard, it is notable that the interwar attempts proceeded without an institutional structure that provides a set of rules under which governments could conduct negotiations, understand clearly their obligations, and enforce compliance. Without this structure, the initial multilateral efforts among governments, while well-intentioned, failed to get traction.

Over the interwar period, trade-policy cooperation instead took place through bilateral trade agreements. In the United States, Secretary of State Cordell Hull's efforts led to the U.S. Reciprocal Trade Agreement Act of 1934. An important advocate of reciprocity, Hull proposed that the United States offer import tariff reductions in exchange for reciprocal reductions in foreign import tariffs. Hull also offered support for the principle of nondiscrimination: when the United States lowered a tariff in a bilateral negotiation, that tariff cut would extend without discrimination to all trading partners of the United States that had been granted MFN status.

Encouraged by its success in the bilateral arena, the United States sought to build upon the key components of the Reciprocal Trade Agreements Act and establish a multilateral institution. In 1946, negotiations began for the creation of an International Trade Organization (ITO). Under the ITO, negotiations between governments would result in reciprocal and mutually advantageous reductions in tariffs, and the principle of nondiscrimination would then ensure that the reduced tariffs would be extended to all member countries. An interim agreement, known as the General Agreement on Tariffs and Trade (1947), was reached in 1947. While GATT was intended as an interim agreement, the ITO was never ratified by the U.S. Congress.

What is the purpose of GATT? According to the Preamble of GATT, the objectives of the contracting parties include "raising standards of living, ensuring full employment and a large and steadily growing volume

of real income and effective demand, developing the full use of the resources of the world and expanding the production and exchange of
goods." The Preamble also states the contracting parties' belief that
"reciprocal and mutually advantageous arrangements directed to the substantial reduction in tariffs and other barriers to trade and to the elimination of discriminatory treatment in international commerce" would
contribute toward these goals. Importantly, "free trade" is not the stated
objective of GATT.

There have been eight rounds of GATT negotiations. The primary focus of the earlier rounds was the reduction of import tariffs on goods.
In the most recent round, known as the Uruguay Round, governments
ventured into a number of new issues (for example, investment and intellectual property) and formed the WTO. This organization embraces the
rules and agreements made in GATT negotiations, but it is also a full-
fledged international organization, with an explicit organizational char-
ter and a unified dispute-settlement system. In effect, with the creation
of the WTO, participating governments fulfilled their original quest with
the ITO for an official international organization.

3.2. The Rules of GATT/WTO

GATT/WTO membership carries with it an obligation to abide by a set
of rules. GATT listed these rules in a series of thirty-nine articles. The
WTO has incorporated these GATT articles, and extended the principles
embodied in them to a variety of new issues. Here, we simply offer an
overview of the GATT/WTO legal structure by focusing on the principles
embodied in these articles.

To understand this structure, it is useful to distinguish between three
elements: substantive obligations, exceptions, and dispute settlement procedures. The substantive obligations of a GATT/WTO member refer to
tariff commitments, MFN treatment, and a set of other commitments that
together comprise a "code of conduct" in the international-trade arena.
Broadly speaking, these provisions define an obligation to concentrate
national protective measures into the form of tariffs, to apply them on
a nondiscriminatory basis, and to honor any tariff bindings made in a
GATT/WTO negotiation.

GATT/WTO also provides for exceptions to these obligations. One
class of exceptions is for "original" actions, such as when a member seeks
to withdraw a previous concession through renegotiation. The rationale
for including exceptions is that a government is more likely to make a

substantial tariff commitment, if the government knows that the legal system has "safeguards" so that its concessions can be withdrawn under appropriate conditions. Of course, a tariff commitment is meaningful only if exceptions for original actions are subject to some disciplining structure. For this reason, GATT/WTO rules also permit a second class of exceptions for "retaliatory" actions. In particular, if a government seeks to withdraw a previous concession, then GATT/WTO rules recognize the cost borne by its trading partner. This partner may seek "compensation" from the government (for example, a tariff reduction on some other good), and if this fails, it is allowed to achieve compensation through retaliation. The meaning of retaliation is that the trading partner can then reciprocate by withdrawing a concession of a "substantially equivalent" nature.

But how are these rules enforced? This question leads to the third element mentioned above: the GATT/WTO dispute settlement procedures. In GATT/WTO disputes, a central issue is whether the actions by one country serve to "nullify or impair" the benefits expected under the agreement by another country. Nullification or impairment includes actions taken by one country "which harmed the trade of another, and which 'could not reasonably have been anticipated' by the other at the time it negotiated for a concession" (Jackson 1997, 115). The typical case is a "violation complaint." This occurs when a country is alleged to have failed to carry out its GATT/WTO obligations, as when a tariff binding is broken.

It is important to distinguish between the procedures associated with safeguard exceptions and those that are associated with nullification or impairment. The safeguard procedures provide for the lawful withdrawal of negotiated concessions and specify the permissible retaliatory responses of trading partners. The dispute settlement procedures govern retaliation against a country that takes a harmful action which its trading partners could not have anticipated under GATT/WTO rules. In the typical case, the offending country has violated GATT/WTO rules, and retaliation here is more directly concerned with the enforcement of rules.

The procedure for settling disputes involves three stages: consultation among the involved parties; investigation, ruling, and recommendation by a GATT/WTO Panel (or Appellate Body); and as a last resort, authorization of retaliation. Resolution may be achieved in the first stage or it may follow the Panel ruling. If the Panel finds that nullification or impairment has occurred, then it recommends that the offending country correct any illegal measures. The offending country may be unwilling to do so, however. In this case, it may seek a negotiated resolution by offering the harmed country compensation via MFN tariff reductions on some other goods. If compensation is not offered, or rejected, then the harmed country may follow through with the last-resort response: an authorized and discriminatory suspension of tariff concessions. In practice, the number of authorized retaliations has been small.[11] As Rhodes (1993, 109) argues, however, the threat of authorized retaliation is often the catalyst that ensures resolution in the earlier stages.

3.3. Reciprocity in GATT/WTO

As the preceding discussion confirms, the enforcement provisions of GATT/WTO are elaborate. The representation of reciprocity in GATT/WTO, however, may be less apparent. In GATT/WTO, the principle of reciprocity refers to the ideal of mutual changes in trade policy which bring about changes in the volume of each country's imports that are of equal value to changes in the volume of its exports. The preceding discussion contains two instances in which a reference to reciprocity arises. First, when governments negotiate in GATT/WTO rounds, they do so with the presumed goal of obtaining mutually advantageous arrangements through reciprocal reductions in tariff bindings. In particular, it is often observed that governments approach negotiations seeking a "balance of concessions," whereby the tariff reduction offered by one government is balanced against an "equivalent" concession from its trading partner. Second, when a government seeks to renegotiate and withdraws a previous concession as an original action, GATT/WTO rules allow that substantially affected trading partners may retaliate in a reciprocal manner, by withdrawing "substantially equivalent concessions."

4. THE THEORY OF GATT/WTO

We now consider the theoretical interpretation of two key GATT/WTO features: reciprocity and enforcement.

We begin with the principle of reciprocity. While we describe above the ideal of reciprocity, our first task here is to offer a formal definition of reciprocity. Utilizing the general equilibrium model of trade presented above and following Bagwell and Staiger (1999), our next task is to show that the concept of reciprocity can be given a very simple formal

---

[11] Under GATT, retaliation was authorized in only one case, concerning the United States and the Netherlands, and even then the Netherlands never acted on that authorization (Jackson 1997, 116). The dispute settlement procedures under the WTO are considerably strengthened. Under the WTO, further cases have emerged in which retaliation has been authorized – and used. These include the well-known banana and beef-hormone cases. Further discussion is offered by Mavroidis (2000) and WTO (2001, 28).

characterization. Finally, we consider in further detail the application of reciprocity in GATT/WTO.

How might the concept of reciprocity be formally defined? Suppose that a tariff negotiation results in a change from an initial pair of tariffs, (τ^0, τ^{*0}), to a subsequent pair of tariffs, (τ^1, τ^{*1}). The initial world and domestic local prices may be denoted as $\tilde{p}^{w0} \equiv \tilde{p}^w(\tau^0, \tau^{*0})$ and $p^0 \equiv p(\tau^0, \tilde{p}^{w0})$; likewise, the subsequent world and domestic local prices may be represented as $\tilde{p}^{w1} \equiv \tilde{p}^w(\tau^1, \tau^{*1})$ and $p^1 \equiv p(\tau^1, \tilde{p}^{w1})$. We may now say that the tariff changes conform to *the principle of reciprocity* provided that

$$\tilde{p}^{w0}[M_x(p^1, \tilde{p}^{w1}) - M_x(p^0, \tilde{p}^{w0})] = [E_y(p^1, \tilde{p}^{w1})$$
$$- E_y(p^0, \tilde{p}^{w0})] \tag{4.1}$$

where changes in trade volumes are valued at the existing world price.

We next use the trade balance condition (2.1) and offer a characterization of reciprocity. Given balanced trade at the initial tariffs, we know that $\tilde{p}^{w0} M_x(p^0, \tilde{p}^{w0}) = E_y(p^0, \tilde{p}^{w0})$; thus, (4.1) may be rewritten as $\tilde{p}^{w0} M_x(p^1, \tilde{p}^{w1}) = E_y(p^1, \tilde{p}^{w1})$.

Balanced trade at the subsequent tariffs means that $\tilde{p}^{w1} M_x(p^1, \tilde{p}^{w1}) = E_y(p^1, \tilde{p}^{w1})$; therefore, with this further application of the trade balanced condition, (4.1) may be rewritten as

$$[\tilde{p}^{w1} - \tilde{p}^{w0}]M_x(p^1, \tilde{p}^{w1}) = 0 \tag{4.2}$$

We thus come to a striking characterization: mutual changes in trade policy conform to the principle of reciprocity if and only if the world price is unchanged.

The potential significance of this characterization is apparent, when it is recalled from Section 2 that a government sets its tariffs in an inefficient manner if and only if it is motivated by the change in the world price that its tariff choice implies. To gain further insight, we consider the application of reciprocity within GATT/WTO practice. As discussed above, reciprocity arises in GATT/WTO practice in two ways.

The first application of reciprocity reflects the balance of concessions that governments seek through a negotiated agreement. This informal principle of reciprocity contrasts with a standard economic argument that free trade is a country's optimal unilateral policy. As we now demonstrate, however, the terms-of-trade theory offers a simple interpretation of this application of reciprocity.

Suppose that governments begin at the Nash equilibrium point. At the Nash point, we may use (2.4), (2.7), and (2.8) to conclude that $W_p < 0 < W^*_{p^*}$. If governments were to reduce tariffs in a reciprocal manner that preserved the world price, then the domestic local price p would fall and the foreign local price p^* would rise; consequently, the domestic-government welfare would rise (as $W_p < 0$) and the foreign-government welfare would also rise (as $W^*_{p^*} > 0$). Intuitively, at the Nash equilibrium, both governments would prefer more trade, if the increase in trade volume could be obtained without a terms-of-trade loss. Neither government is willing to liberalize unilaterally, because its country would then experience a decline in the terms of trade. But if the liberalization occurs under the principle of reciprocity, with one country's tariff reduction balanced against that of the other, then the terms of trade are held constant. Each government can then gain from an expansion in trade volume without experiencing a terms-of-trade loss.

The central ideas are summarized in Figure 3. In Figure 3a, the case of symmetric countries is illustrated. The iso-world-price locus that runs through the Nash point N then also extends to the politically optimal point PO. As governments liberalize under reciprocity, they move down the Nash iso-world-price locus, and each experiences welfare gains along the way until the political optimum is reached. Once the political optimum is obtained, the governments are on the efficiency locus and have no incentive for further negotiations. The case of asymmetric countries is depicted in Figure 3b, wherein the Nash iso-world-price locus does not run through the politically optimal point. Liberalization under reciprocity that begins at the Nash point still raises the welfare of each government;

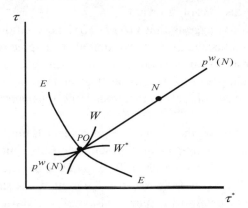

Figure 3a.

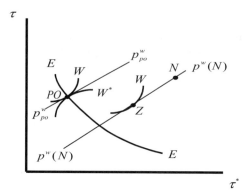

Figure 3b.

however, the mutual benefits from further liberalization are extinguished before the efficiency frontier is reached. For example, in Figure 3b, the mutual benefits from further liberalization terminate at point Z where the home government has achieved its preferred local price (that is, at the Nash world price, $W_p = 0$ at point Z).

The second application of reciprocity in GATT/WTO concerns the rules under which trade agreements may be renegotiated. GATT Article XXVIII allows that a country may propose to withdraw a concession agreed upon in a previous round of negotiation. If the country and its trading partner are unable to agree upon a renegotiated tariff structure, then the country may carry out its proposed change anyway, with the understanding that the trading partner may then reciprocate with its own change. In this context, the notion of reciprocity is used to moderate the response of the trading partner, who is allowed to withdraw substantially equivalent concessions of its own.

This discussion suggests that GATT/WTO negotiations may be understood as a multistage game. Governments first agree to an initial set of tariffs in a round of negotiations. Second, each government considers whether it would prefer to raise its tariff, given that the outcome of any renegotiation must conform to reciprocity and thus preserve the world price.

A figure can capture the key ideas. Figure 4 depicts three possible tariff pairs – A, B, and PO – that might represent an efficient initial agreement. The iso-world-price loci for each tariff pair are also depicted. As well, the loci for which $W_p = 0$ and $W^*_{p^*} = 0$ are represented. For simplicity, these loci are assumed downward sloping. As Bagwell and Staiger (1999) show,

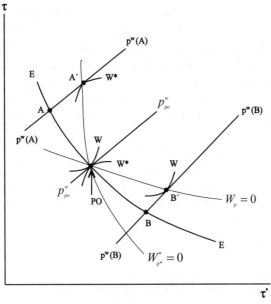

Figure 4.

each locus intersects the efficiency frontier only at the politically optimal point PO.

Now consider an initial agreement at point A. The foreign government would prefer to move up the iso-world-price locus to the point A', where it achieves its preferred local price. It would thus request a renegotiation to raise its tariff to the value corresponding to point A', with the understanding that the domestic government would then withdraw a substantially equivalent concession that would preserve the world price and therefore deliver the tariff pair at point A'. The efficient tariff pair at point A thus fails to be robust against the type of renegotiation that GATT/WTO allows. A similar argument applies for the efficient tariff pair associated with point B. At this tariff pair, it is the domestic government that withdraws its original concession in order to induce the point B'. In fact, there is only one efficient tariff pair that is robust to the possibility of renegotiation. The politically optimal tariff pair is the only point on the efficiency locus at which both governments achieve their preferred local prices given the associated world price.

It is interesting to compare the hypothetical world that led to the definition of politically optimal tariffs with what governments achieve under reciprocity. In the hypothetical world, governments were assumed not to value the terms-of-trade movements caused by their tariff choices, and they were thus led to select politically optimal tariffs. Reciprocity corresponds to a related experiment, in which governments ignore the terms-of-trade movements associated with their tariff increase, because the mutual changes in tariffs under reciprocity guarantee that the terms of trade are, in fact, fixed. Reciprocity thus induces governments to act as if they did not value the terms-of-trade movements caused by their tariff selections.[12]

In effect, governments are "penalized" under the GATT/WTO reciprocity rule if they attempt to negotiate an efficient tariff pair other than the political optimum. Consider, for example, point A in Figure 3. At this point, the home government enjoys greater welfare than it would at the political optimum; however, some of the benefit to the home government of point A would be lost in the subsequent renegotiation to the point A'. The home government therefore may be less desirous of pushing negotiations away from the political optimum and toward point A. As illustrated by this example, the reciprocity rule helps to mitigate the power asymmetries that governments might otherwise wield at the bargaining table. As a consequence, it encourages governments to select the politically optimal tariffs.

4.1. Enforcement

In the context of Figure 2, suppose that governments have formed a trade agreement that specifies rules under which they negotiate from the Nash point N to a point on contract curve, such as the political optimum, PO. How is this agreement enforced?

Unfortunately, the temptation for a government to select a high tariff and shift costs does not evaporate just because an agreement is signed. Each government has a short-term incentive to deviate to a higher-than-is-efficient tariff and enjoy the associated terms-of-trade gain. Unlike many agreements reached under domestic law, a trade agreement is not enforced through the threat of incarceration. There is no "world jail" into which government leaders are thrown if they violate a trade agreement. Rather, a trade agreement must be "self-enforcing": a government will be

---

[12] Formally, as (2.7) indicates, if $\lambda W_{\tilde{p}^w} = 0$, then the domestic government's preferred tariff satisfies $W_p = 0$. In turn, if the government were hypothesized not to value a change in the terms of trade (i.e., if $W_{\tilde{p}^w} \equiv 0$), then W_p would be zero. Likewise, if the government were to expect a reciprocal tariff adjustment from its trading partner that would result in no change in the terms of trade (i.e., if $\lambda = 0$), then W_p would be zero.

dissuaded from violating the agreement only if the short-term gains lead to long-term losses, once other governments retaliate in kind. Viewed this way, the tariffs that governments can achieve as part of a self-enforcing trade agreement reflect a balance between the short-term benefit of protection and the long-term cost of retaliation. The "most-cooperative" tariffs that governments can enforce may not be fully efficient, but the most-cooperative tariffs are more efficient than Nash tariffs.

As McMillan (1986, 1989), Dixit (1987), and Bagwell and Staiger (1990) emphasize, the theory of repeated games may be used to analyze the enforcement issues that are associated with trade agreements. Formally, we may regard the static framework described above as the stage game of an infinitely repeated game. As governments cooperate by imposing low tariffs that rest below the tariff reaction functions, each government perceives a short-run benefit from a unilateral tariff increase. Each government, however, may be concerned that such a deviation, once discovered, could lead to retaliation. At the extreme, recalcitrant behavior could undermine the entire agreement and ultimately lead countries back to the inefficient Nash outcome. This long-term cost may serve as an effective deterrent, provided that the short-term incentive to cheat is not too great. Thus, even if governments cannot cooperate fully, some cooperation can be sustained.

We now argue that this repeated-game perspective is consistent with the GATT/WTO enforcement provisions as described in Section 3. The creation of GATT and its nullification-or-impairment procedures may be interpreted as an attempt to replace the Nash outcome with a more efficient equilibrium outcome. To accomplish this, governments agreed through GATT to limit the use of retaliation along the equilibrium path and reposition it as an off-equilibrium-path threat that enforces rules. It must be stressed, however, that a limited role for retaliation indeed does arise along the equilibrium path. This occurs, for example, when a government seeks a retaliatory exception to obtain compensation for an original tariff modification by its trading partner, where the original modification is a legal exception such as allowed under GATT Article XXVIII (renegotiation). The role of retaliation in GATT/WTO is thus more subtle than a standard application of repeated-game theory might suggest.

The distinction between the on- and off-equilibrium-path roles of retaliation may be further clarified with the consideration of two situations. First, suppose that a foreign government raises its tariff above its bound rate and justifies its behavior as a legal exception under the rules for renegotiation. If the parties are unable to reach an agreement on compensation, then the home government may take its own retaliatory exception, with a "substantially equivalent" tariff hike. Here, retaliation is best interpreted as an on-equilibrium-path event. It serves to discipline the use of legal exceptions, so that their application reflects a legitimate purpose (for example, changed circumstances) rather than an opportunistic desire to shift costs onto a trading partner.

Second, suppose that the home government complains that the foreign trade policy has changed in a manner that nullifies or impairs the access to the foreign market that the home government initially expected. Suppose further that the case is brought before a dispute panel, the panel finds in favor of the foreign government, and the home government nevertheless imposes unauthorized retaliatory tariffs. Such defiant behavior is best interpreted as an off-equilibrium-path deviation. What deters this deviant behavior?

Of course, the foreign government then may be authorized to retaliate against the unauthorized retaliatory tariffs. But this may only extend the cycle: the home government may respond with yet another unauthorized retaliatory response. The fundamental deterrent to such contumacious behavior, and the deterrent that rests at the foundation of all others, is the fear of initiating a breakdown in the entire cooperative arrangement and thereby causing a "trade war" (that is, a return to the Nash point, N). As in the repeated-game model, this breakdown threat is the ultimate off-equilibrium-path retaliation, and it discourages deviant behavior of this second kind.

5. CONCLUSION

In the discussion above, we offer two main conclusions. First, whether or not governments have political motivations, the purpose of a trade agreement is to offer a means of escape from a terms-of-trade-driven Prisoners' Dilemma. Second, GATT/WTO's reciprocity and enforcement rules are well designed to facilitate such an escape.

Given space restrictions, there are a number of further issues that are not treated here. We refer the reader to our book (Bagwell and Staiger, 2002) for a more thorough treatment of the topics raised above, an analysis of the efficiency properties of other GATT/WTO rules (for example, the MFN rule and those rules that concern the treatment of preferential trading agreements and agricultural subsidies), a discussion of several new trade-policy issues that currently confront the WTO (for example, the treatment of labor and environmental standards as well as competition policy), and a variety of important modeling extensions (for example, many goods, multiple trading partners). Instead, we use this concluding section to highlight three important areas for future research.

A first area concerns the purpose of a trade agreement. Our representation of government preferences includes those used in the leading political-economy models of trade policy. Nevertheless, an alternative formulation might point to a novel problem that a trade agreement could solve. One approach is to allow that governments face a time-consistency problem, in which case a government might use a trade agreement to facilitate its commitment to a liberalization process. Recent analyses that emphasize this possibility are offered by Maggi and Rodriguez (1998), McLaren (1997), and Staiger and Tabellini (1999). A second approach is to relax the market-clearing assumption that underlies our general equilibrium model. For example, in line with Keynesian theory, if markets are characterized by rigid markups, then the externalities from trade policy are not channeled through changes in the terms of trade; rather, an import tariff harms foreign exporters by reducing the trade volume on which they enjoy fixed markups. It remains to be seen if these alternative approaches offer an interpretation of the rules of GATT/WTO. This is an important direction that should be pursued in future research.

A second area concerns the role of the GATT/WTO institution in achieving a cooperative trade-policy outcome. At a theoretical level, given the efficiency-enhancing properties of the rules of GATT/WTO, it is not obvious why governments could not come to a tacit understanding to follow these rules. Why is it necessary to have an actual institution? The natural response to this question emphasizes the coordination difficulties in achieving a common and cooperative understanding between multiple participants over a complex set of issues. In particular, although GATT/WTO rules may be understood as the codification of supergame strategies, in the real world, it may be difficult for a large number of countries trading thousands of goods to come to a common and tacit understanding of such strategies. The failed attempts at cooperation in the 1920s and 1930s are indicative of this formidable coordination problem. An actual institution, with a set of rules that makes explicit the obligations of governments and the manner in which these obligations are enforced, may be necessary to get traction in the multilateral journey from a noncooperative relationship toward the efficiency frontier. Ambitious future work would provide a theoretical framework on the basis of which this response might be affirmed or rejected.[13]

Relatedly, it is not obvious why governments should favor a rules-based institution like GATT/WTO over a power-based approach. While we argue that the existing rules-based approach has an attractive design, could not governments do better by eliminating the constraints that rules imply and negotiating directly over tariffs on the efficiency frontier? This question suggests that future work might look for a problem that arises under power-based negotiations and is moderated or eliminated under a rules-based approach. One such problem may be associated with equity considerations: a power-based approach favors the strong, and this may be objectionable on equity grounds. Another approach is to argue that power-based negotiations lead to inefficiencies. Building on McLaren's (1997) ideas, we argue in Bagwell and Staiger (1999, 2002) that power-based negotiations may lead to inefficient participation, as weaker governments may fear being "held up" in subsequent negotiations with stronger governments. Power-based negotiations also may lead to inefficiencies, if governments dissipate rents (for example, through signaling activities) in order to become (or seem) stronger, so as to enjoy the greater benefits that stronger parties enjoy in a power-based system. A rules-based approach may limit such inefficiencies. Important future work would explore a broader game, with potential inefficiencies for power-based negotiations, and determine the equity and efficiency differences between rules- and power-based approaches to trade-policy negotiations.

A third area for future research is empirical. Our discussion emphasizes the terms-of-trade externality as the reason for a trade agreement. In Bagwell and Staiger (2002), we argue that there is strong support for the presumption that trade policies generate important terms-of-trade externalities. But this area of work is still quite new, and there is much more to be learned about the size and pattern of terms-of-trade externalities across trading partners.

---

[13] One thought is that an explicit multilateral institution enhances cooperation by facilitating the exchange of information. For example, as Maggi (1999) suggests, GATT/WTO may provide a forum in which deviations may be publicized, so that third-party punishments may be brought forth. Likewise, as Athey and Bagwell (2001) argue in the context of collusion theory, actual meetings may be necessary, if the form of optimal cooperation requires the (incentive-compatible) communication of private information.

REFERENCES

Athey, Susan and Kyle Bagwell. 2001. "Optimal Collusion with Private Information," *The Rand Journal of Economics* 32.3, Autumn, 428–65.

Bagwell, Kyle and Robert W. Staiger. 1990. "A Theory of Managed Trade," *American Economic Review* 80, September 1990, 779–95.

Bagwell, Kyle and Robert W. Staiger. 1999. "An Economic Theory of GATT," *American Economic Review* 89.1, March, 215–48.

Bagwell, Kyle and Robert W. Staiger. 2001. "Reciprocity, Non-Discrimination and Preferential Agreements in the Multilateral Trading System," *European Journal of Political Economy* 17, 281–325.

Bagwell, Kyle and Robert W. Staiger. 2002. *The Economics of the World Trading System*. Cambridge: The MIT Press.

Baldwin, Richard. 1987. "Politically Realistic Objective Functions and Trade Policy," *Economics Letters* 24, 287–90.

Brock, William A. and Stephen P. Magee. 1978. "The Economics of Special Interest Politics," *American Economic Review* 68, May, 246–50.

Caves, Richard A. 1976. "Economic Models of Political Choice: Canada's Tariff Structure," *Canadian Journal of Economics* 9, May, 278–300.

Dixit, Avinash. 1987. "Strategic Aspects of Trade Policy," in Truman F. Bewley, ed., *Advances in Economic Theory: Fifth World Congress*. New York: Cambridge University Press.

Feenstra, Robert and Jagdish Bhagwati. 1982. "Tariff Seeking and the Efficient Tariff," in Jagdish Bhagwati, ed., *Import Competition and Response*. Chicago: University of Chicago Press.

Findlay, Ronald and Stanislaw Wellisz. 1982. "Endogenous Tariffs, the Political Economy of Trade Restrictions and Welfare," in Jagdish Bhagwati, ed., *Import Competition and Response*. Chicago: University of Chicago Press.

Grossman, Gene M. and Elhanan Helpman. 1994. "Protection for Sale," *American Economic Review* 84, September, 833–50.

Grossman, Gene M. and Elhanan Helpman. 1995. "Trade Wars and Trade Talks," *Journal of Political Economy* 103, August, 675–708.

Hillman, Arye L. 1982. "Declining Industries and Political-Support Protectionist Motives," *American Economic Review* 72, 1180–7.

Hudec, Robert E. 1990. *The GATT Legal System and World Trade Diplomacy*, 2nd ed. New York: Praeger Publisher.

Jackson, John. 1997. *The World Trading System*, 2nd ed. Cambridge: The MIT Press.

Johnson, Harry G. 1953–4. "Optimum Tariffs and Retaliation," *Review of Economic Studies* 1.2, 142–53.

Kennan, John and Raymond Reizman. 1988. "Do Big Countries Win Tariff Wars?" *International Economic Review* 29, 81–5.

Maggi, Giovanni. 1999. "The Role of Multilateral Institutions in International Trade Cooperation," *American Economic Review* 89.1, March, 190–214.

Maggi, Giovanni and Andres Rodriguez-Clare. 1998. "The Value of Trade Agreements in the Presence of Political Pressures," *Journal of Political Economy* 106.3, 574–601.

Mavroidis, Petros C. 2000. "Remedies in the WTO Legal System: Between a Rock and a Hard Place," *European Journal of International Law* 11.4, 763–813.

Mayer, Wolfgang. 1981. "Theoretical Considerations on Negotiated Tariff Adjustments," *Oxford Economic Papers* 33, 135–53.

Mayer, Wolfgang. 1984. "Endogenous Tariff Formation," *American Economic Review* 74, 970–85.

McLaren, John. 1997. "Size, Sunk Costs, and Judge Bowker's Objection to Free Trade," *American Economic Review* 87, 400–20.

McMillan, John. 1986. *Game Theory in International Economics.* New York: Harwood.

McMillan, John. 1989. "A Game-Theoretic View of International Trade Negotiations: Implications for Developing Countries," in John Whalley, ed., *Developing Countries and the Global Trading System: Volume 1.* London: Macmillan.

Mill, John Stuart. 1844. *Essays on Some Unsettled Questions of Political Economy.* London: Parker.

Olson, Mancur. 1965. *The Logic of Collective Action.* Cambridge: Harvard University Press.

Rhodes, Carolyn. 1993. *Reciprocity, U.S. Trade Policy, and the GATT Regime,* Ithaca, NY: Cornell University Press.

Staiger, Robert W. and Guido Tabellini. 1999. "Do GATT Rules Help Governments Make Domestic Commitments?," *Economics and Politics* XI.2, July, 109–44.

Torrens, Robert. 1844. *The Budget: On Commercial Policy and Colonial Policy.* London: Smith, Elder.

WTO. 2001. *Annual Report 2001.* Geneva.

8

What's New in Development Economics?

Debraj Ray

1. INTRODUCTION

This essay is meant to describe the current frontiers of development economics, as I see them. I may as well throw up my hands at the onset and say, There are too many frontiers. In recent years, the subject has made excellent use of economic theory, econometric methods, sociology, anthropology, political science, and demography and has burgeoned into one of the liveliest areas of research in all the social sciences. And about time, too: the study of economic development is probably the most challenging in all of economics, and – provided we are patient about getting to "the bottom line" and the "policy implications" – it can have enormous payoffs.

Fortunately, considerations of space allow me to use brevity as an excuse for selectivity. So rather than attempt an exhaustive review of several areas, I would like to concentrate on a few methodological points around which recent literature appears to have clustered. More than anything else, I want to underscore a certain way of *thinking* about development that has become increasingly influential over the last few decades, one that is changing and will continue to change the face of research in this discipline.

The main trend I would like to try and document is a move – welcome, in my opinion – away from a traditional preoccupation with the notion of *convergence*. This is the basic notion that given certain parameters, say savings or fertility rates, economies inevitably move toward some steady state. If these parameters are the same across economies, then in the long run all economies converge to one another. I review this approach very briefly in Section 2. I then explain why this view leads to (1) a limited depth in the way we ask development questions, and (2) a certain type of policy bias. In Section 3, I discuss the first of two types of theories that take us away from the determinism inherent in the convergence idea. This is an approach based on the notion of multiple equilibria – several dramatically different outcomes can occur given the same fundamentals. In Section 4, I return to equilibria that are determined fundamentally by historical conditions. That is, given a particular historical experience, the outcome that results is fully pinned down, but the influence of that historical experience persists through time in observed outcomes. In either case, there is no presumption of convergence or ahistoricity. I will argue that this approach gives us different insights, both in the way we ask questions and with regard to policy.

Although I am tempted by fashionable trends in nomenclature, I hesitate to call this the "New Development Economics." If writers such as Paul Rosenstein-Rodan or Albert Hirschman were to encounter such a phrase (and the subsequent accompanying description), they would be scandalized. Much of recent thinking in development can be traced back to the insights of these two eminent writers, and the retracing of their paths continues to bring to light fresh insights and arguments.

2. A TRADITIONAL VIEW

Open a book – almost any book – on the economics of developing countries, and it will begin with the usual litany of woes. Developing countries, notwithstanding the enormous strides they have made in the last few decades, display fundamental economic inadequacies in a wide range of indicators. Levels of physical capital per person are small. Nutrition levels are low. Other indicators of human capital such as education – both at the primary and secondary levels – are well below developed-country benchmarks. So are access to sanitation, safe water, and housing. Population growth rates are high, and so too are infant mortality rates. One could expand this list indefinitely.

Notice that some of these indicators – infant survival rates or life expectancy, for instance – may be regarded as *defining* features of underdevelopment, so in this respect the above list may be viewed, not as a statement of correlations, but as a definition of what we mean by development (or the lack of it). But other indicators, such as low quantities of physical capital per capita, or population growth rates, are at least one step removed. These features don't define underdevelopment. For instance, it is unclear whether low fertility rates are an intrinsic feature of economic welfare or development: surely, many families in rich countries may take great pleasure in having a large number of offspring. Likewise, large holdings of physical capital may well have an instrumental value to play in the development process, but surely the mere existence of such holdings does not constitute a defining characteristic of economic welfare.

And indeed, that is how it should be. We do not make a list of the features that go hand-in-hand with underdevelopment simply to define the term. We do so because – whether implicitly or explicitly – we are looking for answers to the question, Why are some countries underdeveloped and others not?[1] One way of addressing this question is to look at empirical relationships between some measure of development (say per-capita GDP) and other (presumably exogenous) factors. For instance, one might regress per-capita income on variables such as the rate of savings (or investment) or population growth rates (see, for example, Mankiw, Romer, and Weil 1992).

The background hypothesis of *convergence* – which goes back to Solow (1956), but also has a parallel in the theory of optimal growth[2] – has often been invoked to interpret empirical work of this sort. The basic idea of convergence is very simple indeed. Suppose that all production is carried out using capital and labor, and a constant fraction of national income is saved. Then countries with a low endowment of capital relative to labor will have a high rate of return to capital (by the "law" of diminishing returns). Consequently, a given addition to the capital stock will have a larger impact on per-capita income. It follows that, controlling for savings rates, poorer countries will tend to grow faster and hence will catch up, converge.

To be sure, the savings rate is not the only factor that qualifies the argument. Anything that systematically affects the marginal addition to per-capita income must be controlled for, including sharp quantifiables such as population growth rates (which affect the denominator of per-capita income) or looser concepts such as "political climate" or "corruption" (which might affect the rate of return to capital).

---

[1] Perhaps the word "underdeveloped" does not constitute politically correct usage, so that several publications – those by well-known international organizations chief among them – use the more hopeful and placatory term "developing." I will refrain from such niceties in this article because it should be clear – or at least it is clear in my mind – that *economic* underdevelopment pins no derogatory social label on those who live in, or come from, such societies.

[2] See the literature on turnpike theory inspired initially by the work of von Neumann (1945), followed by several writers – see McKenzie (1976) for a survey.

Thus the convergence hypothesis, properly interpreted, does not really mean that all countries do actually converge. But it does mean that a failure to observe convergence must be traced to one or another of the so-called exogenous factors that we have just described. This has two important – and unfortunate – implications for the way we think about development.

First, it limits our search for deep explanations. It is not uncommon to find economists "explaining" intercountry variation by stating that one country is more corrupt than another, or more democratic, or is imbued with some particularly hard-working cultural ethic. One might even hang one's hat on the following sort of theory: Different societies have some *intrinsic* difference in their willingness – or ability – to save, or to procreate. Therefore such-and-such country is poor or underdeveloped because it is populated by people who habitually save very little, or procreate a lot.

At some level these "explanations" are perfectly valid. But they are not very deep. We would like to have a theory that – while not belittling or downplaying the role of social, cultural, and political factors – does not simply stop there. We would like to know, for instance, whether low incomes provoke, in turn, low savings rates so that we have a genuine chicken-and-egg problem. The same is true of demographics – might underdevelopment be a cause of high population growth rates, just as high population growth rates themselves retard the development process? More boldly, we might seek a theory of corruption that views corruption just as much an outcome as a cause.

Now simply asserting that "nothing is truly exogenous" doesn't take us very far. The question is whether one can study these interactions in a way that yields new insights. In what follows, I will try and argue that this can be (and is being) done.

The second problem with the convergence approach is that it generates a particular set of attitudes toward economic *policy*. By stressing the role of factors such as savings, population growth, or levels of corruption that might actually be symptoms rather than causes of underdevelopment, they promote superficial (and sometimes wrong) policy interventions. If these factors are a *result* of underdevelopment rather than simply its cause, they are unlikely to be prone to manipulation by simple-minded policy tinkering. And even if the policies are effective, such approaches can lead to misjudgment on the required duration of necessary interventions. For instance, suppose we believe that Bangladeshi growth rates are low because Bangladeshi society somehow promotes high fertility (the outcome, let us say, of religious or cultural attitudes). If the fertility rate is truly believed to be exogenous as a consequence, a policy of of lowering fertility (say, through monetary incentives) will certainly have an effect on growth rates. But the incentives would have to be offered *indefinitely*. In contrast, an interactive approach to the fertility-growth problem may suggest permanent effects of one-time interventions, an issue we shall return to below in more detail.

In the two sections of the essay that follow, I outline theories that go beyond the convergence idea. In these theories, *societies that are fundamentally similar in all respects might behave differently, and persistently so*. I shall discuss two reasons for this persistent difference. The first is based on the notion of underdevelopment as a self-fulfilling failure of expectations. According to this approach (Section 3), economies exhibit multiple equilibria. Some societies may be stuck in the "bad" equilibrium, exhibiting shortfalls in familiar development indicators. Simultaneously, such societies may display low savings rates or "cultures of corruption," but this latter set of features cannot be related causally to the former.

The second set of theories (Section 4) is based on the notion of underdevelopment as a persistent outcome of certain historical configurations. Once again, two blueprints of two societies may be the same, but differences in certain initial conditions cause persistent differences in subsequent trajectories. In particular, we will focus on differences in initial economic inequality, although all sorts of other initial conditions could profitably be considered.

3. UNDERDEVELOPMENT AND EXPECTATIONS

3.1. Multiple Equilibria

Paul Rosenstein-Rodan (1943) and Albert Hirschman (1958) argued that economic development could be thought of as a massive *coordination failure*, in which several investments do not occur simply because other complementary investments are not made, and similarly, these latter investments are not forthcoming simply because the former are missing. Thus one might conceive of *two* equilibria *under the very same fundamental conditions*, one in which active investment is taking place, with each industry's efforts motivated and justified by the expansion of other industries, and another equilibrium involving persistent stagnation, in which the inactivity of one industry seeps into another. This serves as a potential explanation of why similar economies may behave very differently.

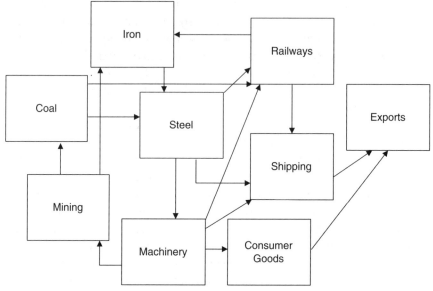

Figure 1. Interindustry links.

The work of these two writers brings out the essential feature that is needed for "multiple equilibria" to arise, at least for multiple equilibria that can be ranked by some welfare criterion such as Pareto-dominance. This is the basic idea of *complementarity*: a particular form of external-ity in which the taking of an action by an agent increases the marginal benefit to other agents from taking the same (or similar) action. As ex-amples, consider the two main sources of coordination failure discussed by Rosenstein-Rodan and Hirschman.

1. **Interindustry Links**. The expansion of a particular production sector will have both direct and indirect implications for other sectors through these links. For instance, the development of a transportation network, such as railways, will facilitate the export of certain types of products, and thereby encourage their production. This is an example of what might be called a *supply link*, one that works by lowering the cost of inputs to another sector. At the same time, the expansion of railways will raise the demand for railway inputs, such as steel. This is an example of a *demand link*.

Supply and demand links may, in turn, be direct or indirect. For in-stance, it is possible for railways to have a direct demand link to the coal in-dustry (at least in the days when steam engines were in operation), as well as an indirect demand link to the coal industry (via steel, for instance). The entire productive sector of an economy is covered by a web of such links.

Figure 1 provides a (vastly oversimplified) picture of what these links might look like.

As an illustration of complementarity, suppose that the "action" in question is as follows: the maginitude of investment in a particular industry. Then a complementarity exists if the links are "positive," as in the examples given above. For instance, an investment expansion in railways increases the incentive to invest in steel. In such cases, it is possible that *the very same economy* may be plunged into a low level of activity for no other reason than the fact that sectoral depressions are self-reinforcing. At the same time, there may exist another (self-fulfilling) level of economic activity that is better for all concerned.

2. **Demand Complementarities**. An entirely different set of connections is also emphasized in this early literature. This is the possibility that an expansion in some industries will serve to raise income, and in this way, generate demand for the product of *other* industries. Once again, there is a potential complementarity here, at least across the producers of noninferior goods. An expansionary investment in some subset of sectors will increase the incentives of other sectors to follow suit, because there is now a greater demand for their products.

As usual, this complementarity raises the possibility of multiple equilibria. Each entrepreneur would invest if he or she were to believe that demand would be high, and if all entrepreneurs harbored such optimism, demand would indeed be high – these expectations would be self-fulfilling. But pessimism may also be self-fulfilling, because lack of investment would lower demand in general for all products.

The argument here is that an enhanced level of economic activity generates greater national income, and the generation of national income creates additional demand to justify that activity.

Notice that such "indirect" complementarities (not via specific interindustry links, but through the economy as a whole) do not need to work through demand alone. Suppose that the expansion of some sectors contributes to the generation of a skilled, reliable, educated workforce. Then the supply of a labor pool of high quality will stimulate the development of other industries. This is a complementarity that works by facilitating production, not by raising the demand for products.

Complementarities lead to a view of the world that is essentially non-deterministic. In its purest form, the theory says nothing about *which* equilibrium will prevail.[3] Interpreted with care and some imagination, it also acts as a critique of the convergence-based methodology in the previous section. For instance, it is possible for the same economy to be in a low-income/high-fertility trap, or in a high-income/low-fertility growth phase. In this view, fertility rates are not *causally* responsible for income, nor are fertility rates some exogenous social characteristic impeding intercountry convergence.

Once complementarities – and their implications for equilibrium multiplicity – enter our way of thinking, they seem to pop up everywhere. The Rosenstein-Rodan view of demand complementarities was given new life in a paper by Murplhy, Shleifer, and Vishny (1989). Since then, there has been an explosion of interest in demand complementaries (although the equally important study of complementarity via direct interindustry links has been surprisingly dormant). See, for example, Rodriguez (1996), Ciccone and Matsuyama (1996), and other papers in a 1996 issue of the *Journal of Development Economics* dedicated to this topic.

To be sure, there is no need to restrict the analysis to cross-industry interactions. As Arthur (1983) and David (1985) have argued, it is possible to show how the presence of complementarities can stifle the arrival of new technologies and new standards. As discussed by Acemoglu and Zilibotti (1997) and others, complementarities can be invoked to explain low financial depth in developing countries. Complementarities make an appearance in the theory of economic growth, as in the pioneering work of Romer (1986), Lucas (1990), and others. Complementarities can be used to understand spatial trends in crime, corruption, or large-scale defaults on debt. See Ray (1998, Ch. 4) for an introductory discussion and several other applications of the idea.

3.2. Policy Implications

The methodology of this section has three striking implications for policy.

First, a policy is to be viewed as a device for moving the economy out of one equilibrium into another. This is, conceptually, completely different from the viewpoint implicit in the previous section: there is a single long-run outcome toward which all economies must go, but this

---

[3] This can sometimes be embarrassing, because such a theory is also unable to predict what will happen today even if one of the equilibria has been played repeatedly over the past 100 periods. I return to this theme below.

long-run outcome may display underdevelopment because the underlying parameters of the economy are not right. Policy amounts to a sustained tweaking of these parameters. In contrast, the multiple equilibria context views policy as a way of pulling the economy out of one equilibrium into another.

This sort of view lies at the heart of arguments put forward by Rosenstein-Rodan and Hirschman in the 1950s, arguments that led to a vigorous debate between "balanced versus unbalanced growth" (see Ray 1998 for a description of the two approaches). It is a pity that these arguments have not received the full attention that they deserve from a modern perspective; in the next subsection, I attempt to explain why.

Second, according to the multiple equilibria view, a policy need not be permanent or persistent, precisely because the desired end-state is *also* an equilibrium in the absence of the policy. Indeed, after a temporary phase in which the old, bad equilibrium is artificially ruled out with the imposition of the policy, leaving only the good equilibrium, the policy may be removed in the expectation that the new state of affairs will hold on its own. Several socioeconomic phenomena conform to this view. It may be an equilibrium response for citizens of a society to employ slaves, to burn their wives, to demand dowry, to have many children, to throw garbage in or otherwise soil public places, to not observe codes of orderly conduct, or to bribe and be bribed, *provided everybody else is doing the same thing*. The very same individuals may refrain from all these activities if no one else engages in them. Consider, for instance, a policy in which one or another of these activities is made unlawful, with attendant penalties for breaking the law. It is to be expected that after some time has passed, the law (while still on the statute books in name) will not need to be enforced anymore, *assuming that initially it has been implemented well*. Social pressures may suffice. The same is true of many economic situations, such as those studied by Rosenstein-Rodan and Hirschman.

Finally, although freed of certain responsibilities of persistent implementation, an equilibrium-tipping policy will need to be artfully chosen and closely implemented in the transition, or it can fail badly. Take, for example, the notion of compulsory primary education. The reason that primary education may need to be compulsorily imposed in a society is that its benefits are unclear in a world where labor power is needed for current output and no one else is particularly educated (this was even true of Western Europe, by the way; see, for example, Eckstein and Zilcha 1994). Yet, in a world where everyone else is educating their children, it would be dangerous for a single family not to do so. So this is a classic example of multiple equilibria. Now, if the policy of imposing primary education is not properly implemented, the outcome may be much worse than it ever was. Resources would be committed to schools. Yet children may not be sent to them. Worse still, children (such as young girls) may be selectively removed from school for the purposes of child labor.[4] The point is that at the time of imposition of the policy, it is (still) not optimal to do as the policy says, so if there are resources expended on the policy (such as schools) and other resources spent on avoiding the policy (say, collective "coaxing" of the village headmaster to keep a false attendance register), the resulting outcome may be worse than it was to start with.[5]

3.3. Transitions

I end this section with some comments on the persistence of particular equilibrium outcomes in the mutiple-equilibria framework. I believe that it is our imperfect understanding of these issues that hinder a more careful study of issues such as balanced versus unbalanced growth.

How does an economy "move from one equilibrium to another"? I place this phrase in quotes because it is imprecise: so-called transitions from one "equilibrium" to another must themselves be viewed as the equilibria of some encompassing intertemporal process. Unfortunately, when embedded in an intertemporal setting, the multiple equilibria or coordination-game paradigm is not of much use in this regard beyond the demonstration that multiplicities may exist. In some sense, it avoids alto-gether any answer to the question: Why is one society less developed than another, and what can be done about it? For this would require a theory of where the pessimistic beliefs originally came from. The paradigm is at a loss for *explaining* historical inertia: repeat a story of multiple equilibria story and numerous dynamic equilibria emerge, including those in which the society jumps between the bad and good equilibria in all sorts of deftly coordinated ways. We lack good economic theory that actually identifies the "stickiness"of equilibria.

A small literature – too small, in my opinion – exists on this topic. See, for instance, Krugman (1991), Matsuyama (1991), and Adserà and

---

[4] For a distinct but related view on child labor and multiple equilibria, see Basu and Van (1998).
[5] For an interesting theoretical discussion of the appearance of (policy-induced) worse equilibria in the Murphy-Shleifer-Vishny model, see Bond and Pande (1999).

Ray (1998) in the development literature. There is also a corresponding smattering of literature among macroeconomists studying business-cycle models based on coordination failure (see, for example, Chamley and Gale 1994 and Cooper 1999), and among theorists (see, for example, Morris and Shin 1998 and Frankel and Pauzner 2000).

As an example of the various approaches, the Adserà-Ray paper embeds a coordination game into a real-time model of "intersectoral choice" (the choices corresponding to the actions of the static coordination game). Now agents may switch sectors (more than once, if they so desire), and their returns are added over time, by applying a discount factor. The objective of the paper is to give meaning to the notion of inertia, to the idea that historical predominance of a "sector" might impede the development of a Pareto-superior "sector." The main result is that if externalities manifest themselves with a lag (which may be arbitrarily small), and if there are no congestion costs in intersectoral migration, then initial conditions *do* pin down equilibria – there is inertia. The paper suggests a research program in which the study of lagged externalities may be fruitful, as also the study of moving costs (a topic given more emphasis in the Krugman and Matsuyama papers).

There is much work to be done in the area of intertemporal persistence of equilibrium. In particular, only after we have a theory of "inter-equilibrium transition" can we get to the serious details of policy interventions.

4. UNDERDEVELOPMENT AND HISTORY

4.1. Historical Legacies

Underdevelopment – viewed as a coordination failure – is a story of *multiple equilibria*, and therefore directs our attention to the beliefs or expectations of the economic agents that shore up one or another of the equilibria. In particular, one might ask – and we did ask this above – how the formation of such expectations may be significantly conditioned by history. But history may dictate much more than expectation-formation; it may actually pin down the values of certain tangible variables and influence future developments. Put another way, historical legacies may actually select among *different sets* of equilibria (quite apart from the possible multiplicities in each set).

Once again, variations in historical legacies – or initial conditions – are not to be thought of as variations in the fundamental makeup of the economy. For instance, two economies may have the same technological possibilities and individual preferences, but differ, perhaps, in the size of the initial capital stock. The capital stock is the legacy; technology and preferences represent the fundamentals. Can the former have persistent effects even if the latter are all the same? As we have seen, the convergence hypothesis says no.

Historical legacies need not be limited to a nation's inheritance of capital stock or GDP from its ancestors. Factors as diverse as legal structure, traditions, or group reputations may serve as initial conditions (see, for example, the review in Ray 1998 or Hoff and Stiglitz 2001). But of all these, perhaps the darkest shadow is cast by historically given *inequalities* in the distribution of asset ownership. With imperfect capital markets, the poor are limited in their access to credit necessary for production and investment (this includes investment not only in projects but also in themselves, via education or nutrition). Hence increased inequality can exert negative effects on both levels and growth rates of per capita income. High initial inequalities may also create conditions for self-perpetuation, generating a lock-in effect with economic stagnation. The very same fundamental economy would perform differently were initial inequality to be altered.

4.2. Inequality

One may think of the literature that addresses this sort of question as studying the *functional role* of inequality, as opposed to the intrinsic merits and demerits of unequal treatment. The question is: what effects does inequality have on other variables of interest, such as aggregate output, employment, efficiency, or growth? The relevant literature includes Dasgupta and Ray (1986, 1987), Baland and Ray (1991), Banerjee and Newman (1993), Galor and Zeira (1993), Lundqvist (1993), Ray and Streufert (1993), Bowles and Gintis (1994, 1995), Hoff (1994), Hoff and Lyon (1995), Legros and Newman (1996), Aghion and Bolton (1997), Mookherjee (1997), Piketty (1997), and others.

Some of the current literature based on dynamic models finds its roots – paradoxically enough – in a paper that did *not* depart from the convergence idea (Loury 1981). Nevertheless, this pioneering paper did pin down the crucial interaction between limited capital markets and dynamic inefficiency. The inefficiency of limited access to capital is a theme that is common to several of the papers, although they depart significantly from the Loury model in other aspects.

As an illustration, consider the simplest version of the Galor-Zeira (1993) model. It shows how the convergence prediction of the neoclassical growth model can be overturned by dropping the assumptions of a convex technology and perfect capital markets. With setup costs in the acquisition of certain occupations or skills, and borrowing constraints for poor agents, the initial distribution of wealth will influence the aggregate skill composition of the economy and total output, resulting in reinforcement of those very same initial conditions. Poor families will not find it worthwhile to invest in the education of their children, locking their descendants into a poverty trap. High initial inequalities thus tend to perpetuate themselves. Moreover, countries with a historially higher poverty rate will have a persistently lower per capita income.

The demonstration of history-dependence in the simple version of the Galor-Zeira model can be criticized. Even in the presence of indivisibilities in investment, substantial stochastic perturbations might restore ergodicity, by simply permitting different wealth levels to communicate (although possibly with very small probability). For instance, in the presence of random elements reflecting luck, a poor family may tip over the required threshold and join the ranks of the prosperous, just as wealthy families may encounter a string of failures and temporarily drift into poverty.

A rebuttal to this criticism would argue that under the conditions of the Galor-Zeira model, those in poverty would remain locked there for a long period of time; the problem would appear in the guise of a low degree of wealth mobility. In part this is a signal that ergodicity (and convergence, more generally) is itself a problematic concept, a topic that would take me somewhat afield of my current program. But in part, it points to a second inadequacy of these simple models, which is that they are not interactive across agents. The economy is just several copies of isolated agents (or families) running in parallel. Then inequality has no aggregate effects that are not simply trivial sums of individual effects. The model misses the interdependence in the evolution of fortunes of different families in a given society, which may strengthen the tendency toward lock-in.

In contrast, the more complicated interactive models – such as those in the later part of the Galor-Zeira paper, and in several of the other papers cited above – do not allow us to conclude anything from the behavior of a single family or dynasty of families. The joint behavior of all families affects important economic variables such as commodity prices, wage rates, or the rate of interest, and these in turn feed back on the decision making of individuals.

Although the following comments do run the risk of some mathematical abstraction, they permit me to quickly illustrate a number of the models in the relevant literature by adopting a framework from Mookherjee and Ray (2000).[6]

Let H be some list of *occupations*, over which a population of unit size is distributed at any date t. The date t is to be interpreted as the lifetime of the generation alive at t.

For each λ, λ', to be interpreted as occupational distributions (of successive generations), a *wage function* $w = w(h)$, for $h \in H$ is defined on H. These define the incomes earned by different occupations.

A wage function w on H in turn helps determine a *cost function* $x = x(h), h \in H$, also defined on H. This can be interpreted as the cost, payable in the current date, of acquiring skills necessary for occupation h for members of the next generation.

Thus given a sequence $\{\lambda_t\}_{t=0}^{\infty}$ of occupational distributions on H, we obtain a sequence $\{w_t, x_t\}_{t=0}^{\infty}$ of wage and cost functions defined on H, where each wage function w_t depends on the neighboring occupational distributions $(\lambda_t, \lambda_{t+1})$, and each cost function x_t is determined in turn by this wage function. We can then say that $\{w_t, x_t\}_{t=0}^{\infty}$ is *generated* by $\{\lambda_t\}_{t=0}^{\infty}$.

Individuals only foresee the wage-cost sequence (the actual generation of this sequence is of little import to them). They care about their own income, and those of their descendants. For an individual i (or current representative of family i) with $h_0(i)$ given, the problem is to

$$\max \sum_{t=0}^{\infty} \beta^t u(c_t) \tag{1}$$

subject to the constraints

$$y_t = w_t(h_t) \tag{2}$$

$$y_t = c_t + x_t(h_{t+1}) \tag{3}$$

for all t. (Above, u is a single-period utility function and β the discount factor.) As in Loury (1981), this formulation presumes that parents care about the utility (rather than just the consumption or income levels) of their descendants in a consistent fashion, so bequests or educational investments in children will be nonpaternalistic, thus removing

---

[6] Note: This research has since been published in somewhat different form, although the basic contours of the framework are broadly the same. See Mookherjee and Ray (2002, 2003).

one potential source of market imperfection. However, capital markets are missing: investments must be financed entirely from current income. The maximization problem above will result in a sequence of occupational choices made by successive generations, which we may denote by $\{h_t(i)\}_{t=0}^{\infty}$ for each family i.

Aggregate these occupational choices across families by defining, for each t, $\lambda_t(h)$ to be the measure of individuals i such that $h_t(i) = h$. [Of course, the distribution λ_0 is exogenously given.] This generates a sequence of occupational distributions: we may describe $\{\lambda_t\}_{t=0}^{\infty}$ as an *aggregate response* to $\{w_t, x_t\}_{t=0}^{\infty}$ (for given λ_0).

An *equilibrium* (given the historical distribution λ_0) is a sequence of succeeding occupational distributions, income, and cost profiles $\{\lambda_t, w_t, x_t\}_{t=0}^{\infty}$ such that (a) $\{w_t, x_t\}_{t=0}^{\infty}$ is generated by $\{\lambda_t\}_{t=0}^{\infty}$ and (b) $\{\lambda_t\}_{t=0}^{\infty}$ is an aggregate response to $\{w_t, x_t\}_{t=0}^{\infty}$. In such an equilibrium, all families have perfect foresight concerning the future evolution of the economy and the returns to different occupations; their optimal responses in turn justify their beliefs.

It is possible to embed several well-known models within this framework. Consider the following examples:

1. **Models of Noninteracting Agents**. H is the set of all capital stocks, $w(h)$ is *independent* of the occupational distribution, and equals some production function $f(h)$, while $x(h) = h$. This is the framework (with uncertainty added) studied in Loury (1981), under the assumption that f is a "standard" concave production function. Alternatively, one might interpret H as some discrete set of skills. This is the first model studied in Galor-Zeira (1993) (they also use a simpler paternalistic "warm-glow" formulation of the bequest motive).

2. **Entrepreneurship**. $H = 1, 2$. 1 stands for worker; 2 stands for employer. $x(h)$, the cost function, is independent of the wage function: it is 0 if $h = 1$, and is S, a setup cost for entrepreneurship, if $h = 2$. To determine the wage function, suppose that there is a production function F defined on the amount of employed labor. Each entrepreneur chooses L to maximize

$$F(L) - w(1)L,$$

where $w(1)$ is the wage rate for labor. In equilibrium, L is just the employment per capitalist, which is $\lambda(2)/\lambda(1)$. So $w(1)$ is given by

$$F'\left(\frac{\lambda(2)}{\lambda(1)}\right) = w(1),$$

while $w(2)$ is the resulting profit:

$$w(2) = F\left(\frac{\lambda(2)}{\lambda(1)}\right) - F'\left(\frac{\lambda(2)}{\lambda(1)}\right)\frac{\lambda(2)}{\lambda(1)}.$$

This is essentially the Banerjee and Newman (1993) model. Like Galor and Zeira, they employ a warm-glow model of bequests, and assume a fundamental indivisibility in the occupational structure (there are two discretely different occupations). The evolution of wealth and of occupational decisions is, however, fundamentally interdependent across different families. The resulting dynamics are complicated. Banerjee and Newman manage to describe the nature of this dynamic in a number of special cases, and show how distinct occupational structures and related production systems (such as the factory system rather than independent cottage production) may evolve in the long run, depending on historical conditions.

Further developments of a related model with a divisible investment technology and random shocks were subsequently explored by Piketty (1997), who showed that the interactive nature of the wealth dynamic may still result in multiple long-run steady states from different historical conditions. In this sense, historical lock-in can persist even in the presence of wealth mobility at the level of individual families, and the presence of a convex technology.

3. **Demand Effects**. H is a finite set of commodities. A person with occupation h can produce one unit of the specialized commodity h. Again, take $x(h)$ as independent of other variables.

Let $\mathbf{p} = p(h), h \in H$ be a *price vector* on H. Given income y, a consumer generates a demand vector $c(P, y)$ on H.

An equilibrium price vector will equate supply and demand. But the demand by occupants of occupation h is just $c(\mathbf{p}, p(h))\lambda(h)$, so that equilibrium prices must be given by the solution to the system

$$\sum_{h \in H} c(\mathbf{p}, p(h))\lambda(h) = \lambda.$$

By constant returns to scale, take $p(h) = w(h)$ for all h. A model of this kind is studied by Mani (1998).

4. **Labor Skills**. This is the approach followed by Lundqvist (1993). $H = 1, 2$. 1 stands for unskilled worker; 2 stands for skilled worker. The production function $F(a_1, a_2)$ defines output produced by a_1 and a_2 units of unskilled and skilled labor, respectively. This determines the wage pattern:

$$w(h) = F_h(a(1), a(2))$$

for $h = 1, 2$. The function $x(h)$ defining the cost of training for different occupations in turn depends on the wage function: it is 0 if $h = 1$, and is $\alpha w(2)$ if $h = 2$. The idea is that to acquire skill a worker needs to be trained by α units of currently skilled workers, who need to be paid their opportunity cost of not working in the production sector and earning the wage $w(2)$. Skilled workers in the economy thus divide themselves between the production and training sectors, depending on the demand in the two sectors. Unskilled workers work only in the production sector. In equilibrium, the occupational distributions at successive dates will determine the allocation of skilled workers in the following manner. Let λ and λ' denote the occupational distributions for succeeding generations. Then notice that

$$a(1) = \lambda(1),$$

while

$$a(2) = \lambda(2) - \alpha\lambda'(2),$$

so that the wage function is ultimately related to the successive occupational distributions:

$$w(h) = F_h(\lambda(1), \lambda(2)) - \alpha\lambda'(2)$$

It is precisely the dependence of the wage and training cost functions on the occupational distribution that generates new insights. There are three consequences that merit particular emphasis.

First, *even if there is perfect equality to start with, the subsequent evolution of inequality is inevitable*. To illustrate this, suppose all individuals in a particular generation have equal wealth. Is it possible for all of them to make the same *choices*? The answer is, in general, no. If all of them choose to leave their descendants unskilled, then the return to skilled labor will become enormously high, encouraging some fraction of the population to educate their children. Similarly, it is not possible for all parents to educate their children, if unskilled labor is also necessary in production. Thus identical agents are forced to take nonidentical actions, precisely because of the interdependence of decisions made by different families. This means, of course, that in the *next* generation some inequality must emerge.

Indeed, following this logic, it is possible to show that *every* steady state of the system described above *must* involve inequality. The evolution of unequal treatment is not precipitated by random factors such as bad luck; it is part of the inner logic of the economic system.

Second, this inequality, in turn, leads to a lack of efficiency. Individuals cannot simply compensate for their unequal positions by taking recourse to a credit market. In the models studied here, there isn't a credit market; or if there is one, it is imperfect. It is this imperfection that underlies the inefficiency of inequality. Individuals with low wealth may be unable to take advantage of profitable opportunities open to them, be these in the form of skill acquisition, certain occupational advantages, or remunerative investment opportunities.

However, I should note that lack of efficiency in this sense (in the sense of the inability to take advantage of productive opportunities) does not necessarily imply that there are other *equilibria* that are Pareto-superior. This has policy implications that I note below.

Third, there may be several steady states, in the sense that many wealth distributions (and associated levels of national output and prices) may all be self-reinforcing. One must be careful not to interpret these as "multiple equilibria" – *given* the initial historical conditions, multiplicity of steady states perfectly consistent with the idea that the economy follows a unique path.[7] As we shall see, the policy implications are different in each case.

Finally, as we have already noted, inequality fundamentally affects the working of equilibrium prices – broadly defined – and in so doing it affects the dynamic fate of individuals in a way that cannot be disentangled by simple stochastic perturbations of individual outcomes. Thus it is perfectly possible that a particular regime displays full mobility of individual dynasties, while there are many such regimes (depending on history).

4.3. Policy Revisited

The policy implications of history-dependence have sharper political edges than the ones implied by multiple equilibria. If multiple equilibria are Pareto-ranked, then an equilibrium-tipping policy will – at least in the long run – benefit all the agents in the economy. To be sure, there are serious problems of implementation. Nevertheless, if the policy works, it

---

[7] To be sure, it is possible that multiple equilibria and history-dependence coexist in the same model. That is, it may be true both that equilibria vary with history, *and* that there are several equilibria for each history. This can be shown to happen, for instance, in the model studied by Romer (1986).

will benefit all concerned,[8] and this knowledge can serve to dilute opposition to the policy.

These conditions are significantly harder to meet in situations of history-dependence, especially those in which the relevant historical variable is asset inequality. The sharpest expression of this possibility is in the static model of inequality and undernutrition studied in Dasgupta and Ray (1986). Under some mild conditions, *every* competitive equilibrium in that model is Pareto-efficient, even though it may display undernutrition, low output (compared to other equilibria), and involuntary unemployment. It follows that – in the Dasgupta-Ray model – every policy designed to reduce undernutrition and unemployment must hurt some segment of the population. In this scenario, the roots of opposition are not very far underground.

Admittedly, the Dasgupta-Ray model is an extreme illustration. Inefficiency appears as soon as we turn to a dynamic formulation. But here too, we must step carefully. As already discussed, the inefficiency of a particular equilibrium simply points to the fact that there are allocations that make all agents better off. But there is no guarantee that such allocations can themselves serve as equilibria. The reason I highlight this concern is that, if we wish to continue the view of economic policy as an ephemeral device, the final outcome of the policy intervention must itself be an equilibrium. But if the latter equilibrium is not Pareto-superior to the former, there may be serious opposition to the policy.

Leaving aside issues of opposition, let us take a closer look at the nature of these policies. In contrast to the policies for eliminating bad equilibria in a multiple-equilibria framework, the objective here is to change initial conditions, thereafter permitting equilibrium outcomes to be generated in accordance with the changed history.

The models discussed above generally have the property that *steady state* equilibria in which the distribution of wealth is relatively equal are "better" from the point of view of (productive and allocative) efficiency, output and employment, and possibly the rate of growth. This suggests that a redistributive change in initial asset inequalities in favor of those who are relatively deprived will be beneficial from the point of view of other important economic indicators. But I must emphasize that the previous two sentences are not necessarily connected by infallible logic. The

---

[8] Of course, this is not true if the multiple equilibria under consideration are not Pareto-ranked. Sometimes this is indeed the case, as in the model of child labor studied by Basu and Van (1999).

former assertion concerns steady states. For the latter assertion to be valid, distributions which are originally more equal must lead to steady states that are more equal as well. But there is no guarantee that this is true – at present we know too little about the out-of-steady-state behavior of these models to tell with any certainty. What we *do* know is that future research will have to study carefully – and in more detail – the subtle and often complex connections between initial conditions and final steady states.

In addition, the first assertion may be wrong as well. It is sometimes true that *extremely* poor societies may gain in functional efficiency if there is some inequality (see, for example, Ray 1998, Chapters 7 and 8, or Matsuyama (2002)). We are then caught in a genuine tradeoff between efficiency and equality. A more complex phenomenon is the possibility of "wrong" responses to small or half-hearted changes, as discussed for employment in Dasgupta and Ray (1987). In these cases, a small degree of redistribution may be worse than no redistribution at all.

The discussion so far may give the impression that we can say very little about the policy prescriptions of these models. This is not entirely true. Remember, the most important policy prescription is that in many cases, one-time interventions can have persistent, permanent effects. Where I have tried to be careful is in cautioning against a cavalier approach to such one-time interventions, arguing that there is still much to be done in connecting initial conditions to final steady state outcomes.

4.4. Concluding Remarks

As mentioned in the introduction, my goal in this essay has been particular in nature, rather than comprehensive. I wanted to write about innovative approaches in the theory of development economics that view underdevelopment not as a failure of some fundamental economic parameters, or sociocultural values, but as an interacting "equilibrium" that hangs together, precipitated by expectational inertia or by historical conditions.

Why is this view of the development process an important one? There are three reasons why I feel this view should be examined very seriously.

First, this point of view leads to a theory, or a set of theories, in which economic "convergence" (of incomes, wealth, levels of well-being) across countries is not to be automatically had. Actually, the intelligent layperson reading these words will find this reasoning a bit abstruse: why on earth would one expect convergence in the first place? And why, indeed, should I find a theory interesting on the grounds that it does *not* predict convergence, when I knew that all along? This is not a bad line of reasoning, but to appreciate why it is misguided, it is important to refer to a venerable tradition in economics that has convergence as its very core prediction. The idea is based – roughly – on the argument that countries that are poor will have higher marginal products of capital, and consequently a higher rate of return to capital. This means that a dollar of extra savings will have a higher payoff in poor countries, allowing it to grow faster. The prediction: poorer countries will tend to grow faster, so that over time rich and poor countries will come together, or "converge."

Of course, I have not examined the convergence hypothesis in detail, as my intention is to cover other views of development.[9] But one should notice that convergence theories in the raw form described above have rarely been found acceptable, and there are several subtle variants of the theory. Some of these variants still preserve the idea that "other things" being equal, convergence in some conditional sense is still to be had. It is only if we start accepting the possibility that these "other things" – such as savings or fertility rates – often *cannot* be kept equal, that the notion of conditional convergence starts losing its relevance and very different views of development, not at all based on the idea of convergence, must be sought.

The second reason why I find these theories important is that they do not rely on "fundamental" differences across peoples or cultures. Thus we may worry about whether Confucianism is better than the Protestant ethic in promoting hard-headed, successful economic agents, and we might certainly decry Hindu fatalism as deeply inimical to purposeful, economic self-advancement, but we have seen again and again that when it comes down to the economic crunch and circumstances are right, both Confucian and Hindu will make the best of available opportunities – and so will a host of other religions and cultures besides. Once again, this is not the place to examine in detail fundamentalist explanations based on cultural or religious differences, but I simply don't find them very convincing. This is not to say that culture – like conditional convergence – does not play a role. But I also take the view that culture, along with several other economic, social, and political institutions, are all part of some broader interactive theory in which "first cause" is to be found – if at all – in historical legacies. And, yes – if we do insist on recursing history backward to find the "original cause" – I would reply that there is no such thing, that small initial "butterfly effects" have magnified consequences.

---

[9] On the convergence postulate and studies stemming from it, see, e.g., Barro and Xala-i-Martin (1995), Jones (1997), and Ray (1998).

The third reason why I wish to focus on these theories is that they create a very different role for government policy. Specifically, I have argued that these theories place a much greater weight on one-time, or temporary, interventions than theories that are based on fundamentals. For instance, if we were to observe that Indian savings rates are low compared to other East Asian countries, and we were to believe that Hindu fatalism is somehow responsible for this outcome, then a policy of encouraging savings (say, through tax breaks) will certainly have an effect on growth rates. But there is no telling when that policy can be taken away, or indeed, if it can be taken away at all. For in the absence of the policy, the theory would tell us that savings would revert to the old Hindu level. In contrast, a theory that is based on an interactive "chicken-and-egg" approach would promote a policy that attempts to push the chicken–egg cycle into a new equilibrium. Once that happens, *the policy can be removed.* This is not to say that once-and-for-all policies are the only correct ones, but to appreciate that the interactive theories that we have discussed have very different implications from the traditional ones.

I have discussed only one of several frontiers in development economics, but I believe this particular frontier to be particularly important. Because it is more abstract than, say, an account of the latest research on labor markets, it is more a methodological frontier than anything else, and permeates much of our thinking about various theories. Of course, even the practitioners of traditional convergence theories are aware of the viewpoints expressed here, and many are even sympathetic to it. But one hopes that future researchers will embrace this methodology not just from a distance, but in the essential way in which their models are constructed.

REFERENCES

Acemoglu, D. and Zilibotti. 1997. "Was Prometheus Unbound by Chance? Risk, Diversification and Growth," *Journal of Political Economy* 105, 709–51.

Adserà, A. and D. Ray. 1998. "History and Coordination Failure," *Journal of Economic Growth* 3, 267–76.

Aghion, P. and P. Bolton. 1997. "A Theory of Trickle-Down Growth and Development," *Review of Economic Studies* 64, 151–72.

Arthur, W. B. 1983. "On Competing Technologies and Historical Small Events: The Dynamics of Choice under Increasing Returns," mimeograph, Department of Economics, Stanford University.

Baland, J-M. and D. Ray. 1991. "Why Does Asset Inequality Affect Unemployment? A Study of the Demand Composition Problem," *Journal of Development Economics* 35, 69–92.

Banerjee, A. V. and A. Newman. 1993. "Occupational Choice and the Process of Development," *Journal of Political Economy* 101, 274–98.

Barro, R. J. and X. Sala-i-Martin. 1995. *Economic Growth.* New York: McGraw-Hill.

Basu, K. and P. H. Van. 1998. "The Economics of Child Labor," *American Economic Review* 88, 412–27.

Bond, P. and R. Pande. 1999. "Implementing the 'Big Push': The Limits of Policy Activism," mimeograph, Department of Economics, Columbia University.

Bowles, S. and H. Gintis. 1994. "Credit Market Imperfections and the Incidence of Worker Owned Firms," *Metroeconomica* 45, 209–23.

Bowles, S. and H. Gintis. 1995. "The Distribution of Wealth and the Assignment of Control Rights," mimeograph, Department of Economics, University of Massachusetts, Amherst.

Chamley, C. and D. Gale. 1994. "Information Revelation and Strategic Delay in a Model of Investment," *Econometrica* 62, 1065–85.

Ciccone, A. and K. Matsuyama. 1996. "Start-up Costs and Pecuniary Externalities as Barriers to Economic Development," *Journal of Development Economics* 49, 33–59.

Cooper, R. 1999. *Coordination Games: Complementarities and Macroeconomics.* Cambridge University Press.

Dasgupta, P. and D. Ray. 1986. "Inequality as a Determinant of Malnutrition and Unemployment: Theory," *Economic Journal* 96, 1011–34.

Dasgupta, P. and D. Ray. 1987. "Inequality as a Determinant of Malnutrition and Unemployment: Policy," *Economic Journal* 97, 177–88.

David, P. A. 1985. "Clio and the Economics of QWERTY," *American Economic Review* 75, 332–7.

Eckstein, Z. and I. Zilcha. 1994. "The Effect of Compulsory Schooling on Growth, Income Distribution and Welfare," *Journal of Public Economics* 54, 339–59.

Galor, O. and J. Zeira. 1993. "Income Distribution and Macroeconomics," *Review of Economic Studies* 60, 35–52.

Hirschman, A. O. 1958. *The Strategy of Economic Development.* New Haven, CT: Yale University Press.

Hoff, K. 1994. "The Second Theorem of the Second Best," *Journal of Public Economics* 45, 223–42.

Hoff, K. and A. Lyon. 1995. "Non-Leaky Buckets: Optimal Redistributive Taxation and Agency Costs," *Journal of Public Economics* 58, 365–90.

Hoff, K. and J. Stiglitz. 2001. "Modern Economic Theory and Development," in G. Meier and J. Stiglitz (eds.), *Frontiers of Development Economics.* New York: Oxford University Press.

Jones, C. 1998. *Introduction to Economic Growth.* W. W. Norton.

Krugman, P. 1991. "History versus Expectations," *Quarterly Journal of Economics* 106, 651–67.

Legros, P. and A. Newman. 1996. "Wealth Effects, Distribution and the Theory of Organization," *Journal of Economic Theory* 70, 312–41.

Loury, G. C. 1981. "Intergenerational Transfers and the Distribution of Earnings," *Econometrica* 49, 843–67.

Lucas, R. E. 1988. "On the Mechanics of Economic Development," *Journal of Monetary Economics* 22, 3–42.

Lundqvist, L. 1993. "Economic Underdevelopment: The Case of a Missing Market for Human Capital," *Journal of Development Economics* 40, 219–39.

Mani, A. 1998. "Income Distribution and the Demand Constraint," mimeograph, Department of Economics, Vanderbilt University.

Mankiw, N. G., P. Romer, and D. Weil. 1992. "A Contribution to the Empirics of Economic Growth," *Quarterly Journal of Economics* 107, 407–38.

Matsuyama, K. 1991. "Increasing Returns, Industrialization, and Indeterminacy of Equilibrium," *Quarterly Journal of Economics* 106, 617–50.

Matsuyama, K. 2002. "The Rise of Mass Consumption Societies," *Journal of Political Economy* 110, 1035–1070.

McKenzie, L. 1976. "Turnpike Theory," *Econometrica* 44, 841–65.

Mookherjee, D. and D. Ray. 2000. "Persistent Inequality and Endogenous Investment Thresholds," mimeograph, Department of Economics, Boston University.

Mookherjee, D. and D. Ray. 2002. "Is Equality Stable?" *American Economic Review* 92, 253–9.

Mookherjee, D. and D. Ray. 2003. "Persistent Inequality," *Review of Economic Studies* 70, 369–93.

Murphy, K., A. Shleifer, and R. Vishny. 1989a. "Industrialization and the Big Push," *Journal of Political Economy* 97, 1003–26.

Neumann, J. V. 1945–6. "A Model of General Economic Equilibrium," *Review of Economic Studies* 13, 1–9.

Piketty, T. 1997, "The Dynamics of the Wealth Distribution and the Interest Rate with Credit Rationing," *Review of Economic Studies* 64, 173–89.

Ray, D. 1998. *Development Economics*. Princeton: Princeton University Press.

Ray, D. and P. Streufert. 1993. "Dynamic Equilibria with Unemployment Due to Undernourishment," *Economic Theory* 3, 61–85.

Rodriguez-Clare, A. 1996. "The Division of Labor and Economic Development," *Journal of Development Economics* 49, 3–32.

Romer, P. 1986. "Increasing Returns and Long-Run Growth," *Journal of Political Economy* 92, 1002–37.

Rosenstein-Rodan, P. 1943. "Problems of Industrialization of Eastern and Southeastern Europe," *Economic Journal* 53, 202–11.

Solow, R. 1956. "A Contribution to the Theory of Economic Growth," *Quarterly Journal of Economics* 70, 65–94.

Morris, S. and H. Shin. 1998. "Unique Equilibrium in a Model of Self-Fulfilling Currency Attacks," *American Economic Review* 88, 587–97.

Frankel, D. and A. Pauzner. 2000. "Resolving Indeterminacy in Dynamic Settings: The Role of Shocks," *Quarterly Journal of Economics* 115, 285–304.

PART IV

CONTRACTS, LAW, AND GAMING

9

Contract or War? On the Consequences of a Broader View of Self-Interest in Economics

Michelle Garfinkel and Stergios Skaperdas

The first principle of Economics is that every agent is actuated only by self-interest. The workings of this principle may be viewed under two aspects, according as the agent acts without, *or* with, *the consent of others affected by his actions. In wide senses, the first species of action may be called* war; *the second,* contract. [Edgeworth (1881), pp. 16, 17; emphasis in the original.]

1. INTRODUCTION

Edgeworth's characterization, made more than a century ago, of the species of actions called "war" appears rather benign; yet the prominent British marginalist proceeded to examine only the case of contract. He left the analytical study of war itself and, perhaps more importantly, the study of what leads to contract and what leads to war for others to pursue. In the intervening years, however, very few economists have followed such a line of inquiry. The study of war – broadly construed – has fallen mostly into the hands of political scientists. The synthetic, integrated study of war and contract has also been claimed by scholars of political science and other social scientists, but not by economists.

In fact, many economists today would cringe at the idea that *homo economicus* – instead of just trucking, bartering, and trading – could also beat, cheat, and steal from others. On a closer look, the notion of *homo economicus* is a bit puzzling in what it requires of a human being: he or she will haggle to death to get a better price, though never think about grabbing what the other person has if given the chance to do so. This is an image of well-defined ruthlessness within a bubble of sainthood. But, real human beings everywhere – from Russia, to Somalia, to Colombia, to inside U.S. prisons as well as boardrooms, to name just a few places – are often so ruthless that they burst this bubble.

If, following Edgeworth, we were to consider the first principle of economics to be that "every agent is actuated only by self-interest," then how can we leave out the possibility of grabbing and all activities that have been variously characterized as "appropriative," "predatory," "redistributive," "enforcive," or "conflictual"? Even if we were to view Edgeworth's principle as too doctrinaire and confining, we would nevertheless have plenty of other reasons for studying such activities. These other reasons revolve around our quest for a scientific understanding of a wide range of problems that we think fall firmly within the realm of the economic. For example, did the revolt in the Southern Mexican state of Chiapas in 1994 have any economic causes, and did it have any economic effects? If the answer to both parts of this question is affirmative as most informed participants would argue, how can economists make any sense of it? Or, should the problem just be left to other social scientists or, worse yet, to journalists? Closer to home, should academic economists have anything to say about the UPS strike in the summer of 1997 or the NBA lockout throughout most of the 1998–99 basketball season? Do we have much to say about the formation of unions and their effects? Should we?

The reader can easily guess our own answers to such questions. There is too much territory that economists have conceded to others that needs to be reclaimed, not for opportunistic, imperialistic reasons, but because economists can genuinely contribute to an improved understanding with their theoretical discipline and powerful empirical techniques. In this essay, we argue for the importance of such an expanded domain of economic inquiry, and present a sample of findings from research that allows for both ordinary, productive economic activity (creating one's own) and appropriation (taking from others).

In the next section we provide examples of substantive areas in which conflict and appropriation are an important part of economic activity. In Section 3 we show how allowing for conflict and appropriation can change many of the findings that are typically robust in the absence of conflict and appropriation. Section 4 concludes by discussing some of the organizations and institutions that typically emerge to manage conflict.

2. THE DARK SIDE OF THE ECONOMY[1]

Recent work in macroeconomics (e.g., Easterly and Levine 1997 and Rodrik 1999) shows what other social scientists and most educated laypersons consider obvious: Conflict and how conflict is managed can make a big difference for economic performance. In much of the developing world, conflict takes on many forms: warfare between countries; civil war; suppression of individuals and groups through political, judicial, military, and police actions; low-level insurgency and open revolts; military coups; gang warfare and other organized crime activity; political and economic protests; strikes and lockouts; and, of course, ordinary crime. All of these involve either the actual use or the threat of violence, but their economic costs and effects on economic performance go well beyond the consequences of the occasional use of force.

First, there are resources directly expended on such activities – resources which could have been used for ordinary production or consumption: military, paramilitary, and police expenditures; the guns and labor of antigovernment forces and organized crime groups; the private security expenditures undertaken by ordinary citizens. We do not claim, of course, that all such expenditures are unnecessary. All societies spend some of their resources on providing security. What we claim is that a certain level of security is compatible with many different levels of expenditures on its provision, depending on the organization of the state and the institutions of conflict management. While Colombia spends more on security than Argentina, for example, Colombia is less secure.[2]

The direct resource costs of appropriation can be substantial, but there are other effects on economic activity as well – namely, allocative distortions. The higher costs of operation due to the higher expenditures on security reduce economic activity and, at the same time, bias investment against anything that is vulnerable. Insecurity and uncertainty about contract enforcement stifle trade. Generations of youths grow up learning how to be soldiers or guerrillas only, and this is what they do for the rest of their lives even if conditions change later. In total, such distortionary (or indirect) costs could easily dwarf all the direct resource costs.

---

[1] The title of this section was inspired by Hirshleifer (1994), entitled "The Dark Side of the Force."

[2] The two countries have made about the same amount of military expenditures during the 1990s (see SIPRI 1998, Table 6A4, 233), yet Colombia has made many more expenditures on police, paramilitaries, drug traffickers, and guerrillas.

Conflict and its costs, of course, are not confined to developing countries. They have also been an integral part of the history of developed countries. Europe was devastated twice in the first half of the twentieth century and, over the past two centuries, was the site of many other episodes of physical combat, which although on a smaller scale than the two world wars, were significantly damaging. This experience appears to have led to institutional adaptations, which have reduced the instances of blood-and-gore conflict and its associated costs, but have not completely eliminated conflict.

Moreover, there are other, more refined forms of conflict and appropriation that have taken on greater importance in developed countries. Instead of fighting it out on the battlefield, different individuals and groups in mature, industrialized nation-states compete for political influence and the economic advantage this confers through lobbying, rent-seeking, and litigation. The resources expended on these activities – like those involving force (the actual use or threat thereof) – could have been used directly for production and consumption, and there are other indirect costs associated with the resultant allocative distortion. Hence, it should be of no surprise that the thinking and modeling of rent-seeking has many similarities with that of conflict and appropriation.

A variety of other forms of appropriation that have received scant attention can be found in both public and private hierarchical organizations. Employees in such organizations typically devote time trying to influence their bosses, and much of this activity is not to convey needed information but to obfuscate and to deceive.[3] Such influence activities occur even at the highest echelons of hierarchical pyramids, between corporate managers and shareholders, where the possibilities for deception and stealing can be the greatest.[4]

Overall, then, the tradeoff between producing and grabbing (or, in Edgeworth's words, between contract and war) exists in many different facets of economic life, from the earlier forms of human interaction to today's corporate offices. Although one can discuss this tradeoff in ordinary language, the problem of incorporating it into the scholarly economic discourse until recently might have been due, at least in part, to the absence of an appropriate model. This absence, however, can no longer serve as an

---

[3] See Milgrom (1988) and Milgrom and Roberts (1990) for pioneering analyses along these lines.

[4] For an overview of the problem and for examples across the world, see Shleifer and Vishny (1997).

excuse to ignore grabbing, conflict, and influence activities in mainstream economics.

3. HOW INCORPORATING DARKNESS MAKES A DIFFERENCE

We now develop a simple model which features the tradeoff between production and appropriation and shows how the results can differ significantly from the comparable economic models that do not allow for such a tradeoff. The earliest such model appeared in Haavelmo (1954, 91–8), followed by Bush and Mayer (1974) and Hirshleifer (1988). Our presentation below is based on a simplified version of Skaperdas (1992). We consider a setting with two risk-neutral agents. These agents can be thought of as either individuals or groups thereof – for example, tribes or nations.[5] Each agent i, $i = 1, 2$, is identically endowed with R units of an inalienable resource – for example, labor. These resources cannot be consumed directly. Rather, they are allocated to productive and appropriative activities that together deliver goods for consumption at the end of the period.

In this model, the total amount of goods for consumption is produced by the two agents jointly. Let agent i's allocation to production (an intermediate input) be denoted by x_i and that to appropriation (guns or arms) be denoted by g_i, where these allocations satisfy the resource constraint, $R = x_i + g_i$, for $i = 1, 2$. Then, the production technology is –

$$F(x_1, x_2) = A_1 x_1 + A_2 x_2, \tag{1}$$

where $A_i > 0 \, (i = 1, 2)$ denotes agent i's marginal productivity. Each term, $A_i x_i$ for $i = 1, 2$, represents the compensation that agent i would receive for his or her input xi in a competitive world. It is increasing in

---

[5] Although treating a collection of individuals as a unitary agent abstracts from the sources of disagreement among the individuals about their share of the secured product and their relative contributions to production and appropriation, adding another layer of conflict would add considerably to the complexity of the model without offering much additional insight. Indeed, Skaperdas and Syropoulos (1997), who allow members within each group to choose their individual allocations to production and their own contributions to the group's appropriative efforts assuming that each member's share of the group's secured product is predetermined, find that neither the size of the two groups nor the distribution of the (fixed) resource endowment within each group has any relevance for the each group's equilibrium aggregate allocation. However, the results of Lee and Skaperdas (1998) suggest that, if members of each group could allocate some of their individual endowments to influence their own shares of the group's secured product, then a *free-rider* problem would emerge. Conflict between members within a group over the distribution of that group's secured product would reduce the amount of resources available for production even further.

his or her marginal productivity, A_i, as well as his or her choice of the input, x_i.[6]

In this analysis, however, where the conventional assumption that property rights are perfectly and costlessly enforced is abandoned, the compensation that each agent i would receive in a competitive world is subject to appropriation by the other agent. In other words, the actual distribution of total output among the two agents is a matter of conflict between them. To be more precise, we assume the quantities of guns, g_i, chosen by the two agents determine each agent's consumption share of the total product.[7] For agent 1 this share is $s(g_1, g_2)$, and for agent 2 it is $s(g_2, g_1) \equiv 1 - s(g_1, g_2)$, where

$$s(g_1, g_2) = \frac{g_1}{g_1 + g_2}. \tag{2}$$

According to equation (2), agent 1's share of total output depends positively on his own choice of arms, g_1, and negatively on that of his opponent, g_2. Similarly, agent 2's share depends positively on g_2 and negatively on g_1. By virtue of the symmetry of this specification, $s(g_1, g_2) = 1 - (g_1, g_2) = \frac{1}{2}$ when $g_1 = g_2 > 0$.[8]

Agents 1 and 2 choose their own allocations, $g_i = R - x_i$, simultaneously to maximize their individual payoffs, given by

$$V^1(g_1, g_2) = s(g_1, g_2)F(R - g_1, R - g_2). \tag{3}$$

$$V^2(g_1, g_2) = [1 - s(g_1, g_2)]F(R - g_1, R - g_2). \tag{4}$$

---

[6] Many analyses found in the literature assume a more general production technology wherein the marginal product of each input is positive, diminishing, and positively related to the level of the other input. But, the specification in (1) assumes that production is separable in the two arguments. Hence, $F(x_1, x_2)$ need not be interpreted as a joint production process; it could be viewed simply as total production that depends on two separate technologies, one for each agent.

[7] One can think of the share for each agent i as representing the fraction of the agent's own product, $A_i x_i$, that he successfully defends and the fraction of other agent's product, $A_j x_j$ $(i \neq j)$, that he or she confiscates with his or her choice of g_i, given the other agent's choice of arms. For an interesting analysis that allows for a meaningful distinction between defense and offense, see Grossman and Kim (1995).

[8] Skaperdas (1996) axiomatizes a general class of contest success functions, $s(g_1, g_2) = h(g_1)/[h(g_1) + h(g_2)]$, where $h(g_i)$ is a nonnegative, increasing function. See Hirshleifer (1989), who considers the implications of two functional forms for $h(g_i)$: (i) the *ratio or power success function*, where $h(g_i) = g_i^\eta$ and $\eta > 0$; and, (ii) the *logit success function*, where $h(g_i) = e_i^{\eta g}$ and $\eta > 0$. For any ratio success function, including the one shown in Equation (2) with $\eta = 1$, the peaceful outcome (i.e., the outcome where $g_1 = g_2 = 0$) is undefined. Such an outcome would be possible, by contrast, if a difference-logistic success function were adopted.

Once these choices are made, the level of total output and the two agents' shares of that output are realized.[9] The first-order conditions to agent 1's and agent 2's optimization problems are given respectively by

$$
\frac{\partial V^1}{\partial g_1} \equiv V_1^1 = \frac{g_2}{(g_1 + g_2)^2}[R(A_1 + A_2) - A_1 g_1 - A_2 g_2]
$$
$$
- \frac{g_1}{g_1 + g_2} A_1 = 0 \tag{5}
$$

$$
\frac{\partial V^2}{\partial g_2} \equiv V_2^2 = \frac{g_1}{(g_1 + g_2)^2}[R(A_1 + A_2) - A_1 g_1 - A_2 g_2]
$$
$$
- \frac{g_2}{g_1 + g_2} A_2 = 0, \tag{6}
$$

reflecting the tradeoff between appropriative and productive uses of the endowment. The first term in both expressions represents the marginal benefit of allocating one more unit of the endowment to appropriation in terms of the implied increase in the share of total output it yields for agent i. The second term is the marginal cost of doing so in terms of the resulting decrease in total output weighted by the agent's share of total output. At the interior optimum, this marginal cost is balanced against the marginal benefit such that the solutions, $g_1^*, g_2^* \in (0, R)$, are implicitly defined by the two conditions in (5) and (6) as strict equalities.[10]

With the solutions for arms, g_i^* ($i = 1, 2$), the two agents' intermediate input choices (x_i^*) are determined from their respective resource constraints, and then total output can be found by using the production specification (1), $F(x_1^*, x_2^*)$. Furthermore, we can solve for the agents'

---

[9] Under the maintained assumption of risk-neutrality, the agents' output shares may be interpreted alternatively as probabilities of winning the conflict and taking the entire prize – that is, total output; the losing party consumes nothing. Under this interpretation, the expressions in Equations (3) and (4) would be the agents' expected payoffs. For any linearly homogeneous production function, which is increasing in each input at a diminishing rate, risk-neutrality implies that the agents are indifferent between this conflict where the winner takes all and that where the agents share total output according to the winning probabilities.

[10] That a pure-strategy equilibrium, with neither agent allocating his or her entire endowment to appropriative activities, exists and is unique follows from our specifications of the contest success function (2) and the production technology (1). (Proofs for more general specifications can be found in Skaperdas and Syropoulos 1997.) Furthermore, as noted earlier, "full cooperation" where $g_1 = g_2 = 0$ is not defined in our model. One can also rule out "partially cooperative" outcomes where $g_1 = 0$ and $g_2 > 0$ or $g_1 > 0$ and $g_2 = 0$. Specifically, from the first-order condition for agent 1 (5) as a strict inequality, $g_1 = 0$ requires that $g_2 > R(A_1 + A_2)/A_2 > R$, which is not feasible. Similar reasoning establishes that $g_2 = 0$ is not an equilibrium outcome in this model. Hence, the unique pure-strategy equilibrium (for $g_i < R, i = 1, 2$) is an interior solution.

equilibrium shares from (2), $s(g_1^*, g_2^*)$ for agent 1 and $1 - s(g_1^*, g_2^*)$ for agent 2. To economize on notation, we indicate $F(x_1^*, x_2^*)$ by F^* and $s(g_1^*, g_2^*)$ by s^*. Then, the agents' payoffs can be found by substituting in the value total of output F^* and the agents' output shares s^* and $1 - s^*$ into Equations (3) and (4). In what follows, based on these solutions, we highlight some of the more interesting implications of conflict in the equilibrium allocation of resources.

3.1. Conflict and Output Losses

To draw out one obvious implication of conflict, reflected in the equilibrium allocation of resources, we consider here the symmetric case of the model in which the agents' marginal productivities are identical: $A_1 = A_2 = A$. From Equations (5) and (6), this assumption implies a symmetric equilibrium, $g_1^* = g_2^* = g^*$ and $s^* = 1 - s^* = \frac{1}{2}$, such that $g^* = \frac{1}{2} R$. Then, from the resource constraints, we have $x_1^* = x_2^* = x^* = \frac{1}{2} R$. Hence, the production technology, (1) with $A_1 = A_2 = A$, implies that $F^* = AR$, which is divided equally among the two agents, yielding the payoffs: $V^i(g^*, g^*) = \frac{1}{2} AR$ for $i = 1, 2$.

Now consider, as a benchmark for comparison, the outcome that would emerge in a competitive economic setting – that is, if property rights were perfectly and costlessly enforced. In such a hypothetical setting, the distribution of output would be determined by the factor shares, $A_i x_i / (A_1 x_1 + A_2 x_2)$, or $\frac{1}{2}$ for $i = 1, 2$ when $A_1 = A_2 = A$. Without conflict, each agent would allocate his or her entire endowment, R, to the production of goods for consumption, $x_1 = x_2 = R$, implying $F(R, R) = 2AR$ and $V^i(0, 0) = AR$ for $i = 1, 2$.

A comparison of the two sets of payoffs reveals immediately that conflict over the distribution of total output has negative welfare implications. By diverting the flow of resources away from the production of goods for consumption, conflict reduces total output (that is, the entire prize), leaving the two agents' shares unchanged. In the symmetric case, that output loss, AR, is borne equally by the two agents.

However, once we move outside the context of our model, the output loss is not easily measured, as we cannot know the hypothetical level of output that would have been produced in the absence of conflict. Nevertheless, the amount of resources that are diverted from productive uses and consumption to engage in conflictual activities (that is, the direct resource costs of conflict and appropriation) provides some indication of the output losses.[11] The direct resource costs would include expenditures such as military spending by the federal government, spending by state and local governments to support police forces, and spending by businesses and households on privately provided security services as well as on weapons. But, our confidence in even an estimate of the direct resource costs of conflict would have to be small, primarily because many of the components – for example, expenditures made by underground communities for offensive and defensive purposes – are not easily observable.

In any case, as one continues to think about the many ways in which conflict, whether it be actual or the threat thereof, influences the allocation of resources within an economy, one implication becomes clear: Our aggregate measures of income and production (for example, GDP) are likely to be misleading measures of the economy's overall performance. Specifically, insofar as the expenditures that reflect the diversionary effects of conflict are included in measures of aggregate income/production as positive components, such measures are likely to overstate the amount of aggregate economic activity. As mentioned earlier, while some security expenditures may be necessary to facilitate trade between agents within an economy or perhaps even between economies, a certain level of security could be supported by many different levels of such expenditures. Furthermore, these expenditures do not add directly to the current or future value of final goods and services. Thus, an increase in GDP (the total value of final goods and services produced in an economy) need not reflect an improvement in economic performance, particularly if it is fueled by sharply rising expenditures on the military, police, and/or privately provided security services.

3.2. Differences in Productivity and Distributive Asymmetries

Now we turn to the conflict equilibrium of the asymmetric case (that is, where $A_1 \neq A_2$). This equilibrium exhibits a similar type of inefficiency identified in the symmetric case above. That is, at least one agent could be made better-off relative to the conflict equilibrium, without making the other worse-off. In the asymmetric equilibrium with conflict, however,

---

[11] A measure of the indirect costs of conflict induced by the distortionary effects of conflict and appropriation mentioned in Section 2 would provide, with a measure of the direct costs, a more complete picture; however, such costs are typically unobservable.

one of the two agents will emerge as the "winner," seizing a greater share of total output. Thus, the inefficiency of conflict generally will not be reflected equally in terms of lower payoffs for both players as in the symmetric case. Indeed, conflict can augment the payoff for one agent by a sufficient amount to make him or her better-off relative to what his or her situation would be in the competitive outcome.

To fix ideas, suppose that agent 1 is more productive than agent 2: $A_1 > A_2$. Tedious algebra, using the agents' first-order conditions (5) and (6) as strict equalities, shows that the agents' optimizing choices of guns are

$$g_1^* = \frac{(A_1 + A_2)R}{2(A_1 - A_2)}[1 - \sqrt{A_2/A_1}] \text{ and } g_2^* = \frac{(A_1 + A_2)R}{2(A_1 - A_2)}[\sqrt{A_1/A_2} - 1].$$
(7)

As revealed by comparing these two expressions, because $A_1 > A_2$ by assumption, agent 2 allocates a relatively greater fraction of his or her resources to arm: $g_1^* < g_2^*$. In turn, the conflict technology (2) implies that the more productive agent (agent 1) receives a smaller share of total output. Interpreting each agent's equilibrium share of output as his or her power, the more productive agent is generally less powerful.

This result might seem surprising at first glance. After all, according to the typical textbook treatment of the competitive world as previously mentioned, each owner of a factor of production is compensated by his or her factor share of total output: $A_i/(A_1 + A_2)$, in our model without conflict, since $x_i = R$ for $i = 1, 2$. Hence, contrary to the prediction of the model with conflict, in a competitive world the more productive agent, agent 1 in our example, enjoys the greater share of total output.

The intuition for the direction of distributive asymmetry in the conflict equilibrium, however, is perfectly consistent with economic theory. Suppose that, starting from the symmetric equilibrium where $A_1 = A_2 = A$ and $g_1 = g_2 = \frac{1}{2} R$, agent 1's productivity improves, while that of agent 2 deteriorates. Assume that the increase in A_1 and the decrease in A_2 are of equal magnitude (i.e., $dA_1 = -dA_2 > 0$) such that, at the initial allocation of resources, output is left unchanged. Accordingly, the marginal benefit from arming for both agents is also unchanged. The marginal cost of arming, however, changes for both agents. For agent 1, it rises by $\frac{1}{2} dA_1$ — the output that agent 1 sacrifices when he or she allocates an additional unit of his or her resource endowment to guns. Hence, the more productive agent has a smaller incentive to arm [see Equation (5)]. At the same time for agent 2, the marginal cost of arming falls by $\frac{1}{2} dA_1 = -\frac{1}{2} dA_2 > 0$, giving him or her a greater incentive to arm [see Equation (6)]. With a greater incentive to arm, the less productive agent is favored in the conflict equilibrium.[12]

Although based on a simple model of conflict, this finding is fairly robust. In particular, it holds for a general class of symmetric conflict technologies, with a more general specification for the production technology than that assumed here.[13] Skaperdas and Syropoulos (1997) show that an analogous result would obtain if, instead, the source of the asymmetry were in terms of the agents' efficiency in transforming their endowments into the intermediate input.[14]

Whereas the less productive agent enjoys a larger share of total output than he or she would in the hypothetical outcome without conflict, conflict itself results in a lower level of total output to share. Hence the sign of the impact of conflict on this agent's payoff is generally ambiguous. See Figure 1, which shows both possibilities. In the figure, the downward sloping line (with a slope of -1) running through point C represents all constrained efficient distributions of the total product F^*, given the equilibrium allocations to guns by both agents, g_1^* and g_2^*. The dashed line drawn from the origin through point C has a slope equal to $[s^*/(1-s^*)] < 1$. Hence, point C shows the payoffs for the two agents in the conflict equilibrium. The outer downward sloping line similarly represents all distributions of total output, but given the efficient output level where $g_1 = g_2 = 0$, $F(R, R) > F^*$. The area within the triangle CB_1B_2 shows all hypothetical outcomes where at least one agent is made better-off without the other

---

[12] Note that, at the (initial) symmetric equilibrium, $\partial^2 V^1/\partial g_1 \partial g_2 = \partial^2 V^2/\partial g_2 \partial g_1 = 0$. Hence, the predicted adjustment made by each agent in response to the changes in the agents' marginal productivities is independent of the other agent's adjustments.

[13] In particular, Skaperdas (1992) assumes that the production technology $F(x_1, x_2)$ is linearly homogeneous, increasing in each of the two inputs, $x_i (i = 1, 2)$ at a diminishing rate and exhibiting some degree of complementarity. For conflict technologies of the general form $s(g_1, g_2) = h(g_1)/[h(g_1 + g_2)]$ where $h(g_i)$ is a nonnegative increasing function, a key restriction is that $s_{11}s < s_1^2$ and $-s_{22}(1-s) < s_2^2$, where $s_i \equiv \partial s/\partial g_i$ and $s_{ij} \equiv \partial^2 s/\partial g_i \partial g_j$. Note that this condition is necessarily satisfied if $s_{11} < 0$, but imposing concavity on the conflict technology is not required.

[14] To allow for such a possibility, the resource constraints could be written as $R = a_i x_i + g_i$, where $a_i > 0$, for $i = 1, 2$. Then, a greater efficiency in transforming the endowment into x_i for agent i would be reflected in a smaller value of a_i.

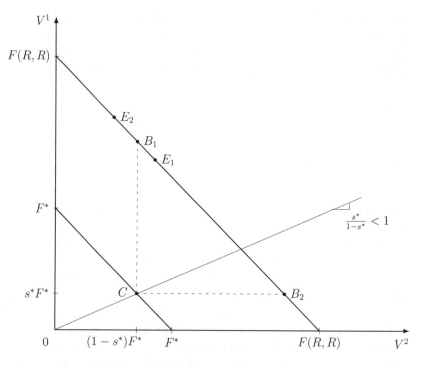

Figure 1. Asymmetric outcomes with and without conflict.

being made worse-off, with the points along the segment $B_1 B_2$ representing those alternative outcomes that yield the maximal joint improvement relative to the conflict equilibrium. The competitive equilibrium would be at the point where a line from the origin with slope $(A_1/A_2) > 1$ intersects the efficient frontier, that is, $F(R,R)F(R,R)$. Because $(A_1/A_2) > 1 > s^*/(1-s^*)$, this point would lie to the left of the midpoint of the efficient frontier. If that point lies to the right of B_1 on the frontier, such as point E_1, then the more powerful agent, like the less powerful one, finds himself to be worse off in the conflict equilibrium than he would be in the hypothetical competitive equilibrium. If, however, that point lies to the left of B_1 on the frontier, such as point E_2, the less productive agent is sufficiently more powerful than the other agent to make him prefer conflict, despite the effect of conflict to lower the level of total output.

As suggested by our earlier comparative static exercise, it should be clear from this figure that, when the difference between the two agents' productivity is greater, the less productive agent is more likely to benefit from the absence of perfectly and costlessly enforced property rights.[15] Nevertheless, even in this case, the less productive agent as well as the more productive agent would prefer to "cooperate" somehow to avoid the output losses due to conflict.[16]

3.3. Prospects for "Cooperation" in a Noncooperative Equilibrium

In the context of our simple, one-period model of conflict, it would appear that cooperation, where at least one of the two agents allocates all of his or her endowment to production, cannot be supported in the equilibrium when the two players behave noncooperatively (that is, taking the other agent's resource allocation as given).[17] But, because each agent is aware of the room for improvement in both of their payoffs, it seems reasonable to imagine that they would try to "coordinate" their actions, decreasing their allocations to guns and increasing their allocations to production, whereby they could effect an outcome closer to one along the efficient frontier.

---

[15] With the resource constraints, the solutions shown in Equation (7) imply that the more powerful agent (agent 2 given $A_1 > A_2$) will prefer conflict if and only if $A_1^2(A_1 - 3A_2) - 4A_2^3 > 0$. This condition is more likely to be satisfied the larger is A_1 given A_2, provided that $A_1 > 2A_2$. But a necessary condition is that $A_1 > 3A_2$.

[16] Recall that, in Figure 1, all distributions in the triangle CB_1B_2 (excluding C) represent Pareto improvements relative to the conflict equilibrium. See Garfinkel and Lee (2000), who study conflict in a somewhat different setting. In particular, agents having different preferences can allocate resources in an attempt to induce the policymaker to choose a tax-spending policy that they find more appealing. While this form of conflict (i.e., lobbying) is generally thought to be costly, Garfinkel and Lee show that, if preferences are not too diverse, lobbying might lead to a better outcome from a social welfare perspective, when policy is already distorted by the policymaker's inability to commit to future policy. This distortion alone imparts a positive bias in taxes, implying that those with the greatest incentive to lobby are precisely those agents who prefer lower taxes. Hence, the "distortion" attributed to lobbying tends to offset the positive bias on taxes and public spending due to the policymaker's inability to commit to future policy. However, the outcome is only a second-best one in the sense that some resources are "wasted" in the lobbying process.

[17] The absence of such cooperation in the equilibrium of this model, however, is not a robust result. (See, for example, Skaperdas 1992 and Neary 1996.) Rather, it is an artifact of our simple specifications. More generally, depending on the specification of the conflict technology as well as on that of the production technology, the equilibrium where agents behave noncooperatively could be fully or partially cooperative. Skaperdas (1992) demonstrates that full cooperation is more likely to be supported when the conflict technology is sufficiently ineffective (in the sense that $\partial s/\partial g_1$, evaluated at $g_1 = g_2 = 0$, is smaller than some critical value) and the agent's marginal productivities, evaluated at full cooperation, are sufficiently close to one another. Partial cooperation is more likely to emerge in equilibrium when the conflict technology is sufficiently ineffective (but not as ineffective as is necessary for full cooperation) and the two agents' marginal products evaluated at full cooperation are sufficiently diverse.

Returning to the symmetric case, for example, suppose that the two agents agree to reduce their allocations to guns, $g_1 = g_2 = \alpha R$ with $0 < \alpha < \frac{1}{2}$, in hopes of recovering at least some of the output lost as a result of the conflict between them.[18] However, under the belief that the other agent adheres to the agreement, each agent would have an incentive to "renege," arming by more than the amount specified in the agreement.[19] That is to say, this alternative sort of cooperation is not incentive compatible. Without some set of institutions to enforce such agreements, neither agent would expect the other to follow through on an agreement to cooperate in the noncooperative equilibrium.[20] Accordingly, based on this one-period setting, we would not expect to observe any sort of cooperation by the agents in equilibrium.

Matters differ, however, if we suppose that the two agents interact repeatedly over time. Suppose that the events of the (static) one-period model are repeated over an infinite time horizon, $t = 1, 2, \ldots, \infty$. Such repetition introduces the possibility of strategic dynamics whereby each agent can influence the other agent's future actions with his or her current actions. Focusing again on the symmetric case, consider the following trigger strategy: Each agent i $(i = 1, 2)$ agrees to cooperate by setting, $g_{it} = \alpha R$ with $0 < \alpha < \frac{1}{2}$, in the first period $t = 1$, and to continue cooperating by setting $g_{it} = \alpha R$ in each future period, $t > 1$, provided that the other agent has not cheated in the past N periods. Cheating by either agent triggers a punishment by the other, involving a return to the equilibrium of the one-period model for the following N periods. The punishment phase may be as short as one period ($N = 1$) like Axelrod's (1984) *tit for tat* strategy, but it could last forever ($N = \infty$) as considered, for example, by Garfinkel (1990).

For any given N-period punishment, there is a continuum of possible trigger strategies which vary by the value of $\alpha \in (0, \frac{1}{2})$ – that is, by the fraction of resources diverted from production when both agents adopt the strategy. But not all of these strategies are supported in equilibrium.

---

[18] As the conflict technology is not defined at $g_1 = g_2 = 0$, we cannot analyze the incentive compatibility of an agreement with $\alpha = 0$.

[19] Substituting $g_2 = \alpha R$ into agent 1's first-order condition (5) and then solving for g_1 shows that agent 1's cheating solution is $g = (\sqrt{2\alpha} - \alpha)R > \alpha R$ for $\alpha < \frac{1}{2}$. Analogous calculations show the same cheating solution for agent 2.

[20] Even if we were to assume that such institutions exist (e.g., a judicial system), additional resources would have to be diverted from production to make enforcement effective (e.g., court costs and lawyer fees). As enforcement generally is not perfect or costless, some degree of conflict remains, although the structure of the "game" is different. We return to this and related issues below in Section 4.

The set of equilibrium trigger strategies, all with a given N-period punishment, is defined by an incentive compatibility constraint, requiring that the current one-period temptation to cheat (that is, the difference between the one-period payoff under cheating and the payoff under cooperation) be less than or equal to the losses associated with the punishment (that is, the difference between the discounted sum of the following N future payoffs when both cooperate and the discounted sum of future payoffs over the same N periods when both choose their allocations as in the one-period model). For equilibrium trigger strategies, then, neither agent ever has an incentive to cheat, implying that the punishment period is never observed in equilibrium. As such, each agent effectively induces the other to "cooperate" in the future, by cooperating today, with the threat of punishment for cheating (lost gains from cooperation) lurking in the background. The set of equilibrium trigger strategies with an infinite-period punishment is the largest, and contains that strategy which implies the greatest gains from maintained cooperation – that is, the smallest value of α which is incentive compatible. The more the two agents care about the future relative to the present (as reflected in the agents' discount factor), the more effective is the threat of that punishment to induce cooperative behavior and reduce the severity of the remaining conflict between them and the resulting output losses.[21]

The importance of the future in promoting cooperation, however, might have been overstated in the preceding. Suppose that the one-period model is repeated only a finite number of times. Then, in the final period, each agent will rationally choose to cheat, because there is no future period in which a punishment can be imposed. Recognizing this, the equilibrium of the final period is simply that of the one-period model. Given that equilibrium, the threat of a punishment in the last period for cheating behavior in the second to last period is irrelevant. Indeed, the trigger-strategy solution unravels, so that the only equilibrium when the time horizon is finite is the one of the one-period model.[22]

Moreover, as shown by Skaperdas and Syropoulos (1996), the importance of the future might make cooperation a less likely outcome if there is structural time dependence – specifically, economic growth. Suppose

---

[21] For a more complete analysis of threats and punishments which identifies other parameters that are key to determining how much conflict can be avoided in equilibrium, see Garfinkel (1990).

[22] Note that, in the infinite horizon case, the possibility of renegotiation between the two agents in the future to wipe the slate clean, if one were to cheat, would similarly cause this solution to unravel.

that, by securing a larger share of total product today, an agent can obtain even more resources in the future for him- or herself, which in turn enhances his or her ability to secure more resources thereafter. The potential for growth in the agents' resource endowment in the future based on their respective current payoffs can give each agent a greater incentive to arm today. Hence, instead of promoting cooperation, the importance of the future can intensify the conflict between the two agents. In such a setting, the more each agent cares about the future (that is, the larger is discount factor), the greater is his or her incentive to arm today.[23]

4. MANAGING CONFLICT

Rarely do most of us witness explosions of violence – other than on television and film. The ordinary life of most human beings is overwhelmingly peaceful. Yet there are plenty of signs everywhere of the potential for the use of force: there are armies and armaments, there are police, and there are guns. Although the potential for the breakout of actual conflict is always present, conflict is somehow controlled and managed. We have seen the possibility, yet far from the necessity, of reducing the resources expended on conflict when the future is important and the contending parties follow regular self-interested actions. There are many other ways, however, to manage conflict, and we shall conclude with a brief discussion of two broad mechanisms through which societies manage conflict: the state and societies' belief systems.

The settlement of conflicting claims among individual agents has typically been facilitated by the intervention of third parties – the village elders in traditional communities; the police, the courts, and the halls of politics of modern states. That is, conflict in the battlefield can be transformed into the more "civilized," and usually less socially wasteful, forms of conflict

---

[23] An analogous result concerning the discount factor is obtained by Garfinkel (1994), who focuses primarily on a single democratic state in which there is some disagreement about the composition of peaceful production (private versus public consumption goods), but there is no disagreement about spending on guns that enable the nation to secure resources for the next period (given another nation's guns allocation). In this setting, electoral uncertainty associated with competition between two political parties, each representing a specific group of the electorate, imparts a negative bias on the nation's guns allocation. That is, the possibility of being replaced by another policymaker with different preferences prevents the incumbent from fully internalizing the benefits of current spending on guns realized beyond the current electoral term. Thus, electoral uncertainty, like a smaller discount factor, reduces a nation's incentive to arm, which may in turn reduce the intensity of conflict between nations.

of litigation and political contests. How you move from one level of conflict to another, less wasteful one is an important topic for research, yet one that has barely been studied. Acemoglu and Robinson (2000) and Rosendorff (2001) represent two early attempts in that direction. They both view the extension of the democratic franchise respectively in nineteenth century Britain and twentieth century South Africa, as a rational response on the part of the power-wielding elites to the endemic social conflict that was plaguing, and was expected to continue to plague, their countries. The elites relinquished some political power and, as a result, also part of their share of the total economic pie in exchange for less conflict and the resultant increase in the total size of the pie. Learning more about the details of such institutional transitions is, in our view, much more important for understanding economic development than continuing to rely on extant growth models that assume the presence of perfectly functioning institutions and markets.

In its early forms, the state had been just another contender in the arena of conflict, albeit a bigger one that could subjugate and pacify most of the "small" contenders in their areas of influence. Any savings from this pacification were typically appropriated by the rulers themselves, while the mass of the population could suffer even more privations than in the absence of lords and kings.[24] Such conditions still prevail today in some third-world countries in which the state can be accurately described as predatory.[25]

Besides the carrot-and-stick methods used by states to manage conflict, a major class of mechanisms that control conflict resides, simply, in our heads. Human beings have the capacity to empathize with others and the need for a spiritual being in their corner. These human traits are reinforced in a variety of ways – especially during childhood – in all societies. Ethical beliefs and norms against violence and conflict then serve the very practical purpose of minimizing conflict within a community but also across communities. Religions that have spread beyond the confines of a community have also helped along the same lines. Another trait of humans, however, is the ability to rationalize almost any action with a moral veneer. When the material stakes are high enough, even the most

---

[24] McGuire and Olson (1996) have argued that everybody benefits from the presence of a king; Moselle and Polak (2001) and Konrad and Skaperdas (1999), however, identify the circumstances in which the presence of a king can lead to a worse outcome for everybody but the king, despite the higher level of security that the king may provide.

[25] For conditions that induce such behavior on the part of rulers, see Robinson (1997). For an in-depth economic analysis of dictatorial rule in general, see Wintrobe (1998).

morally abhorrent acts can somehow be justified and rationalized as a necessary means, even morally so with some strange twist of logic.

Perhaps one instance of such justification and rationalization is that the emperor or king is God's single representative on earth or holds the "Mandate of Heaven." This way, absolutist rule acquires the aura of divine rule and therefore the "legitimacy" that makes subjects acquiesce to that rule. The economic effects of such an ideology can be substantial as pacification becomes hard-wired in people's minds and does not require much expenditure of real resources. In modern nation-states, the ideological function of the divine mandate is played by the "imagined community"[26] of the citizens of the nation-state who are bound by a common destiny.

The same force of nationalism that serves the purpose of internal cohesion and pacification can also be held responsible for much of the conflict that has prevailed in the world during the last two centuries. The formal anarchy of the international order today, however, is increasingly mediated and governed through a growing thicket of norms, international law (frequently violated by those who can get away with it – more often than not the more powerful), and a number of international organizations that adjudicate disputes from trade conflicts, to environmental and labor regulation as well as to sovereignty over underseas wealth. This new trend appears to have led to increasing speculation about the nation-state being dead in evolutionary terms. But, even if this speculation were true, it could be another century before the nation-state actually dies. After all, it took longer for absolutist empires to die out after enlightenment thinkers had declared it a dead end in the eighteenth century. War, in the meantime, will continue to be dancing around along with contract as the two ways in which human beings and collectivities pursue their respective interests.

REFERENCES

Acemoglu, Daron and Robinson, James A. "Why Did the West Extend the Franchise? Democracy, Inequality and Growth in Historical Perspective," *Quarterly Journal of Economics* 115(4), November 2000, 1167–99.

Anderson, Benedict. *Imagined Communities. Reflection on the Origin and Spread of Nationalism.* (New York: Verso, 1991), revised edition (originally published in 1983).

---

[26] The term is due to Anderson (1991), who traces the origins of nationalism to the spread of print media.

Axelrod, Robert. *The Evolution of Cooperation.* (New York: Basic Books, 1984).

Bush, Winston C. and Mayer, Lawrence S. "Some Implications of Anarchy for the Distribution of Property," *Journal of Economic Theory* 8(2), August 1974, 401–12.

Easterly, William and Levine, Ross. "Africa's Growth Tragedy: Policies and Ethnic Divisions," *Quarterly Journal of Economics* 112(4), November 1997, 1203–50.

Edgeworth, Francis Ysidro. *Mathematical Psychics.* (London: C. Kegan Paul & Co., 1881).

Garfinkel, Michelle R. "Arming as a Strategic Investment in a Cooperative Equilibrium," *American Economic Review* 80(1), March 1990, 50–68.

Garfinkel, Michelle R. "Domestic Politics and International Conflict," *American Economic Review* 84(5), December 1994, 1292–309.

Garfinkel, Michelle R. and Lee, Jaewoo. "Political Influence and the Dynamic Consistency of Policy," *American Economic Review* 90(3), June 2000, 649–66.

Grossman, Herschel I. and Kim, Minseong. "Swords or Plowshares? A Theory of the Security of Claims to Property," *Journal of Political Economy* 103(6), December 1995, 1275–88.

Haavelmo, Trygve. *A Study in the Theory of Economic Evolution.* (Amsterdam: North-Holland, 1954).

Hirshleifer, Jack. "The Analytics of Continuing Conflict," *Synthese* 76(2), August 1988, 201–33.

Hirshleifer, Jack. "Conflict and Rent Seeking Functions: Ratio vs. Difference Models of Relative Success," *Public Choice* 63(2), November 1989, 101–12.

Hirshleifer, Jack. "The Dark Side of the Force," *Economic Inquiry* 32(1), January 1994, 1–10.

Konrad, Kai A. and Skaperdas, Stergios. "The Market for Protection and the Origin of the State," Department of Economics, University of California Irvine, 1999.

Lee, Jaewoo and Skaperdas, Stergios. "Workshops or Barracks? Productive versus Enforcive Investment and Economic Performance," in Michael R. Baye (ed.), *Advances in Applied Microeconomics,* vol. 7 (Stamford, CT: JAI Press, 1998).

McGuire, Martin and Olson, Mancur. "The Economics of Autocracy and Majority Rule: The Invisible Hand and the Use of Force," *Journal of Economics Literature* 34(1), March 1996, 72–96.

Milgrom, Paul. "Employment Contracts, Influence Activities, and Efficient Organization Design," *Journal of Political Economy* 96(2), February 1988, 42–60.

Milgrom, Paul and Roberts, John. "The Efficiency of Equity in Organizational Decision Processes," *American Economic Review* 90(2), May 1990, 154–9.

Moselle, Boaz and Polak, Ben. "A Model of a Predatory State," *Journal of Law, Economics, and Organization,* April 2001, 1–33.

Neary, Hugh M. "Equilibrium Structure in an Economic Model of Conflict," *Economic Inquiry* 35(3), July 1996, 480–94.

Robinson, James A. "When Is the State Predatory?" Department of Economics, University of Southern California, 1997.

Rodrik, Dani. "Where Did All the Growth Go? External Shocks, Social Conflict, and Growth Collapses," *Journal of Economic Growth* 4, December 1999, 385–412.

Rosendorff, B. Peter. "Choosing Democracy: The Transition in South Africa," *Economics and Politics* 13(1), 2001, 1–29.

Shleifer, Andrei and Vishny, Robert. "A Survey of Corporate Governance," *Journal of Finance* 52(2), June 1997, 737–83.

Skaperdas, Stergios. "Cooperation, Conflict, and Power in the Absence of Property Rights," *American Economic Review* 82(4), September 1992, 720–39.

Skaperdas, Stergios. "Contest Success Functions," *Economic Theory* 7(2), February 1996, 283–90.

Skaperdas, Stergios and Syropoulos, Constantinos. "Can the Shadow of the Future Harm Cooperation?" *Journal of Economic Behavior and Organization* 29(3), May 1996, 355–72.

Skaperdas, Stergios and Syropoulos, Constantinos. "The Distribution of Income in the Presence of Appropriative Activities," *Economica* 64, February 1997, 101–17.

SIPRI (Stockholm International Peace Research Institute) Yearbook 1998, *Armaments, Disarmament, and International Security*. (Oxford: Oxford University Press, 1998).

Wintrobe, Ronald. *The Political Economy of Dictatorship*. (New York: Cambridge University Press, 1998).

10

New Directions in Law and Economics

Alan O. Sykes

Law and economics began at the University of Chicago with the pioneering work of Henry Simons in the tax area and Aaron Director on antitrust. Ronald Coase contributed "The Problem of Social Cost," sometimes said to be the most cited article in the history of economics, and launched the serious study of tort and property law from the economic perspective. The antitrust mantle was carried forward by such Chicago-connected scholars as Robert Bork, Frank Easterbrook, William Landes, and Richard Posner. Their critique of antitrust doctrine as it had emerged in the 1960s and 1970s revolutionized the field, so much so that Robert Bork claims substantial victory for Chicago school ideas in the afterword to the most recent edition of *The Antitrust Paradox*. Guido Calabresi at Yale introduced basic ideas of economics to the field of accident law, as Landes, Posner, and Steven Shavell at Harvard also labored to understand the economic implications of negligence, strict liability, joint and several liability, and other central features of tort doctrine. Serious work on contract law soon followed, such as Shavell's seminal work on contract remedies. The corporate area was also a natural target for economically oriented research. Chicago scholars Easterbrook and Daniel Fischel focused on the law governing changes in corporate control, for example, while Ralph Winter at Yale thoughtfully rebutted the suggestion that the state of Delaware had led corporate law racing toward the bottom, and Henry Manne wondered about the logic of insider trading rules.

These vintage subjects retain their vitality. *United States v. Microsoft* is one of many recent cases proving that difficult challenges remain in understanding the economics of important business practices under the antitrust laws, particularly in high-tech industries. The "patient's bill of rights" debate raises intriguing theoretical and empirical issues about the optimal tort liability system for a complex entity such as a managed care organization. The early work on optimal contracting, and its relationship to the law of contract has burgeoned into a vast enterprise on agency, mechanism design, employment contracting, and many other topics. The fallout from the collapse of Enron is already central to the scholarly agenda of many who labor in the cooperate area.

A great deal of the action has now shifted to other areas, however, many of which will be relatively unfamiliar to readers without significant legal training. Subjects such as civil procedure, criminal law, constitutional law, employment law, family law, insurance law, international law, and intellectual property law now weigh heavily in the research agenda. My goal in this essay is to familiarize the reader with *some* of these newer lines of research in law and economics, which I believe offer important opportunities for innovative work by young scholars.

The survey is unavoidably selective and illustrative rather than comprehensive. I choose to write about fields with which I am relatively familiar for obvious reasons, and on that basis and in the interests of brevity I will limit my survey to criminal law, international law, and insurance law. I do not purport to have identified the work that is necessarily the "best" or most influential, and I apologize in advance to the many superb scholars whose work I am unable to highlight in this brief essay. The objective here is not to honor the finest but to convey the breadth of new research as well as a sense of its depth, commenting on some unanswered questions along the way.

1. CRIMINAL LAW

I begin with criminal law not only because of the valuable work done on the subject in recent years, but also because it typifies an important trend in law and economics – an increasing emphasis on careful empirical work. Accordingly, much of the work discussed below is empirical, although there have been some important theoretical advances to be sure.

Despite the prominence of crime in the press and in the political arena, many basic issues have received only modest attention from economists. For example, what is the social cost of crime? A sense of the answer to that question is essential to judgments about the proper level of anticrime enforcement. Many crimes involve transfers (theft of one sort or another), but there are substantial resource costs to crime as well – death and disability of victims, the cost of precautions against crime, the opportunity costs of labor for those incarcerated, the costs of the criminal justice system, and so on. Anderson (1999) is perhaps the first effort to quantify in rough fashion all of the costs of crime net of transfers for the United States – his (pre-September 11) estimate of an annual cost exceeding $1 trillion is assuredly subject to quibbles, but underscores the importance of the subject and the potential returns to cost-effective policies for crime control.

Other recent work focuses on the costs of particular crimes, such as the work of Levitt and Porter (2001) on drunk driving. Using data on fatal crashes, they devise a clever method for measuring the harm of drinking by using information on two-driver crashes to identify the marginal risk caused by drinking. They conclude that of about 12,000 alcohol-related fatalities each year, approximately 3,000 are "externalities" (harm to people other than the drinking driver), and that to externalize this externality would require that drivers arrested for driving under the influence be fined approximately $8,000 per offense.

Modern theoretical work on crime and the criminal law begins with Becker (1968) and Stigler (1970). They assumed that criminals make rational choices about how to behave just like anyone else, with the decision to commit a criminal act dependent on such factors as the probability of apprehension and the magnitude of punishment. Among other things, this framework can be used to analyze basic optimal deterrence problems, such as what is the least costly way for society to deter crime. Assume that a fine can impose costs on criminals more cheaply than incarceration (enforcement costs to the side, fines are transfers rather than resource expenditures); that the costs of imposing fines rise less than proportionally with the magnitude of the fine; and that the costs of increasing the probability of apprehending criminals rise more than proportionally with that probability. These seemingly plausible assumptions yield an important insight that is the starting point for much economic thinking on the subject – fines are a more efficient penalty than incarceration, and an optimal system of deterrence using fines may achieve a given expected penalty most cheaply by imposing a large fine with a low probability (thereby reducing the need for investments in catching criminals).

This proposition is at odds with much of what we observe in the criminal justice system. Fines are the exclusive penalty for crime primarily for minor offenses, and incarceration is used extensively even when criminals apparently have assets that the state could seize. Nor is it clear that fines when used are calibrated with regard to the probability of apprehension – the "seriousness" of the crime seems to be the primary consideration.

What explains this divergence? A partial answer is that many criminals are judgment-proof and cannot pay fines, but this is too simple. Many criminals have considerable wealth that the state does not take, and still others have human capital that can be taxed through the years. The desire of the state to incapacitate criminals is often invoked as another reason for the widespread use of incarceration, but the very need for incapacitation presupposes that deterrence in a world of fines is inadequate, which returns full circle to the judgment-proofness issue and to the puzzle of why fines are not used as much as they might be in practice. A system that allowed the wealthy to avoid jail time by paying fines might seem inequitable and thus politically unpalatable, but that objection seems to imagine that fines cannot be set high enough to punish the wealthy criminal as much as the jail time that is imposed in its stead – if the criminal with assets suffers disutility from a fine comparable to the jail time imposed currently, what would make the fine unjust? The puzzle is not easily laid to rest.

Levitt (1997) responds with the observation that a system of fines will not work unless criminals can be coerced to pay them, and the primary device for coercion is a threat of prison. Fines and imprisonment must be "incentive compatible" in the sense that fines are useless if criminals would prefer to accept the jail penalty for not paying them. He further imagines that criminals often have private information about their wealth, and that the ability to tax their human capital turns on the government's ability to maintain work incentives in the face of an inability to observe work effort directly. Because the government cannot identify the criminals with greater assets well or those with greater earning capacity, it must confront all offenders with the same fine/jail tradeoff, and the result is an equilibrium in which many offenders opt for jail. Although the argument is a useful extension of standard explanations for imprisonment, it still fails to explain the commonly observed fact that criminals with a great deal of verifiable wealth are allowed to retain much of it while being sent to jail for lengthy periods. As a positive matter, therefore, it remains an open question as to why fines are used to a limited extent in the criminal justice system, particularly for white collar offenders with substantial assets or human capital.

To be sure, there is some evidence that criminal penalties are sensitive to efficiency considerations even if not "optimal," at least in certain contexts. For example, Waldfogel (1995) studies sentencing patterns for a large sample of convicted federal fraud offenders. He finds that proxies for ability to pay – such as monthly income prior to conviction and age of the offender – are positively correlated with the magnitude of fines, and that the length of the prison sentence is negatively correlated with the size of the fine, other things being equal.

Related to work on the optimal mix of fines and incarceration is a growing body of literature on alternative penalties. Rasmusen (1996) considers the role of "stigma" in deterrence, which he defines as a labor market penalty imposed on convicted criminals, either because employers find criminals repugnant and will sacrifice profit to avoid them, or because criminality is correlated with factors that reduce a worker's productivity. As long as criminality is not so widespread that a criminal record loses its informativeness (as might be the case in high crime areas in the inner city), equilibria may emerge in which stigma deters crimes quite effectively for all but the most criminally inclined. Stigma also has the virtue that it is not subject to the judgment-proof problem (like fines), and it is not costly to impose on criminals (like prison). Indeed, it may be productive in the sense of yielding better labor market sorting. A further implication of treating stigma as a component of the penalty system is that there is no longer a simple case to be made for high penalties coupled with low probabilities of apprehension – a high probability of apprehension becomes more useful because of the information that a conviction conveys about an individual. Where stigma is a useful component of deterrence, state efforts to disseminate information regarding convictions (thereby increasing stigma) will often be valuable.

Closely connected is the work of Kahan and Posner (1999) on punishment for white collar offenders. They begin with the premise that a substitution of fines for imprisonment in this category of offenses is for some reason politically infeasible. They then observe that shaming penalties – such as publicizing the white collar offender's name widely in the newspaper or on billboards – may yield social and labor market penalties that, like fines, can deter crime much more cheaply than prison. This observation is at odds with the trend in the Federal Sentencing Guidelines toward higher prison sentences for these offenders, although they find evidence of the creative use of shaming penalties in some state courts.

Some consumers of the law and economics literature on crime reject its premises, however, and thus see little merit in its efficiency propositions. The assumption that criminals act "rationally," for example, so that an increase in the punishment or the probability of apprehension will reduce crime at the margin, is not considered at all obvious by many scholars of criminal law. In response to this critique, a vast literature has emerged that seeks to test a most basic notion – that punishment deters crime, and that incremental punishment deters crime at the margin.

A confounding factor in much of this research is the fact that the deterrent effect of punishment is difficult to separate from the incapacitation effect. If prison sentences increase and crime falls, is that because potential criminals are deterred by a prospect of prison, or because would-be recidivists are locked away and unable to commit new crimes?

Kessler and Levitt (1999) devise a clever strategy for differentiating between the two effects in one particular setting. At times states will enact "sentence enhancement" laws that ratchet upward the penalties for particular offenses. Immediately after such laws are passed, there is no increase in incapacitation inasmuch as the enhancements do not apply retroactively to people already in prison, and those newly sentenced to prison would have been sent to jail for a significant period anyway even without the sentence enhancement. The increase in incapacitation will be seen only after the prison terms that would have been imposed under prior law elapse and the sentence enhancement begins. Thus, any impact on crime rates on the "short run" must be attributable to increased deterrence rather than to incapacitation. Looking at data on crime in California immediately after the passage of the sentence enhancements embodied in Proposition 8 of 1982, Kessler and Levitt indeed find a decrease in crime (other things equal) for the crimes covered by Proposition 8, but not for other crimes.

Another dimension to the deterrent effect of the criminal law relates to this issue of "marginal deterrence." If the penalty for a modest crime is severe enough, there may be little reason for criminals to eschew more severe crimes. More broadly, the importance of maintaining marginal deterrence raises a host of empirical questions about the structure of penalties in the criminal justice system, such as the question whether modern "get tough on crime" policies may have some unfortunate unintended consequences. A robber faced with a prospect of life in prison for robbery may elect to kill the witnesses, for example, on the premise that the penalty for murder is no worse. Marvell and Moody (2001) study the effects of "three-strikes" laws, enacted in many jurisdictions in the 1990s, which typically provide that criminals convicted of three felony offenses during their lifetime will receive mandatory life sentences. Using panel data, they find that three strikes laws result in about a 10 percent to 12 percent increase in homicides shortly after their passage and nearly a 30 percent increase in the long run. Their findings too tend to confirm the "rationality" model of criminal actors, as well as to remind us that increasing the penalties for crime will not always move behavior in the right direction.

Of course, many things affect the crime rate besides simply the penalties for crime, and a vast literature exists on the broader causes of crime. For example, it is well known that crime rates are much higher in cities. Why is this so? Is there more wealth to be stolen? Does the greater density of victims somehow increase the returns to crime? Are there more poor people whose best option to earn money is criminal behavior? Is it easier for criminals to avoid arrest in an urban setting? Glaeser and Sacerdote (1999) explore the issue using three different data sets on crime. Their most striking finding is that the higher incidence of crime in cities relates heavily to the higher percentage of families in cities in which women are the head of the household. They are cautious in drawing conclusions about the nature of the causal link here (and acknowledge possible simultaneity problems), but the tentative hypothesis deserving of further study is that the offspring in female-headed households are more likely to become criminals.

Another well-publicized phenomenon is the decline in crime rates nationally over the past decade or so. An extended period of economic prosperity no doubt holds some part of the explanation, but Donahue and Levitt (2001a) offer a controversial suggestion that legalized abortion has had much to do with the drop in crime. They observe that crime rates began to fall approximately eighteen years after *Roe v. Wade* legalized abortion on a national scale, and note how abortion might be expected to affect crime rates – it reduces the number of unwanted children, who tend to be born into more difficult circumstances and are more likely to turn to crime as teenagers and adults. Their analysis employs panel data to explore the relationship between abortion rates and crime rates across states, and concludes that as much as 50 percent of the reduction in crime since the early 1990s may be due to the availability of abortions.

Even more controversial has been the work of Lott (1998) and Lott and Mustard (1997) on the relationship between guns and crime. Lott and Mustard study the effects of "right to carry" laws, which provide that any citizen of legal age and without any disabling factor (such as a criminal record) shall be issued a permit to carry a concealed weapon. Using panel data at the county level, they find that right to carry laws significantly reduce several categories of violent crimes in the jurisdictions that have them, without increasing accidental deaths. They also find some increase in crime within those jurisdictions for categories of crime (such as burglary) that do not involve direct contact with victims following the passage of right to carry laws, as well as some increase in violent crime in jurisdictions adjacent to those that have right to carry laws (suggesting that criminals cross the border to commit their crimes).

I should note that both Donahue and Levitt (2001b) and Lott and Mustard (1997) are not without their critics, and work is ongoing that questions their findings. Neither matter has been laid to rest by any means.

Among the most vexing issues in the criminal justice system is the question whether it is able to function in an unbiased fashion, particularly as regards the issue of race. Readers will no doubt recall the extensive publicity given to so-called racial profiling in recent years, for example. A number of empirical analyses have been undertaken to examine such issues, and the findings are not always comforting.

Donahue and Levitt (2001b) study the relationship between the race of police officers and the arrest rate by race. Using panel data from the 122 largest U.S. cities, they find that an increase in the number of white police officers produces a significant increase in the number of arrests of nonwhite suspects, but has little impact on the number of arrests of white suspects. Similarly, an increase in the number of nonwhite police officers leads to an increase in the number of arrests of white suspects, and to fewer arrests of nonwhite suspects. The proper interpretation of these findings remains an open question. It is conceivable that racial bias explains the pattern, and that an increase in the number of (white/nonwhite) officers tends to increase the number of innocent (nonwhite/white) individuals who are arrested. But it is also possible, for example, that same-race policing is for some reason more effective, so that an increase in the number of officers of one race reduces crime by members of that race and leads to fewer arrests. More remains to be done to sort out such issues.

Mustard (2001) considers another set of issues – how do race, ethnicity, and gender affect the length of prison sentences, controlling for other variables that might bear on the proper length of sentence. He examines data for over 75,000 individuals convicted in Federal court, and controls for the offense at issue, the criminal history of the defendant, and the District Court in which the defendant is tried. He finds that minorities tend to receive longer prison sentences, other things being equal, as do males and lower-income defendants. Again, the interpretation of the results requires some care, as unobservable variables correlated with race, ethnicity, gender, or income (perhaps the likelihood of recidivism or the ability to pay fines?) may enter into the thinking of judges and lead to the erroneous impression that discrimination is the driving force behind these differences. Again, more research is plainly in order.

I conclude this section with a note on "corporate crime" – the imposition of criminal penalties on companies rather than individuals. Plainly, corporations cannot be put in jail, and corporate criminal penalties are inevitably monetary (although, of course, corporate agents can be incarcerated). Here, therefore, the issue is not what type of penalty to employ, but at what level to set the monetary penalty, and how to coordinate it with the civil damages that often attach to the same conduct in private litigation and with the criminal penalties that agents of the corporation may also incur. In this regard, corporate criminal liability differs in a fundamental respect from the criminal liability of individuals. Many crimes – murder and robbery being examples – are socially unproductive, and the "optimal" level of such crimes would be zero (perhaps putting aside the starving man who steals a loaf of bread) if enforcement costs were zero. In this sense, we do not worry in general about "overdeterring" individual crimes, and thus do not worry much about calibrating the penalty imposed for an individual crime to its social cost. But the optimal deterrence problem for corporate crime involves another margin. Corporate crime is committed by corporate agents, and their superiors must choose how much to monitor them for the purpose of preventing criminal acts. If the penalty imposed on a corporation for a crime by its agent exceeds the social cost of the crime, corporate monitoring to prevent crime will tend to exceed its socially optimal level. This is the essential point in Fischel and Sykes (1996), who go on to argue that much of the criminal liability imposed on corporations presently is excessive for this reason.

It is worth noting that the problem of calibrating corporate criminal penalties appropriately is essentially identical to the problem of setting punitive damages appropriately for corporations (see Polinsky and Shavell 1998). The expected penalty to be paid by the corporation should equal the social costs of the crime that its agents commit. The penalty must be adjusted downward to account for any individual penalties imposed on corporate agents, as shown in Polinsky and Shavell (1993). A further complication is the fact that corporations may suffer substantial market penalties for criminal acts, because in many instances the entities harmed by corporate crime are its customers or creditors. Karpoff and Lott (1993) use an event study to examine public announcements of corporate fraud, and find that corporations suffer substantial declines in market value following such announcements, declines far in excess of their expected legal fees. Their findings suggest that a considerable market penalty is exacted for fraud. The penalties imposed by the criminal justice system on top of those imposed by the market must be calibrated to ensure that the total penalty does not exceed the social costs of misconduct. Otherwise, corporations will overinvest in the prevention of crime.

2. INTERNATIONAL LAW

I now turn to two other fields that are of great importance in law but that remain relatively unexplored territory for law and economics research. The first of these fields is international law.

International law scholars conventionally divide the field into "public" and "private" international law. Public international law refers to the law that governs the relationship among nations, whereas private international law refers to the law governing individuals. The line between them is often hazy, but an international treaty is a classic example of public international law (even if it has important effects on private citizens), while the International Sale of Goods Convention (an international convention on the law of contracts for the sale of goods that parties may choose to govern their transactions) provides a nice illustration of private international law. Almost all of the law and economics research in the field is in the public law area, and of that, by far the bulk pertains to the law of international trade.

I begin, however, with the topic of "customary international law," defined by the Restatement of Foreign Relations as "a general and consistent practice of states followed by them from a sense of legal obligation." A familiar example of customary international law is diplomatic immunity, whereby host nations extend civil and criminal immunity to diplomats from other nations.

Customary law raises numerous puzzles. How are these "general and consistent legal practices" established? Why do nations adhere to them? In particular, given that no formal enforcement mechanism exists to compel adherence to these norms, why would any nation adhere out of a "sense of legal obligation?" The first and, in many respects, only serious effort to answer such questions from an economic perspective is that of Goldsmith and Posner (1999). They argue that customary international law, as conventionally defined, does not exist – "legal obligation," they contend, has nothing to do with the behavior of nations acting in accordance with customary norms. Adopting a simple game theoretic framework, they argue that international norms arise out of purely self-interested behavior on the part of nations. Some norms represent a simple coincidence of unilateral interest, for example, whereas others represent the solution to iterated games such as a repeated Prisoners' Dilemma (the latter being the explanation offered for diplomatic immunity, one of the case studies that they examine in detail). They further show how adherence to many ostensible norms is fragile, and tends to break down precisely when theory suggests that cooperative behavior cannot sustain itself, such as in end game conditions. But many puzzles remain. If customary law is nothing more than a coincidence of interest or cooperative moves in a repeated game, why bother to codify it in places such as the Restatement of Foreign Relations? Does codification not impede useful change and evolution? These and other questions suggest that a good deal of further thinking remains ahead.

The preceding discussion of customary law touches on a more fundamental issue – given the absence of a centralized enforcement mechanism with coercive authority (putting aside occasional UN resolutions authorizing military force and WTO sanctions, for a moment), why do nations comply with any form of international law? The answer is that international law must be self-enforcing, but what makes it so? The conventional response is that some combination of reputational considerations and unilateral retaliation for noncompliance must be operative. The notion that nations care about their reputations for compliance with international law raises a host of issues, many empirical, that have not been examined. For example, what is the nature of the private information that makes reputation valuable (especially in an open society like the United States or the European Union)? Can one observe the effects of reputation on compliance behavior? How durable is reputation over time, such as when political leadership changes? Does "reputation" cut across subject areas (for example, does a violation of a trade agreement jeopardize reputation with respect to human rights agreements)?

Although the importance of reputation has been postulated but never carefully studied, unilateral sanctions have been examined in various contexts, both theoretically and empirically. A number of basic analyses have made the point that unilateral sanctions can support a "tit for tat" type of equilibrium that is known to support mutually advantageous equilibria in noncooperative games of indefinite duration. Eaton and Engers (1992) develop a more formal analysis of international sanctions, identifying some conditions under which a threat of sanctions can induce a target nation to do something that it would not do otherwise. They observe that the need for credibility limits the effectiveness of sanctions, especially when they are costly to the nation that imposes them. Their core results support some simple intuitions, such as the proposition that the effectiveness of sanctions (if they are effective at all) declines with the cost of the sanction to the nation that uses it, and increases with the harm done to the target. A number of empirical studies, more accurately described as collections of case studies, also suggest that sanctions are effective at times, and that they may have played a useful role in holding together international agreements such as GATT. Most of the literature is collected and surveyed in Eaton and Sykes (1998).

Moving on to the study of treaties, a number of writers have made the point that treaties are nothing more than contracts among nations. As such, the theoretical techniques long employed to model optimal contracting behavior should be more or less directly applicable to treaties. Parties to treaties will strive to achieve their Pareto frontier, and thus treaties represent the solution to the problem of maximizing a weighted sum of the parties' welfare. They will need to cope with conditions of uncertainty just like private contracting parties, and can benefit from a system of remedies for breach that promotes efficient compliance but allows efficient adjustment of the bargain to changing circumstances. See, for example, Schwartz and Sykes (2002).

One difficulty in modeling treaties from the optimal contracting perspective relates to the assumptions about the welfare maximand of parties to treaties. One possible assumption is that the representatives of each nation seek to maximize national economic welfare, but this is unrealistic in general. Treaties are negotiated by political representatives, and the theory of public choice suggests that political agents in democracies respond to organized interest groups. Because interest groups differ in their ability to organize and influence policy, there is no reason to suppose that political agents will maximize their welfare in the aggregate. Further, many of the parties to treaties are nondemocracies, and there is very little theorizing about the objective functions of their leaders. Nevertheless, a number of writers have undertaken to model the treaty formation process with some success, almost always with reference to international trade treaties.

Bagwell and Staiger (1999) model trade agreements on the simple assumption that governments care about their "terms of trade" with other countries (the relative prices of their imports and exports), and that they can each influence the terms of trade through their tariff policies (hence, that they are "large" countries and not international price takers). Their results are much the same as one would obtain by assuming that nations maximize national economic welfare – when acting unilaterally in Nash equilibrium, large nations acting unilaterally have long been imagined to seek the "optimal tariff" that maximizes national welfare by holding constant the trade policies of trading partners. Bagwell and

Staiger find the same tendency with their more general formulation of the welfare measure. The external harm to trading partners that is ignored with unilateral policy making can be averted through cooperative agreements that reduce tariffs, and this is the role of trade agreements in their model.

Grossman and Helpman (1995a) develop a model of trade policy and trade agreements with more political structure. They assume that some industries are organized and some not, and that the organized interests make donations to political authorities to promote their interests through trade policy. The equilibrium under unilateral policy making involves protection for well-organized import competing industries, which increases with the size of the industry (and thus its willingness to make donations to secure protection). When nations cooperate in a trade agreement, the degree of organization in foreign export industries will affect each nation's policies. The greatest levels of protection under trade agreements will tend to emerge when the import-competing industry is large and well-organized, while their foreign competitors are poorly organized. Grossman and Helpman (1995b) adapt the model to the study of free trade agreements that liberalize trade preferentially between two nations while maintaining protection vis-à-vis third countries, and derive conditions under which preferential agreements are politically feasible.

A number of writers have studied particular features of international trade agreements with the goal of offering a positive theory of their inclusion. For example, why does the GATT agreement (now part of the WTO) require that all trade concessions be granted on a most-favored-nation basis (that is, extended to all members) unconditionally? Does this rule not create a massive free rider problem in trade negotiations, with nations offering few concessions of their own and waiting to free ride on concessions offered to others? Schwartz and Sykes (1996) argue that the most-favored-nation principle has two key properties that outweigh the free rider concern: (1) it maximizes global tariff revenue conditional on the level of protection for each industry in each country (because it avoids any trade diversion), and thus promotes joint political welfare on the assumption that each nation's political welfare is increasing in its tariff revenue; and (2) it protects the value of negotiated tariff concessions against erosion by ensuring that no future negotiating partner will get a better deal. The free rider problem is addressed through various other devices, such as across-the-board tariff cut formulas and (perhaps) the opportunity to deviate from the most-favored-nation principle in free trade agreements.

In a similar vein, it is interesting to note that trade agreements constrain a wide variety of government policy instruments besides tariffs. Were it otherwise, nations could protect their domestic industries through domestic tax and regulatory polices just as effectively as through traditional instruments of trade policy, and concessions on trade policy alone would be largely worthless. Some attention has been paid to the nature of the constraints on domestic policy instruments, and some puzzles have arisen. For example, although the law of the WTO allows nations to protect their industries with tariffs unless they have made a promise not to with respect to a particular industry, it generally prohibits them altogether from using domestic regulatory measures for the purpose of protecting any domestic industry. Why allow one form of protection and not the other? Sykes (1999) argues that the system is the product of two goals: to reduce the transaction costs of trade negotiations by channeling protectionist measures into as few policy instruments as possible; and in that process to select the policy instruments that impose the smallest economic welfare loss conditional on the level of protection that remains. Regulatory protectionism is particularly disfavored because it typically raises the prices of imports through policies that create deadweight losses. Tariffs, by contrast, achieve protection in substantial part through transfers.

A good deal more has been done on a variety of topics in the trade realm, and interested readers may wish to consult another recent survey by the author for more detail (Sykes 2000). Rather than continuing to discuss prior work here, I will conclude this section with some thoughts on future directions for research.

As the discussion above indicates, very little has been done by law and economics scholars in the international area on topics other than international trade. In this respect, political scientists have far outstripped those operating from the economic perspective. Snidal (1997) provides a nice window into the political science literature, much of which has useful things to say to economists.

A brief look at any international law textbook will suggest a wide range of topics on which both positive and normative analysis is lacking, from the law of the sea to the law of war to international human rights agreements. Take the latter types of agreements as an example. Why do nations bother to create them, given that they obligate most signatories to do nothing more than to obey their domestic laws already in place? What impact do they have, given that most of them (outside of Europe) have no enforcement mechanism? Is it possible to demonstrate empirically that these agreements have any impact on the behavior of signatory governments? These sorts of basic questions are untouched by economists to my knowledge.

In the trade area, much work also remains to be done. Consider the following puzzles: (1) Economic writing has long been critical of antidumping law, which is a limited prohibition of export sales that are accompanied by price discrimination *in favor* of the importing nation, or of sales below fully allocated production costs (including fixed costs). If such laws are so foolish, why have they not been eliminated unilaterally or through international trade negotiations? Plainly, the political equilibrium so far requires their retention, but no fully developed explanation for this state of affairs has emerged. (2) Why are trade agreements enforced with the use of trade sanctions? Retaliatory trade sanctions impose deadweight costs, and one can readily imagine other devices (such as monetary transfers) that deter breach of agreement more cheaply. (3) What explains the pattern of private rights of action under international trade agreements? Why is it that a citizen of New York aggrieved by a protectionist regulatory policy in New Jersey can sue to strike it down under the U.S. Constitution (so too in Europe under the Treaty of Rome), but a citizen of the United States has no standing to invoke WTO law that prohibits an identical policy in France (so too for a dispute within NAFTA)? Why are the only private rights of action in NAFTA pursuant to the investor rights provisions, and why are similar private rights of action available under most bilateral investment treaties?

If economic scholars can manage to educate themselves in a rudimentary way about these and other important features of international law, the potential for new research on untouched subjects is enormous. No field of law (save perhaps constitutional law) covers such a wide range of intriguing issues with respect to which so little has yet been done.

3. INSURANCE LAW

The events of September 11, 2001 have brought some attention to a field of law that receives relatively little attention from legal scholars themselves, let alone law and economics scholars – insurance law. The fascinating issues in this field warrant much greater attention than they receive, and economic tools are particularly suited to addressing them.

To take an issue of immense practical importance in current litigation, if insurance coverage is limited to $X billion "per occurrence" that causes loss, is the attack on the World Trade Center one occurrence or two? Here, perhaps what matters from an economic perspective is that the coverage of policies be clarified so that insurers can price their products appropriately and insureds can purchase efficient coverage. But there may be more at stake – I am not aware of any theorizing on the rationale for separate per occurrence limits in casualty of liability policies.

The fallout from September 11 is much broader than just the coverage disputes now in litigation, however, with many insurers now seeking to exclude terrorist acts from coverage. State regulators will weigh in, and regardless of the regulatory response, the willingness of global insurers and reinsurers to assume such risks is now very much in question. What are the economic consequences of diminished availability of coverage? Is the problem a lasting one or merely a transitional one, like the "insurance crises" in medical malpractice coverage of the 1980s? Should the government become involved in offering its own "coverage" in some manner?

The problem extends beyond the issue of terrorism coverage to all manner of catastrophic events. The insurance industry is exposed to catastrophic losses running into the $100 billion or more range from natural disasters that are not all that unusual, such as Hurricane Andrew. Such exposure is a high percentage of total capital and reserves in the domestic industry, and offshore reinsurance markets for catastrophic risk are quite thin. The thinness of reinsurance options and the high cost associated with reinsurance for catastrophic loss is actually an intriguing economic puzzle in itself. The collection of papers in Froot (1999) provide an excellent introduction to both the theoretical and empirical issues here. The suggestion that government enter the market to facilitate broader risk distribution often follows these observations. Historical experience with the government provision of insurance, however, is unsettling. Rarely does government price coverage appropriately, and there is ample evidence that government "insurance" and disaster relief programs have begotten substantial moral hazard (Priest 1996). The proper responses to these problems are no doubt subtle and turn importantly on the type of insurance at issue.

Putting aside catastrophic losses, law and economics scholars have paid very little attention to insurance regulation despite the fact that insurance is among the most heavily regulated industries. Insurers are subject to extensive solvency regulation, and often to rate regulation and line of business regulation. The need for rate regulation is certainly unclear given competition in most lines of insurance, and even the need for solvency regulation is hardly obvious given public ratings agencies that can ensure a market penalty for insurers that are imprudently operated. What makes the matter all the more complicated in the United States is the fact that almost all of this regulation occurs at the state level, even though many insurance companies have national operations. The logic of this federalist approach, and its attendant costs, deserves much closer scrutiny.

To be sure, some work has been done on particular issues. Epstein (1999) is highly critical of state regulations that effectively prohibit insurers from exiting a certain line of coverage (such as efforts by the State of Florida to prevent insurers from curtailing coverage for wind damage after Hurricane Andrew). He argues that the ability of firms to exit is essential to discipline overzealous state regulators, who can otherwise distort the efficiency of the market by mandating that insurers provide some lines of coverage at a loss. Danzon and Harrington (2001) examine state regulation of workers' compensation premiums. They test whether price constraints on carriers might actually lead to an increase in losses because the price controls eliminate the marginal incentive (via premium increases) for employers to avoid workplace accidents, and find that price suppression indeed produces an increase in the rate of growth of covered losses. Gron (1994) examines the effects of state regulations that limit the volume of premiums to a fixed percentage of capital, ostensibly to ensure solvency. She finds that such regulations have the effect of creating capacity constraints for significant periods of time and may contribute to periodic "crises" in certain lines of insurance.

Beyond the intriguing range of regulatory issues in insurance law lies a vast body of common law decisions on the construction of insurance contracts. Only a handful of the doctrines that emanate from this body of decisions have been closely examined through the lens of insurance economics.

Rea (1993) examines some of the most basic common law principles, such as the principle that insureds must possess an insurable interest in the subject matter of the insurance contract if the contract is to be enforceable. He explains this doctrine as a response to the moral hazard problem that would arise in its absence. The rule that allows the insurer to raise the insurable interest issue after a covered loss arises, even if it sold the policy in full awareness of the insured's lack of insurable interest, protects third parties whose life or property might be jeopardized by this moral hazard.

A complex issue that has received considerable attention concerns the conflict of interest that may arise between insurers and insureds under liability policies that require the insurer to defend suits against the insured. Liability policies invariably have coverage limits, and a judgment against the insured in an amount that exceeds the coverage limit will harm the insured but not the insurer. The insurer, controlling the defense and thus deciding whether to settle or litigate a claim, may thus be tempted to "roll the dice" on litigation at the insured's expense. The law has responded with a "duty to settle" on insurers, often stated to require the insurer to behave "as if" it had no policy limit. Putting aside the administrability of such a rule, its efficiency has been questioned. Meurer (1992) suggests that the absence of a duty to settle may benefit the parties to an insurance contract because it makes the insurer a tougher bargainer during settlement negotiations, allowing it to extract more of the surplus from settlement. Social optimality and private optimality may diverge, however, because the absence of a duty to settle may result in more costly litigation – the "as if" requirement may then be socially optimal but privately suboptimal. Sykes (1994) develops a contrary result. He notes that the "as if" requirement may make little sense for the parties to an insurance contract when the policyholder lacks the assets to pay a judgment substantially in excess of the policy limits, a common situation. Nonetheless, an insured may benefit from a duty to settle because it lowers the coverage level necessary to induce settlement rather than litigation by the insurer. Because the insured may purchase lower levels of coverage under the "as if" requirement, however, more of the harm that he or she causes will be externalized and social welfare may decline. Based on the competing analyses to date, therefore, no simple legal rule seems able to accommodate all of the factors in play.

Another line of cases addresses the "bad faith" denial of claims by insurers under first-party policies. Increasingly, state courts allow insureds to collect punitive damages against insurers who are found to have denied claims without adequate basis, despite the general rule of contract law that disallows punitive damages in other contexts. A possible justification is that in the absence of punitive damages, insurers can exploit the high "discount rate" of insureds with an acute need for cash to induce them to settle for less than they are entitled to receive. But punitive damages may also have some unintended consequences. Sykes (1996) argues that insurers often lack the information to distinguish legitimate from fraudulent claims, and that litigation may then be valuable as a screening device – only insureds with valid claims will press them in litigation. Related work by Crocker and Tennyson (2002) suggests that insurers will optimally tend to underpay claims when fraud is possible and hard to detect. They find empirical confirmation in the fact that reported underpayments are greater in categories of claims in which losses are easier to exaggerate. The imposition of punitive damages on insurers that deny claims that are adjudged by a court to be valid after litigation may discourage these valuable strategies for policing fraud.

Economic analysis has much to say about other types of disputes between insurers and insureds. For example, suppose that an insured who is injured by a negligent motorist collects his or her medical expenses from a first-party insurer, which has a contractual right to be reimbursed in the event that the insured collects a tort judgment from the negligent party. The injured party indeed obtains a judgment against the negligent driver in court, but the driver only has the assets to pay only part of it. Should the medical insurer be reimbursed under these circumstances, even if the injured insured would then be left with less than full compensation for his or her other losses (lost wages, pain and suffering, and so on)? The tendency of the cases is to answer "no," but Sykes (2001) argues that the answer should be "yes." The reason is that the problem only arises when the insured's first-party coverage is inadequate to cover all of his or her losses (the award for pain and suffering, say). But if it was optimal for the insured to forego coverage for some of the loss that occurred, it will also be optimal for the insurer to be reimbursed for its costs even ahead of the insured receiving full compensation for the loss.

CONCLUSION

I reiterate that this survey of work in new areas of law and economics research is highly selective and biased toward the particular interests of the author. There are many new areas that I do not touch here, some no doubt as fertile and important as the subjects above. My goal has been merely to demonstrate that law and economics is making valuable contributions in areas beyond those in which its founders and early adherents labored most intensively. If some of the older fields seem mature and perhaps to have reached a point of diminishing returns, vast areas remain little explored and offer excellent research opportunities for younger scholars.

REFERENCES

Anderson, David (1999), "The Aggregate Burden of Crime," *Journal of Law and Economics* 42, 611–42.

Bagwell, Kyle and Staiger, Robert (1999), "An Economic Theory of GATT," *American Economic Review* 89, 215–48.

Becker, Gary (1968), "Crime and Punishment: An Economic Approach," *Journal of Political Economy* 76, 169–217.

Crocker, Keith and Tennyson, Sharon (2002), "Insurance Fraud and Optimal Claims Settlement Strategies," *Journal of Law and Economics* 469–508.

Danzon, Patricia and Harrington, Scott (2001), "Workers' Compensation Rate Regulation: How Price Controls Increase Costs," *Journal of Law and Economics* 44, 1–36.

Donahue, John and Steven Levitt (2001a), "The Impact of Legalized Abortion on Crime," *Quarterly Journal of Economics* 116, 379–420.

Donahue, John and Steven Levitt (2001b), "The Impact of Race on Policing and Arrests," *Journal of Law and Economics* 44, 367–94.

Eaton, Jonathan and Engers, Marco (1992), "Sanctions," *Journal of Political Economy* 100, 899–928.

Eaton, Jonathan and Sykes, Alan (1998), "International Sanctions," in *New Palgrave Dictionary of Economics and the Law* Vol. II, Peter Newman, ed. (New York: Stockton Press), 352–9.

Epstein, Richard (1999), "Exit Rights and Insurance Regulation: From Federalism to Takings," *George Mason Law Review* 7, 293–511.

Fischel, Daniel and Sykes, Alan (1996), "Corporate Crime," *Journal of Legal Studies* 25, 319–50.

Froot, Kenneth, ed. (1999), *The Financing of Catastrophe Risk* (Chicago: NBER).

Glaeser, Edward and Sacerdote, Bruce (1999), "Why Is There More Crime in Cities?" *Journal of Political Economy* 107, S225–S258.

Goldsmith, Jack and Posner, Eric (1999), "A Theory of Customary International Law," *University of Chicago Law Review* 66, 1113–77.

Gron, Anne (1994), "Evidence of Capacity Constraints in Insurance Markets," *Journal of Law and Economics* 37, 349–77.

Grossman, Gene and Helpman, Elhanan (1995a), "Trade Wars and Trade Talks," *Journal of Political Economy* 103, 675–708.

Grossman, Gene and Helpman, Elhanan (1995b), "The Politics of Free Trade Agreements," *American Economic Review* 85, 667–90.

Kahan, Dan and Posner, Eric (1999), "Shaming White Collar Criminals: A Proposal for the Reform of the Federal Sentencing Guidelines," *Journal of Law and Economics* 42, 365–91.

Karpoff, Jonathan and Lott, John (1993), "The Reputational Penalty Firms Bear for Committing Criminal Fraud," *Journal of Law and Economics* 36, 757–802.

Kessler, Daniel and Steven, Levitt (1999), "Using Sentence Enhancements to Distinguish Between Deterrence and Incapacitation," *Journal of Law and Economics* 42, 343–64.

Levitt, Steven (1997), "Incentive Compatibility Constraints as an Explanation for the Use of Prison Sentences Instead of Fines," *International Review of Law and Economics* 17, 179–92.

Levitt, Steven and Porter, Jack (2001), "How Dangerous Are Drinking Drivers?" *Journal of Political Economy* 109, 1198–1237.

Lott, John (1998), *More Guns, Less Crime* (Chicago: University of Chicago Press).

Lott, John and Mustard, David (1997), "Crime, Deterrence and Right to Carry Concealed Handguns," *Journal of Legal Studies* 26, 1–68.

Marvell, Thomas and Moody, Carlisle (2001), "The Lethal Effects of Three-Strikes Laws," *Journal of Legal Studies* 30, 89–106.

Meurer, Michael (1992), "The Gains from Faith in an Unfaithful Agent: Settlement Conflicts Between Defendants and Liability Insurers," *Journal of Law, Economics and Organization* 8, 502–22.

Mustard, David (2001), "Racial, Ethnic and Gender Disparities in Sentencing: Evidence from the U.S. Federal Courts," *Journal of Law and Economics* 44, 285–314.

Polinsky, A. Mitchell and Shavell, Steven (1993), "Should Employees Be Subject to Finds and Imprisonment Given the Existence of Corporate Liability?" *International Review of Law and Economics* 13, 239–57.

Polinsky, A. Mitchell and Shavell, Steven (1998), "Punitive Damages: An Economic Analysis," *Harvard Law Review* 111, 869–962.

Priest, George (1996), "The Government, The Market and the Problem of Catastrophic Loss," *Journal of Risk and Uncertainty* 12, 219–37.

Rasmusen, Eric (1996), "Stigma and Self-Fulfilling Expectations of Criminality," *Journal of Law and Economics* 39, 519–43.

Rea, Samuel (1993), "The Economics of Insurance Law," *International Review of Law and Economics* 13, 145–62.

Snidal, Duncan (1997), "International Political Economy Approaches to International Institutions," in *Economic Dimensions in International Law*, Jagdeep Bhandari and Alan Sykes, eds. (Cambridge: Cambridge Press), 477–512.

Schwarz, Warren and Sykes, Alan (1996), "Toward a Positive Theory of the Most Favored Nation Obligation and Its Exceptions in the WTO/GATT System," *International Review of Law and Economics* 16, 27–52.

Schwarz, Warren and Sykes, Alan (2002), "The Economic Structure of Renegotiation and Dispute Settlement in the WTO/GATT System," *Journal of Legal Studies* Vol. 31, S179–S204.

Sykes, Alan (1994), "Bad Faith Refusal to Settle by Liability Insurers: Some Implications of the Judgment Proof Problem, *Journal of Legal Studies* 23, 77–110.

Sykes, Alan (1999), "Regulatory Protectionism and the Law of International Trade," *University of Chicago Law Review* 66, 1–46.

Sykes, Alan (2000), "International Trade," in *Encyclopedia of Law and Economics* Vol. III, Boudewijn Bouckaert and Gerrit De Geest, eds. (Northampton, MA: Edward Elgar), 1114–32.

Sykes, Alan (2001), "Subrogation and Insolvency," *Journal of Legal Studies* 30, 383–400.

Stigler, George (1970), "The Optimum Enforcement of Law," *Journal of Political Economy* 78, 1526–36.

Author Index

Subject Index